Alfonso Maria de Liguori

Dignity and Duties of the Priest

Selva

Alfonso Maria de Liguori

Dignity and Duties of the Priest
Selva

ISBN/EAN: 9783337340575

Printed in Europe, USA, Canada, Australia, Japan

Cover: Foto ©Lupo / pixelio.de

More available books at **www.hansebooks.com**

The Centenary Edition.

DIGNITY AND DUTIES OF THE PRIEST;

OR,

SELVA.

A COLLECTION OF MATERIALS FOR ECCLESIASTICAL RETREATS. RULE OF LIFE AND SPIRITUAL RULES.

BY

St. ALPHONSUS DE LIGUORI,

Doctor of the Church.

EDITED BY

REV. EUGENE GRIMM,

Priest of the Congregation of the Most Holy Redeemer.

NEW YORK, CINCINNATI, CHICAGO:

BENZIGER BROTHERS

Printers to the Holy Apostolic See.

R. WASHBOURNE,   M. H. GILL & SON,
18 Paternoster Row, London.   50 Upper O'Connell Street, Dublin.

APPROBATION.

By virtue of the authority granted me by the Most Rev. Nicholas Mauron, Superior-General of the Congregation of the Most Holy Redeemer, I hereby sanction the publication of the work entitled "DIGNITY AND DUTIES OF THE PRIEST," etc., which is Volume XII. of the new and complete edition in English of the works of St. Alphonsus de Liguori, called "The Centenary Edition."

ELIAS FRED. SCHAUER,

Sup. Prov. Baltimorensis.

BALTIMORE, MD., August 15, 1888.

NOTICE.

WE begin the series of works composed especially for the clergy.[1] The work that comes first appeared in 1760 after the *True Spouse of Jesus Christ*, when the author had attained the age of sixty-four. It is the fruit of researches and of studies that he had made during nearly forty years, either for the purpose of regulating his own conduct, or of directing ecclesiastical retreats, and exercises which, by order of the archbishop, he preached for the first time to the clergy of Naples, in 1732, when he had been a priest only six years. He was then regarded as a model for imitation, and as a master worthy of being intrusted with the duty of educating ministers of the sanctuary of every grade.

This book is one that has had most success, thus giving us a high idea of the good that it has effected. It was at once translated into the principal languages of Europe. There are at least five translations of it in French, among which the translation by Mgr. Gaume, an author of very many valuable works, deservedly holds a high rank. To several of these translations the first word of the Italian title *Selva*[2] has been given, the word *Selva* meaning *wood, forest, material, collection of*

[1] Volumes XIII. and XIV. treat of the Holy Mass and of the divine Office; volumes XV. and XVI. of missions and of preaching, and a subsequent volume containing *Pastoral letters*.

[2] *Selva di materie predicabili ed istruttive, per dare gli esercizj ai Preti, ed anche per uso di lezione privata a proprio profitto ;* the translation of this we give as the sub title of the work.

matter. We have, however, preferred to give to this work and to this volume a title that clearly expresses its aim, namely, DIGNITY AND DUTIES OF THE PRIEST.

The author informs us in his preface that he did not endeavor to put much order into the collection of ideas suitable for each subject; we, however, perceive that there is more order in it than he would have us believe. In order the better to understand the author, we have, as much as possible, divided each subject into paragraphs; by such an arrangement the subjects are not only more easily grasped and retained, but we may most conveniently use this book either for meditation or for spiritual reading.

We think it to be not amiss if we call to mind what we have elsewhere said, namely, that all the citations from authors, accompanied by references to the margin, have been carefully verified and corrected when necessary. St. Alphonsus was not always able to draw from original sources: he was often obliged to content himself with what was offered him by the authors whom he had at hand, and who themselves only reproduced the mistakes of their predecessors, which were increased by the mistakes of copyists or of printers. Hence it was necessary to consult the original texts in order to obtain exact citations.

As to the value and utility of this Collection, we take pleasure in quoting the following passage from the preface of Mgr. Gaume:

"We have *Massillon, Sevoy, le Miroir du clergé*. What have you?—three authorities that are without doubt respectable; but they are, after all, private authorities, and your reason, so often the dupe of such authorities, hesitates, distrusts, and using its right, judges, adopts, rejects, and never raises itself to a philosophical faith. Useful at all times, these works—monuments of eloquence or of piety—suffice no longer at the present day.

To the vast development of error we must oppose the analogous development of truth; to this invasion of private spirit we must oppose the imposing authority of the Catholic spirit. Read *Selva*, and say whether it is possible to reach this end in a better manner. Here is not man's thought that is given to you as a rule for your thought: it is the thought of ages; it is not the Bishop of St. Agatha;[1] it is solely tradition that preaches that instructs, that forbids, that commands, that encourages, or that terrifies. This book is as a sacred tribune from which speak one after another the prophets, the apostles, the apostolic men, the martyrs, the solitaries, the most illustrious pontiffs of the East and the West, the most famous Doctors, the most skilful masters of the science of the saints, the successors of St. Peter and the councils, the organs of the Holy Ghost; in a word, antiquity, the middle ages, modern times, the entire Church.

"In the midst of this august assembly what does the holy bishop do? Nearly always he limits his task to the modest *rôle* of a narrator; often even he leaves to you the care of drawing conclusions. There are no long reasonings, inductions, special interpretations. In this consist the particular merit and providential character of *Selva*. More than at any other epoch did the world and the clergy, who should save the world, stand in need of Catholic thought, and the saint gives it pure and entire; he feared to weaken it by mingling his own with it. . . ."[2]

[1] St. Alphonsus was not yet a bishop when he published this work; he was appointed to this office two years later.

[2] We read in a treatise entitled L'INFALLIBILITÉ ET LE CONCILE GÉNÉRAL, ch. 8, written by Cardinal Dechamps, a note that is to the point. After having called St. Alphonsus "the most faithful and the most powerful Echo of tradition in modern times," the eloquent Cardinal explains that our author was, however, not a simple echo in his dogmatical, in his moral, or in his ascetical works, on which he passes

This is the language of Mgr. Gaume, and we must acknowledge that such is in fact the power of this book; but this power is equalled by the unction that accompanies it, as is the case with the other works of this author, and both its unction and its power are supported by the example of his life. One may in some manner say of him what was said of our divine Saviour: *Cœpit facere, et docere*—" He began to do and to teach " (Acts ii.). The following are the rules of conduct that he composed for himself at the time he entered the ecclesiastical state, to serve for his guidance as a candidate for the priesthood:

1. The cleric should frequent the society of holy priests, to be edified by their example.

2. He should spend at least one hour daily in mental prayer, that he may live in fervor and recollection.

3. He should visit the Blessed Sacrament frequently, especially during the time of exposition.

4. He should read the lives of holy priests, that he may imitate their virtues.

5. He must cultivate a special devotion to the Holy

a eulogy which he concludes as follows: " Among his ascetical works there is one that St. Alphonsus has modestly entitled a COLLECTION of texts. At first sight one might believe that this is true; but if one reads the book attentively one sees that the thought of the author is the framework of the whole, and that the strongest and the sweetest that tradition contains he skilfully adapts to the service of his pen. We know that nothing is more difficult than the composing of such a work, in which the texts are not in juxtaposition, but are united by a living thought that revivifies them. If St. Alphonsus is an echo, it is after the fashion of St. Bernard." This judgment seems to us to be perfectly just; we thence conclude that our venerated author is an echo that thinks, that admirably chooses the most proper sounds to express his thought with an irresistible energy; but he also knows how to speak in another manner when the subject demands it, as one may especially see in his Fourth Instruction, in which he speaks of preaching and the administration of the sacrament of Penance.

Virgin, the Mother and Queen of the clergy, and consecrate himself particularly to her service.

6. For the honor of the ecclesiastical state he must be most careful of his reputation.

7. He should flee from worldly conversation, and not be too familiar with the laity, especially women.

8. Seeing God in his Superiors, he must obey them, because such is the divine will.

9. He should be modest, but without affectation, severity, or fastidiousness; and he should always wear the cassock and tonsure.

10. He should be quiet and gentle at home, exemplary in class, and edifying in church, especially during the public offices.

11. He should confess every eight days, and communicate still oftener.

12. He should live free from sin, and practise every virtue.

The young Levite, whose virtue and talents we have admired in another career, edified the whole city of Naples by a constantly increasing fervor while ascending the different degrees of the sanctuary. At the end of a preparation of three years he was judged worthy to be elevated by a dispensation to the dignity of the priesthood. This took place December 21, 1726. He then wrote the following resolutions:

1. I am a priest; my dignity is above that of the angels. I should then lead a life of angelic purity, and I am obliged to strive for this by all possible means.

2. A God deigns to obey my voice. I should with far greater reason obey his speaking to me through his inspirations or my Superiors.

3. The holy Church has honored me: I must therefore honor myself by sanctity of life, by my zeal and labors, etc.

4. I offer to the Eternal Father Jesus Christ, his Son:

it is then my duty to clothe myself with the virtues of Jesus Christ, that I may become fit for my office.

5. Christian people see in me a minister of reconciliation, a mediator between God and man; consequently I must always keep myself in the grace and friendship of God.

6. The faithful desire to see in me a model of the virtues to which they should aspire; I must then be edifying always and under all circumstances.

7. Poor sinners that have lost the light of grace come to me to be spiritually resuscitated: I must therefore aid them by my prayers, exhortations, and good example.

8. Courage is necessary to triumph over the world, the flesh, and the devil; I must then correspond with divine grace that I may combat these virtues victoriously.

9. To defend religion and fight against error and impiety, one must have knowledge. I will then strive, by every means within my reach, to acquire the necessary knowledge.

10. Human respect and worldly friendships dishonor the priesthood; I will then avoid them.

11. Ambition and self-interest have often caused priests to lose their faith; I must then abhor these vices as sources of reprobation.

12. Gravity should accompany charity in a priest; I will then be prudent and reserved, especially with regard to women, without being proud, rough, or disdainful.

13. I can please God only by recollection, fervor, and solid virtue, which nourish the holy exercise of prayer; I will then neglect nothing which may tend to their acquisition.

14. I should seek only the glory of God, my own sanctification, and the salvation of souls; consequently, I must achieve these ends though it should cost my life.

15. I am a priest; it is my duty to inspire virtue in all with whom I come in contact, and to glorify Jesus Christ, the eternal High-priest.[1]

Such was the aurora of this star that was to pass through so grand a career, and raise itself to so high a perfection. *Quasi lux splendens, procedit, et crescit usque ad perfectam diem*—" As a shining light goeth forwards and increaseth even to perfect day" (Prov. iv. 18). Our saint is already recognized as one of the purest lights that God has sent to illumine the world. *Quasi sol refulgens, sic ille effulsit in templo Dei*—" As the sun when it shineth, so did he shine in the temple of God" (Ecclus. l. 7). A new ray has been added to his glory: he has been declared a Doctor of the Church. Let us not omit to profit by his teachings and imitate his virtues in order that we may one day share in his eternal happiness.

Live Jesus, Mary, Joseph, and Alphonsus!

[1] *Villecourt*, l. 1, ch. 11.

CONTENTS.

	PAGE
APPROBATION,	4
NOTICE,	5
ADMONITIONS NECESSARY FOR HIM WHO GIVES THE SPIRITUAL EXERCISES TO PRIESTS,	19

PART I.

MATERIAL FOR SERMONS.

CHAPTER I. THE DIGNITY OF THE PRIESTHOOD . . . 23
   I. Idea of the priestly dignity, 23.
   II. Importance of the priestly office, 24.
   III. Grandeur of the priestly power, 26.
   IV. The dignity of the priest surpasses all other created dignities, 29.
   V. Elevation of the post occupied by the priest, 33.
   VI. Conclusion, 37.

CHAPTER II. THE END OF THE PRIESTHOOD, ... 39
   I. The priesthood appears to the saints a formidable charge, 39.
   II. What is the end of the priesthood, 41.
   III. Principal duties of the priest, 43.

CHAPTER III. THE SANCTITY NECESSARY FOR THE PRIEST, . 48
   I. What should be the sanctity of the priest by reason of his dignity, 48.
   II. What should be the sanctity of the priest as the minister of the altar, 55.
   III. What should be the sanctity of the priest as mediator between God and man, 59.
   IV. What should be the sanctity of the priest given to the people to be their model, 62.
   V. Practical consequences, 64.

CHAPTER IV. GRIEVOUSNESS AND CHASTISEMENT OF SIN IN A PRIEST, ... 70
   I. Grievousness of sin in a priest, 70.
   II. Chastisement of the sinful priest, 75.
   III. Exhortation, 82.

Contents.

CHAPTER V. THE INJURY THAT TEPIDITY DOES TO A PRIEST, 88
 I. To what the tepid priest is exposed, 88.
 II. A priest cannot be satisfied with avoiding grievous sins, 97.
 III. Exhortation, 101.

CHAPTER VI. THE SIN OF INCONTINENCE, ... 107
 I. Necessity of purity in the priest, 107.
 II. Malice of impurity in the priest, 109.
 III. Sad effects of impurity, 113.
  Blindness of the soul, 113. Obstinacy of the will, 117. Eternal damnation, 119.
 IV. Remedies for incontinence, 120.

CHAPTER VII. THE SACRILEGIOUS MASS, ... 122
 I. Purity required in the priest to celebrate worthily, 122.
 II. How great is the crime of the priest that celebrates Mass in mortal sin, 125.

CHAPTER VIII. THE SIN OF SCANDAL, ... 138

CHAPTER IX. THE ZEAL OF THE PRIEST, ... 154
 I. The obligation of every priest to labor for the salvation of souls, 154.
 II. The pleasure that a priest who labors for the salvation of souls gives to God, 166.
 III. How secure the priest who labors for the salvation of souls renders his own salvation, and how great the reward that he shall receive in heaven, 172.
 IV. The end, the means, and the labors of the priest who has zeal, 177.
  The end to be proposed, 177. Means to be employed, 178. Works of a zealous priest, 180.

CHAPTER X. THE VOCATION TO THE PRIESTHOOD, . . . 185
 I. Necessity of a divine vocation to take Holy Orders, 185.
 II. Marks of a divine vocation to the sacerdotal state, 189.
  1. Purity of intention, 192. 2. Science and talents, 193. 3. Positive goodness of character, 194.
 III. To what dangers one exposes one's self by taking Holy Orders without a vocation, 198.

PART II.

MATERIAL FOR INSTRUCTIONS.

INSTRUCTION I. THE CELEBRATION OF MASS, ... 208
 I. Importance of the Holy Sacrifice and what it exacts of the priest, 208.
 II. The preparation for Mass, 213.
 III. The reverence and the devotion with which the priest should celebrate Mass, 217.
 IV. Thanksgiving after Mass, 226.
 V. The priest who abstains from saying Mass, 228.

INSTRUCTION II. THE GOOD EXAMPLE THAT THE PRIEST SHOULD
GIVE, ... 230
INSTRUCTION III. THE CHASTITY OF THE PRIEST, . . . 243
   I. The merit of this virtue, and its necessity to the priest, 240.
   II. Means of preserving chastity, 247.
      Flight of the occasion, 248. Mortification, 258. Prayer, 261.
INSTRUCTION IV. PREACHING AND THE ADMINISTRATION OF THE
SACRAMENT OF PENANCE, ... 265
   I. Preaching, 265.
   II. Administration of the Sacrament of Penance, 271.
      Grave responsibility of confessors, 271. The knowledge required to hear confessions well, 273. Charity and firmness that the confessor should have, 274. How to act in regard to those living in the occasion of sin and those who are relapsing sinners, 281.
INSTRUCTION V. MENTAL PRAYER, ... 289
   I. Necessity of mental prayer for priests, 289.
   II. Answer to excuses, 293.
   III. The recitation of the divine Office, 302.
INSTRUCTION VI. HUMILITY, ... 305
   I. Necessity of humility, 305.
   II. The practice of humility, 309.
      To have a horror of pride, 309. Not to glory in the good that we do, 312. We must distrust ourselves, 315. To accept humiliations, 319.
INSTRUCTION VII. MEEKNESS, ... 322
   I. We must repress anger, 323.
   II. We must bear contempt, 330.
INSTRUCTION VIII. MORTIFICATION, AND PARTICULARLY INTERIOR MORTIFICATION, . . . 337
   I. Necessity of mortification in general, 337
   II. Necessity of interior mortification, 341.
   III. The practice of interior mortification, 345.
      Property, 345. Honors, 351. Relatives, 354. Self-will, 357. Means of conquering self-will, 360.
INSTRUCTION IX. EXTERIOR MORTIFICATION, ... 362
   I. Necessity of exterior mortification, 362.
   II. Practice of exterior mortification, 366.
      The eyes and the whole exterior, 367. The taste or appetite, 374. The touch, 377. Involuntary mortifications, 379.
   III The good that is derived from a mortified life, 380.
INSTRUCTION X. THE LOVE OF GOD, ... 384
   I. Special obligation for the priest to belong entirely to God, 384.
   II. Means to be employed for belonging entirely to God, 391.
      Desire for perfection, 391. The intention of pleasing

God in all things, 395. Patience in pains and humiliations, 399. Conformity to the will of God, 403.

INSTRUCTION XI. DEVOTION TO MOST HOLY MARY, . . 409

I. Moral necessity of the intercession of the Blessed Virgin, 409.
II. Confidence that we should have in the intercession of the Mother of God, 414.
III. Practice of devotion to the Blessed Virgin, 421.

APPENDIX.

RULE OF LIFE FOR A SECULAR PRIEST, ... 427

I. Morning exercises, 427.
The first acts on rising, 427. Mental prayer, 428. The holy Mass, 428. Confessions and study, 429. Remark in regard to the order of the exercises, 430. Dinner, 430.
II. Exercises after dinner, 431.
Spiritual reading, 431. The visit to the Blessed Sacrament and to the Blessed Virgin, 432. Recreation, 433.
III. Exercises of the evening, 433.
Before supper, 433. Supper, 433. The last acts before going to bed, 434.
IV. Exercises that are not performed every day, 434.
Confession, 434. The monthly retreat, 434. Special counsels, 435.

SPIRITUAL RULES FOR A PRIEST WHO ASPIRES TO PERFECTION, 436

To avoid sin, and trouble after sin, 436. Efficacious desire to advance in the love of God, 437. Devotion to the Passion of our Lord and to the Blessed Sacrament, 438. The intention of doing all for God, 439. Love of solitude and of silence, 439. Conformity to the will of God, 441. Desire for death, 442. Devotion to the Blessed Virgin, 442. To be humble of heart, 443. To render good for evil, 444. Interior and exterior mortification, 444. To pray without ceasing, 445.

SPIRITUAL MAXIMS FOR A PRIEST, ... 446

EXHORTATION TO YOUNG MEN WHO DEVOTE THEMSELVES TO THE STUDY OF THE ECCLESIASTICAL SCIENCES, . . . 449

They should, above all, endeavor to make progress in the science of the saints, 449.

DISCOURSE ON THE NECESSITY OF MENTAL PRAYER FOR PRIESTS, 454

I. Without mental prayer it is difficult for a priest to save his soul, 455.
II. Without mental prayer it is impossible for the priest to attain perfection, 462.

INDEX, ... 463

Dignity and Duties of the Priest;

OR SELVA,

A COLLECTION OF MATERIAL FOR SERMONS AND INSTRUCTIONS,
FOR ECCLESIASTICAL RETREATS,

AND ALSO FOR PRIVATE SPIRITUAL READING.

DIGNITY AND DUTIES OF THE PRIEST.

Admonitions Necessary for Him who gives the Spiritual Exercises to Priests.

THE present little work is entitled "A Collection of Materials,"[1] and not Discourses or Spiritual Exercises, because although I have endeavored to collect the material belonging to each subject, I have not observed the order necessary for a regular discourse, nor have I extended the thoughts. They are given without order, and expressed briefly, that the reader may select the authorities, subjects, and thoughts that are most pleasing to him, and may afterwards arrange and extend them as he pleases, and thus make the discourse his own. For experience shows, that a preacher will scarcely deliver sentiments with fervor and zeal unless he has first made them his own, at least by selecting them from among others, and arranging and extending them, in composing the discourse. Hence, I have taken from different authors several passages that have the same signification, so that the preacher may select those that please him most.

I have said so much to explain the aim of the work. Let him who gives the spiritual exercises to priests be careful, first of all, to propose to himself a good end in his instructions:

I. This end must be not to gain the character of a man of learning, of talent, and of eloquence, but only to give glory to God by the sanctification of his hearers.

---
[1] *Selva*. . . . See Notice, page 5.

II. Let him be careful not to seek to introduce into his sermons ideas foreign to the subject, nor new and lofty thoughts that serve only to fix the mind on the beauty of the conceptions, but leave the will dry and without fruit; let him be careful to say what he considers best calculated to move his hearers to make some good resolution.

III. In order to attain that end, let him in his sermons frequently remind the hearers of the truths of eternity, by the consideration of which perseverance is obtained, according to the words of the Holy Ghost: *In all thy works remember thy last end, and thou shalt never sin.*[1] It is true, indeed, that certain priests dislike sermons on the last things, and are offended at seeing themselves treated like seculars, as if they were not, as well as seculars, to die and be judged. Let him, then, who gives the spiritual exercises not omit at least to remind the audience several times of death, of judgment, and of eternity. These are the truths best calculated to effect a change of life in all that meditate upon them.

IV. Let the preacher be careful to inculcate as much as possible what is practical. For example, the method of making mental prayer, thanksgiving after Mass, the correction of sinners, and above all the mode of hearing confessions, particularly the confessions of relapsing sinners, or of those that are in the proximate occasion of sin. In hearing the confessions of these two classes of penitents, many confessors err, either by an excess of rigor, or by too great a facility of giving absolution (the latter is more frequent), and thus they are the cause of the damnation of so many souls. Latin passages are soon forgotten; only what is practical remains in the mind.

V. Let the preacher be careful to treat with respect

[1] "Memorare novissima tua, et in æternum non peccabis."—*Ecclus.* vii. 40.

and sweetness the priests who listen to him. With *respect;* showing a veneration for them, often calling them men of learning and of sanctity, and when he inveighs against any vice, let him always speak in general terms, protesting that he speaks not of those that are present. Let him guard, in a special manner, against censuring any defect of any particular person, as also against speaking in a tone of authority; but let him endeavor to preach in a familiar style, which is the best calculated to persuade and move. With respect and with *sweetness;* let him, then, never appear angry, nor ever break out into injurious words, which tend more to irritate the mind than to excite piety.

VI. In sermons that are apt to strike terror, let him not induce his hearers to despair of salvation or of amendment. Let him always leave to all, however abandoned, a means by which they may hope to change their lives; animating them to confidence in the merits of Jesus Christ, and in the intercession of the divine Mother, and to have recourse by prayer to these two great anchors of hope. Let the preacher, in almost all his sermons, frequently and strongly recommend the exercise of prayer, that is, the prayer of petition, which is the only means of obtaining the graces necessary for salvation.

VII. Finally, above all, let the preacher be careful to expect the fruit not from his own labors, but from the divine mercy, and from his prayers, begging of God to give strength to his words. For we know that, ordinarily, sermons produce scarcely any fruit in priests, and to induce, in the spiritual exercises, a priest to change his life if he is a sinner, or to become fervent if he is tepid, is almost a miracle, which seldom occurs. Hence, the conversion of priests must be the fruit of prayer more than of study.

PART I.

MATERIAL FOR SERMONS.

CHAPTER I.

THE DIGNITY OF THE PRIESTHOOD.

I.

Idea of the Priestly Dignity.

IN his epistle to the Christians of Smyrna, St. Ignatius, Martyr, says that the priesthood is the most sublime of all created dignities: "The apex of dignities is the priesthood."[1] St. Ephrem calls it an infinite dignity: "The priesthood is an astounding miracle, great, immense, and infinite."[2] St. John Chrysostom says, that though its functions are performed on earth, the priesthood should be numbered among the things of heaven.[3] According to Cassian, the priest of God is exalted above all earthly sovereignties, and above all celestial heights —he is inferior only to God.[4] Innocent III. says that the

---

[1] "Omnium apex est Sacerdotium."—*Epist. ad Smyrn.*

[2] "Miraculum est stupendum, magna, immensa, infinita Sacerdoti dignitas."—*De Sacerdotio.*

[3] "Sacerdotium in terris peragitur sed in rerum cœlestium ordinem referendum est."—*De Sacerd.* l. 3.

[4] "O Sacerdos Dei ! si altitudinem cœli contemplaris, altior es; si omnium dominorum sublimitatem, sublimior es; solo tuo Creatore inferior es."—*Catal. gloriæ mundi,* p. 4, cons. 6.

priest is placed between God and man; inferior to God, but superior to man.[1]

St. Denis calls the priest a divine man.[2] Hence he has called the priesthood a divine dignity.[3] In fine, St. Ephrem says that the gift of the sacerdotal dignity surpasses all understanding.[4] For us it is enough to know, that Jesus Christ has said that we should treat his priests as we would his own person: *He that heareth you, heareth me; he that despiseth you, despiseth me.*[5] Hence St. John Chrysostom says, that "he who honors a priest, honors Christ, and he who insults a priest, insults Christ."[6] Through respect for the sacerdotal dignity, St. Mary of Oignies used to kiss the ground on which a priest had walked.

II.

Importance of the Priestly Office.

The dignity of the priest is estimated from the exalted nature of his offices. Priests are chosen by God to manage on earth all his concerns and interests. "Divine," says St. Cyril of Alexandria, "are the offices confided to priests."[7] St. Ambrose has called the priestly office a divine profession.[8] A priest is a minister destined by God to be a public ambassador of the whole Church, to honor him, and to obtain his graces for all

[1] "Inter Deum et hominem medius constitutus; minor Deo, sed major homine."—*In Consecr. Pont.* s. 2.

[2] "Qui Sacerdotem dixit, prorsus divinum insinuat virum."—*De Eccl. Hier.* c. 1.

[3] "Angelica, imo divina est dignitas."—*Ibid.*

[4] "Excedit omnem cogitationem donum dignitatis sacerdotalis."—*De Sacerd.*

[5] "Qui vos audit, me audit; et qui vos spernit, me spernit."—*Luke*, x. 16.

[6] "Qui honorat Sacerdotem Christi, honorat Christum; et qui injuriat Sacerdotem Christi, injuriat Christum."—*Hom.* 17.

[7] "Genus divinis ministeriis mancipatum."—*De Adorat.* l. 13.

[8] "Deifica professio."—*De Dignit. sac.* c. 3.

the faithful. The entire Church cannot give to God as much honor, nor obtain so many graces, as a single priest by celebrating a single Mass; for the greatest honor that the whole Church without priests could give to God would consist in offering to him in sacrifice the lives of all men. But of what value are the lives of all men compared with the sacrifice of Jesus Christ, which is a sacrifice of infinite value? What are all men before God but a little dust? *As a drop of a bucket, ... as a little dust.*[1] They are but a mere nothing in his sight: *All nations are before him as if they had no being at all.* Thus, by the celebration of a single Mass, in which he offers Jesus Christ in sacrifice, a priest gives greater honor to the Lord, than if all men by dying for God offered to him the sacrifice of their lives. By a single Mass, he gives greater honor to God than all the angels and saints, along with the Blessed Virgin Mary, have given or shall give to him; for their worship cannot be of infinite value, like that which the priest celebrating on the altar offers to God.

Moreover, in the holy Mass, the priest offers to God an adequate thanksgiving for all the graces bestowed even on the Blessed in Paradise; but such a thanksgiving all the saints together are incapable of offering to him. Hence it is, that on this account also the priestly dignity is superior even to all celestial dignities. Besides, the priest, says St. John Chrysostom, is an ambassador of the whole world, to intercede with God and to obtain graces for all creatures.[2] The priest, according to St. Ephrem, "treats familiarly with God."[3] To priests every door is open.

[1] "Quasi stilla situlæ, . . . pulvis exiguus. . . . Omnes gentes, quasi non sint, sic sunt coram eo."—*Isa.* xl. 15, 17.
[2] "Pro universo terrarum orbe legatus intercedit apud Deum."—*De Sacerd.* l. 6.
[3] "Cum Deo familiariter agit."—*De Sacerdotio.*

Jesus has died to institute the priesthood. It was not necessary for the Redeemer to die in order to save the world; a drop of his blood, a single tear, or prayer, was sufficient to procure salvation for all; for such a prayer, being of infinite value, should be sufficient to save not one but a thousand worlds. But to institute the priesthood, the death of Jesus Christ has been necessary. Had he not died, where should we find the victim that the priests of the New Law now offer? a victim altogether holy and immaculate, capable of giving to God an honor worthy of God. As has been already said, all the lives of men and angels are not capable of giving to God an infinite honor like that which a priest offers to him by a single Mass.

III.
Grandeur of the Priestly Power.

The dignity of the priest is also estimated from the power that he has over the real and the mystic body of Jesus Christ.

With regard to the power of priests over the real body of Jesus Christ, it is of faith that when they pronounce the words of consecration the Incarnate Word has obliged himself to obey and to come into their hands under the sacramental species. We are struck with wonder when we hear that God obeyed the voice of Josue—*The Lord obeying the voice of man*[1]—and made the sun stand when he said *move not, O sun, towards Gabaon, . . . and the sun stood still.*[2] But our wonder should be far greater when we find that in obedience to the words of his priests—HOC EST CORPUS MEUM—God himself descends on the altar, that he comes wherever they call him, and as often as they call him, and places

---

[1] "Obediente Domino voci hominis."—*Jos.* x. 14.

[2] "Sol, contra Gabaon ne movearis. . . . Stetit itaque sol in medio cœli."—*Ibid.* x. 12.

himself in their hands, even though they should be his enemies. And after having come, he remains, entirely at their disposal; they move him as they please, from one place to another; they may, if they wish, shut him up in the tabernacle, or expose him on the altar, or carry him outside the church; they may, if they choose, eat his flesh, and give him for the food of others. " Oh, how very great is their power," says St. Laurence Justinian, speaking of priests. " A word falls from their lips and the body of Christ is there substantially formed from the matter of bread, and the Incarnate Word descended from heaven, is found really present on the table of the altar ! Never did divine goodness give such power to the angels. The angels abide by the order of God, but the priests take him in their hands, distribute him to the faithful, and partake of him as food for themselves." [1]

With regard to the *mystic* body of Christ, that is, all the faithful, the priest has the power of the keys, or the power of delivering sinners from hell, of making them worthy of paradise, and of changing them from the slaves of Satan into the children of God. And God himself is obliged to abide by the judgment of his priests, and either not to pardon or to pardon, according as they refuse or give absolution, provided the penitent is capable of it. " Such is," says St. Maximus of Turin, " this judiciary power ascribed to Peter that its decision carries with it the decision of God."[2] The sentence of the priest precedes, and God subscribes to it,

---

[1] " Maxima illis est collata potestas! Ad eorum pene libitum, corpus Christi de panis transsubstantiatur materia; descendit de cœlo in carne Verbum, et altaris verissime reperitur in mensa! Hoc illis prærogatur ex gratia, quod nusquam datum est Angelis. Hi assistunt Deo; illi contrectant manibus, tribuunt populis, et in se suscipiünt."— *Serm. de Euchar.*

[2] " Tanta ei (Petro) potestas attributa est judicandi, ut in arbitrio ejus poneretur cœleste judicium."—*In Nat. B. Petri, hom.* 3.

writes St. Peter Damian.[1] Hence St. John Chrysostom thus concludes: " The Sovereign Master of the universe only follows the servant by confirming in heaven all that the latter decides upon earth."[2]

Priests are the dispensers of the divine graces and the companions of God. " Consider the priests," says St. Ignatius, Martyr, " as the dispensers of divine graces and the associates of God."[3] " They are," says St. Prosper, " the glory and the immovable columns of the Church; thay are the doors of the eternal city; through them all reach Christ; they are the vigilant guardians to whom the Lord has confided the keys of the kingdom of heaven; they are the stewards of the king's house, to assign to each according to his good pleasure his place in the hierarchy."[4]

Were the Redeemer to descend into a church, and sit in a confessional to administer the sacrament of penance, and a priest to sit in another confessional, Jesus would say over each penitent, "Ego te absolvo," the priest would likewise say over each of his penitents, "Ego te absolvo," and the penitents of each would be equally absolved. How great the honor that a king would confer on a subject whom he should empower to rescue from prison as many as he pleased ! But far greater is the power that the eternal Father has given to Jesus Christ, and that Jesus Christ has given to his priests, to rescue from hell not only the bodies but also

[1] " Præcedit Petri sententia sententiam Redemptoris."—*Serm.* 26.
[2] " Dominus sequitur servum; et quidquid hic in inferioribus judicaverit, hoc ille in supernis comprobat."—*De Verbis Is. hom.* 5.
[3] " In domo Dei, divinorum bonorum œconomos, sociosque Dei, Sacerdotes respicite."—*Ep. ad Polyc.*
[4] " Ipsi sunt Ecclesiæ decus, columnæ firmissimæ; ipsi januæ Civitatis æternæ, per quos omnes ingrediuntur ad Christum; ipsi janitores, quibus claves datæ sunt regni cœlorum; ipsi dispensatores regiæ domus, quorum arbitrio dividuntur gradus singulorum."—*De Vita cont.* l. 2, c. 2.

the souls of the faithful: " The Son," says St. John Chrysostom, "has put into the hands of the priests all judgment; for having been as it were transported into heaven, they have received this divine prerogative. If a king gave to a mortal the power to release from prison all prisoners, all would pronounce such a one happy; but priests have received from God a far greater power, since the soul is more noble than the body." [1]

IV.

The Dignity of the Priest Surpasses all other Created Dignities.

Thus the sacerdotal dignity is the most noble of all the dignities in this world. "Nothing," says St. Ambrose, "is more excellent in this world." [2] It transcends, says St. Bernard, "all the dignities of kings, of emperors, and of angels." [3] According to St. Ambrose, the dignity of the priest as far exceeds that of kings, as the value of gold surpasses that of lead. [4] The reason is, because the power of kings extends only to temporal goods and to the bodies of men, but the power of the priest extends to spiritual goods and to the human soul. Hence, says St. Clement, "as much as the soul is more noble than the body, so much is the priesthood more excellent than royalty." [5] "Princes," says St. John

[1] "Omne judicium a Filio illis traditum. . . . . Nam, quasi in cœlum translati, ad principatum istum perducti sunt. Si cui rex hunc honorem detulerit, ut potestatem habeat quoscunque in carcerem conjectos laxandi, beatus ille judicio omnium fuerit; at vero qui tanto majorem a Deo accepit potestatem, quanto animæ corporibus præstant."—*De Sacerd.* 1. 3.

[2] "Nihil in hoc sæculo excellentius."—*De Dignit. sac.* c. 3.

[3] "Prætulit vos, Sacerdotes, regibus et imperatoribus; prætulit Angelis."—*Serm. ad Pastor. in syn.*

[4] "Longe erit inferius, quam si plumbum ad auri fulgorem compares."—*De Dignit. sac.* c. 2.

[5] "Quanto anima corpore præstantior est, tanto est Sacerdotium regno excellentius."—*Constit. apost.* l. 2, c. 34.

Chrysostom, "have the power of binding, but they bind only the bodies, while the priest binds the souls."[1]

The kings of the earth glory in honoring priests: "It is a mark of a good prince," says Pope St. Marcellinus, "to honor the priests of God."[2] "They willingly," says Peter de Blois, "bend their knee before the priest of God; they kiss his hands, and with bowed down head receive his benediction."[3] "The sacerdotal dignity," says St. Chrysostom, "effaces the royal dignity; hence the king inclines his head under the hand of the priest to receive his blessing."[4] Baronius relates that when the Empress Eusebia sent for Leontius, Bishop of Tripoli, he said that if she wished to see him, she should consent to two conditions: first, that on his arrival she should instantly descend from the throne, and bowing down her head, should ask his benediction; secondly, that he should be seated on the throne, and that she should not sit upon it without his permission: he added, that unless she submitted to these conditions he should never go to the palace. Being invited to the table of the Emperor Maximus, St. Martin, in taking a draught, first paid a mark of respect to his chaplain, and then to the emperor. In the Council of Nice, the Emperor Constantine wished to sit in the last place, after all the priests, and on a seat lower than that which they occupied; he would not even sit down without their permission. The holy king St. Boleslans had so great a veneration for priests, that he would not dare to sit in their presence.

[1] "Habent principes vinculi potestatem, verum corporum solum; Sacerdotes vinculum etiam animarum contingit."—*De Sacerd.* l. 3.

[2] "Boni principis est Dei Sacerdotes honorare."—*Cap. Boni princ. dist.* 96.

[3] "Reges flexis genibus offerunt ei munera, et deosculantur manum, ut ex ejus contactu sanctificentur."—*Serm.* 47.

[4] "Major est hic principatus quam regis; propterea rex caput submittit manui Sacerdotis."—*De Verbis Is. hom.* 4.

The Dignity of the Priesthood.

The sacerdotal dignity also surpasses the dignity of the angels, who likewise show their veneration for the priesthood, says St. Gregory Nazianzen.[1] All the angels in heaven cannot absolve from a single sin. The angels guardian procure for the souls committed to their care grace to have recourse to a priest that he may absolve them: "Although," says St. Peter Damian, "angels may be present, they yet wait for the priest to exercise his power, but no one of them has the power of the keys— of binding and of loosening."[2] When St. Michael comes to a dying Christian who invokes his aid, the holy archangel can chase away the devils, but he cannot free his client from their chains till a priest comes to absolve him. After having given the order of priesthood to a holy ecclesiastic, St. Francis de Sales perceived, that in going out he stopped at the door as if to give precedence to another. Being asked by the saint why he stopped, he answered that God favored him with the visible presence of his angel guardian, who before he had received priesthood always remained at his right and preceded him, but afterwards walked on his left and refused to go before him. It was in a holy contest with the angel that he stopped at the door. St. Francis of Assisi used to say, "If I saw an angel and a priest, 1 would bend my knee first to the priest and then to the angel."

Besides, the power of the priest surpasses that of the Blessed Virgin Mary; for, although this divine Mother can pray for us, and by her prayers obtain whatever she wishes, yet she cannot absolve a Christian from even the smallest sin. "The Blessed Virgin was eminently

---

[1] "Sacerdotium ipsi quoque Angeli venerantur."—*Orat. ad Naz. tim. pere.*

[2] "Licet assistant Angeli, præsidentis (Sacerdotis) imperium exspectantes, nullus tamen eorum ligandi atque solvendi possidet potestatem."—*Serm.* 26.

more perfect than the apostles," says Innocent III.; " it was, however, not to her, but only to the apostles, that the Lord intrusted the keys of the kingdom of heaven." [1] St. Bernardine of Sienna has written: " Holy Virgin, excuse me, for I speak not against thee: the Lord has raised the priesthood above thee." [2] The saint assigns the reason of the superiority of the priesthood over Mary; she conceived Jesus Christ only once; but by consecrating the Eucharist, the priest, as it were, conceives him as often as he wishes, so that if the person of the Redeemer had not as yet been in the world, the priest, by pronouncing the words of consecration, would produce this great person of a Man-God. " O wonderful dignity of the priests," cries out St. Augustine; " in their hands, as in the womb of the Blessed Virgin, the Son of God becomes incarnate." [3] Hence priests are called the parents of Jesus Christ: [4] such is the title that St. Bernard gives them, for they are the active cause by which he is made to exist really in the consecrated Host.

Thus the priest may, in a certain manner, be called the creator of his Creator, since by saying the words of consecration, he creates, as it were, Jesus in the sacrament, by giving him a sacramental existence, and produces him as a victim to be offered to the eternal Father. As in creating the world it was sufficient for God to have said, Let it be made, and it was created—*He spoke,*

[1] " Licet Beatissima Virgo excellentior fuerit Apostolis, non tamen illi, sed istis Dominus claves regni coelorum commisit."—*Cap. Nova quædam. De Pænit.*

[2] " Virgo benedicta, excusa me, quia non loquor contra te: Sacerdotium ipse prætulit supra te."—T. 1, s. 20, a. 2, c. 7.

[3] " O veneranda Sacerdotum dignitas, in quorum manibus, velut in utero Virginis, Filius Dei incarnatur."—*Molina. Instr. Sacerd.* tr. 1, c. 5, § 2.

[4] " Parentes Christi."—*S. ad Past. in syn.*

and they were made,¹—so it is sufficient for the priest to say, "Hoc est corpus meum," and behold the bread is no longer bread, but the body of Jesus Christ. "The power of the priest," says St. Bernardine of Sienna, "is the power of the divine person; for the transubstantiation of the bread requires as much power as the creation of the world."² And St. Augustine has written, "O venerable sanctity of the hands! O happy function of the priest! He that created (if I may say so) gave me the power to create him; and he that created me without me is himself created by me!"³ As the Word of God created heaven and earth, so, says St. Jerome, the words of the priest create Jesus Christ. "At a sign from God there came forth from nothing both the sublime vault of the heavens and the vast extent of the earth; but not less great is the power that manifests itself in the mysterious words of the priest."⁴ The dignity of the priest is so great, that he even blesses Jesus Christ on the altar as a victim to be offered to the eternal Father. In the sacrifice of the Mass, writes Father Mansi, Jesus Christ is the principal offerer and victim; as minister, he blesses the priest, but as victim, the priest blesses him.

V.

Elevation of the Post Occupied by the Priest.

The greatness of the dignity of a priest is also estimated from the high place that he occupies. The

¹ "Ipse dixit, et facta sunt."—*Ps.* xxxii. 9.

² "Potestas Sacerdotis est sicut potestas Personarum divinarum; quia, in panis transsubstantiatione, tanta requiritur virtus, quanta in mundi creatione."—*Loco cit.*

³ "O venerabilis sanctitudo manuum! o felix exercitium! Qui creavit me (si fas est dicere) dedit mihi creare se; et qui creavit me sine me ipse creavit se mediante me!"

⁴ "Ad nutum Domini, ex nihilo substiterunt excelsa cœlorum, vasta terrarum; ita parem potentiam in spiritualibus Sacerdotis verbis præbet virtus."—*Hom. de Corpore Chr.*

priesthood is called, at the synod of Chartres, in 1550, the seat of the saints. Priests are called Vicars of Jesus Christ, because they hold his place on earth. "You hold the place of Christ," says St. Augustine to them; "you are therefore his lieutenants."[1] In the Council of Milan, St. Charles Borromeo called priests·the representatives of the person of God on earth.[2] And before him, the Apostle said: *For Christ we are ambassadors, God, as it were, exhorting by us.*[3]

When he ascended into heaven, Jesus Christ left his priests after him to hold on earth his place of mediator between God and men, particularly on the altar. "Let the priest," says St. Laurence Justinian, "approach the altar as another Christ."[4] According to St. Cyprian, a priest at the altar performs the office of Christ.[5] When, says St. Chrysostom, you have seen a priest offering sacrifice, consider that the hand of Christ is invisibly extended.[6]

The priest holds the place of the Saviour himself, when, by saying "Ego te absolvo," he absolves from sin. This great power, which Jesus Christ has received from his eternal Father, he has communicated to his priests. "Jesus," says Tertullian, "invests the priests with his own powers."[7] To pardon a single sin requires all the omnipotence of God. "O God, who chiefly manifestest Thy almighty power in pardoning and showing mercy,"[8] etc., says the holy Church in one of her

[1] "Vos estis Vicarii Christi, qui vicem ejus geritis."—*Ad Fr. in cr.* s. 36.
[2] "Dei personam in terris gerentes."
[3] "Pro Christo legatione fungimur, tamquam Deo exhortante per nos."—2 *Cor.* v. 20.
[4] "Accedat Sacerdos ad altaris tribunal ut Christus."—*Serm. de Euchar.*
[5] "Sacerdos vice Christi vere fungitur."—*Ep. ad Cæcil.*
[6] "Cum videris Sacerdotem offerentem, consideres Christi manum invisibiliter extensam."—*Ad pop. Ant. hom.* 60.
[7] "De suo vestiens Sacerdotes."
[8] "Deus, qui omnipotentiam tuam parcendo maxime et miserendo manifestas."—*Dom.* 10 *post Pent.*

prayers. Hence, when they heard that Jesus Christ pardoned the sins of the paralytic, the Jews justly said: *Who can forgive sins but God alone?*[1] But what only God can do by his omnipotence, the priest can also do by saying "Ego te absolvo a peccatis tuis;" for the forms of the sacraments, or the words of the forms, produce what they signify. How great should be our wonder if we saw a person invested with the power of changing a negro into a white man; but the priest does what is far more wonderful, for by saying "Ego te absolvo" he changes the sinner from an enemy into the friend of God, and from the slave of hell into an heir of paradise.

Cardinal Hugo represents the Lord addressing the following words to a priest who absolves a sinner: "I have created heaven and earth, but I leave to you a better and nobler creation; make out of this soul that is in sin a new soul, that is, make out of the slave of Satan, that the soul is, a child of God. I have made the earth bring forth all kinds of fruit, but to thee I confide a more beautiful creation, namely, that the soul should bring forth fruits of salvation."[2] The soul without grace is a withered tree that can no longer produce fruit; but receiving the divine grace, through the ministry of a priest, it brings forth fruits of eternal life. St. Augustine says, that to sanctify a sinner is a greater work than to create heaven and earth.[3] *And hast thou*, says Job, *an arm like God, and canst thou thunder with a voice like Him?*[4] Who is it that has an arm like the arm

[1] "Quis potest dimittere peccata, nisi solus Deus?"—*Luke*, v. 21.

[2] "Ego feci cœlum et terram; verumtamen meliorem et nobiliorem creationem do tibi: fac novam animam quæ est in peccato. Ego feci ut terra produceret fructus suos; do tibi meliorem creationem, ut anima fructus suos producat."

[3] "Prorsus majus hoc esse dixerim, quam est cœlum et terra, et quæcunque cernuntur in cœlo et in terra."—*In Jo. tr.* 72.

[4] "Et si habes brachium sicut Deus, et si voce simili tonas?"—*Job*, xl. 4.

of God, and thunders with a voice like the thundering voice of God? It is the priest, who, in giving absolution, exerts the arm and voice of God, by which he rescues souls from hell.

According to St. Ambrose, a priest, in absolving a sinner, performs the very office of the Holy Ghost in the sanctification of souls.[1] Hence, in giving priests the power of absolving from sin, the Redeemer *breathed on them, and said to them, Receive ye the Holy Ghost: whose sins you shall forgive, they are forgiven; and whose sins you shall retain, they are retained.*[2] He gave them his own Spirit, that is, the Holy Ghost, the sanctifier of souls, and thus made them, according to the words of the Apostle, his own coadjutors: *We are God's coadjutors.*[3] "On priests," says St. Gregory, "it is incumbent to give the final decision, for by the right that they have received from the Lord they now remit, now retain sins."[4] St. Clement, then, had reason to say that the priest is, as it were, a God on earth.[5] *God*, said David, *stood in the congregation of the gods.*[6] These gods are, according to St. Augustine, the priests of God.[7] Innocent III. has written: "Indeed, it is not too much to say that in view of the sublimity of their offices the priests are so many gods."[8]

[1] "Munus Spiritus Sancti, officium Sacerdotis."

[2] "Insufflavit, et dixit eis: Accipite Spiritum Sanctum: quorum remiseritis peccata, remittuntur eis; et quorum retinueritis, retenta sunt."—*John*, xx. 22.

[3] "Dei enim sumus adjutores."—1 *Cor.* iii. 9.

[4] "Principatum superni judicii sortiuntur; ut, vice Dei, quibusdam peccata retineant, quibusdam relaxent."—*In Evang. hom.* 26.

[5] "Post Deum, terrenus Deus."—*Const. apost.* l. 2, c. 26.

[6] "Deus stetit in synagoga Deorum."—*Ps.* lxxxi. 1.

[7] "Dii excelsi, in quorum synagoga Deus Deorum stare desiderat."—*Ad Fr. in er.* s. 36.

[8] "Sacerdotes, propter officii dignitatem, Deorum nomine nuncupantur."—*Can. Cum ex injuncto. De Hæret.*

VI.
Conclusion.

How great, then, says St. Ambrose, the disorder to see in the same person the highest dignity and a life of scandal, a divine profession and wicked conduct![1] What, says Salvian, is a sublime dignity conferred on an unworthy person but a gem enchased in mire?[2]

Neither doth any man, says St. Paul, *take the honor to himself, but he that is called by God, as Aaron was. For Christ did not glorify Himself that He might be made a high priest; but He that said unto Him: Thou art my Son; this day have I begotten Thee.*[3] Let no one, he says, dare to ascend to the priesthood, without first receiving, as Aaron did, the divine call; for even Jesus Christ would not of himself assume the honor of the priesthood, but waited till his Father called him to it. From this we may infer the greatness of the sacerdotal dignity. But the greater its sublimity, the more it should be dreaded. "For," says St. Jerome, "great is the dignity of priests; but also, when they sin, great is their ruin. Let us rejoice at having been raised so high, but let us be afraid of falling."[4] Lamenting, St. Gregory cries out: "Purified by the hands of the priest the elect enter the heavenly country, and alas! priests precipitate themselves into

[1] "Ne sit honor sublimis, et vita deformis; deifica professio, et illicita actio. Actio respondeat nomini."—*De Dignat. sac.* c. 3.

[2] "Quid est dignitas in indigno, nisi ornamentum in luto?"—*Ad Eccl. cath.* l. 2.

[3] "Nec quisquam sumit sibi honorem, sed qui vocatur a Deo, tamquam Aaron. Sic et Christus non semetipsum clarificavit ut Pontifex fieret, sed qui locutus est ad eum: Filius meus es tu; ego hodie genui te."—*Heb.* v. 4.

[4] "Grandis dignitas Sacerdotum, sed grandis ruina eorum, si peccant. Lætemur ad ascensum, sed timeamus ad lapsum."—*In Ezech.* c. 44.

the fire of hell!"[1] The saint compares priests to the baptismal water which cleanses the baptized from their sins, and sends them to heaven, "and is afterwards thrown into the sink."[2]

[1] "Ingrediuntur electi, Sacerdotum manibus expiati, cœlestem patriam; et Sacerdotes ad inferni supplicia festinant!"
[2] "Et ipsa in cloacas descendit!"—*In Evang. hom.* 17.

CHAPTER II

THE END OF THE PRIESTHOOD.

1.

The Priesthood Appears to the Saints a Formidable Charge.

ST. CYPRIAN said, that all those that had the true spirit of God were, when compelled to take the order of priesthood, seized with fear and trembling, as if they saw an enormous weight placed on their shoulders, by which they were in danger of being crushed to death. "I see," said St. Cyril of Alexandria, "all the saints frightened at the sacred ministry, as at an immense charge."[1] St. Epiphanius writes, that he found no one willing to be ordained a priest. A Council held in Carthage ordained that they that were thought worthy, and refused to be ordained, might be compelled to become priests.

St. Gregory Nazianzen says: "No one rejoices when he is ordained priest."[2] In his life of St. Cyprian, Paul the Deacon states that when the saint heard that his bishop intended to ordain him priest, he through humility concealed himself.[3] It is related in the life of St. Fulgentius that he too fled away and hid himself.[4] St. Athanasius also, as Sozomen relates, took flight in order to escape the priesthood. St. Ambrose, as he himself

---
[1] "Omnes sanctos reperio divini ministerii ingentem veluti molem formidantes."—*De Fest. pasch. hom.* 1.

[2] "Nemo læto animo creatur Sacerdos."

[3] "Humiliter secessit."—*Vita S. Cypr.*

[4] "Vota eligentium velociori præveniens fuga, latebris incertis absconditur."—*Vita S. Fulg.* c. 16.

attests, resisted for a long time before he consented to be ordained.[1] St. Gregory, even after it was made manifest by miracles that God wished him to be a priest, concealed himself under the garb of a merchant, in order to prevent his ordination.

To avoid being ordained, St. Ephrem feigned madness; St. Mark cut off his thumb; St. Ammonius cut off his ears and nose, and because the people insisted on his ordination, he threatened to cut out his tongue, and thus they ceased to molest him.

It is known to all, that St. Francis remained a deacon, and refused to ascend to the priesthood, because he learned by revelation, that the soul of a priest should be as pure as the water that was shown to him in a crystal vessel. The Abbot Theodore was only a deacon, but he would not exercise the duties of the Order he had received because during prayer he was shown a pillar of fire, and heard the following words: "If you have a heart as inflamed as this pillar, you may then exercise your Order." The Abbot Motuès was a priest, but always refused to offer the holy Mass, saying that he had been compelled to take holy Orders, and that because he felt himself unworthy, he could not celebrate.

Formerly there were but few priests among the monks, whose lives were so austere; and the monk who aspired to the priesthood was considered to be a proud man. Hence, to try the obedience of one of his monks, St. Basil commanded him to ask in public the Order of priesthood; his compliance was regarded as an act of heroic obedience, because by his obedience in asking to be ordained priest he, as it were, declared himself to be a man filled with the spirit of pride.

But how, I ask, does it happen that the saints, who live only for God, resist their ordination through a sense

---

[1] "Quam resistebam, ne ordinarer!"—*Epist.* 82.

of their unworthiness, and that some run blindly to the priesthood, and rest not until they attain it by lawful or unlawful means? Ah, unhappy men! says St. Bernard, to be registered among the priests of God shall be for them the same as to be enrolled on the catalogue of the damned. And why? Because such persons are generally called to the priesthood, not by God, but by relatives, by interest, or ambition. Thus they enter the house of God, not through the motive that a priest should have, but through worldly motives. Behold why the faithful are abandoned, the Church dishonored, so many souls perish, and with them such priests are also damned.

II.

What is the End of the Priesthood.

God wills that all men should be saved, but not in the same way. As in heaven he has distinguished different degrees of glory, so on earth he has established different states of life, as so many different ways of gaining heaven. On account of the great ends for which it has been instituted, the priesthood is of all these the most noble, the most exalted and sublime. What are these ends? Perhaps the sole ends of the priesthood are to say Mass, and to recite the Office, and then to live like seculars? No, the end for which God has instituted the priesthood has been to appoint on earth public persons to watch over the honor of his divine majesty, and to procure the salvation of souls. *For every high priest*, says St. Paul, *taken from among men, is ordained for men in the things that appertain to God, that he may offer up gifts and sacrifices for sins: who can have compassion on them that are ignorant and that err.*[1] *To execute the office of the priest-*

---

[1] "Omnis namque Pontifex, ex hominibus assumptus, pro hominibus constituitur in iis quæ sunt ad Deum, ut offerat dona et sacrificia pro peccatis; qui condolere possit iis qui ignorant et errant."—*Heb.* v. 1.

hood and to have praise.[1] "That is," says Cardinal Hugo, "to perform the office of praising God."[2] And Cornelius à Lapide says: "Just as it is the office of the angels to praise God without ceasing in heaven, so it is the office of priests to praise God without ceasing on earth."[3]

Jesus Christ has made priests, as it were, his co-operators in procuring the honor of his eternal Father and the salvation of souls, and therefore, when he ascended into heaven, he protested that he left them to hold his place, and to continue the work of redemption which he had undertaken and consummated. "He made them," says St. Ambrose, "the vicars of his love."[4] And Jesus Christ himself said to his disciples: *As the Father hath sent Me, I also send you.*[5] I leave you to perform the very office for which I came into the world; that is, to make known to men the name of my Father. And addressing his eternal Father, he said: *I have glorified Thee on earth; I have finished the work which Thou gavest me to do; I have manifested Thy name to the men.*[6] He then prayed for his priests: *I have given them Thy word. . . . Sanctify them in truth. . . . As Thou hast sent me into the world, I also have sent them.*[7] Thus, priests are placed in the world to make known to men God and his perfections, his justice and mercy, his commands, and to procure the respect, obedience, and love that he deserves. They are appointed to seek the lost sheep, and when

---

[1] "Fungi sacerdotio et habere laudem."—*Ecclus.* xlv. 19.

[2] "'Habere laudem,' id est, officium laudandi Deum."

[3] "Sicut Angelorum est perpetim laudare Deum in cœlis, sic Sacerdotum officium est eumdem jugiter laudare in terris."

[4] "Amoris sui velut vicarium (Petrum) relinquebat."—*In Luk.* l. 10, c. *ult.*

[5] "Sicut misit me Pater, et ego mitto vos."—*John*, xx. 21.

[6] "Ego te clarificavi super terram; opus consummavi. . . . Manifestavi nomen tuum hominibus."—*John*, xvii. 4.

[7] "Ego dedi eis sermonem tuum. . . . Sanctifica eos in veritate. . . . Sicut tu me misisti in mundum, et ego misi eos."—*Ibid.* xvii. 18.

necessary, to give their lives for them. This is the end for which Jesus Christ has come on earth, for which he has constituted priests: *As the Father hath sent me, I also send you.*

III.
Principal Duties of the Priest.

Jesus came into the world for no other purpose than to light up the fire of divine love. *I am come to cast fire on the earth, and what will I but that it be kindled.*[1] And the priest must labor during his whole life, and with his whole strength, not to acquire riches, honors, and worldly goods, but to inspire all with the love of God. "Therefore," says the author of the Imperfect Work, "has Christ sent us not that we may do what is to our profit, but what is for the glory of God. . . . . True love does not seek its own advantage, but it wishes in all things only what is the good pleasure of the person loved."[2] In the Book of Leviticus the Lord says to his priests: *I have separated you from other people, that you should be Mine.*[3] Mark the words *that you should be Mine;* that you may be employed in my praises, devoted to my service, and to my love: "The co-operators and dispensers of my sacraments," says St. Peter Damian.[4] "*Mine,*" says St. Ambrose, "that you may be the guides and the rulers of the flock of Christ."[5] "*Mine,*" for, according to the same Doctor, the minister of the altar

---

[1] " Ignem veni mittere in terram; et quid volo, nisi ut accendatur?"—*Luke*, xii. 49.

[2] " Ideo vocati sumus a Christo, non ut operemur quæ ad nostrum pertinent usum, sed quæ ad gloriam Dei. . . . Verus amor non quærit quæ sua sunt, sed ad libitum amati cuncta desiderat perficere."—*Hom.* 34.

[3] " Separavi vos a cæteris populis, ut essetis mei."—*Levit.* xx. 26.

[4] " Sacramentorum Dei cooperatores et dispensatores."—*Opusc.* 27, c. 3.

[5] " Duces et rectores gregis Christi."—*De Dignit. sac.* c. 2.

belongs not to himself, but to God.[1] The Lord separates his priests from the rest of his people in order to unite them entirely to himself. *Is it a small thing unto you that the God of Israel hath separated you from all the people, and joined you to Himself.*[2]

If, said the Redeemer, *any man minister unto Me, let him follow Me.*[3] *Let him follow Me;* he should follow Jesus Christ by shunning the world, by assisting souls, by promoting the love of God, and extirpating vice. *The reproaches of them that reproached thee have fallen upon Me.*[4] The priest, who is a true follower of Jesus Christ, regards injuries done to God as offered to himself. Seculars, devoted to the world, cannot render to God the veneration and the gratitude that are due to him: hence, says a learned author, Father Frassen, it has been necessary to select certain persons, that by the fulfilment of their peculiar office and obligations they may give due honor to the Lord.[5]

In every government ministers are appointed to enforce the observance of the laws, to remove scandals, to repress the seditious, and to defend the honor of the king. For all these ends the Lord has constituted priests the officers of his court. Hence St. Paul has said: *Let us exhibit ourselves as the ministers of God.*[6] Ministers of state always endeavor to procure the respect due to their sovereign, and to extend his glories; they always speak of him in terms of praise, and should they hear a word against their master, with what zeal

---

[1] "Verus minister altaris Deo, non sibi, natus est."—*In Ps.* 118, s. 8.

[2] "Separavit vos Deus Israel ab omni populo, et junxit sibi."—*Num.* xvi. 9.

[3] "Si quis mihi ministrat, me sequatur."—*John*, xii. 26.

[4] "Opprobria exprobrantium tibi ceciderunt super me."—*Ps.* lxviii. 10.

[5] "Fuit necessarium aliquos e populo seligi ac destinari, qui ad impendendum debitum Deo cultum, et sui status obligatione et institutione, intenderent."—*Scotus acad. De Ord.* d. 1, a. 1, q. 1.

[6] "Exhibeamus nosmetipsos sicut Dei ministros."—2 *Cor.* vi. 4.

do they reprove the author of it? They study to gratify his inclinations, and even expose their life in order to please him. Is it thus that priests act for God? It is certain that they are his ministers of state: by them are managed all the interests of his glory. Through them sins should be removed from the world: this is the end for which Jesus Christ has died. *Crucified, that the body of sin may be destroyed.*[1] But on the day of judgment how can the judge acknowledge as his true minister the priest who, instead of preventing the sins of others, is the first to conspire against Jesus Christ? What would you say of ministers who should neglect to attend to the interests of their sovereign, and should refuse to assist him when he stood in need of their aid? But what would you say if these ministers also spoke against their master, and endeavored to deprive him of his throne by entering into an alliance with his enemies?

Priests are the ambassadors of God, says the Apostle: *For Christ we are ambassadors.*[2] They are his coadjutors in procuring the salvation of souls: *For we are God's coadjutors.*[3] For this end Jesus Christ gave them the Holy Ghost, that they might save souls by remitting their sins. *He breathed on them, and He said to them: Receive ye the Holy Ghost: whose sins you shall forgive, they are forgiven them.*[4] Hence the theologian Habert has written that the essence of the priesthood consists in seeking ardently to procure first the glory of God, and then the salvation of souls.[5]

The business, then, of every priest is to attend, not to

---

[1] "Crucifixus est, ut destruatur corpus peccati."—*Rom.* vi. 6.

[2] "Pro Christo legatione fungimur."—2 *Cor.* v. 20.

[3] "Dei enim sumus adjutores."—1 *Cor.* iii. 9.

[4] "Insufflavit, et dixit eis: Accipite Spiritum Sanctum: quorum remiseritis peccata, remittuntur eis."—*John*, xx. 22.

[5] "Ingenium sacerdotale essentialiter consistit in ardenti studio promovendi gloriam Dei et salutem proximi."—*De Ord.* p. 3, c. 5, q. 3.

the things of the world, but to the things of God: *He is ordained in the things that appertain to God.*[1] Hence St. Silvester ordained that for ecclesiastics the days of the week should be called *Feriæ*, or vacant or free days; and he says: "It is every day that the priest, free from earthly occupations, should occupy himself entirely with God."[2] By this he meant that we, who are ordained priests, should seek nothing but God and the salvation of souls, an office which St. Denis called "the most divine of all the divine offices."[3] St. Antonine says that the meaning of *sacerdos* is *sacra docens*, one that teaches sacred things.[4] And Honorius of Autun says that *presbyter* signifies *præbens iter*, one that shows the way.[5] Hence St. Ambrose calls priests *the guides and rectors of the flock of Christ.*[6] And St. Peter calls ecclesiastics *a kingly priesthood, a holy nation, a purchased people.*[7] A people destined to acquire not riches, but souls. St. Ambrose calls the sacerdotal office "an office that should acquire not money, but souls."[8] Even the Gentiles wished their priests to attend only to the worship of their gods, and therefore they would not permit them to hold the office of secular magistrates.

Hence, speaking of priests, St. Gregory says, with tears, it is our duty to abandon all earthly business in order to attend to the things of God, but we do the

[1] "Constituitur in iis quæ sunt ad Deum."—*Hebr.* v. 1.
[2] "Quo significaretur quotidie clericos, abjecta ceterarum rerum cura, uni Deo prorsus vacare debere."—*Breviar.* 31 *Dec.*
[3] "In hoc sita est Sacerdotis perfectio, ut ad divinam promoveatur imitationem, quodque divinius est omnium, ipsius etiam Dei cooperator existat."—*De Cæl. Hierarch.* c. 3.
[4] "Sacerdos—Sacra docens."—*Summ.* p. 3, tr. 14, c. 7, § 1.
[5] "Presbyter—Præbens iter."—*Gemma an.* l. 1, c. 181.
[6] "Duces et Rectores gregis Christi."—*De Dignit. Sacerd.* c. 2.
[7] "Regale Sacerdotium, Gens Sancta, Populus acquisitionis."—1 *Pet.* ii. 9.
[8] "Officium quæstus, non pecuniarum, sed animarum."—*Serm.* 78.

The End of the Priesthood. 47

very contrary, "for we desert the cause of God and devote all our care to the things of the earth."[1] After being appointed by God to attend only to the advancement of his glory, Moses spent his time in settling the disputes of the people. Jethro rebuked him for his conduct, saying: *Thou art spent with foolish labor. . . . Be thou to the people in the things that pertain to God.*[2] But what would Jethro say if he saw our priests employed in mercantile affairs, acting as the servants of seculars, or occupied in arranging marriages, but forgetful of the works of God; if, in a word, he saw them seeking, as St. Prosper says, " to advance in wealth, but not in virtue, and to acquire greater honors, but not greater sanctity!"[3] . . . "Oh! what an abuse," exclaims Father John d'Avila, "to make heaven subordinate to earth!" "What a misery," says St. Gregory, "to see so many priests seeking, not the merits of virtue, but the goods of this life!"[4]

Hence, says St. Isidore of Pelusium, in the very works of their ministry they regard not the glory of God, but the reward annexed to them.[5]

(Many other things that might be added to this chapter are omitted, because they are contained in the following chapter, which treats of the offices of a priest.)

[1] " Dei causam relinquimus, et ad terrena negotia vacamus."—*In Evang. hom.* 17.

[2] "Stulto labore consumeris. . . . Esto tu populo in his quæ ad Deum pertinent."—*Exod.* xviii. 18.

[3] " Non ut meliores, sed ut ditiores fiant; non ut sanctiores, sed ut honoratiores sint!"—*De Vita cont.* l. 1, c. 21.

[4] " Non virtutum merita, sed subsidia vitæ præsentis exquirunt."—*Mor.* l. 23, c. 26.

[5] " Ad stipendia dumtaxat oculos habent."—*Epist.* l. 1, *ep.* 447.

CHAPTER III.

THE SANCTITY NECESSARY FOR THE PRIEST.

I.

What should be the Sanctity of the Priest by Reason of his Dignity.

GREAT is the dignity of the priesthood, but great also are its obligations. Priests ascend to a great height, but in their ascent they must be assisted by great virtue; otherwise, instead of meriting a reward, they shall be reserved for severe chastisement. "The sacerdotal dignity," says St. Laurence Justinian, "is great, but great is the burden. Raised to this high degree of honor, it is necessary that priests sustain themselves by great virtue; otherwise they will have to expect instead of great merit great punishment."[1] And St. Peter Chrysologus says: "The priests are honored, but I say that they are burdened."[2] The honor of the priesthood is great, but its burden is also great; great, too, is the account that priests have to render to God. "Priests," says St. Jerome, "will save themselves, not by their dignity, but by the works that correspond to their dignity."[3]

Every Christian should be perfect and holy, because every Christian professes to serve a God of holiness.

---

[1] "Magna dignitas, sed majus est pondus. In alto gradu positi sunt; oportet quoque ut in sublimi virtutum culmine sint erecti; alioquin, non ad meritum, sed ad proprium præsunt judicium."—*De Inst. præl.* c. 11.

[2] "Sacerdotes honorati; dicam autem, onerati."

[3] "Non dignitas, sed opus dignitatis salvare consuevit."—*Ad Sophon.* 3.

CHAP. III.] *Sanctity Necessary for the Priest.*

"In this," says St. Leo, "a Christian consists, that he gets rid of the earthly and puts on the heavenly man."[1] Hence Jesus Christ has said: *Be you therefore perfect, as also your heavenly Father is perfect.*[2] But the sanctity of the priest should be very different from that of seculars. "Between priests and the rest of men," says St. Ambrose "there should be nothing in common as to works and as to conduct."[3] And the saint adds, that as greater grace is given to the priest, so his life should be more holy than that of seculars.[4] And St. Isidore of Pelusium says that between the sanctity of a priest and a good secular the difference should be as great as between heaven and earth.[5]

St. Thomas teaches that every one is obliged to practise what is suited to the state that he has chosen.[6] And according to St. Augustine, a man by entering the ecclesiastical state imposes on himself the obligation of being holy.[7] And Cassiodorus calls the clerical profession a heavenly life.[8] The priest is, as Thomas à Kempis says, bound to greater perfection than all others,[9] because the priesthood is the most sublime of

[1] "Dum terreni hominis imago deponitur, et cœlestis forma suscipitur."—*De Pass.* s. 14.
[2] "Estote ergo vos perfecti, sicut et Pater vester cœlestis perfectus est."—*Matth.* v. 48.
[3] "Nihil in Sacerdote commune cum studio atque usu multitudinis."—*Epist.* 6.
[4] "Debet præponderare vita sacerdotis, sicut præponderat gratia."—*Epist.* 82.
[5] "Tantum inter Sacerdotem et quemlibet probum interesse debet, quantum inter cœlum et terram discriminis est."—*Epist.* l. 2, *ep.* 205.
[6] "Quicunque profitetur statum aliquem, tenetur ad ea quæ illi statui conveniunt."
[7] "Clericus duas res professus est, et sanctitatem et clericatum."—*Serm.* 355, *E. B.*
[8] "Professio clericorum, vita cœlestis."
[9] "Sacerdos ad majorem tenetur perfectionem sanctitatis."—*Imit. Chr.* l. 4, c. 5.

all states. Salvian adds, that in things in which God counsels perfection to seculars, he makes it imperative on ecclesiastics.[1]

The priests of the Old Law carried on their forehead a plate on which was engraved the words *Sanctum Domino*,[2] that they might be reminded of the sanctity that they should profess. The victims offered by the priests should be entirely consumed. And why? "It was," says Theodoret, "to symbolize the complete sacrifice that the priest has made of himself to the Lord."[3] St. Ambrose says that to offer sacrifice worthily the priest ought first to sacrifice himself by the oblation of his whole being to God.[4] And Hesychius has written that from youth till death the priest should be a perfect holocaust of perfection.[5] Hence God said to the priests of the Old Law: *I have separated you from other people, that you should be mine.*[6] Now, in the New Law, the Lord commands his priests far more strictly to abstain from worldly business that they may labor only to please that God to whom they have dedicated themselves. *No man*, says St. Paul, *being a soldier to God, entangleth himself with secular business that he may please him to whom he hath engaged himself.*[7] And the holy Church requires of those that enter the sanctuary by taking the first

[1] " Clericis suis Salvator, non ut cæteris voluntarium, sed imperativum officium perfectionis indicit."—*De Eccl. Cathol.* l. 2.

[2] "Sanctum Domini."—*Exod.* xxxix. 29.

[3] " Ut integritas Sacerdotis monstraretur, qui totum se Deo dicaverit." —*In Levit.* q. 3.

[4] " Hoc enim est sacrificium primitivum, quando unusquisque se offert hostiam, et a se incipit, ut postea munus suum possit offerre."— *De Abel,* l. 2, c. 6.

[5] " Sacerdos continuum holocaustum offerre præcipitur, ut, a perfecta sapientia incipiens, in eadem finiat, et totam vitam suam componat ad perfectionem."—*In Levit.* l. 2, c. 1.

[6] " Separavi vos a cæteris populis, ut essetis mei."—*Levit.* xx. 26.

[7] " Nemo, militans Deo, implicat se negotiis sæcularibus, ut ei placeat, cui se probavit."—2 *Tim.* ii. 4.

tonsure, to promise that they shall not engage in secular pursuits, and to declare that thenceforward they will have no other inheritance than the Lord. *The Lord is the portion of my inheritance and of my cup; it is Thou that wilt restore my inheritance to me.*[1] St. Jerome says that the clerical dress, the very state, calls for and demands sanctity of life.[2] Thus the priest should keep not only at a distance from every vice, but should also make continual efforts to arrive at perfection. In this consists, according to St. Bernard, the perfection that can be attained in this life.[3]

St. Bernard weeps at the sight of so many that run to Holy Orders without considering the sanctity necessary for those that wish to ascend to such a height.[4] St. Ambrose says, "Those are very rare that can say, 'The Lord is my portion.' Those are very rare whom passion does not inflame, or whom cupidity does not actuate, or whom terrestrial cares do not absorb."[5]

St. John the Evangelist writes: *Who hath made us a kingdom, and priests to God and His Father.*[6] In explaining the word *kingdom*, Tirinus with other interpreters says, that priests are the kingdom of God: first, because in them God reigns in this life by grace, and in the next by glory:[7] secondly, because they are made kings to reign over vice.[8] St. Gregory says, that the priest ought to

---

[1] "Dominus pars hereditatis meæ et calicis mei; tu es qui restitues hereditatem meam mihi."—*Ps.* xv. 5.

[2] "Clamat vestis clericalis, clamat status professi animi sanctitatem."

[3] "Jugis conatus ad perfectionem, perfectio reputatur."—*Epist.* 254.

[4] "Curritur passim ad sacros Ordines sine consideratione."—*De Conv. ad cler.* c. 20.

[5] "Quam rarus, qui potest dicere: Portio mea, Dominus; quem non inflammet libido, non stimulet avaritia, non aliqua negotiorum sæcularium cura sollicitet!"—*In Ps.* cxviii. s. 8.

[6] "Fecit nos regnum et Sacerdotes Deo et Patri suo."—*Apoc.* i. 6.

[7] "In quo Deus regnat nunc per gratiam, postea per gloriam."—

[8] "Fecit nos reges; regnamus enim cum ipso, et imperamus vitiis."

be dead to the world and to all the passions, in order to lead a life altogether divine.[1] The present priesthood is the same as that which Jesus Christ has received from his Father: *And the glory which Thou hast given to Me, I have given to them.*[2] Since, then, says St. Chrysostom, the priest represents Jesus Christ, he ought to have as much purity as would entitle him to stand in the midst of the angels.[3]

St. Paul requires that the priest should be irreprehensible: *It behoveth a bishop to be blameless.*[4] In the word *bishop*, the Apostle certainly includes priests; for from bishops he passes to deacons, without making mention of priests: *Deacons in like manner chaste,*[5] etc. Hence he intended to comprehend them under the word bishop. This passage is understood in this sense by St. Augustine and St. John Chrysostom, who in speaking on this point says, "What he said of bishops he also meant for priests."[6] Now the word *irreprehensibilem—blameless*—every one knows, implies the possession of all virtues. "It comprises all virtues,"[7] says St. Jerome. And in explaining this word, Cornelius à Lapide says "that it is meant for him who is not only exempt from all vice, but who is adorned with all virtues."[8]

For eleven centuries, all that fell into mortal sin after baptism were excluded from the priesthood. This we

[1] " Necesse est ut, mortuus omnibus passionibus, vivat vita divina."
[2] " Et ego claritatem, quam dedisti mihi, dedi eis."—*John*, xvii. 22.
[3] " Necesse est Sacerdotem sic esse purum, ut, in ipsis coelis collocatus, inter coelestes illas virtutes medius staret."—*De Sacerd.* l. 3.
[4] " Oportet ergo Episcopum irreprehensibilem esse."—1 *Tim.* iii. 2.
[5] " Diaconos similiter pudicos."
[6] " Quæ de Episcopis dixit, etiam Sacerdotibus congruit."—*In* 1 *Tim. hom.* 11.
[7] " Omnes virtutes comprehendit."—*Ep. ad. Occanum.*
[8] " Qui non tantum vitio careat, sed qui omnibus virtutibus sit ornatus."

learn from the Council of Nice,[1] from the Council of Toledo,[2] from the Council of Elvira,[3] and from the Fourth Council of Carthage.[4] And if a priest after his ordination had fallen into sin, he was deposed, and shut up in a monastery, as may be observed from several canons.[5] In the sixth canon, the following reason is assigned: "Above all, what the Church wishes is perfect innocence. Those that are not holy should not touch holy things."[6] And in the several canons we read: "Since the clerics have taken the Lord for their inheritance, let them not have intercourse with the world."[7] The Council of Trent declared, "Wherefore clerics called to have the Lord for their portion ought by all means so to regulate their whole life and conversation as that in their dress, comportment, gait, discourse, and all things else, nothing appear but what is grave, regulated, and replete with religiousness."[8] In ecclesiastics the Council requires sanctity in dress as well as in conduct, language, and every action. St. John Chrysostom says, that priests should be so holy that all may look to them as models of sanctity; because God has placed them on earth that they may live like angels, and be luminaries and teachers of virtue to all others.[9]

[1] *Can.* 9, 10.   [2] I. *Can.* 2.   [3] *Can.* 76.   [4] IV. *Can.* 68.
[5] *Corp. Jur. Can. dist.* 81.
[6] "In omnibus enim quod irreprehensibile est, Sancta defendit Ecclesia. Qui sancti non sunt, sancta tractare non possunt."—*Dist.* 81. *can.* 4–6.
[7] "Clerici, quibus pars Dominus est, a sæculi segregati vivant."
[8] " Decet omnino clericos, in sortem Domini vocatos, vitam moresque suos componere, ut habitu, gestu, sermone, aliisque rebus, nil nisi grave ac religione plenum præ se ferant."—*Sess.* 2, *cap.* 1, *de Ref.*
[9] "Sacerdos debet vitam habere immaculatam, ut omnes in illum veluti in aliquod exemplar excellens intueantur. Idcirco enim nos (Deus) elegit, ut simus quasi luminaria, et magistri cæterorum efficiamur, ac veluti angeli cum hominibus versemur in terris."—*In* 1 *Tim. hom.* 10,

The word *ecclesiastic*, according to St. Jerome, signifies a person who has taken God for his inheritance. This made the holy Doctor say: " Let the cleric then understand the signification of his name, and let him put his life in harmony with his title."[1] Let ecclesiastics understand the signification of their name, and live according to it; and since God is their portion, let them live for God alone, says St. Ambrose.[2]

The priest is a minister destined by God for two most noble and exalted offices—to honor him by sacrifices and to sanctify souls: *Every high priest taken from among men is ordained for men in the things that appertain to God.*[3] " Hence," says St. Thomas on this passage, " it is for the things that refer to God that the priest receives his mission, and by no means that he may acquire glory or amass riches."[4] Every priest is chosen by the Lord, and placed in the world to labor, not to acquire wealth nor applause, nor to indulge in amusements, nor to advance his family, but only to promote the interests of God's glory. " He is ordained for the things that appertain to God." Hence, in the Scriptures, the priest is called a man of God.[5] A man that belongs not to the world, nor to relatives, nor to himself, but only to God, and that seeks nothing but God. Hence to priests should be applied the words of David: *This is the generation of them that seek him, of them that seek the face of the God of Jacob.*[6] Behold the generation that seek only

---

[1] " Clericus interpretetur primo vocabulum suum, et nitatur esse quod dicitur."—*Ep. ad Nepotian.*

[2] " Cui Deus portio est, nihil debet curare, nisi Deum."—*De Esau.* c. 2.

[3] " Omnis namque Pontifex, ex hominibus assumptus, pro hominibus constituitur in iis quæ sunt ad Deum."—*Hebr.* v. 1.

[4] " Non propter gloriam, non propter cumulandas divitias."—*In Hebr.* v. *lect.* 1.

[5] " Homo Dei."—1 *Tim.* vi. 11.

[6] " Hæc est generatio quærentium cum."—*Ps.* xxiii. 6.

God! As in heaven God has appointed certain angels to assist at his throne, so on earth, among men, he has destined priests to procure his glory. Hence he says to them, *I have separated you from other people*.[1] St. John Chrysostom writes: "Therefore has God chosen us, that like angels we may live with men on earth."[2] And God himself says, *I will be sanctified in them that approach to Me*.[3] "That is," adds the commentator, "my sanctity shall be shown forth by the sanctity of my ministers."[4]

II.

What Should be the Sanctity of the Priest as the Minister of the Altar.

St. Thomas says, that greater sanctity is required in a priest than in religious, on account of the most sublime functions of his ministry, particularly in the oblation of the sacrifice of the Mass. "Hence," adds the holy Doctor, "the cleric who is ordained sins more grievously under similar circumstances if he does anything contrary to the sanctity of his state than the religious who is not ordained."[5] Listen to the celebrated maxim of St. Augustine: "A good monk will hardly become a good cleric."[6] Hence no one can be called a good ecclesiastic unless he surpasses a good monk in virtue. "A true minister of the altar," says St. Ambrose, "is

[1] "Separavi vos a cæteris populis, ut essetis mei."—*Levit.* xx. 26.
[2] "Idcirco enim nos (Deus) elegit, ut veluti angeli cum hominibus versemur in terris."—*In* 1 *Tim. hom.* 10.
[3] "Sanctificabor in iis qui appropinquant mihi."—*Levit.* x. 3.
[4] "Agnoscar sanctus ex sanctitate ministrorum."
[5] "Quia, per sacrum Ordinem, aliquis deputatur ad dignissima ministeria, quibus ipsi Christo servitur in Sacramento altaris; ad quod requiritur major sanctitas interior, quam requirit etiam religionis status. Unde gravius peccat, cæteris paribus, clericus in sacris Ordinibus constitutus, si aliquid contrarium sanctitati agat, quam aliquis religiosus qui non habet Ordinem sacrum."—2. 2, q. 184, a. 3.
[6] "Bonus monachus vix bonum clericum facit."—*Epist.* 60, *E. B.*

born for God, not for himself."[1] That is, a priest should disregard his conveniencies, his interests, and amusements; he should consider that from the day that he has received the priesthood, he belongs not to himself, but to God; and should attend only to the interests of God. The Lord evidently wishes his priests to be pure and holy; that being cleansed from every defect, they may approach the altar to offer sacrifice to him: *And*, says the Prophet Malachy, *He shall sit refining and cleansing the silver, and He shall purify the sons of Levi, and shall refine them as gold and as silver, and they shall offer sacrifices to the Lord in justice.*[2] In the book of Leviticus he says: *They shall be holy to their God, and shall not profane His name; for they offer the burnt offerings of the Lord, and the bread of their God, and therefore they shall be holy.*[3] The priests of the Old Law, then, were commanded to be holy, because they offered to God incense and the loaves of proposition, that were but a figure of the most holy Sacrament of the altar. How much greater should be the purity and sanctity of the priests of the New Law that offer to God the immaculate Lamb, his own very Son? Estius says that we do not offer calves or incense, as the priests of the Old Law did, "but the body of Christ who was hanging on the cross."[4] Hence Bellarmine says: "Woe be to us miserable beings, to

[1] "Verus minister altaris Deo, non sibi, natus est."—*In Ps.* cxviii s. 3.

[2] "Et sedebit conflans et emundans argentum; et purgabit filios Levi, et colabit eos quasi aurum et quasi argentum; et erunt Domino offerentes sacrificia in justitia."—*Mal.* iii. 3.

[3] "Sancti erunt Deo suo et non polluent nomen ejus; incensum enim Domini et panes Dei sui offerunt, et ideo sancti erunt."—*Levit.* xxi. 6.

[4] "Ipsum videlicet Corpus Domini, quod in ara crucis pependit. Ideoque sanctitas requiritur, quæ sita est in puritate animi; sine qua, quisquis ad hæc tremenda mysteria accedit, immundus accedit."—*In Levit.* xxi. 6.

whom the highest office has been assigned, yet we are so far from the fervor that God required of the priests of the Old Law, who were in comparison with us only shadows."[1]

The Lord commanded even those that carried the sacred vessels to be free from all stain: *Be ye clean, you who carry the vessels of the Lord.*[2] "How much greater," says Peter de Blois, "should be the purity of priests who carry Jesus Christ in their hands and in their breasts?"[3] "He that holds in his hands not only golden vessels," says St. Augustine, "but those vessels in which the death of the Lord is commemorated, must be pure."[4] The Blessed Virgin Mary should be holy and free from all stain, because she was to carry in her womb, and to treat as a mother, the Incarnate Word. "Why, then," says St. John Chrysostom, "should not sanctity shine forth with greater splendor than the sun, in the hand that touches the flesh of a God? in the mouth that is filled with celestial fire? and in the tongue that is purpled with the blood of Jesus Christ?"[5] The priest on the altar holds the place of Jesus Christ. "He should, then," says St. Laurence Justinian, "approach the altar to offer sacrifice like Jesus Christ; imitating as much as possible the purity and sanctity of Jesus Christ."[6] How great the sanctity that a confessor requires in a

[1] "Væ nobis miseris, qui, ministerium altissimum sortiti, tam procul absumus a fervore quem Salomon in umbraticis Sacerdotibus exigebat."—*In Ps.* cxxxi. 7.

[2] "Mundamini, qui fertis vasa Domini."—*Is.* lii. 11.

[3] "Quanto mundiores esse oportet, qui in manibus et corpore portant Christum!"—*Epist.* 123.

[4] "Oportet mundum esse, qui non solum vasa aurea debet tractare, sed etiam illa in quibus Domini mors exercetur."

[5] "Quo solari radio non splendidiorem oportet esse manum Carnem hanc dividentem, os quod igne spirituali repletur, linguam quæ tremendo nimis Sanguine rubescit?"—*Ad pop. Ant. hom.* 60.

[6] "Accedat ut Christus, ministret ut sanctus."—*S. de Euchar.*

nun, in order to permit her to communicate every day? And why is not the same perfection required in a priest that celebrates every morning?

"It must be confessed," says the Council of Trent, "that man can perform no action more holy than the celebration of Mass."[1] Hence the holy Council adds, that priests should be most careful to offer this holy sacrifice with the greatest possible purity of conscience.[2] "But," says St. Augustine, "what a horrible thing to hear the tongue that calls down the Son of God from heaven to earth speaking against God; and to see the hands that are bathed in the blood of Jesus Christ polluted with the filthiness of sin."[3]

If God required so much purity in those that were to offer the sacrifice of animals and of bread, and if he forbid these oblations to be made by him who had any blemish,— *Whosoever hath a blemish, he shall not offer bread to his God*,[4]—" how much greater purity," says Cardinal Bellarmine, "is required in those that have to offer to God his own Son, the divine Lamb?"[5] St. Thomas says that the word *macula* includes every defect: "Whoever is addicted to any vice should not be admitted to Holy Orders."[6] In the Old Law, the blind,

[1] "Necessario fatemur nullum aliud opus adeo sanctum ac divinum tractari posse, quam hoc tremendum mysterium."

[2] "Satis apparet omnem operam in eo ponendam esse, quanta ut maxima fieri potest interiori cordis munditia peragatur."—*Sess.* 22, *decr. de Observ.*

[3] "Ne lingua, quæ vocat de cœlo Filium Dei, contra Dominum loquatur; et manus, quæ intinguntur sanguine Christi, polluantur sanguine peccati."—*Molina, Instr. Sac. tr.* 1, c. 5, § 2.

[4] "Qui habuerit maculam, non offeret panes Deo suo."—*Levit.* xxi. 17.

[5] "Si tanta sanctitas requirebatur in Sacerdotibus qui sacrificabant oves et boves, quid, quæso, requiritur in Sacerdotibus qui sacrificant divinum Agnum?"—*In Ps.* cxxxi. 7.

[6] "Qui est aliquo vitio irretitus, non debet ad ministerium Ordinis accedere."—*Suppl.* q. 36, a. 1.

the lame, the lepers, were forbidden to offer sacrifice. *Neither shall he approach to minister to him, if he be blind, if he be lame, if he be crooked-backed, if he have a continual scab.*[1] Understanding the preceding defects in a spiritual sense, the holy Fathers say, that the *blind*, that is, they that shut their eyes to the light of God; the *lame*, that is, slothful priests that never advance in the way of God, and live always with the same defects, without mental prayer, and without recollection; the *crooked-backed*, that are, by worldly attachments, always bent down to the earth, to riches, to empty honors, and worldly amusements; and the *scabious*, that is, the voluptuous, that always wallow in sensual pleasures, *The sow that was washed to her wallowing in the mire*,[2]—are unfit to offer sacrifice; in a word, that he that is not holy is unworthy to approach the altar, because by the stains that he brings with him he contaminates the sanctuary of God. Let him not *approach the altar, because he hath a blemish, and he must not defile my sanctuary.*[3]

III.

What should be the Sanctity of the Priest as Mediator between God and Man.

The priest should be holy, because he holds the office of dispenser of the sacraments;[4] and also because he is a mediator between God and sinners. "Between God and man the priest stands," says St. John Chrysostom, "by communicating to us God's benefits, and by offer-

---

[1] " Nec accedet ad ministerium ejus, si cæcus fuerit, si claudus, . . . si gibbus, . . . si habens jugem scabiem."—*Levit*. xxi. 18.
[2] " Sus lota in volutabro luti."—2 *Pet*. ii. 22.
[3] " Nec accedat ad altare, quia maculam habet, et contaminare non debet sanctuarium meum."—*Levit*. xxi. 23.
[4] " Oportet sine crimine esse, sicut Dei dispensatorem."—*Tit*. i. 7.

ing him our petitions; he reconciles the angry Lord, and wards from us the blows of his justice."[1]

Through priests, God communicates his grace to the faithful in the sacraments. Through them he makes us his children, and saves us by baptism: *Unless a man be born again he cannot see the kingdom of God.*[2] Through them he heals the infirm, and even resuscitates, by the sacrament of penance, sinners that are dead to divine grace. Through them he nourishes souls, and preserves in them the life of divine grace, by means of the sacrament of the Eucharist: *Except you eat the flesh of the Son of man, and drink His blood, you shall not have life in you.*[3] Through them he gives strength to the dying, to overcome the temptations of hell, by means of the sacrament of Extreme Unction.

In a word, St. John Chrysostom says, that without priests we cannot be saved.[4] By St. Prosper priests are called judges of the divine will.[5] By St. Chrysostom, the walls of the Church.[6] By St. Ambrose, the camps of sanctity,[7] and by St. Gregory Nazianzen, the foundations of the world, and the pillars of the faith.[8] Hence St. Jerome says, that the priest by the power of his sanctity has to carry the weight of all the sins

---

[1] "Medius stat Sacerdos inter Deum et naturam humanam; illinc venientia beneficia ad nos deferens, et nostras petitiones illuc perferens Dominum iratum reconcilians, et nos eripiens ex illius manibus."—*De Verbis Is. hom.* 5.

[2] "Nisi quis renatus fuerit denuo, non potest videre regnum Dei."— *John*, iii. 3.

[3] "Nisi manducaveritis carnem Filii hominis, . . . non habebitis vitam in vobis."—*John*, vi. 54.

[4] "Sine his, salutis compotes fieri non possumus."—*De Sacerd.* l. 3.

[5] "Divinæ voluntatis Indices."—*De Vita cont.* l. 2, c. 2.

[6] "Muros Ecclesiæ."—*Hom.* 10.

[7] "Castra sanctitatis."—*De Offic.* l. 1, c. 50.

[8] "Mundi Fundamenta et Fidei Columnas."—*Carm. ad Episc.*

of the world.[1] Oh, what a tremendous weight! *And the priest shall pray for him, and for his sins before the Lord, ... and the sin shall be forgiven.*[2] It is on this account that the holy Church obliges priests to recite the Office every day, and to celebrate Mass at least several times in the year. St. Ambrose says that priests should never cease by night or by day to pray for the people.[3]

But to obtain graces for others the priest must be holy. "Those that are mediators between God and the people," says St. Thomas, "must shine before God with a good conscience, and with a good reputation before men."[4] St. Gregory says that it would be temerity in a mediator to present himself before a prince to ask pardon for rebels, if he himself stood charged with the guilt of treason.[5] They that wish to intercede for another, adds the same saint, must stand high in the estimation of the king; for should they be objects of his hatred, their intercession will only increase the indignation of the sovereign.[6] Hence, according to St. Augustine, the priest must have such merit before God that he may be able to obtain for the people what they, on account of their demerits, cannot hope to receive.[7] And

[1] "Sacerdotes onus totius orbis portant humeris sanctitatis."—*Hom. de Dedic. eccl.*
[2] "Orabitque pro eo Sacerdos et pro peccato ejus coram Domino, et repropitiabitur ei, dimitteturque peccatum."—*Levit.* xix. 22.
[3] "Sacerdotes die noctuque, pro plebe sibi commissa, oportet orare."—*In* 1 *Tim.* c. 3.
[4] "Medii inter Deum et hominem plebem, debent bona conscientia nitere quoad Deum, et bona fama quoad homines."—*Suppl.* q. 36, a. 1.
[5] "Qua mente apud Deum intercessoris locum pro populo arripit, qui familiarem se ejus gratiæ esse per vitæ merita nescit?"—*Past.* p. 1, c. 11.
[6] "Cum is qui displicet, ad intercedendum mittitur, irati animus ad deteriora provocatur."
[7] "Talem esse oportet Domini Sacerdotem, ut, quod populus pro se apud Deum non valuerit, ipse pro populo mereatur impetrare."—*In Ps.* xxxvi. s. 2.

Pope Hormisdas has said, "The priest must be holier than the people, because he must pray for them."[1]

But St. Bernard says, with tears, "Behold, the world is full of priests, and still there are but few mediators."[2] Yes; for few priests are holy and worthy of being mediators. Speaking of bad ecclesiastics, St. Augustine says: "To the Lord is more pleasing the barking of dogs than the prayer of such priests."[3] Father Marchese, in his Journal of the Dominicans, writes that when a servant of God of the Order of St. Dominic implored the Lord to have pity on the people through the merits of priests, he said to her that, by their sins, priests provoked rather than appeased his anger.

IV.

What should be the Sanctity of the Priest given to the People to be their Model.

Priests should be holy; because God has placed them in the world as models of virtue. They are called by St. John Chrysostom, "Teachers of piety;"[4] by St. Jerome, "Redeemers of the world;"[5] by St. Prosper, "Gates to the eternal city for all nations;"[6] and by St. Peter Chrysologus, "Models of virtue."[7] Hence St. Isidor has said, "Whoever leads people on the road of

---

[1] "Emendatiorem esse convenit populo, quem necesse est orare pro populo."—*Dist.* 61, *can. Non negamus.*

[2] "Ecce mundus Sacerdotibus plenus est, et rarus invenitur mediator."
—(We have not found these words in St. Bernard, but the following are St. Gregory's words: "Ecce mundus Sacerdotibus plenus est; sed tamen in messe Dei rarus valde invenitur operator."—*In Evang. hom.* 17.)

[3] "Plus placet Deo latratus canum, quam oratio talium clericorum."
—*Cornel. à Lapid. in Lev.* i. 17.

[4] "Doctores pietatis."—*Hom.* 10.

[5] "Salvatores mundi."—*In Abdiam*, 21.

[6] "Januae civitatis aeternae."—*De Vita cont.* l. 2, c. 2.

[7] "Forma virtutum."—*Serm.* 26.

virtue, must himself be holy and blameless."[1] Pope Hormisdas has written: "Let him be blameless that presides over others in order to reform them."[2] And St. Denis has pronounced that celebrated sentence, that no one should dare to become the guide of others, unless by his virtues he has made himself most like to God.[3] And according to St. Gregory, the sermons of the priest whose life is not edifying, excite contempt and produce no fruit.[4] St. Thomas adds, " For the same reason are disregarded all the spiritual functions of such a one."[5] Speaking of the priest of God, St. Gregory Nazianzen writes: "The priest must first be cleansed before he can cleanse others; he must first himself approach God before he can lead others to him; he must first sanctify himself before he can sanctify others; he must first be himself a light before he can illumine others."[6]

The hand that must wash away the stains and defilements of others must not be polluted, says St. Gregory.[7] In another place he says that the torch that does not

---

[1] "Qui in erudiendis atque instituendis ad virtutem populis præerit, necesse est ut in omnibus sanctus sit, et in nullo reprehensibilis."—*De Offic. eccl.* l. 2, c. 5.

[2] "Irreprehensibiles esse oportet, quos necesse est præesse corrigendis."—*Ep. ad Episc. Hispan.*

[3] "In divino omni non audendum aliis ducem fieri, nisi, secundum omnem habitum suum, factus sit deiformissimus et Deo simillimus."—*De Eccl. Hier.* c. 3.

[4] "Cujus vita despicitur, restat ut ejus prædicatio contemnatur."—*In Evang. hom.* 12.

[5] "Et eadem ratione, omnia spiritualia ab eis exhibita."—*Suppl.* q. 36, a. 4.

[6] "Purgari prius oportet, deinde purgare; ad Deum appropinquari, et alios adducere; sanctificari, et postea sanctificare; lucem fieri, et alios illuminare."—*Apologet.* 1.

[7] "Necesse est ut esse munda studeat manus, quæ aliorum sordes curat."—*Past.* p. 2, c. 2.

burn, cannot inflame others.[1] And St. Bernard says, that to him that loves not, the language of love is a strange and a barbarous tongue.[2] Priests are placed in the world as so many mirrors, in which seculars should look at themselves: *We are made a spectacle to the world, and to angels and to men.*[3] Hence the Council of Trent, speaking of ecclesiastics, says, "Others fix their eyes upon them as upon a mirror, and derive from them what they are to imitate."[4] Philip the Abbot used to say that priests are chosen to defend the people, but for this their dignity is not sufficient; sanctity of life is also necessary.[5]

V.

Practical Consequences.

Hence the Angelic Doctor, considering all that has been said on the sanctity necessary for the priesthood, has written, that to exercise Holy Orders worthily more than ordinary virtue is required.[6] Again he says, "Those that devote themselves to the celebration of the divine mysteries should be perfect in virtue."[7] In another place he says, "In order to exercise this office in a

[1] "Lucerna quæ non ardet, non accendit."—*In Ezech. hom.* 11.
[2] "Lingua amoris, ei qui non amat, barbara est."—*In Cant.* s. 79.
[3] "Spectaculum facti sumus mundo, et Angelis et hominibus."—1 *Cor.* iv. 9.
[4] "In eos, tanquam in speculum, reliqui omnes oculos conjiciunt, ex iisque sumunt quod imitentur."—*Sess.* 22, c. 1, *de Ref.*
[5] "De medio populi segregantur, ut, non solum seipsos, verum et populum tueantur; vero, ad hanc tuitionem, clericalis non sufficit prærogativa dignitatis, nisi dignitati adjungatur cumulus sanctitatis."—*De Dignit. cler.* c. 2.
[6] "Ad idoneam executionem Ordinum, non sufficit bonitas qualiscumque, sed requiritur bonitas excellens."—*Suppl.* q. 35, a. 1.
[7] "Illi, qui in divinis mysteriis applicantur, perfecti in virtute esse debent."—*In* 4 *Sent.* d. 24, q. 3, a. 1.

worthy manner interior perfection is required."[1] Priests should be holy, that they may give glory, and not dishonor to that God whose ministers they are: *They shall be holy to their God, and shall not profane His name.*[2] Were a minister of state seen playing in the public places, frequenting public-houses, associating with the rabble, speaking and acting in a manner calculated to reflect dishonor on the king, what regard could such a minister entertain for his sovereign? By bad priests, who are his ministers, Jesus Christ is covered with shame. St. John Chrysostom says that of unholy priests the Gentiles might say, "What kind of a God have those that do such things? Would he bear with them if he did not approve of their conduct?"[3] Were the Chinese, the Indians, to see a priest of Jesus Christ leading a scandalous life, they might say, how can we believe that the God whom such priests preach is the true God? were he the true God, how could he bear them in their wickedness without being a party to their crimes?

Hence the exhortation of St. Paul: *In all things let us exhibit ourselves as ministers of God.*[4] Let us, he says, addressing priests, appear as true ministers of God, *in much patience*—bearing with peace, poverty, infirmity, persecutions; *in watchings and fastings*—vigilant in what regards the glory of God, mortifying the senses; *in chastity, in knowledge, in sweetness, in charity unfeigned*—in guarding holy purity, in attending to study in order to assist souls, in practising meekness and true charity to our neighbor;

[1] "Interior perfectio ad hoc requiritur, quod aliquis digne hujusmod actus exerceat."—2. 2, q. 184, a. 6.
[2] "Sancti erunt Deo suo, et non polluent nomen ejus."—*Levit.* xxi. 6.
[3] "Qualis est Deus eorum, qui talia agunt? numquid sustineret eos talia facientes, nisi consentiret eorum operibus?"—*Hom.* 10.
[4] "In omnibus exhibeamus nosmetipsos sicut Dei ministros: in multa patientia, in vigiliis, in jejuniis, in castitate, in scientia, in suavitate, in caritate non ficta: quasi tristes, semper autem gaudentes; tanquam nihil habentes, et omnia possidentes."—2 *Cor.* vi. 4.

as sorrowful, yet always rejoicing—appearing afflicted at being deprived of the pleasures of the world, but enjoying the peace which is the portion of the children of God; *as having nothing, but possessing all things*—poor in earthly goods, but rich in God; for he that possesses God, possesses all things.

Such ought priests to be. In a word, they ought to be holy; because they are the ministers of the God of holiness: *Be holy, because I am holy.*[1] They ought to be prepared to give their lives for souls, because they are the ministers of Jesus Christ, who, as he himself has said, came to die for us who are his sheep: *I am the good shepherd. The good shepherd giveth His life for His sheep.*[2] They ought, in fine, to be entirely employed in inflaming all men with the holy fire of divine love; because they are the ministers of the Incarnate Word, who came into the world for that purpose: *I am come to cast fire on the earth, and what will I but that it be kindled.*[3]

David earnestly besought the Lord to grant, for the benefit of the whole world, that his priests might be clothed with justice: *Let the priests be clothed with justice.*[4] Justice comprises all virtues. Every priest should be clothed with faith, by living according to the maxims not of the world, but of faith. The maxims of the world are: It is necessary to possess wealth and property, to seek the esteem of others, to indulge in every amusement within our reach. The maxims of faith are: Happy are the poor; we should embrace contempt, deny ourselves, and love suffering. The priest must be clothed with holy confidence; hoping for all things not from

---

[1] "Sancti estote quia ego sanctus sum."—*Levit.* xi. 44.

[2] "Ego sum Pastor bonus. Bonus Pastor animam suam dat pro ovibus suis."—*John*, x. 11.

[3] "Ignem veni mittere in terram; et quid volo, nisi ut accendatur?" *Luke*, xii. 49.

[4] "Sacerdotes tui induantur justitiam."—*Ps.* cxxxi. 9.

creatures, but only from God. He must be clothed with humility, considering himself worthy of all punishment and contempt; with meekness, being sweet to all, particularly to the rude and passionate; with charity towards God and man: towards God, living in an entire union of his soul with God, and making his heart, by means of mental prayer, an altar on which the fire of divine love always burns; and towards man, fulfilling the instruction of the Apostle: *Put ye on, therefore, as the elect of God, holy and beloved, the bowels of mercy;*[1] and endeavoring to the best of his ability to relieve all in their spiritual and temporal necessities. I say all—even his persecutors and those that treat him with ingratitude.

St. Augustine says: "Nothing in this world is more advantageous or more honorable in the eyes of men than the priestly office. But in the eyes of God nothing is more formidable, important, and dangerous."[2] It is a great happiness and advantage to be a priest, to have the power of making the Incarnate Word descend from heaven into his hands, and of delivering souls from sin and hell, to be the vicar of Jesus Christ, the light of the world, the mediator between God and men, to be raised and exalted above all the monarchs of the earth, to have greater power than the angels, in a word, to be, as St. Clement says, a God on earth: *nothing more advantageous.* But, on the other hand, *nothing more important and dangerous.*[3] For if in his hands, Jesus Christ descends to be his food, the priest must be more pure than the clearest water, as St. Francis of Assisi was told in a vision. If he is a mediator before God in favor of men,

---

[1] "Induite vos ergo, sicut electi Dei, sancti et dilecti, viscera misericordiæ."—*Col.* iii. 12.

[2] "Nihil in hac vita felicius et hominibus acceptabilius Presbyteri officio; sed nihil apud Deum miserius, et tristius, et damnabilius."—*Epist.* 21, *E. B.*

[3] *Const. Apost.* l. 2, c. 26.

he must not appear before God stained with the guilt of any sin; if he is the vicar of the Redeemer, he must be like him in his life. If he is the light of the world, he must be refulgent with the splendor of all virtues. In fine, if he is a priest he must be holy. If he correspond not with God's graces, the greater the gifts that he has received, the more frightful the account that he shall have to render to God. "For," says St. Gregory, "the gifts of God while augmenting augment the account that one has to render."[1] St. Bernard says that the priest "holds a celestial office, that he is made an angel of the Lord, and [adds the saint], as an angel he is elected to glory or condemned to hell."[2] St. Ambrose says that a priest should be exempt even from the smallest faults. "Not a mediocre and ordinary virtue is suitable to the priest," says the same holy Doctor; "he must be on his guard not only against shameful falls, but even against light faults."[3]

Hence, if a priest is not holy, he is in great danger of being lost. What do some, or rather the greater number of priests do in order to acquire sanctity? They say the Office and Mass, and do nothing more: they live without making mental prayer, without mortification, without recollection. Some will say, It is enough for me to be saved. "No," says St. Augustine, "it is not enough; if you say that it is enough, you will be lost."[4] To be holy, the priest must lead a life of detachment from all things, from worldly society, empty honors, etc.: and particularly from inordinate attachment to relatives.

[1] "Cum enim augentur dona, rationes etiam crescunt donorum."—*In Evang. hom.* 9.

[2] "Cœleste tenet officium, angelus Domini factus est; tanquam angelus, aut eligitur, aut reprobatur."—*Declam.* n. 24.

[3] "Neque enim mediocris virtus sacerdotalis est, cui cavendum, non solum ne gravioribus flagitiis sit affinis, sed ne minimis quidem."—*Epist.* 82.

[4] "Si dixeris. Sufficit;—et peristi."—*Serm.* 169, *E. B.*

CHAP. III.] *Sanctity Necessary for the Priest.* 69

When they see him attend but little to the advancement of his family, and wholly devoted to the things of God, they say to him: *Why dost thou do so to us?*[1] He must answer them in the words of the Infant Jesus to his mother when she found him in the temple: *How is it that you sought Me? did you not know that I must be about My Father's business?*[2] Such should be the answer of a priest to his relatives. Have you, he should say to them, made me a priest? Do you not know that a priest should attend only to God? Him only do I wish to seek.

[1] " Quid facis nobis sic ?"
[2] " Quid est quod me quærebatis ? nesciebatis quia, in his quæ Patris mei sunt, oportet me esse ?"—*Luke*, ii. 49.

CHAPTER IV.

GRIEVOUSNESS AND CHASTISEMENT OF SIN IN A PRIEST.

I.

Grievousness of Sin in a Priest.

THE sin of a priest is very grievous, because he sins in view of the light: in consenting to sin he knows well what he does. On this account St. Thomas says, "that the sin of a Christian is more grievous than the sin of an infidel: because he knows the truth."[1] But the light of a secular, though a Christian, is very different from that of a priest. The priest is so well instructed in the divine law that he teaches it to others. *The lips of the priest shall keep knowledge, and they shall seek the law of his mouth.*[2] Hence St. Ambrose says, "that the sins of those who know the law are very grievous, because they are not excused by ignorance."[3] Poor seculars sin, but they sin in the midst of the darkness of the world, at a distance from the sacraments, badly instructed in spiritual things, and immersed in worldly business; they have but little knowledge of God, and consequently they see but imperfectly the evil that they do in consenting to sin. To use the words of David, they *shoot in the dark.*[4] But priests are so full of light that they are the luminaries by which the people are enlightened:

[1] "Propter notitiam veritatis."—2. 2, q. 10, a. 3.
[2] "Labia enim Sacerdotis custodient scientiam, et legem requirent ex ore ejus."—*Mal.* ii. 7.
[3] "Scienti legem, et non facienti, peccatum est grande."—*De Dignit. sac.* c. 3.
[4] "Sagittant in obscuro."—*Ps.* x. 3.

You are the light of the world.[1] They are well instructed by so many books that they have read, by so many sermons that they have heard, by so many considerations that they have made, by so many admonitions that they have received from Superiors. In a word, to priests is given to know the mysteries of God.[2] Hence they well understand the claims that God has to our love and service, the malice of mortal sin, which is an enemy so opposed to God that were he capable of destruction a single mortal sin would, as St. Bernard says, destroy him;[3] and in another place the saint says: "Sin, as far as in it lies, aims at the destruction of God."[4] Thus, according to St. Chrysostom, the sinner, as far as his will is concerned, puts God to death.[5] Hence Father Medina writes that mortal sin does so much dishonor, and gives so much displeasure to God, that were he capable of grief, sin would make him die through pure sorrow.[6] All this the priest understands well: he has also a perfect knowledge of his obligations by which as a priest, whom the Lord has so highly favored, he is bound to serve and love God. The more perfectly, then, he sees the enormity of the injury that he does to God by committing sin, the more grievous the malice of his sin,[7] says St. Gregory.

— Every sin of a priest is a sin of malice; it is like the sin of the angels that sinned in view of the light, says St. Bernard, speaking of a priest; hence he adds, " He has become an angel of the Lord, and sinning as a

[1] "Vos estis lux mundi."—*Matth.* v. 14.
[2] "Vobis datum est nosse mysterium regni Dei."—*Luke*, viii. 10.
[3] "Peccatum est destructivum divinæ bonitatis."
[4] "Peccatum, quantum in se est, Deum perimit."—*In Temp. Pasch.* s. 3.
[5] "Quantum ad voluntatem suam, occidit Deum."—*Hom.* 40.
[6] "Peccatum mortale, si possibile esset, destrueret Deum, eo quod esset causa tristitiæ (in Deo) infinitæ."—*De Satisf.* q. 1.
[7] "Quo melius videt, eo gravius peccat."

priest he sins in heaven."[1] He sins in the midst of light, and therefore his sin, as has been said, is a sin of malice: he cannot allege ignorance, for he knows the great evil of mortal sin: he cannot plead weakness, because he knows the means by which, if he wishes, he can acquire strength; if he is unwilling to adopt the means, the fault is entirely his own. *He would not understand that he might do well.*[2] According to St. Thomas, the sin of malice is that which is committed with knowledge.[3] And in another place he says: "Every sin committed through malice is against the Holy Ghost."[4] We know from St. Matthew that the sin against the Holy Ghost *shall not be forgiven, neither in this world nor in the world to come.*[5] That is, on account of the blindness caused by sins of malice they shall be pardoned only with great difficulty.

Our Saviour prayed on the cross for his persecutors, saying, *Father, forgive them, for they know not what they do.*[6] But for bad priests this prayer was a source rather of condemnation than of salvation: for they *know what they do.*[7] Jeremias said with tears, *How is the gold become dim, the finest color is changed.*[8] "The gold which has been obscured," says Cardinal Hugo, "is the sinful priest who ought to shine forth with divine love; but by committing sin he becomes black, and an object of horror even to hell, and becomes more hateful to God than

---

[1] "Angelus Domini factus est. In clero quippe, tanquam in cœlo gerens iniqua."—*Declam.* n. 24.
[2] "Noluit intelligere, ut bene ageret."—*Ps.* xxxv. 4.
[3] "Scienter eligitur."—1. 2, q. 78, a. 1.
[4] "Omne peccatum ex malitia est contra Spiritum Sanctum."—*D. Malo*, q. 3, a. 14.
[5] "Non remittetur ei, neque in hoc sæculo, neque in futuro."— *Matth.* xii. 32.
[6] "Pater, dimitte illis; non enim sciunt quid faciunt."—*Luke*, xxiii. 34.
[7] "Sciunt quid faciunt."
[8] "Quomodo obscuratum est aurum, mutatus est color optimus!"

other sinners." St. John Chrysostom says that the Lord is not so much enraged against any sinner as against him who, while he shines with the splendor of the sacerdotal dignity, insults the divine majesty.[1] The malice of the sins of a priest is increased by his ingratitude to God, by whom he has been so highly exalted. St. Thomas teaches that the grievousness of sin increases in proportion to the ingratitude of the sinner. "We ourselves," says St. Basil, "are not so indignant at any offence as at that which we receive from a friend and familiar acquaintance."[2] For this reason priests are called by St. Cyril the most intimate friends of God.[3] What greater exaltation can God give to a man than by raising him to the dignity of his own priest? "Enumerate all the honors, all the dignities," says St. Ephrem; "the priest surpasses them all."[4] What greater honor, what more exalted rank, could God confer upon him than that of being his own representative, his coadjutor, the sanctifier of souls, and the dispenser of his sacraments? Priests are called by St. Prosper "Dispensers in the royal house."[5] The Lord has chosen the priest from among so many men for his own minister to offer to him in sacrifice his own very Son. *He chose him*, says the Holy Ghost, *out of all men living to offer sacrifice to God.*[6] He has given him power over the body of Jesus Christ, he has placed in his hands the keys of paradise, he has raised him above all the kings of the earth, and above all the angels in heaven; in a word, he has made

---

[1] "Nulla re Deus magis offenditur, quam quando peccatores Sacerdotii dignitate præfulgent."—*In Matth. hom.* 41.

[2] "Naturaliter magis indignamur his qui nobis familiarissimi sunt, cum in nos peccaverint."—*Glossa, in* 1 *Pet.* iv.

[3] "Dei intimi familiares."

[4] "Enumera honores, dignitates; omnium apex est Sacerdos."

[5] "Dispensatores regiæ domus."

[6] "Ipsum elegit ab omni vivente, offerre sacrificium Deo."—*Eccius.* xlv. 20.

him, as it were, a God on earth: "A God on earth."[1] *What is there that I ought to do more to my vineyard that I have not done?*[2] (Here God appears to speak only of priests.) How horrible, then, the ingratitude of the priest whom God has loved so tenderly, and who insults the Lord in his own very house? *What is the meaning*, says Jeremias, *that my beloved hath wrought much wickedness in my house?*[3] Hence St. Gregory weeps and says, "Alas! my Lord God, those that should govern Thy Church persecute you more than the rest."[4]

It appears, also, that it was of bad priests that God complained when he called on heaven and earth to witness the ingratitude with which he was treated by his own children. *Hear, O ye heavens, and give ear, O earth. ... I have brought up children and exalted them, but they have despised me.*[5] And who are these children but priests who, after being raised by God to such an elevation, and nourished at his table with his own flesh, dare to despise his love and his grace? Of this he also complained by the mouth of David: *If my enemy had reviled me I would verily have borne it.*[6] Were my enemy, were an idolater, a heretic, or a worldling to offend me, I would bear with him, but how can I bear to see myself insulted by you, my priest, who are my friend and fellow-guest? *But thou, a man of one mind, my guide and*

---

[1] "Deus terrenus."
[2] "Quid est quod debui ultra facere vineæ meæ, et non feci?"—*Is.* v. 4.
[3] "Quid est, quod dilectus meus, in domo mea, fecit scelera multa?" —*Jer.* xi. 15.
[4] "Heu, Domine Deus, quia ipsi sunt in persecutione tua primi, qui videntur in Ecclesia tua gerere principatum."—*In Convers. S. Pauli*, s. 1.
[5] "Audite, cœli, et auribus percipe, terra. . . . filios enutrivi et exaltavi; ipsi autem spreverunt me."—*Is.* i. 2.
[6] "Si inimicus maledixisset mihi, sustinuissem utique, . . . tu vero, homo unanimis, dux meus et notus meus, qui simul mecum dulces capiebas cibos!"—*Ps.* liv. 13.

my familiar, who didst take sweetmeats together with me. The Prophet Jeremias weeps and exclaims: *They that were fed delicately, . . . they that were brought up in scarlet, have embraced the dung.*[1] Oh! what a misery, what a horrible thing, to see the man that fed on celestial food and was clad in purple wearing the sordid garment of sin, and feeding on filth and dung! By the word *croceis* the interpreters (resting on the Hebrew text *that were brought up in scarlet*[2]) understand the purple; and priests are said to be honored with the purple on account of their regal dignity: *You are a chosen nation, a kingly priesthood.*[3]

II.

Chastisement of the Sinful Priest.

But let us now see the chastisement that awaits the sinful priest—a chastisement proportioned to the grievousness of his sin. *According to the measure of the sin shall the measure also of the stripes be.*[4] St. John Chrysostom gives up as lost the priest that commits a single mortal sin after his elevation to the priesthood.[5] Terrible indeed are the threats that the Lord has pronounced, by the mouth of Jeremias, against priests who fall into sin. *For the prophet and the priest are defiled, and in my house I have found their wickedness, saith the Lord. Therefore, their way shall be as the slippery way in the dark; for they err and fall therein.*[6] What hope of life would you give to him who, without light to guide his steps, should

---

[1] "Qui vescebantur voluptuose, . . . qui nutriebantur in croceis, amplexati sunt stercora!"—*Lam.* iv. 5.

[2] "Qui in purpura educati fuerunt."

[3] "Vos autem genus electum, regale Sacerdotium."—1 *Pet.* ii. 9.

[4] "Pro mensura peccati erit et plagarum modus."—*Deut.* xxv. 2.

[5] "Si privatim pecces, nihil tale passurus es; si in Sacerdotio peccas, periisti."—*In Act. Ap. hom.* 3.

[6] "Propheta namque et Sacerdos polluti sunt, et in domo mea inveni malum eorum, ait Dominus. Idcirco via eorum erit quasi lubricum in tenebris; impellentur enim, et corruent in ea."—*Jer.* xxiii. 11.

walk on a slippery way along the brink of a precipice, and who should from time to time be violently assailed by enemies endeavoring to cast him down the precipice? This is the miserable state into which a priest who commits mortal sin has brought himself.

The slippery way in the dark. By sin the priest loses light and becomes blind. *It had been better for them not to have known the way of justice, than after they had known it, to turn back.*[1] How much better would it be for the priest that falls into sin to have been a poor uninstructed peasant, who had never known the law! For, after so much knowledge learned from books, from sermons, from directors, and after so many illuminations received from God, the miserable man, by yielding to sin and trampling under foot all the graces that God had bestowed upon him, shall make all the lights received serve to increase his blindness, and to keep him in the state of perdition. "Greater knowledge is followed by greater punishment," says St. John Chrysostom.[2] And the saint adds: "The sin to which the priest consents may be committed by many seculars, but his chastisement shall be far more severe, because his blindness shall be far greater than theirs." He shall receive the punishment threatened by the Prophet: *That seeing they may not see, and hearing may not understand.*[3]

"And this," says the same St. John Chrysostom, "we know from experience that a secular after committing sin is easily induced to do penance."[4] A secular who falls into sin, if he attends a mission, or is present at a sermon in which he hears some eternal truth regarding

[1] "Melius erat illis non cognoscere viam justitiæ, quam, post agnitionem, retrorsum converti."—2 *Pet.* ii. 21.

[2] "Major scientia majoris pœnæ fit materia. Propterea Sacerdos, si eadem cum subditis peccata committit, non eadem, sed multa acerbiora patietur."—*Ad pop. Ant. hom.* 77.

[3] "Ut videntes non videant, et audientes non intelligant."—*Luke*, viii. 10; *Isa.* vi. 9.

[4] "Sæcularis homo, post peccatum, facile ad pœnitentiam venit."

the malice of sin, the certainty of death, the rigor of the divine judgment, or the pains of hell, easily enters into himself and returns to God; "because," says the saint, "these truths are new to him, and fill him with terror."[1] But what impression can the eternal truths and the menaces of the holy Scriptures make on a priest that has trampled on the grace of God, and on all the lights and knowledge that he has received? "All that is contained in Scripture," continues the holy Doctor, "appears to him as something obsolete and worthless, for everything terrible has by use lost its power."[2] Hence he concludes that there is nothing more impossible than to reform a person who sins with a perfect knowledge of the law.[3]

"Great indeed," says St. Jerome, "is the dignity of priests, but great also is their perdition, if in the priesthood they turn their back on God."[4] "The greater the height," says St. Bernard, "to which God has raised them, the more precipitous and ruinous shall be their fall."[5] He that falls on level ground is seldom severely hurt, but the man that falls from a great height is said not to fall, but to be precipitated, and therefore his fall is mortal. "As when we fall on a plain, we do ourselves rarely any harm," says St. Ambrose, "so when we fall from a height, we not only fall, but are precipitated, and the fall becomes more dangerous."[6] "Let us

---

[1] "Quia, quasi novum aliquid audiens, expavescit."

[2] "Omnia enim quæ sunt in Scripturis ante oculos ejus inveterata et vilia æstimantur; nam quidquid illic terribile est, usu vilescit."

[3] "Nihil autem impossibilius, quam illum corrigere qui omnia scit."
—*Hom.* 40.

[4] "Grandis dignitas Sacerdotum; sed grandis ruina eorum, si peccant."
—*In Ezech.* xliv.

[5] "Ab altiori gradu fit casus gravior."—*Declam.* n. 25.

[6] "Ut levius est de plano corruere, sic gravius est qui de sublimi ceciderit dignitate; quia ruina quæ de alto est, graviori casu colliditur."
—*De Dignit. sac.* c. 3.

who are priests," says St. Jerome, "rejoice at our elevation to so great a height, but let our fear of falling be proportioned to our exaltation."[1] It is to the priest that the Lord appears to speak by the Prophet Ezechiel, when he says, *I set thee on the holy mountain of God, and thou hast sinned; and I cast thee out from the mountain of God and destroyed thee.*[2] O priests! says the Lord, I have placed you on my holy mountain, and have made you the luminaries of the world: *You are the light of the world. A city seated on a mountain cannot be hid.*[3] Justly, then, has St. Laurence Justinian said that the greater the grace that God has bestowed on priests, the more severe the chastisement that their sins deserve; and the more elevated the state to which he has raised them, the more disastrous shall be their fall.[4] He that falls into a river sinks deeper in proportion to the height from which he has fallen,[5] says Peter de Blois. Beloved priest, remember that in elevating you to the sacerdotal state God has raised you up to heaven, by making you a man no longer earthly, but altogether celestial: If you sin, you fall from heaven. Consider, then, how ruinous and destructive shall be your fall. "What is higher than heaven?" says St. Peter Chrysologus; "he therefore falls from heaven that mingles sin with heavenly functions."[6] Your fall, according to St. Bernard, shall be like that of a thunderbolt, which rushes headlong with vehement impetuosity.[7] That is, your destruction is

[1] "Lætemur ad ascensum, sed timeamus ad lapsum."—*In Ezech.* xliv.

[2] "Posui te in monte sancto Dei, . . . et peccasti; et ejeci te de monte Dei, et perdidi te."—*Ezech.* xxviii. 14.

[3] "Vos estis lux mundi. Non potest civitas abscondi, supra montem posita."—*Matt.* v. 14.

[4] "Quo est gratia cumulatior, et status sublimior, eo casus est gravior, et damnabilior culpa."—*De Compunct.* p. 1.

[5] "Altius mergitur, qui de alto cadit."

[6] "Quid altius cœlo? De cœlo cadit, in cœlestibus qui delinquit."—*Serm.* 26.

[7] "Tanquam fulgur in impetu vehementi dejicieris."—*Declam.* n. 25.

CHAP. IV.] *Chastisement of the Sinful Priest.* 79

irreparable.[1] In your unhappy soul is verified the threat of the Lord against Capharnaum: *And thou, Capharnaum, which art exalted unto heaven, thou shalt be thrust down to hell.*[2]

Such the chastisement that the priest that falls into sin merits on account of his infinite ingratitude to God. He owes more gratitude to God than others, because he has received greater favors, says St. Gregory.[3] The ungrateful, as a learned author says, deserve to be deprived of all the favors that they have received.[4] Jesus Christ has said: *To every one that hath, shall be given, and he shall abound; but from him that hath not, that also which he seemeth to have shall be taken away.*[5] Upon those that are grateful to God he shall pour his graces more abundantly; but the priest who after so many lights and so many Communions turns his back on God, despises all his favors, and renounces his grace, shall be justly deprived of all. The Lord is liberal to all, but not to the ungrateful. "Ingratitude," says St. Bernard, "dries up the sources of divine favors."[6]

Hence St. Jerome justly says, "There is not in the whole world a monster to be compared with a priest in the state of sin, for the unfortunate man will not bear with correction."[7] And St. John Chrysostom, or the author of the "Imperfect Work," writes: "When laypersons sin, they easily amend. As for priests, once

[1] "Corruent in ea."—*Jer.* xxiii. 12.
[2] "Et tu, Capharnaum, usque ad cœlum exaltata, usque ad infernum demergeris."—*Luke*, x. 15.
[3] "Cum enim augentur dona, rationes etiam crescunt donorum."—*In Evang. hom.* 9.
[4] "Ingratus meretur beneficii subtractionem."
[5] "Omni enim habenti dabitur, et abundabit; ei autem qui non habet, et quod videtur habere, auferetur ab eo."—*Matt.* xxv. 29.
[6] "Ingratitudo exsiccat fontem divinæ pietatis."—*In Cant.* s. 51.
[7] "Nulla certe in mundo tam crudelis bestia, quam malus Sacerdos; nam corrigi non patitur."—*Eusebius, Ep. ad Dam. de morte Hier.*

bad, they are incorrigible."[1] To priests that fall into sin, we may, with St. Peter Damian,[2] apply in a special manner the words of the Apostle: *It is impossible for those that were once illuminated, have tasted also the heavenly gift, and were made partakers of the Holy Ghost, and are fallen away, to be renewed again to penance.*[3] Who has been more enlightened than the priest? Who has tasted more frequently the heavenly gifts, and partaken more abundantly of the Holy Ghost? St. Thomas says that the rebel angels remained obstinate in sin, because they sinned in view of the light; and St. Bernard writes that God shall treat the sinful priest in a similar manner, that is, "the priest having become an angel of the Lord, must expect either the reward or the reprobation of an angel."[4] Our Lord said to St. Bridget: "I see on earth pagans and Jews, but I see none so wicked as priests; they are guilty of the same sin that Lucifer committed."[5] And let it be observed in this place, that, according to Innocent III., many things are venial sins in seculars that are mortal in ecclesiastics.[6]

To priests we may also apply what St. Paul says in another place: *The earth that drinketh in the rain which cometh often upon it, ... and bringeth forth thorns and briers, is reprobate and very near unto a curse, whose end is*

---

[1] "Laici delinquentes facile emendantur; clerici, si mali fuerint, inemendabiles sunt."—*Hom.* 43.

[2] *Epist.* l. 4, *ep.* 3.

[3] "Impossibile est enim, eos, qui semel sunt illuminati, gustaverunt etiam donum cœleste, et participes facti sunt Spiritus Sancti, . . . et prolapsi sunt, rursus renovari ad pœnitentiam."—*Heb.* vi. 4.

[4] "Angelus Domini factus est; tanquam angelus, aut eligitur, aut reprobatur."—*Declam.* n. 24.

[5] "Ego conspicio paganos et Judæos; sed nullos video deteriores quam Sacerdotes: ipsi sunt in eodem peccato quo cecidit Lucifer."—*Rev.* l. 1, c. 47.

[6] "Multa sunt laicis venialia, quæ clericis sunt mortalia."—*In Consecr. Pont.* s. 1.

CHAP. IV.] *Chastisement of the Sinful Priest.* 81

*to be burnt.*¹ What showers of grace has the priest continually received from God! And, after all, he brings forth briers and thorns instead of fruit. Miserable man! he is on the point of being reprobated, of receiving the final malediction, and of being sent in the end, after so many favors from God, to burn forever in the fire of hell. But what dread has the priest that turns his back on God of the fire of hell? Priests who fall into sin lose light, and lose also the fear of God. Behold, the Lord himself assures us of this. *If I be a master, where is My fear*, saith the Lord of Hosts, *to you, O Priests, that despise My name?*² St. Bernard says that priests falling from on high remain so immersed in their malice, that they forget God, and disregard the divine threats to such a degree that the danger of their damnation has no longer any terror for them.³

But why should that excite our wonder, since by committing sin the priest falls from an immense height into a deep pit, in which he is bereft of light, and therefore despises all things; verifying in himself the words of the Wise Man: *The wicked man when he is come into the depth of sins, contemneth.*⁴ *The wicked man:* this wicked man is the priest that sins through malice: *into the depth;* by a single mortal sin, the priest sinks to the depth of misery and remains in blindness; *contemneth;* and thus he despises chastisements, admonitions, the presence of Jesus Christ who is near him on the altar:

¹ "Terra enim sæpe venientem super se bibens imbrem, . . . profer ens autem spinas ac tribulos, reproba est, et maledicto proxima: cujus consummatio in combustionem."—*Heb.* vi. 11.
² "Si Dominus ego sum, ubi est timor meus? dicit Dominus exercituum ad vos, o Sacerdotes, quid despicitis nomen meum!"—*Mal.* i. 6.
³ "Alto quippe demersi oblivionis somno, ad nullum Dominicæ comminationis tonitruum expergiscuntur, ut suum periculum expavescant." *In Cant.* s. 77.
⁴ "Impius, cum in profundum venerit peccatorum, contemnit."— *Prov.* xviii. 3.

he despises all, and blushes not to surpass in malice Judas, the betrayer of Jesus Christ. Of this our Lord complained to St. Bridget: "Such priests are not my priests, but they are real traitors."[1] Yes, real traitors, who avail themselves of the celebration of Mass to outrage Jesus Christ by sacrilege.

But what shall be the unhappy end of such priests? Behold it: *In the land of the saints he hath done wicked things, and he shall not see the glory of the Lord.*[2] The end shall be, first, abandonment of God, and then the fire of hell. But, Father, some may say, this language is too terrific. Do you, they ask, wish to drive us to despair? I answer with St. Augustine, "being myself frightened, I frighten others."[3] Then a priest who has offended God since his ordination may ask, Is there no hope of pardon for me? Yes, there is hope, if he repents and entertains a horror for the evil he has done. Let such a priest, then, thank the Lord with his whole heart if he, too, finds himself aided by divine grace; but he must instantly give himself to that God who calls him. "Let us listen to the Lord," says St. Augustine, "while he is calling us, lest he may turn a deaf ear to us when he judges us."[4]

III.

Exhortation.

From this day forward, let us, dearly beloved priests, learn to esteem our noble elevation, and regarding our-

---

[1] "Tales Sacerdotes non sunt mei Sacerdotes, sed veri proditores."—*Rev.* l. 1, c. 47.

[2] "In terra sanctorum iniqua gessit, et non videbit gloriam Domini."—*Isa.* xxvi. 10.

[3] "Territus, terreo."—*Serm.* 40, *E. B.*

[4] "Audiamus illum, dum regat, ne nos postea non audiat, dum judicat."—*Serm.* 29, *E. B. app.*

CHAP. IV.] *Chastisement of the Sinful Priest.* 83

selves as ministers of a God, let us blush to become the slaves of sin and of the devil, says St. Peter Damian.[1] Let us not imitate the folly of seculars that think only of the present. *It is appointed unto men once to die, and after this the judgment.*[2] We must all appear at this judgment: *We must all be manifested before the judgment seat of Christ, that every one may receive the proper things of the body, according as he hath done.*[3] To each of us the Judge shall say: *Give an account of thy stewardship.*[4] That is, of your priesthood; how have you exercised it? for what end have you exercised it? Dearly beloved priest, were you now to be judged, would you feel satisfied and content with the manner in which you have discharged your ministry? Or would you not say: *When he shall examine, what shall I answer him?*[5] When the Lord chastises a people, the chastisement begins with the priest, for he is the cause of the sins of the people, either by his bad example, or by his negligence in attending to their sanctification. Hence the Lord says, *The time is that judgment should begin at the house of God.*[6] In the slaughter described by Ezechiel, God wished the priests to be the first victims of his vengeance: *Begin ye at my sanctuary.*[7] That is, says Origen, "with the priests." *A most severe judgment,* says the Wise Man, *for them that bear rule.*[8] *And unto whom,* says Jesus Christ, *much is*

---

[1] "Nobilem necesse est esse Sacerdotem, ut, qui minister est Domini, erubescat se servum esse peccati."—*Opusc.* 25, c. 2.
[2] "Statutum est hominibus semel mori; post hoc autem, judicium."—*Heb.* ix. 27.
[3] "Omnes nos enim manifestari oportet ante tribunal Christi, ut referat unusquisque propria corporis, prout gessit."—2 *Cor.* v. 10.
[4] "Redde rationem vilicationis tuæ."—*Luke,* xvi. 2.
[5] "Cum quæsierit, quid respondebo illi?"—*Job,* xxxi. 14.
[6] "Tempus est ut incipiat judicium a domo Dei."—1 *Pet.* iv. 17.
[7] "A sanctuario meo incipite."—*Ezech.* ix. 6.
[8] "Judicium durissimum, his qui præsunt, fiet."—*Wisd.* vi. 6.

given, of him much shall be required.[1] The author of the "Imperfect Work" says, "On the day of judgment the secular will receive the priestly stole, but the sinful priest will be deprived of the priestly dignity, and ranked among infidels and hypocrites."[2] *Hear ye this, O priests!* says the Prophet Osee, . . . *for there is judgment against you.*[3]

And as the judgment of priests is most rigorous, so also shall their damnation be most miserable. *With a double destruction destroy them*, says Jeremias.[4] A Council of Paris repeats these words of St. Jerome, already cited: "Great is the dignity of priests, but if they happen to fall into sin, very great will also be their ruin."[5] And St. John Chrysostom says, "If a priest were to commit only the sins of which the simple faithful become guilty, he would incur not a similar but a more rigorous chastisement."[6] It was revealed to St. Bridget that priests who are sinners "will find themselves deeper in hell than all the other damned."[7] Oh! how great the rejoicing of the devils when a priest enters hell? All hell is in confusion to meet the priest who comes. *Hell below*, says Isaias, *was in an uproar to meet thee at thy coming. . . All the princes of the earth have risen from*

[1] "Omni autem cui multum datum est, multum quæretur ab eo."—*Luke*, xii. 48.

[2] "Laicus, in die judicii, stolam sacerdotalem accipiet; Sacerdos autem peccator spoliabitur dignitate, et erit inter infideles et hypocritas."—*Hom.* 40.

[3] "Audite hoc, Sacerdotes: . . . quia vobis judicium est."—*Osee*, v. i.

[4] "Duplici contritione contere eos."—*Jer.* xvii. 18.

[5] "Grandis dignitas Sacredotum, sed grandis ruina, si peccant."—*In Ezech.* xliv.

[6] "Sacerdos, si eadem cum subditis peccata committit, non eadem, sed multo acerbiora patietur."—*Ad pop. Ant. hom.* 77.

[7] "Præ omnibus diabolis, profundius submergentur in infernum."—*Rev.* l. 4, c. 135.

CHAP. IV.] *Chastisement of the Sinful Priest.* 85

their thrones. All the princes of that land of woe rise up to give the first place of torment to the damned priest. *All*, continues the prophet, *shall answer and say to thee: Thou also art wounded as well as we, thou art become like unto us.*[1] O priest, you once ruled over us, you have so often made the Incarnate Word descend on the altars, you have delivered so many souls from hell, and now you have become like us, miserable and tormented as we are: *Thy pride is brought to hell.* Your pride, by which you have despised God and your neighbor, has in the end brought you to this land of misery, *Thy carcass is fallen down: under thee shall the moth be strewed, and worms shall be thy covering.*[2] As a king you shall have a royal couch and a purple robe: behold, fire and worms shall forever corrode your body and your soul. Oh! how shall the devils then scoff at all the Masses, sacraments, and sacred functions of the damned priest! *And have mocked at her sabbaths.*[3]

Be attentive, dearly beloved priests, for the devils tempt one priest more than a hundred seculars; because a priest that is lost brings with him many seculars to hell. St. Chrysostom says, "To take away the shepherds is to scatter the flocks."[4] In a work that is found among the works of St. Cyprian we read this very just remark: "In war, the combatants endeavor first of all to kill the enemy's commanders."[5] St. Jerome adds:

[1] "Infernus subter conturbatus est in occursum adventus tui. . . . Omnes principes terræ surrexerunt de soliis suis. . . . Universi respondebunt, et dicent tibi: Et tu vulneratus es sicut et nos, nostri similis effectus es."—*Isa.* xiv. 9, 10.
[2] "Detracta est ad inferos superbia tua, concidit cadaver tuum; subter te sternetur tinea, et operimentum tuum erunt vermes."—*Ibid.* 11.
[3] "Et deriserunt sabbata ejus."—*Lam.* i. 7.
[4] "Qui pastorem de medio tulerit, totum gregem dissipat."—*In* 1 *Tim. hom.* 1.
[5] "Plus duces, quam milites, appetuntur in pugna."—*Inter op. S. Cypr. De Singul. cler.*

"The devil does not go in search of infidels and those that are outside" (that is, who are outside of the sanctuary); "he looks for booty in the Church of Christ, for according to Habacuc they are his choice food."[1] To the devils, the souls of ecclesiastics are the most delicious food.

[What follows may serve to supply motives of compunction in the act of contrition.]

Dearly beloved priests, the Lord appears to say to you what he said to the Jewish people:

What have I done to thee? Or in what have I grieved thee? Answer me? Tell me, what evil have I done you: have I not, on the contrary, bestowed many favors upon you?

I brought thee out of the land of Egypt. I have drawn you out of the world, I have selected you from among so many seculars, to make you my priest, my minister, my familiar: *thou hast prepared a cross for thy Saviour:* and you, for a miserable interest, for a vile pleasure, have again nailed me to the cross.

I fed thee with manna in the desert: in the wilderness of this earth I have fed you every morning with the celestial manna, that is, with my divine flesh, and with my blood: *and thou hast beaten me with buffets and stripes.*

What more should I have done to thee, and have not done? I have planted thee for my most beautiful vineyard; and thou hast proved very bitter to me. I have destined you for the vineyard of my delight, planting in you so many lights and so many graces, that they might pro duce sweet and precious fruits; and you have given me only fruits of bitterness.

I gave thee the royal sceptre. I have made you a king, and have exalted you above all the kings of the earth:

---

[1] "Non quærit diabolus homines infideles, non eos qui foris sunt; de Ecclesia Christi rapere festinat; escæ ejus, secundum Habacuc, electæ sunt."—*Ep. ad Eustoch.*

and thou hast given me a crown of thorns, by the bad thoughts to which you have consented.

I raised thee on high. I have raised you to the dignity of my representative, and have given you the keys of heaven; I have, in fine, made you, as it were, a God on earth: *And thou hast hanged me on the gibbet of the cross*,[1] and you have despised all my graces, my friendship, nailing me again to the cross, etc.

[1] " Quid feci tibi, aut in quo contristavi te ? responde mihi.
Eduxi te de terra Ægypti: et tu parasti crucem Salvatori tuo.
Ego te pavi manna per desertum: et tu me cecidisti alapis et flagellis.
Quid ultra debui facere tibi, et non feci? Ego plantavi te vineam speciosissimam: et tu facta es mihi nimis amara.
Ego dedi tibi sceptrum regale: et tu dedisti capiti meo spineam coronam.
Ego te exaltavi: et tu me suspendisti in patibulo crucis."—*Improperia, sung on Good Friday.*

CHAPTER V.

THE INJURY THAT TEPIDITY DOES TO THE PRIEST.

I.

To what the Tepid Priest is Exposed.

THE Lord commanded St. John in the Apocalypse to write to the Bishop of Ephesus the following words: *I know thy works, and thy labor, and thy patience.*[1] I know well all that you do; I know your labors for my glory; I know your patience in the toils of your office. But he adds: *But I have somewhat against thee, because thou hast left thy first charity.*[2] But I must reprove you for having fallen away from your first fervor. But what great evil was there in this? What great evil? Listen to what our Lord adds: *Be mindful, therefore, from whence thou art fallen; and do penance, and do the first works: or else I come to thee, and will move thy candlestick 'out of its place.*[3] Remember whence you have fallen; do penance, and return to the first fervor, with which, as my minister, you are bound to live, otherwise I will reject you as unworthy of the ministry that I have committed to you.

Is tepidity, then, productive of so much ruin? Yes, it brings with it great ruin, and the greatest evil is, that this ruin is not known, and is, therefore, neither avoided nor dreaded by the tepid, and especially by priests. The

---

[1] "Scio opera tua, et laborem, et patientiam tuam."—*Apoc.* ii. 2.
[2] "Sed habeo adversum te, quod caritatem tuam primam reliquisti."—*Ib.* 4.
[3] "Memor esto itaque unde excideris, et age pœnitentiam, et prima opera fac; sin autem, venio tibi, et movebo candelabrum tuum de loco suo."—*Ib.* 5.

majority of them are shipwrecked on this blind rock of tepidity, and therefore many of them are lost. I call it a blind rock: because the great danger of perdition to which the tepid are exposed consists in this, that their tepidity does not allow them to see the great havoc that it produces in the soul. Many are unwilling to be altogether separated from Jesus Christ; they wish to follow him, but they wish to follow him at a distance, like St. Peter, who, when the Redeemer was seized in the garden, *followed him from afar off*.[1] But they that act in this manner, shall easily fall into the misfortune which befell St. Peter, who, when charged by a servant maid with being a disciple of the Redeemer, thrice denied Jesus Christ.

He that contemneth small things shall fall by little and little.[2] The interpreter applies this passage to the tepid Christian, and says that he shall first lose devotion, and shall afterwards fall,[3] passing from venial sins, which he has disregarded, to grievous and mortal offences. Eusebius Emissenus says that he that is not afraid to offend God by venial faults shall scarcely be exempt from mortal sins.[4] "By a just judgment," says St. Isidore, " the Lord will permit him that despises minor transgressions to fall into grievous crimes."[5] Trifling maladies, when few, do little injury to health, but when they are numerous and frequent, they bring on mortal diseases. "You guard against great faults," says St. Augustine, "but what do you do in regard to light faults? You have shaken the mountain: take care that you be

---

[1] " Petrus autem sequebatur eum a longe."—*Matth.* xxvi. 58.
[2] "Qui spernit modica, paulatim decidet."—*Ecclus.* xix. 1.
[3] " Decidet a pietate, a statu gratiæ in statum peccati."
[4] " Difficile est ut non cadere in gravia permittatur, qui minus gravia non veretur."—*Homil. init. quadr.*
[5] " Judicio autem divino in reatum nequiorem labuntur, qui distringere minora sua facta contemnunt."—*Sent.* l. 2, c. 19.

not crushed by a heap of sand."[1] You are careful to avoid grievous falls, but you fear not small ones; you are not deprived of life by the great rock of any mortal sin, but beware, says the saint, lest by a multitude of venial sins you be crushed as by a heap of sand. We all know that only mortal sin kills the soul, and that venial sins, however great their number, cannot rob the soul of divine grace. But it is also necessary to understand what St. Gregory teaches, that the habit of committing light faults without remorse, and without an effort to correct them, gradually deprives us of the fear of God; and when the fear of God is lost, it is easy to pass from venial to mortal sins.[2] St. Dorotheus adds, that by despising light faults we expose ourselves to the danger of falling into perfect insensibility.[3] He that disregards small offences is in danger of general insensibility, so that afterwards he shall feel no horror even of mortal sins.

St. Teresa, as the Roman Rota attests, never fell into any mortal sin; but still our Lord showed her the place prepared for her in hell, not because she had deserved hell, but because, had she not risen from the state of tepidity in which she lived, she should in the end have lost the grace of God, and should be damned. Hence the Apostle says, *Give not place to the devil.*[4] The devil is satisfied when we begin to open the door to him by disregarding small faults; for he shall then labor to open it perfectly, by leading us into grievous transgressions. "Do not imagine," says Cassian, "that any

---

[1] "Magna præcavisti! de minutis quid agis? Projecisti molem! vide ne arena obruaris."—*In Ps.* xxxix.

[2] "Ut, usu cuncta levigante, nequaquam post committere etiam graviora timeamus."—*Mor.* l. 10, c. 14.

[3] "Periculum est ne in perfectam insensibilitatem deveniamus."— *Doctr.* 3.

[4] "Nolite locum dare diabolo."—*Eph.* iv. 27.

one falls at once into ruin."[1] That is, when you hear of the fall of a spiritual soul, do not imagine that the devil has suddenly precipitated her into sin; for he has first brought her into tepidity, and then has cast her into the precipice of enmity with God. Hence St. John Chrysostom says that he knew many persons adorned with all virtues, who afterwards fell into tepidity, and from tepidity into an abyss of vice.[2] It is related in the Teresian Chronicles, that Sister Anne of the Incarnation once saw in hell a person whom she had regarded as a saint: on her countenance appeared a multitude of small animals, which represented the multitude of defects that she committed and disregarded during life. Of these some were heard to say, *By us you began;* others, *By us you continued;* others, *By us you have brought yourself to hell.*

I know thy works, that thou art neither cold nor hot,[3] says our Lord, through St. John, to the Bishop of Laodicea. Behold the state of a tepid soul, neither cold nor hot. "The tepid person," says Father Menochius in his exposition of this passage, "is one that does not dare offend God knowingly and willingly, but is one that neglects to strive after a more perfect life, and hence easily gives himself up to his passions."[4] A tepid priest is not manifestly cold, because he does not knowingly and deliberately commit mortal sins; but neglecting to seek after the perfection to which he is bound by the

[1] "Lapsus quispiam nequaquam subitanea ruina corruisse credendus est."—*Coll.* 6, c. 17.
[2] "Novimus multos, omnes virtutes numero habuisse, et tamen, negligentia lapsos, ad vitiorum barathrum devenisse."—*In Matth. hom.* 27.
[3] "Scio opera tua, quia neque frigidus es, neque calidus."—*Apoc.* iii. 15.
[4] "Tepidus est qui non audet Deum mortaliter sciens et volens offendere, sed perfectioris vitæ studium negligit, unde facile concupiscentiis se committit."—*In Apoc.* iii. 16.

obligations of his state, he makes little of venial sins, he commits many of them every day without scruple, by lies, by intemperance in eating and drinking, by imprecations, by distraction at the Office and Mass, by detractions, by jests opposed to modesty: he leads a life of dissipation in the midst of worldly business and amusements; he cherishes dangerous desires and attachments; full of vainglory, of human respect and self-esteem, he cannot bear a contradiction or a disrespectful word; he neglects mental prayer, and is destitute of piety. Father Alvarez de Paz says that the defects and faults of a tepid soul are "like those light indispositions that do not cause death, but that weaken the body in such a manner that a grave malady cannot supervene without destroying the body which has no longer the power of resisting."[1] The tepid Christian is like a sick man who has labored under many light maladies, which, because they are incessant, reduce him to such a state of debility, that as soon as he is attacked by any serious disease, that is, by a strong temptation, he has not strength to resist, and falls, but falls with greater ruin.

Hence the Lord continues to address the tepid bishop, saying, *I would thou wert cold or hot, but because thou art lukewarm, I will begin to vomit thee out of My mouth.*[2] Let him that finds himself miserably fallen into the state of tepidity, consider these words and tremble.

I would that thou wert cold! Better, says the Lord, that you were cold, that is, deprived of my grace, for then there should be greater reason to hope for your recovery from so miserable a state; but by remaining in

---

[1] "Sunt velut irremissæ ægrotatiunculæ, quæ vitam quidem non dissolvunt, sed ita corpus extenuant, ut accedente aliquo gravi morbo statim corpus, vires non habens resistendi, succumbat."—*De Perf.* l. 5, p. 2, c. 16.

[2] "Utinam frigidus esses, aut calidus! sed quia tepidus es, et nec frigidus nec calidus, incipiam te evomere ex ore meo."

it, you shall be exposed to greater danger of rushing into grievous sins without any hope of ever emerging from them. "Although he that is cold," says Cornelius à Lapide, " is worse than he that is tepid, yet the condition of the tepid is worse, since the danger of falling is greater, without any hope of recovery."[1] St. Bernard says that it is easier to convert a wicked layman than a tepid ecclesiastic. Pereira adds, that it is more easy to bring an infidel to the faith, than to renew a tepid Christian in the spirit of fervor.[2] And Cassian has said that he saw many sinners consecrate themselves to God with their whole heart, but that he knew no one that had risen from tepidity to fervor.[3] St. Gregory holds out hopes to a sinner not yet converted, but he despairs of him who, after having repented, and given himself to God with fervor, falls into tepidity. Behold his words: " However tepid any one may be, there is always a hope that sooner or later his fervor will be reanimated; but of any one that falls little by little from fervor into tepidity, we must expect nothing. In fact, we may count on a sinner for the grace of conversion, but if after conversion he becomes tepid, we must despair of his return."[4]

In a word, tepidity is a desperate and almost incurable evil. For in order to be able to avoid danger it is necessary to know it. Now the tepid, when they have fallen into that miserable state of darkness, do not even

[1] " Licet frigidus sit pejor tepido, tamen pejor est status tepidi, quia tepidus est in majori periculo ruendi sine spe. resurgendi."—*In Apoc.* iii. 16.

[2] " Facilius enim est quemlibet paganum ad fidem Christi adducere. quam talem aliquem a suo torpore ad spiritus fervorem revocare."

[3] " Frequenter vidimus de frigidis ad spiritalem pervenire fervorem, de tepidis omnino non vidimus."—*Coll.* 4, c. 19.

[4] " Sicut ante teporem frigus sub spe est, ita tepor in desperatione· qui enim adhuc in peccatis est, conversionis fiduciam non amittit; qui vero post conversionem tepuit, et spem, quæ esse potuit de peccatore, subtraxit."—*Past.* p. 3, c. 1, *adm.* 35.

know their danger. Tepidity is like a hectic fever that is scarcely perceived. The tepid man does not see even habitual defects. "Grievous faults," says St. Gregory, "because they are more easily observed, are more readily corrected; but he who disregards light defects continues to commit them, and thus by the habit of despising minor transgressions he shall soon despise grievous sins."[1] Besides, mortal sin always excites a certain horror even in habitual sinners, but to the tepid, his imperfections, inordinate attachments, dissipations, love of pleasure or of self-esteem, cause no horror. These little faults are the more dangerous because they imperceptibly dispose him to ruin. "Great sins," says Father Alvarez de Paz, "are less dangerous for the just than these little faults, because the hideous aspect of the former frightens them, while the others insensibly conduct to ruin."[2]

Hence St. John Chrysostom has written that celebrated sentence, that we ought in a certain manner to be more careful to avoid light faults than grievous sins: "We must use more care to avoid little sins than to avoid great sins; for the latter are already opposed by our nature, and because the former, being small, make us more indolent in our struggles. Since we disregard them, the soul cannot raise itself so generously as to repel them: hence great sins flow from small sins."[3]

---

[1] "Major enim quo citius quia sit culpa agnoscitur, eo etiam citius emendatur; minor vero, dum quasi nulla creditur, eo pejus quo et securius in usu retinetur. Unde fit plerumque ut mens, assueta malis levibus, nec graviora perhorrescat, et in majoribus contemnat."—*Past*. p. 3, c. 1, *adm*. 34.

[2] "Magna peccata eo justis minus periculosa sunt, quod aspectum satis tetrum exherrent; at minima periculosiora videntur, quia latenter ad ruinam disponunt."—*De Perf*. l. 5, p. 2, c. 16.

[3] "Non tanto studio magna peccata esse vitanda, quam parva: illa enim natura adversatur; hæc autem, quia parva sunt, desides reddunt. Dum contemnuntur, non potest ad eorum expulsionem animus generose insurgere; unde cito ex parvis maxima fiunt."—*In Matth. hom*. 87.

Injury Done to the Priest by Tepidity. 95

The reason, then, assigned by the saint is, that mortal sins excite a natural horror, but light faults are disregarded, and therefore they soon become grievous. And the greatest evil is, that small defects that are disregarded render the soul more careless about her spiritual interests, and therefore, because she has been accustomed to despise slight offences, they lead her to think little of grievous transgressions. In the Canticles the Lord says: *Catch us the little foxes that destroy the vines, for our vineyard hath flourished.*[1] Mark the word *foxes:* he does not tell us to catch the lions and tigers, but the foxes. These foxes destroy the vine; they make a multitude of dens, and thus dry up the roots, that is, devotion and good desires, which are the roots of spiritual life. He also says *little.* Why does he tells us to catch the little and not the large foxes? Because the little foxes excite less terror, but often do more mischief than the large ones. For, as Father Alvarez says, small faults when disregarded impede the infusion of divine graces, and thus the soul remains barren, and is finally lost.[2] The Holy Ghost adds: *for our vineyard hath flourished.* How great the evil of venial faults when multiplied and not abhorred? They eat the flowers, that is, they destroy the good desires of advancing in perfection, and when these desires fail, the soul shall always go backward until she finds herself fallen into a precipice from which it will be difficult to rescue her.

I will begin to vomit thee out of My mouth.[3] Let us conclude the exposition of this text of the Apocalypse. A

---

[1] "Capite nobis vulpes parvulas quæ demoliuntur vineas; nam vinea nostra floruit."—*Cant.* ii. 15.

[2] "Culpæ leves et imperfectiones vulpes parvulæ sunt, in quibus nihil nimis noxium aspicimus; sed hæ vineam, id est, animam demoliuntur, quia eam sterilem faciunt, dum pluviam auxilii cœlestis impediunt."—*De Perf.* l. 5, p. 2, c. 16.

[3] "Sed, quia tepidus es, incipiam te evomere ex ore meo."—*Apoc.* iii. 16.

draught that is cold or hot is taken with facility, but when tepid it is taken with great difficulty, because it provokes vomiting. This precisely is what the Lord has threatened against the tepid soul. *I will begin to vomit thee out of My mouth.* In expounding this passage Menochius says, "God begins to vomit forth the tepid man, because the latter as long as he perseveres in his tepidity creates in Him nausea, until finally at his death the Lord vomits him entirely, and he is forever separated from Christ."[1] The tepid are in danger of being vomited forth by God, that is, of being abandoned without hope of remedy. This is what the Lord means by vomiting the soul out of his mouth; for all have a great horror of taking back what they vomit. "For just as," says Cornelius à Lapide, "one refuses to take back what one has rejected, so God has a horror of the tepid whom he has vomited forth."[2] How does God begin to vomit forth the tepid priest? He ceases to give him any longer these loving calls (this precisely means to be vomited forth from the mouth of God), these spiritual consolations, these good desires. In fine, he shall be deprived of spiritual unction. The unhappy man will go to meditation, but shall make it with great tediousness, dissipation, and unwillingness. Hence he shall by degrees begin to omit it, and thus shall cease to recommend himself to God by petitions for his graces, and by neglecting to ask the divine graces he shall always become more poor, and shall go from bad to worse. He shall say Mass and the Office, but they shall be a source of demerit rather than of merit. He shall perform all his functions with difficulty and by force, or without

---

[1] "Porro tepidus incipit evomi, cum, permanens in tepore suo, Deo nauseam movere incipit, donec tandem omnino in morte sua evomatur, et a Christo in æternum separetur."

[2] "Vomitus significat Deum exsecrari tepidos, sicut exsecramur id quod os evomuit."—*In Apoc.* iii. 16.

devotion. You shall, says the Lord, be anointed all over with oil, but you shall remain without unction.[1] The Mass, the divine Office, preaching, hearing confessions, assisting the dying, attending at funerals, are exercises that should excite new fervor; but after all these functions you shall remain dry, without peace, dissipated, agitated by a thousand temptations. *I will begin to vomit thee out of My mouth.* Behold how God begins to vomit you out of his mouth.

II.

A Priest cannot be Satisfied with Avoiding Grievous Sins.

Some priests may say it is enough for me to avoid mortal sins and to save my soul. No, answers St. Augustine, you that are a priest, and therefore obliged to walk in the narrow way of perfection, shall not even save your soul by treading the broad way of tepidity. "When you say it is enough, you are lost."[2] St. Gregory says that they that are to be saved as saints, and wish to be saved as imperfect souls, shall not be saved. And this our Lord one day gave Blessed Angela of Foligno to understand: "They that are enlightened by me to walk in the way of perfection, and through tepidity wish to tread in the ordinary path, shall be abandoned by me."[3] It is certain, as we have seen in the above,[4] that a priest is bound to be holy, as well on account of his dignity as the familiar and minister of God, as on account of his office of offering to God the sacrifice of the Mass, of mediator for the people before the divine Majesty, and of sanctifier of souls by means of the sacraments. The reason is that he may walk in the way of perfection, that God loads him with so many

[1] "Calcabis olivam, et non ungeris oleo."—*Mich.* vi. 15.
[2] "Si dixeris: Sufficit;—et periisti."—*Serm.* 169, *E. B.*
[3] *Vision.* c. 51.
[4] Chap. III.

graces and special helps. Hence, when he exercises his ministry with negligence, amid defects and faults, without even detesting them, God pronounces a malediction against him. *Cursed be he that doth the work of the Lord deceitfully.*[1] This malediction consists in abandonment by God. "God," writes St. Augustine, "is accustomed to abandon the negligent."[2] The Lord, says the saint, usually abandons souls favored by his special graces, when after all his gifts they neglect to live according to the perfection to which they are called. God, observes a certain author, wishes to be served by his priests with the fervor with which the seraphim serve him in heaven; otherwise he will withdraw his graces and permit them to sleep in tepidity, and thence to fall, first into the precipice of sin and afterwards into hell.[3] The tepid priest, weighed down by so many venial sins and by so many inordinate attachments, remains, as it were, in a state of insensibility. Hence the graces received and the obligations of the priesthood make but little impression upon him, and therefore the Lord shall justly withhold the abundant helps that are morally necessary for the fulfilment of the obligations of his state; thus he shall go from bad to worse, and with his defects his blindness shall increase. Perhaps God is bound to make his graces abound in those that are parsimonious and ungenerous to him? No, says the Apostle, he who sows little shall reap but little.[4]

The Lord has declared that to the grateful that preserve his graces he will multiply his favors, but from the ungrateful he shall take away the gifts that had been bestowed upon them. *For to every one that hath shall be*

---

[1] "Maledictus, qui facit opus Domini fraudulenter."—*Jer.* xlviii. 10.
[2] "Negligentes Deus deserere consuevit."—*In Ps.* cxviii. s. 10.
[3] "Deus vult a seraphinis ministrari; tepido gratiam suam subtrahit, sinitque eum dormire, itaque ruere in barathrum."
[4] "Qui parce seminat, parce et metet."—2 *Cor.* ix. 6.

given, and he shall abound ; but from him that hath not, that also which he seemeth to have shall be taken away.[1] Besides, St. Matthew says that when the master receives no fruit from the vineyard, he takes it away from the husbandmen to whom he had given it, and after punishing them consigns it to others. *He will bring those evil men to an evil end, and will let out His vineyard to other husbandmen, that shall render Him fruit in due season.*[2] He afterwards adds: *Therefore I say to you, that the kingdom of God shall be taken from you, and shall be given to a nation yielding the fruits thereof.*[3] That is, God shall take out of life the priest to whom he gave the care of his kingdom, or of procuring his glory, and shall intrust his interests to others who will be grateful for his favors and faithful to his graces. Hence it happens that from so many sacrifices, so many Communions, and so many prayers offered in the Office and in the Mass, many priests draw little or no fruit. *You have sowed much*, says the Prophet Aggeus, *and brought in little, . . . and he that earned wages put them into a bag with holes.*[4] Such the tepid priest! He lays up all his spiritual exercises *in a bag with holes ;* thus no merit remains, but on the contrary, in consequence of committing many defects in the performance of these exercises, he always renders himself more deserving of chastisement. The tepid priest is not far from perdition. The heart of a priest should, as Peter de Blois says, be the altar on which the fire of divine love always burns. But what proof of burning love for God does the priest give who is content with avoiding mortal sin, but takes no

[1] "Omni enim habenti dabitur, et abundabit; ei autem qui non habet, et quod videtur habere, auferetur ab eo."—*Matth*. xxv. 29.

[2] "Malos male perdet, et vineam suam locabit aliis agricolis, qui reddant ei fructum temporibus suis."—*Matth*. xxi. 41.

[3] "Ideo dico vobis quia auferetur a vobis regnum Dei, et dabitur genti facienti fructus ejus."—*Ibid*. 43.

[4] "Seminastis multum, et intulistis parum; . . . et qui mercedes congregavit, misit eas in sacculum pertusum."—*Agg*. i. 6.

trouble to abstain from displeasing God by light faults. "It is a sign of a very tepid love," says Father Alvarez, "to restrict the proofs of love only to the omission of very grave faults against God, and to be troubled very little about offending him with little faults."[1]

To become a good priest, a man requires not the common graces, nor a small number of graces, but special and abundant helps. But how can God be generous and abundant in his graces to him who is appointed to serve him, and who serves him so badly? St. Ignatius of Loyola sent one day for a lay brother who led a very tepid life, and said to him: " Tell me, my brother, for what purpose have you entered religion?" The lay brother answered, "To serve God." "And is it thus," replied the saint, "you serve him? Had you told me that you came to serve a cardinal or an earthly prince, you should be more deserving of compassion; but you tell me that you have come to serve God, and do you serve him so badly?" Every priest enters into the court, not among the servants, but among the familiars of God, who have continually to treat confidentially with him on matters of the utmost importance to his glory. Hence a tepid priest dishonors God more than he honors him; for by his negligent and imperfect life he shows that he regards God unworthy of being served and loved with greater fervor. He declares that in pleasing God he does not find that felicity which is sufficient to make the soul perfectly content; he declares that his divine Majesty is unworthy of the love that obliges us to prefer his glory to all self-gratification.

[1] "Signum est amoris satis tepidi, velle amatum in solis rebus gravibus non offendere, et in aliis, quæ non tanta severitate præcipit, ejus voluntatem procaciter violare."—*De Exterm. mali*, l. 1, c. 12.

III.

Exhortation.

Be attentive, dearly beloved priests; let us tremble lest all the grandeurs and honors by which God has raised us to such an elevation among men should only terminate in our eternal damnation. St. Bernard says that the solicitude of the devils for our destruction should make us solicitous in laboring for salvation.[1] Oh! how active are our enemies in seeking the perdition of a priest. They desire the fall of one priest more ardently than that of a hundred seculars; as well because the victory over a priest is a far greater triumph than a victory over a layman, as because a priest that falls brings many others with him to perdition. But as flies avoid boiling water and run to that which is tepid, so the devils do not tempt the fervent as violently as they tempt the tepid priest, whom they often succeed in bringing from tepidity into the state of mortal sin. Cornelius à Lapide says that the tepid when assailed by any strong temptation are in great danger of yielding to temptations, because they have but little strength to resist; hence it is that in so many occasions of danger they often fall into mortal sin.[2]

It is necessary then to labor to avoid faults that are wilfully and deliberately committed. It cannot be denied that, except Jesus Christ and the divine Mother, who by a singular privilege have been free from all stain of sin, all other men, even the saints, have not been exempt at least from venial sins. *The heavens are*

---

[1] " Hostium malitia, qua tam solliciti sunt in nostram perditionem, nos quoque sollicitos faciat, ut in timore et tremore ipsorum nostram salutem operemur."—*De S. Andrea*, s. 2.

[2] " In magno versatur periculo, sæpeque, inter tot occasiones quibus plena est hæc vita, in mortale prolabitur."—*In Apoc.* iii. 15.

not pure in his sight[1] says Job. St. James says, *In many things we all offend.*[2] Thus every child of Adam must, as St. Leo has written, be defiled with the mire of this earth.[3] But it is necessary to attend to what the Wise Man says on this subject: *For a just man shall fall seven times, and shall rise again.*[4] He that falls through human frailty, without a full knowledge of the malice of the act, and without a deliberate consent, rises easily: *shall fall and rise again.* But how can he rise who knows his defects, commits them deliberately, and instead of detesting them, takes complacency in them?

If we commit faults, says St. Augustine, let us at least confess and detest them, and God will pardon them.[5] *If we confess our sins, He is faithful and just to forgive us our sins.*[6] To obtain the remission of venial faults, Louis de Blois says that it is enough to confess them in general.[7] And in another place he writes[8] that such sins are more easily cancelled by turning to God with humility and love than by stopping to dwell upon them with too much fear. St. Francis de Sales also has written that as the daily faults of spiritual souls are indeliberately committed, so they are indeliberately taken away. He meant to say what St. Thomas teaches, that for the remission of venial sins "it is sufficient to detest them either explicitly or even implicitly, for example,

[1] "Cœli non sunt mundi in conspectu ejus."—*Job*, xv. 15.
[2] "In multis enim offendimus omnes."—*James*, iii. 2.
[3] "Necesse est de mundano pulvere etiam religiosa corda sordescere."—*De Quadr.* s. 4.
[4] "Septies enim cadet justus, et resurget."—*Prov.* xxiv. 16.
[5] "Et si non sumus sine peccatis, oderimus tamen ea."—*Serm.* 181, E. B.
[6] "Si confiteamur peccata nostra, fidelis est et justus, ut remittat nobis peccata nostra, et emundet nos ab omni iniquitate."—1 *John*, i. 9.
[7] "Sane tales culpas generaliter exposuisse satis est."—*Consol. pusill.* c. 1, § 4.
[8] *Brev. Reg. tyr. sp.* § 4.

CH. V.] *Injury Done to the Priest by Tepidity.* 103

by a fervent act of the love of God."[1] The holy Doctor then says: "The remission of venial sins is brought about in three ways: 1. By infusion of divine grace; in this way by means of the Holy Eucharist and the other sacraments such sins are remitted; 2. By acts that include a movement of detestation, and thus by a general confession of sins, by striking the breast, by reciting an *Our Father*, we obtain the remission of such sins; 3. By every act of religion towards God and the things of God, such as the receiving of the blessing from a bishop, to take holy water, to pray in a consecrated church."[2] Speaking of the holy Communion, St. Bernardine of Sienna says: "It may happen that after Communion the soul finds itself so absorbed in God that all venial sins disappear before the fervor of its devotion."[3]

The Venerable Louis da Ponte used to say: "I have committed many faults, but I have never made peace with my faults. Many make peace with their defects, and this shall cause their ruin." St. Bernard says that as long as a person detests his imperfections, there is reason to hope that he shall return to the straight path;

---

[1] "Sufficit actus quo aliquis detestatur peccatum veniale vel explicite vel implicite, sicut cum aliquis ferventer movetur ad Deum."—P. 3, q. 87, a. 3.

[2] "Triplici ratione, aliqua causant remissionem venialium: 1°, per infusionem gratiæ; et hoc modo, per Eucharistiam et omnia Sacramenta, venialia remittuntur; 2°, in quantum sunt cum aliquo motu detestationis; et hoc modo, confessio generalis, tunsio pectoris, et Oratio Dominica, operantur ad remissionem; 3°, in quantum sunt cum aliquo motu reverentiæ in Deum et ad res divinas; et hoc modo, benedictio episcopalis, aspersio aquæ benedictæ, oratio in ecclesia dedicata, et si aliqua sunt hujusmodi, operantur ad remissionem venialium."—*S. Thomas, loco citato.*

[3] "Contingere potest quod tanta devotione mens, per sumptionem Sacramenti, in Domino absorbeatur, quod ab omnibus venialibus expurgetur."—*De Chr. Dom.* s. 12, a. 2, c. 1.

but when he commits faults knowingly and deliberately, and when the commission of them excites neither fear nor remorse, they shall by degrees bring him to ruin. *Dying flies*, says the Holy Ghost, *spoil the sweetness of the ointment*.[1] Dying flies are the faults that are committed but not detested; for they remain dead in the soul. "When a fly," says Denis the Carthusian, "falls into a sweet-smelling ointment and remains therein, it will injure the ointment and its good odor. If we apply this to the spiritual life, the dead flies represent our idle thoughts, illicit affections, voluntary distractions—things that spoil the sweetness of the ointment, that is, the sweetness attached to the exercises of piety."[2]

St. Bernard[3] writes, that to say this is a *light sin* is not a great evil, but to commit it, and take complacency in it, is an evil of great moment, and shall, according to the words of St. Luke, be severely chastised by God. *And that servant that knew the will of his Lord, and did not according to His will, shall be beaten with many stripes; but he that knew not, and did things worthy of stripes, shall be beaten with few stripes.*[4] It is true that even spiritual persons are not free from light transgressions; "but," says Father Alvarez, "they daily diminish the number and grievousness of their faults, and afterwards efface them by acts of divine love." Whoever acts in this manner shall acquire sanctity: neither shall his defects hinder

---

[1] " Muscæ morientes perdunt suavitatem unguenti."—*Eccles.* x. 1.

[2] " Dum musca cadit in unguentum, manendo in illo, destruit ejus valorem atque odorem. Spiritualiter, muscæ morientes sunt cogitationes vanæ, affectiones illicitæ, distractiones morosæ, quæ 'perdunt suavitatem unguenti,' id est, dulcedinem spiritualium exercitiorum."

[3] *In Convers. S. Pauli*, s. 1.

[4] " Qui cognovit voluntatem domini sui, et non præparavit, et non fecit secundum voluntatem ejus, vapulabit multis; qui autem non cognovit, et fecit digna plagis, vapulabit paucis."—*Luke*, xii. 47.

him from tending to perfection. Hence Louis de Blois tells us not to be disheartened by these little faults, because we have several means of expiating them: "If every day we fall several times, it will depend entirely on us to employ every day the means of atoning for our faults."[1] But how can he that entertains an attachment for any earthly good, and voluntarily falls and relapses into that attachment without any wish to get rid of it, advance in the way of God? The bird that escapes from the net instantly takes flight; but as long as it is held even by a slender thread, it remains on the earth. "Every little thread of attachment to this world," says St. John of the Cross, "impedes the spiritual progress of the soul."

Let us, then, guard against falling into this miserable state of tepidity; for, according to what has been already said, to raise a priest from such a state a most powerful grace is necessary. But what reason have we to think that God will give such a grace to priests that provoke him to vomit them out of his mouth? Some person that has fallen into this miserable state may ask, Is there, then, no hope for me? There is ground of hope in the mercy and power of God. *The things that are impossible with men, are possible with God.*[2] It is impossible for the tepid priest to rise, but to raise him up is not impossible to God. However, a desire, at least, is necessary on our part. How can he that does not even desire to rise hope for the divine aid? Let him that has not even this desire ask it of God. If we pray, and persevere in prayer, the Lord shall grant both the desire and the grace to rise. *Ask, and you shall receive.*[3] God has

[1] "Quemadmodum singulis diebus in multis offendimus, ita quotidianas expiationes habemus."—*Parad. an.* p. 1, c. 3.
[2] "Quæ impossibilia sunt apud homines, possibilia sunt apud Deum." —*Luke*, xviii. 27.
[3] "Petite, et accipietis."

promised, and his promise cannot fail. Let us then pray, and say with St. Augustine, "Let my merit be Thy mercy."[1] Lord, I have no claim or merit to be heard by you, but, O eternal Father, your mercy and the merits of Jesus Christ are my merits. To have recourse to the most holy Virgin is also a great means of rising from a state of tepidity.

[1] " Meritum meum, misericordia tua."

CHAPTER VI.

THE SIN OF INCONTINENCE.

I.

Necessity of Purity in the Priest.

INCONTINENCE is called by St. Basil of Seleucia[1] a living plague, and by St. Bernardine of Sienna, the most noxious of all sins; "a terrible gnawing worm."[2] Because, as St. Bonaventure says, impurity destroys the germs of all virtues.[3] Hence St. Ambrose calls it the hot-house and mother of all vices.[4] For it brings with it hatred, thefts, sacrileges, and other similar vices. Hence St. Remigius has justly said: "With the exception of those that die in childhood, most men will be damned on account of this vice."[5] And Father Paul Segneri says that as pride has filled hell with angels, so impurity has filled it with men. In other vices the devil fishes with the hook, in this he fishes with the net; so that by incontinence he gains more for hell than by all other sins. On the other hand, God has inflicted the severest chastisement on the world, sending deluges of water and fire from heaven, in punishment of the sin of incontinence.

Chastity is a most beautiful gem; but, as St. Athana-

---

[1] *Orat.* 5.
[2] "Vermis quo nullus nocentior."—*T. II.* s. 52, a. 3, c. 2.
[3] "Luxuria omnium virtutum eradicat germina."
[4] "Luxuria seminarium et origo vitiorum est."—*St. Thom. de Vill. De S. Ildeph. conc.* 2.
[5] "Demptis parvulis, ex adultis pauci, propter hoc vitium, salvantur." —*Il Crist. istr.* p. 1, *rag.* 24.

sius says, it is a gem found by few on this earth.[1] But if this gem is suitable for seculars, it is absolutely necessary for ecclesiastics. Among the virtues that St. Paul prescribes to Timothy, he recommended chastity in a special manner: *Keep thyself chaste.*[2] Origen says that chastity is the first virtue with which a priest that goes to the altar should be adorned.[3] Clement of Alexandria has written that only they that lead a chaste life are and can be called priests.[4] Hence, then, as purity constitutes priests, so, on the other hand, incontinence robs them, as it were, of their dignity, says St. Isidore.[5]

Hence the holy Church has always endeavored by so many Councils, laws, and admonitions to guard with jealousy the chastity of her priests. Innocent III. made the following ordinance: "No one is to be allowed to be ordained priest unless he is a virgin or his chastity has been proved."[6] He also commanded that the incontinent priest should be excluded "from all ecclesiastical dignities."[7] St. Gregory ordained: "He that has fallen into a carnal sin after ordination should be deprived so far of his office, that he be not permitted to perform any function at the altar."[8] Besides, he ordained,[9] that if a priest committed a sin against purity, he should do penance for ten years. For the first three

[1] "Gemma pretiosissima, a paucis inventa."—*De Virginit.*
[2] "Teipsum castum custodi."—1 *Tim.* v. 22.
[3] "Ante omnia Sacerdos, qui divinis assistit altaribus, castitate debit accingi."—*In Levit. hom.* 4.
[4] "Soli qui puram agunt vitam, sunt Dei Sacerdotes."—*Strom.* l. 4.
[5] "Si pudicitia Sacerdotes creat, libido Sacerdotibus dignitatem abrogat."—*Epist.* l. 3, *ep.* 75.
[6] "Nemo ad sacrum Ordinem permittatur accedere, nisi aut virgo aut probatæ castitatis existat."—*Cap. A Multis. De æt. et qual. ord.*
[7] "Ab omnium graduum dignitate."
[8] "Qui, post acceptum sacrum Ordinem, lapsus in peccatum carnis fuerit, sacro Ordine ita careat, ut ad altaris ministerium ulterius non accedat."—*Cap. Pervenit. dist.* 50.
[9] *Cap. Presbyter. dist.* 82.

months he should sleep on the ground, remain in solitude, have no intercourse with any person, and should be deprived of Communion. He should then fast every day for a year and a half on bread and water, and for the remainder of the ten years he should continue to fast on bread and water only on three days in the week. In a word, the Church regards as a monster the priest that does not lead a life of chastity.

II.

Malice of Impurity in the Priest.

Let us, in the first place, examine the malice of the sin of a priest who violates chastity. A priest is the temple of God, as well by the vow of chastity as by the sacred unction by which he was consecrated to God. *He that hath anointed us in God, who also hath sealed us.*[1] Such is the language of St. Paul, speaking of himself and of his associates in the ministry. Hence Cardinal Hugo has said: "The priest should not pollute the sanctuary of the Lord, because the oil of the holy unction is poured out upon him."[2] The body, then, of the priest is the sanctuary of the Lord. "Keep thyself chaste," says St. Ignatius, Martyr, "as a gift of God and the temple of the Holy Ghost."[3] St. Peter Damian says that the priest that defiles his body by impurity violates the temple of God. He then adds: "Do not change the vessels consecrated to God into vessels of contumely."[4] What would you say of the man that should use a consecrated chalice at table? Speaking of priests, Innocent II. has

---

[1] "Unxit nos Deus, qui et signavit nos."—2 *Cor.* i. 21.
[2] "Sacerdos ne polluat sanctuarium Domini; quia oleum sanctæ unctionis super eum est."
[3] "Teipsum castum custodi, ut domum Dei, templum Christi."—*Ep. ad Heron. Diac.*
[4] "Nonne templum Dei violant? Nolite vasa Deo sacrata in vasa contumeliæ vertere."—*Opusc.* 18, d. 2, c. 47.

said: "Since they should be the temples of the sanctuaries of the Holy Ghost, they are disgraced if they become addicted to impurity."[1] How horrible to see a priest that should send forth in every direction the light and odor of purity, become sordid, fetid, and polluted with sins of the flesh? *The sow that was washed to her wallowing in the mire.*[2] Hence Clement of Alexandria has written that an unchaste priest, as far as in him lies, contaminates God himself, who dwells within him.[3] Of this God himself complains by the mouth of his prophet: *Her priests have despised My law, and have despised My sanctuaries, . . . and I was profaned in the midst of them.*[4] Alas! says the Lord, by the incontinence of my priest, I, too, am defiled: by violating chastity he pollutes my sanctuary, that is, his body which I have consecrated, and in which I often come to dwell. It was this St. Jerome meant when he said: "We defile the body of Christ whenever we approach the altar unworthily."[5]

Besides, the priest on the altar offers to God in sacrifice the immaculate Lamb; that is, the very Son of God. On this account, says St. Jerome, the priest should be so chaste as not only to abstain from every impure action, but also to avoid every indecent glance.[6] St. John Chrysostom likewise has written that a priest should have purity which would make him fit to stand

[1] "Cum ipsi templum et sacrarium Spiritus Sancti debeant esse, indignum est eos immunditiis deservire."—*Cap. Decernimus. dist.* 28.
[2] "Sus lota in volutabro luti!"—2 *Pet.* ii. 22.
[3] "Deum in ipsis habitantem corrumpunt, quantum in se est, et vitiorum suorum conjunctione poluunt."—*Pædag.* l. 2, c. 10.
[4] "Sacerdotes ejus contempserunt legem meam, et polluerunt sanctuaria mea; . . . et coinquinabor in medio eorum."—*Ezech.* xxii. 26.
[5] "Polluimus corpus Christi, quando indigni accedimus ad altare."—*In Mal.* i. 7.
[6] "Pudicitia sacerdotalis, non solum ab opere immundo, sed etiam a jactu oculi sit libera."—*In Tit.* i. 8, 9.

CHAP. VI.]   *The Sin of Incontinence.*   111

in the midst of the angels in heaven.[1] And in another place he has said that by their purity the hands of a priest, which must touch the flesh of Jesus Christ, should be more resplendent than the rays of the sun.[2] On the other hand, St. Augustine asks where can a man be found so wicked as to presume to touch the most holy sacrament of the altar with unclean hands?[3] "But," says St. Bernard, "the priest that dares to ascend the altar, to handle the body of Jesus Christ, after being contaminated with sins of impurity, is guilty of a far more enormous crime."[4] "Ah! priest of God," exclaims St. Augustine, "the hands that you moisten with the blood of the Redeemer do not moisten with the sacrilegious blood of sin."[5] Ah! do not allow the hands which are bathed in the blood of the Redeemer, shed one day for the love of you, to be polluted with the sacrilegious blood of sin.

Moreover, Cassian says that priests must not only touch, but must also eat, the sacred flesh of the Lamb; and therefore they should practise angelic purity.[6] But

[1] "Necesse est Sacerdotem sic esse purum, ut, in ipsis cœlis collocatus, inter cœlestes illas virtutes medius staret."—*De Sacerd.* l. 3.
[2] "Quo solares radios non deberet excedere manus illa, quæ hanc carnem tractat?"—*In Matt. hom.* 83.
[3] "Quis adeo impius erit, qui lutosis manibus Sacratissimum Sacramentum tractare præsumat?" *
[4] "Audent Agni immaculati sacras contingere carnes, et intingere in sanguinem Salvatoris manus, quibus paulo ante carnes attrectaverunt."—*Declam.* n. 13.
[5] "Ne manus quæ intinguntur sanguine Christi, polluantur sanguine peccati."—*Molina, Intr. Sac.* tr. 1, c. 5, § 2.
[6] "Qua puritate oportebit custodire castitatem, quos necesse est quotidie sacrosanctis Agni carnibus vesci!"—*De Cœn. Inst.* l. 6, c. 8.

---

* Instead of these words we read at the place indicated: "Si erubescimus et timemus Eucharistiam manibus sordidis tangere, plus debemus timere ipsam Eucharistiam in anima polluta suscipere."—*Serm.* 292, *E. B. App.*—ED.

according to Peter Comestor, the priest who, while he is defiled with sins against chastity, pronounces the words of consecration, spits, as it were, in the face of Jesus Christ; and in receiving the sacred body and blood into his polluted mouth, he, as it were, casts them into the foulest mire.[1] St. Vincent Ferrer says that such a priest is guilty of a greater impiety than if he threw the consecrated host into a sink.[2] Here St. Peter Damian exclaims, and says, " O priests ! whose duty it is to offer to God the immaculate Lamb, do not first immolate yourself to the devil by your impurities."[3] Hence the saint afterwards calls the unchaste priest a victim of the devils, on which these cruel spirits make a most delicious feast in hell.[4] Besides, the unchaste priest not only brings himself to perdition, but he also causes the damnation of many others. St. Bernard said that incontinence in ecclesiastics was one of the greatest persecutions that the Church could suffer. On the words of Ezechias, *Behold in peace is my bitterness most bitter*,[5] says the holy Doctor, the Church has suffered much from the sword of the tyrant and from the infection of heresy, but she suffers still more from the incontinence of the unchaste ecclesiastic, who by his scandals drags the bowels out of his own mother.[6] "How shameful," says St. Peter Da-

---

[1] " Qui sacra illius verba Sacramenti ore immundo profert, in faciem Salvatoris spuit; et cum in os immundum sanctisimam Carnem ponit, eam quasi in lutum projicit."—*Serm*. 38.

[2] " Majus peccatum est, quam si projiciat Corpus Christi in cloacam."

[3] " Cur, o Sacerdos, qui sacrificium Deo debes offerre, temet ipsum prius maligno spiritui non vereris victimam immolare."—*Opus*. 17, c. 3.

[4] " Vos estis dæmonum victimæ, ad æternæ mortis succidium destinatæ; ex vobis diabolus, tamquam delicatis dapibus, pascitur et saginatur."

[5] " Ecce in pace amaritudo mea amarissima."—*Is*. xxxviii. 17.

[6] " Amara prius in nece Martyrum, amarior in conflictu hæreticorum, amarissima in moribus domesticorum. Pax est, et non est pax: pax a paganis, pax ab hæreticis, sed non profecto a filiis."—*In Cant*. s. 33.

mian, "to see a man who preaches chastity made the slave of lust!"[1]

III.

Sad Effects of Impurity.

Let us now examine the evils that the vice of incontinence produces in the soul, particularly in that of a priest.

1. BLINDNESS OF THE SOUL.

First, this sin blinds the soul, and makes her lose sight of God and of the eternal truths. "Chastity," says St. Augustine, "purifies the mind, and through it men see God."[2] But the first effect of the vice of impurity is, according to St. Thomas, blindness of the understanding. Its effects are thus described by the saint: "The effects of this impure vice are: blindness of the mind, hatred of God, attachment to the present life, horror of the future life."[3] St. Augustine has said that impurity takes away the thought of eternity.[4] When a raven finds a dead body, its first act is to pluck out the eyes; and the first injury that incontinence inflicts on the soul is to take away the light of the things of God. This was felt by Calvin, who was first a parish priest,—a pastor of souls,*—but afterwards, by this vice, became

[1] "Qui prædicator constitutus es castitatis, non te pudet servum esse libidinis!"—*S. ad Past. in syn.*
[2] "Castitas, mundans mentes hominum, præstat videre Deum."—*Serm.* 291, *E. B. app.*
[3] "Cæcitas mentis, odium Dei, affectus præsentis sæculi, horor vel desperatio futuri."—2. 2, q. 153, a. 5.
[4] "Luxuria futura non sinit cogitare."

---

* John Calvin was provided, at the age of twelve, with a chaplaincy in the church of Noyon, and afterwards with the curacy of Pont l'Evêque, near this city, although he was never raised to the dignity of the priesthood. (Dict. hist. de Feller.)

S

an heresiarch; by Henry VIII., first the defender and afterwards the persecutor of the Church. This was also experienced by Solomon; first a saint, and afterwards an idolater. The same happens to the unchaste priest. *They shall*, says the Prophet Sophonias, *walk like blind men, because they have sinned against the Lord.*[1] Miserable man! in the midst of the light of the Masses that he celebrates, of the Offices that he recites, and of the funerals that he attends, he remains as blind as if he believed neither in death that awaits him, nor in a future judgment, nor in hell that he purchases by his sins. *Mayest thou*, says the Lord, *grope at midday as the blind is wont to grope in the dark.*[2] In a word, he is so blinded by the fetid mire in which he is immersed, that after having forsaken God who has raised him so much above others, he does not even think of returning to ask pardon. *They will not*, says the Prophet Osee, *set their thoughts to return to their God; for the spirit of fornication is in the midst of them.*[3] Hence St. John Chrysostom says, that neither the admonitions of Superiors, nor the counsels of virtuous friends, nor the fear of chastisements, nor the danger of shame shall be sufficient to enlighten the unchaste priest.[4]

No wonder: for he is so blind that he can no longer see. *Fire hath fallen on them, and they have not seen the sun.*[5] "This fire is no other than the fire of concupiscence,"[6]

[1] "Ambulabunt ut cæci, quia Domino peccaverunt."—*Soph.* i. 17.

[2] "Percutiat te Dominus amentia, et cæcitate, ac furore mentis, et palpes in meridie, sicut palpare solet cæcus in tenebris, et non dirigas vias tuas."—*Deut.* xxviii. 28.

[3] "Non dabunt cogitationes suas, ut revertantur ad Deum suum; quia spiritus fornicationum in medio eorum, et Dominum non cogno. verunt."—*Os.* v. 4.

[4] "Nec admonitiones, nec consilia, ne aliquid aliud salvare potest animam libidine periclitantem."—*Hom. contra lux.*

[5] "Supercecidit ignis, et non viderunt solem."—*Ps.* lvii. 9.

[6] "'Supercecidit ignis,' id est, concupiscentiæ."—2, 2, q. 15, a. 1.

CHAP. VI.] *The Sin of Incontinence.* 115

says St. Thomas. Hence he afterwards adds, " The sins of the flesh extinguish the light of reason, for carnal delectations cause the soul to be drawn entirely towards the pleasures of the senses."[1] This vice, by its beastly delectation, deprives man even of reason; so that, as Eusebius says, it makes him become worse than the senseless beast.[2] Hence the unchaste priest, blinded by his impurities, shall no longer make any account of the injuries that he does to God by his sacrileges, nor of the scandal that he gives to others. He will even go so far as to dare to say Mass in a state of sin. No wonder; for he that has lost the light, easily abandons himself to the commission of every crime.

Come ye to Him and be enlightened.[3] He that wants light must draw near to God; but because, according to the words of St. Thomas, "a thoroughly impure man is mostly removed from God,"[4] impurity removes man to a great distance from God, the unchaste becomes, as it were, senseless brutes that no longer apprehend spiritual things. *But the sensual man,* says St. Paul, *perceiveth not these things that are of the Spirit of God.*[5] Hell, eternity, and the dignity of the priesthood, no longer make any impression upon the incontinent ecclesiastic: *He perceiveth not.*[6] Perhaps he will, as St. Ambrose says, begin even to entertain doubts about faith: " Whenever one begins

[1] "Vitia carnalia extinguunt judicium rationis. Delectatio quæ est in venereis, totam animam trahit ad sensibilem delectationem."—2. 2, q. 53, a. 6.
[2] " Luxuria hominem pejorem bestia facit."—*Eusebius, Ep. ad Dam. de morte Hier.*
[3] "Accedite ad eum, et illuminamini."—*Ps.* xxxiii. 6.
[4] " Per peccatum luxuriæ, homo videtur maxime a Deo recedere."—*In Job* 31, *lect.* 1.
[5] "Animalis autem homo non percipit ea quæ sunt Spiritus Dei."—1 *Cor.* ii. 14.
[6] "Non percipit."

to be incontinent, one begins to deviate from the faith."[1] Oh! how many miserable priests have by this vice even lost their faith? *His bones*, says Job, *shall be filled with the vices of his youth* (the vices of youth are impurities), *and they shall sleep with him in the dust*.[2] As the light of the sun cannot enter into a vessel filled with earth, so the light of God cannot shine into a soul habituated to sins of the flesh: her vices shall continue to sleep with her till death.

But as that unhappy soul, for the sake of her impurities, forgets God, so shall he forget her, and permit her to remain abandoned in her darkness. *Because*, says the Lord, *thou hast forgotten Me, and hast cast Me off behind thy body, bear thou also thy wickedness and thy fornications*.[3] St. Peter Damian says, "They throw the Lord behind their bodies that obey the voice of their passions."[4] Father Cataneo[5] relates that a sinner who had contracted a habit of impurity, when admonished by a friend to abandon his evil ways, unless he wished to be damned, answered: "Friend, I may indeed go to hell for this habit." He certainly went to that place of torment, for he was suddenly struck dead. A priest who was found in the house of a certain lady whom he went to tempt was compelled by her husband to take a poisonous draught. After returning home he took to his bed, and mentioned to a friend the misfortune that had befallen him. The friend seeing the miserable man so near his end exhorted him to go to confession. No, replied the unhappy man, I cannot go to confession; this favor only

[1] " Ubi cœperit quis luxuriari, incipit deviare a fide recta."—*Epist*. 36.
[2] "Ossa ejus implebuntur vitiis adolescentiæ ejus et cum eo in pulvere dormient."—*Job*, xx. 11.
[3] "Quia oblita es mei, et projecisti me post corpus tuum, tu quoque porta scelus tuum et fornicationes tuas."—*Ezech*. xxiii. 35.
[4] "Illi Deum post corpus suum ponunt, qui suarum obtemperant illecebris voluptatum."—*Opusc*. 18, *diss*. 2, c. 3.
[5] *Esere. della buona m.* p. 1, d. 34.

I ask of you,—go to such a lady, tell her that I die for the love of her. Can greater blindness be conceived?

2. OBSTINACY OF THE WILL.

In the second place, the sin of impurity produces obstinacy of the will. "Once fallen into the snare of the devil, one cannot so easily escape it," says St. Jerome.[1] And according to St. Thomas, there is no sin in which the devil takes so much delight as in impurity; because the flesh is strongly inclined to that vice, and he that falls into it can be rescued from it only with difficulty.[2] Hence the vice of incontinence has been called by Clement of Alexandria "a malady without remedy;"[3] and by Tertullian, "an incurable vice."[4] Hence St. Cyprian calls it the mother of impenitence.[5] "It is impossible," says Peter de Blois, "for him that submits to the domination of the flesh to conquer carnal temptations."[6] Father Biderman relates of a young man, who was in the habit of relapsing into this sin, that at the hour of death he confessed his sins with many tears and died, leaving strong grounds to hope for his salvation. But on the following day his confessor, while saying Mass, felt some one pulling the chasuble; turning round he saw a dark cloud, which sent forth scintillations of fire, and heard a voice saying that was the soul of the young man that had died; that though he had been absolved from his sins, he was again tempted, yielded to a bad thought, and was damned.

[1] " Hoc rete diaboli, si quis capitur, non cito solvitur."—*Eusebius, Ep. ad Dam. de morte Hier.*

[2] "Diabolus dicitur maxime gaudere de peccato luxuriæ, quia est maximæ adhærentiæ, et difficile ab eo homo potest eripi."—1. 2, q. 73, a. 5.

[3] "Morbus immedicabilis."—*Pædag.* 1. 2, c. 10.

[4] "Vitium immutabile."

[5] "Impudicitia mater est impœnitentiæ."—*De Disc. et Bon. pud.*

[6] "Est fere impossibile triumphare de carne, si ipsa de nobis triumphavit."

The prophet and the priest are defiled. . . . Therefore their way shall be as a slippery way in the dark; for they shall be driven on, and fall therein.[1] Behold the ruin of the unchaste ecclesiastic. He walks on a slippery path, in the midst of darkness, and is impelled to the precipice by the devils, and by evil habits. Hence it is impossible for him to escape destruction. St. Augustine says that they that give themselves up to this vice soon contract the habit of it; and the habit soon creates, as it were, a necessity of sinning.[2] The vulture rather than abandon the carcass on which it has begun to feed is content to wait to be killed by the sportsman. This happens to him that contracts a habit of impurity.

Oh! how much greater the obstinacy produced in the priest that submits to the tyrannical rule of this vice, than that which it causes in seculars! This happens both because the priest has had greater light to know the malice of mortal sin, and because in him impurity is a greater sin than it is in a secular. For the unchaste priest not only offends against chastity, but also against religion, by violating his vow, and, generally speaking, he also transgresses against fraternal charity. For the incontinence of a priest is almost always accompanied with most grievous scandal to others. In his book on the " Last Things," Denis the Carthusian relates that a servant of God, conducted in spirit to purgatory, saw there many seculars that were suffering for sins against purity, but very few priests. Having asked the reason, he was told that scarcely any unchaste priest repents sincerely of this sin, and that, therefore, almost all such priests are damned.[3]

[1] " Propheta et Sacerdos polluti sunt; . . . idcirco via eorum erit quasi lubricum in tenebris; impellentur enim, et corruent in ea."— *Jer.* xxiii. 11.

[2] " Dum servitur libidini, facta est consuetudo; et dum consuetudini non resistitur, facta est necessitas."—*Conf.* 1. 8, c. 5.

[3] " Vix aliquis talium veram habet contritionem; idcirco pene omnes æternaliter damnantur."—*Quat. Nov.* p. 3, a. 13.

3. Eternal Damnation.

Finally, this accursed vice leads all, and particularly priests that are infected with it, to eternal damnation. St. Peter Damian says that the altar of God receives no other fire than that of divine love. Hence he that dares to ascend the altar inflamed by the fire of impurity is consumed by the fire of divine vengeance.[1] And in another place he says that all the obscenities of the sinner shall be one day converted into pitch, which shall eternally nourish in his bowels the fire of hell.[2]

Oh! what vengeance does not the Lord inflict on the unchaste priest! How many priests are now in hell for sins against purity! "If," says St. Peter Damian, "the man in the Gospel, who came to the marriage feast without the nuptial garment, was condemned to darkness, what then should he expect who, admitted to the mystical banquet of the divine Lamb, neglects to adorn himself with the brilliant garb of virtues, and even presents himself impregnated with the fetid odors of impurity."[3] Baronius relates that a priest who had contracted a habit of sins against chastity saw at death a multitude of devils coming to carry him away. He turned to a religious who was attending him, and besought him to pray for him. But soon after he exclaimed that he was before the tribunal of God, and cried aloud: "Cease, cease to pray for me, for I am already con-

---

[1] "Altaria Domini, non alienum, sed ignem dumtaxat divini amoris accipiunt; quisquis igitur carnalis concupiscentiæ flamma æstuat, et sacris assistere mysteriis non formidat, ille divinæ ultionis igne consumitur."—*Opusc.* 27, c. 3.

[2] "Veniet, veniet profecto dies, imo nox, quando libido ista tua vertetur in picem, qua se perpetuus ignis in tuis visceribus inextinguibiliter nutriat."—*Opusc.* 17, c. 3.

[3] "Quid illi sperandum, qui, cœlestibus tricliniis intromissus, non modo non est spiritalis indumenti decore conspicuus, sed ultro etiam fœtet sordentis luxuriæ squalore perfusus."—*Opusc.* 18, d. 1, c. 4.

demned, and your prayers can be of no service to me."[1] St. Peter Damian[2] relates that in the city of Parma a priest and a woman with whom he had sinned were suddenly struck dead. In the revelations of St. Bridget[3] we read that an unchaste priest was killed by a thunderbolt; and it was found that the lightning had reduced to ashes only the indelicate members, and left the remainder of the body untouched, as if to show that it was principally for incontinence that God had inflicted this chastisement upon him. Another priest in our own time died suddenly in the act of committing a sin against chastity, and for his greater infamy was exposed in the court of the church. The unchaste priest dishonors the Church, and therefore the Lord justly chastises him by making him the most dishonored of all men. Thus, speaking of priests, God says, by the Prophet Malachy, *But you have departed out of the way, and have caused many to stumble at the law. . . . Therefore I also made you contemptible, and base before all people.*[4]

IV.

Remedies for Incontinence.

The spiritual masters point out many remedies for the vice of impurity; but the principal and the most necessary are the flight of occasions, and prayer. As to the first means, St. Philip Neri used to say that in this warfare cowards, that is, they that avoid dangerous occasions, gain the victory. Let a man use all other possible

---

[1] "Cessa pro me orare, pro quo nullatenus exaudieris."—*Anno* 1100, n. 24.

[2] *Epist.* l. 5, ep. 16.

[3] *Rev.* l. 2, c. 2.

[4] "Vos autem recessistis de via, et scandalizastis plurimos in lege; . . . propter quod et ego dedi vos contemptibiles et humiles omnibus populis."—*Mal.* ii. 8.

CHAP. VI.] *The Sin of Incontinence.* 121

means, unless he flies away he is lost. *He that loveth danger shall perish in it.*[1]

As to the second means, it is necessary to know that we have not strength to resist temptations of the flesh. This strength must be the gift of God. But God grants it to those only that pray and ask for it. The only defence against this temptation, says St. Gregory of Nyssa, is prayer.[2] And before him the Wise Man said: *And as I knew that I could not otherwise be continent, except God gave it, . . . I went to the Lord and besought Him.*[3]

[They that desire more information on the means of overcoming sins of the flesh, and especially on the two means above mentioned,—the avoidance of occasions, and prayer,—should read the instruction on chastity in the second part of this work.]

[1] "Qui amat periculum, in illo peribit."—*Ecclus.* iii. 27.
[2] "Oratio pudicitiæ præsidium est."—*De or. Dom. or.* 1.
[3] "Et ut scivi quoniam aliter nom possem esse continens, nisi Deus det, . . . adii Dominum, et deprecatus sum illum."—*Wisd.* viii. 21.

CHAPTER VII.

THE SACRILEGIOUS MASS.

I.

Purity Required in the Priest to Celebrate Worthily.

"WE must needs confess," says the holy Council of Trent, "that no other work can be performed by the faithful so holy and divine as this tremendous mystery itself."[1] God himself could not enable man to perform a more sublime or sacred action than the celebration of Mass. Oh! how much more excellent than all the ancient sacrifices is our sacrifice of the altar, in which we immolate not an ox, nor a lamb, but the very Son of God? The Jews, says St. Peter of Cluni, had an ox; the Christians have Christ: the sacrifice of the latter as far transcends that of the former, as Christ is more excellent than an ox.[2] The same author adds, that to servants a servile victim was suited, but for friends and children was reserved Jesus Christ—a victim that has delivered us from sin and eternal death.[3] Justly, then, has St. Laurence Justinian said, that there is no oblation greater, more profitable to us, or more pleasing to God, than the offering that is made in the sacrifice of the Mass.[4]

[1] "Necessario fatemur nullum aliud opus adeo sanctum a Christi fidelibus tractari posse, quam hoc tremendum mysterium."—*Sess.* 22, *Decr. de observ. in Missa.*

[2] "Habuit bovem Judæus, habet Christum Christianus, cujus sacrificium tanto excellentius est, quanto Christus bove major est."

[3] "Congrua tunc fuit servilis hostia servis; servata est liberatrix victima jam filiis et amicis."—*Ep. contra Petrobr.*

[4] "Qua oblatione nulla major, nulla utilior, nulloque oculis Divinæ Majestatis est gratior."—*Serm. de Euchar.*

CHAP. VI.] *The Sacrilegious Mass.* 123

According to St. John Chrysostom, during the celebration of Mass the altar is surrounded by angels, who are present to pay homage to Jesus Christ, the victim offered in sacrifice.[1] And St. Gregory asks, " who doubts that at the very hour of immolation, at that voice of the priest, the heavens are opened and the choirs of angels are present at that mystery of Jesus Christ?"[2] St. Augustine says that the angels assist as servants to the priest who offers the sacrifice.[3]

Now the Council of Trent teaches that Jesus Christ himself was the first that offered this great sacrifice of his body and blood, and that he now offers himself by the hands of a priest chosen to be his minister and representative on the altar.[4] St. Cyprian says that "the priest truly holds the place of Christ,"[5] and that, therefore, at the consecration, he says *This is My body: this is the chalice of My blood.*[6] To his disciples Jesus himself said, *He that heareth you, heareth Me; and he that despiseth you, despiseth Me.*[7]

The priests of the Old Law the Lord commanded to be clean, merely because it was their duty to carry the sacred vessels: *Be ye clean, you that carry the vessels of the Lord.*[8] "How much more clean," says Peter de

---

[1] "Locus altari vicinus plenus est Angelorum choris, in honorem illius qui immolatur."—*De Sacerd.* l. 6.

[2] "Quis fidelium habere dubium possit, in ipsa immolationis hora, ad Sacerdotis vocem cœlos aperiri, et in illo Jesu Christi mysterio Angelorum choros adesse ?"—*Dial.* l. 4. c. 58.

[3] "Sacerdos enim hoc ineffabile conficit mysterium. et Angeli conficienti sibi quasi famuli assistunt."—*Molina, Instr. Sac.* tr. 1, c. 5, § 2.

[4] "Idem nunc offerens Sacerdotum ministerio, qui seipsum tunc in cruce obtulit."—*Sess.* 22, cap. 2.

[5] "Sacerdos vice Christi vere fungitur."—*Epist.* 62.

[6] "Hoc est corpus meum; hic est calix sanguinis mei."

[7] "Qui vos audit, me audit; qui vos spernit, me spernit."—*Luke*, x. 16.

[8] "Mundamini, qui fertis vasa Domini."—*Is.* lii. 11.

Blois, "should they be who carry Christ in their hands and in their body?"[1] How much greater purity shall God demand from the priests of the New Law, who must represent the person of Jesus Christ on the altar, in offering to the eternal Father his own very Son! Justly, then, does the Council of Trent require that priests celebrate this sacrifice with the greatest possible purity of conscience: "It is also sufficiently clear, that all industry and diligence are to be applied to this end, that it be performed with the greatest possible inward cleanness and purity of heart."[2] This, says the Abbot Rupert, is what is signified by the *Alb* with which the Church commands the priest to be covered from head to foot in the celebration of the holy mysteries.[3]

It is but just that priests should honor God by innocence of life, since he has honored them so much above others, by making them the ministers of this great mystery. "Behold, O priests," says St. Francis of Assisi, "your dignity; and as the Lord has honored you on account of this mystery, so be careful on your part to love and to honor him."[4] But how shall a priest honor God? Is it by the costliness or vanity of his dress? No, says St. Bernard, but by sanctity of life, by the study of the sacred sciences, and by labor in holy works.[5]

---

[1] "Quanto mundiores esse oportet, qui in manibus et in corpore portant Christum!"—*Epist.* 123.

[2] "Satis apparet omnem operam et diligentiam in eo ponendam esse, ut quanta maxima fieri potest interiori cordis munditia peragatur."—*Sess.* 22, *Decr. de obs. in Missa.*

[3] "Candorem significat vitæ innocentis, quæ a Sacerdote debet incipere."

[4] "Videte dignitatem vestram, Sacerdotes; et sicut super omnes, propter hoc mysterium, honoravit vos Dominus, ita et vos diligite eum et honorate."—*Op.* p. I, ep. 12.

[5] "Honorificabitis autem, non cultu vestium, sed ornatis moribus, studiis spiritualibus, operibus bonis."—*De Mor. et Off. Episc.* c. 2.

II.

How Great is the Crime of the Priest that Celebrates Mass in Mortal Sin.

But does the priest that celebrates in mortal sin give honor to God? As far as regards himself, he treats the Lord with the greatest dishonor that can be offered to him, by despising him in his own person. For by his sacrilege he appears, as far as in him lies, to defile the immaculate Lamb, whom he immolates in the consecrated host. *To you, O priests*, says the Lord by the Prophet Malachy, *who despise My name, . . . you offer polluted bread upon My altar, and you say, wherein have we polluted Thee?*[1] " We," says St. Jerome, in his comment on this passage, " pollute the bread, that is, the body of Christ, when we unworthily approach the altar.[2]

God cannot raise a man to a greater elevation than by conferring on him the sacerdotal dignity. How many selections must the Lord have made in calling a person to the priesthood. First, he must select him from a countless number of possible creatures. He must then separate him from so many millions of pagans and heretics, and, lastly, he must make choice of him from the immense multitude of the faithful. And what power does God confer on this man? If the Lord bestowed only on one man the power of calling down by his words the Son of God from heaven, how great should be his obligations and his gratitude to the Lord! This power God grants to every priest. *Lifting up the poor out of the dunghill, that he may place him with princes, with the princes of his people.*[3]

---

[1] " Ad vos, o Sacerdotes, qui despicitis nomen meum! . . . Offertis super altare meum panem pollutum, et dicitis: In quo polluimus te?" —*Mal.* i. 6.

[2] " Polluimus panem, id est, corpus Christi, quando indigni accedimus ad altare."

[3] " De stercore erigens pauperem, ut collocet eum cum principibus populi sui."—*Ps.* cxii. 6.

The number of persons to whom God has given this power does not diminish the dignity or the obligations of the priesthood. But what does the priest do that celebrates in the state of sin? He dishonors and despises the Lord, by declaring that so great a sacrifice is not deserving of the reverence which would make him dread the sacrilegious oblation of it, says St. Cyril.[1]

The hand, says St. John Chrysostom, that touches the sacred flesh of Jesus Christ, and the tongue that is purpled with his divine blood, should be purer than the rays of the sun.[2] In another place he says that a priest ascending the altar should be possessed of purity and sanctity which would merit for him a place in the midst of the angels.[3] How great, then, must be the horror of the angels when they behold a priest, who is the enemy of God, stretching forth his sacrilegious hands to touch and eat the immaculate Lamb! "Who," exclaims St. Augustine, "shall be so wicked and daring as to touch the most holy sacrament with polluted hands!"[4] Still more wicked is the priest that celebrates Mass with a soul defiled by mortal sin. God turns away his eyes that he may not behold such horrible impiety. *When, says the Lord, you stretch forth your hands, I will turn away My eyes, ... for your hands are full of blood.*[5] To express the disgust that he feels at the sight of such

---

[1] "Qui non adhibet honorem quem debet altari sancto, factis testatur illud esse contemptibile."—*Molina, Instr. Sacerd.* tr. 2, c. 18, § 1.

[2] "Quo igitur solari radio non puriorem esse oportet manum carnem hanc dividentem, linguam quæ tremendo nimis sanguine rubescit?"—*Ad pop. Ant. hom.* 60.

[3] "Nonne accedentem ad altare Sacerdotem sic parum esse oportet, ut, si in ipsis cœlis esset collocatus, inter cœlestes illas virtutes medius staret."—*De Sacerd.* l. 3.

[4] "Quis adeo impius erit, qui lutosis manibus sacratissimum Sacramentum tractare præsumat?"

[5] "Cum extenderitis manus vestras, avertam oculos meos a vobis." —*Is.* i. 15.

sacrilegious priests, the Lord declares that he will scatter the dung of their sacrifices over their faces: *I will scatter upon your face the dung of your solemnities.*[1] It is true, as the Council of Trent teaches, that the holy sacrifice cannot be contaminated by the malice of priests.[2] However, priests who celebrate in the state of sin defile, as far as in them lies, the sacred mystery; and therefore the Lord declares that he is, as it were, polluted by their abominations. *Her priests have defiled My sanctuaries, . . . and I was profaned in the midst of them.*[3]

Alas! O Lord, exclaims St. Bernard, how does it happen that some of those that hold a high place in your Church are the first to persecute you![4] This is, indeed, too true, as St. Cyprian says, that a priest who celebrates Mass in the state of sin insults with his mouth and hands the very body of Christ.[5] Another author, Peter Comeston, adds, that the priest who pronounces the words of consecration in the state of sin spits, as it were, in the face of Jesus Christ; and when he receives the most holy sacrament into his unhallowed mouth he, as it were, casts the body and blood of Jesus Christ into the mire.[6] But why do I say that he casts Jesus Christ into the mire? The soul of a priest in sin is worse than mire; and, as Theophilactus says, the mire is not so un-

---

[1] "Dispergam super vultum vestrum stercus solemnitatum vestrarum."—*Mal.* ii. 3.

[2] "Hæc quidem illa munda oblatio est, quæ nulla malitia offerentium inquinari potest."—*Sess.* 22, cap. 1.

[3] "Coinquinabar in medio eorum."—*Ezech.* xxii. 26.

[4] "Heu, Domine, Deus, quia ipsi sunt in persecutione tua primi, qui videntur in Ecclesia tua gerere principatum."—*In Conv. S. Pauli* s. 1.

[5] "Vis infertur corpori Domini; in Dominum manibus atque ore delinquunt."—*Serm. de Lapsis.*

[6] 'Qui sacra illius verba Sacramenti ore immundo profert, in faciem Salvatoris spuit; et cum in os immundum sanctissimum carnem ponit, eum quasi in lutum projicit."—*Serm.* 38.

worthy of receiving the divine flesh as the heart of a sacrilegious priest.[1] The sacrilegious priest, then, says St. Vincent Ferror, is guilty of greater impiety than if he cast the most holy sacrament into a sink.[2] Such, too, is the doctrine of St. Thomas of Villanova.[3]

- The sins of a priest are always most grievous on account of the injury that they do to God, who has chosen him for his own minister, and has heaped so many favors upon him. It is one thing, says St. Peter Damian, to violate the laws of a sovereign, and another to strike him with your own hands. This is what the priest does that offers sacrifice in the state of mortal sin. "It is one thing to transgress edicts which the king has promulgated, and another to wound him with our own hands. No one sins more grievously than the priest that offers sacrifice unworthily. When we sin in any other way we, as it were, injure God in his property, but when we unworthily offer sacrifice we dare to lay violent hands upon his person.[4] This was the sin of the Jews who had the daring audacity to offer violence to the person of Jesus Christ. But St. Augustine teaches that the sin of the priest that offers sacrifice unworthily is still more grievous: "Those that unworthily offer Jesus Christ in heaven sin more grievously than the Jews who crucified him when he was upon earth.[5] The

[1] "Lutum non adeo indignum est corpore divino, quam indigna est carnis tuæ impuritas."—*In Heb.* 10, 16.

[2] "Majus peccatum est, quam si projiceret corpus Christi in cloacam."

[3] "Quantum flagitium sit in spurcissimam pectoris tui cloacam Christi sanguinem fundere."—*De Sacram. alt.* conc. 3.

[4] "Aliud est promulgata edicta negligere, aliud ipsum regem vibrato propriæ manus jaculo sanciare. Deterius nemo peccat, quam Sacerdos qui indigne sacrificat: aliter in quocumque modo peccantes, quasi Dominum in rebus ejus offendimus; indigne vero sacrificantes, velut in personam ejus manus injicere non timemus."—*Opusc.* 26, c. 2.

[5] "Minus peccaverunt Judæi crucifigentes in terra deambulantem, quam qui contemnunt in cœlo sedentem."—*In Ps.* 68, s. 2.

Jews did not know the Redeemer as priests do. Besides, as Tertullian says, the Jews lay hands on Jesus Christ only once, but the sacrilegious priest dares frequently to repeat this injurious treatment.[1] It is also necessary to remark, that, according to the doctrine of theologians, a priest by the sacrilegious celebration of Mass is guilty of *four* mortal sins: 1. Because he consecrates in the state of sin, 2 Because he communicates in the state of sin, 3 Because he administers the sacrament in the state of sin; and, 4 Because he administers it to an unworthy person, that is, to himself, who is in mortal sin.*

This made St. Jerome foam, through zeal, against the Deacon Sabinian. " Miserable wretch !" said the holy Doctor, " how has it happened that your eyes have not grown dim, that your tongue has not been twisted, that your arms have not fallen to the ground when you dared to assist at the altar in the state of sin."[2] St. John Chrysostom teaches that a priest that approaches the altar with a soul stained with mortal sin is far worse than a devil.[3] For the devils tremble in the presence of Jesus Christ We read in the life of St. Teresa that when she was going to Communion one day she saw with terror a devil on each side of the priest who celebrated Mass in the state of mortal sin. The devils trembled in the presence of the holy sacrament, and manifested a desire to fly away. From the consecrated Host Jesus said to the saint, " Behold the force of the words of consecration, and see, O Teresa, my goodness

---

[1] " Semel Judæi Christo manus intulerunt ; isti quotidie corpus ejus lacessunt. O manus præscindendæ !"—*De Idol.*

[2] ' Miser ' non caligaverunt oculi tui, lingua torpuit, conciderunt brachia !"—*Ep. ad Sabian.*

[3] " Multo dæmonio pejor est, qui, peccati conscius, accedit ad altare."—*In Matt.* hom. 83.

---

* Cfr. our Moral Theology, I. 6, n. 35, and V. *Hinc dicimus.*

which makes me willing to place myself in the hands of my enemy for your welfare, and for the welfare of every Christian !"[1] The devils then tremble before Jesus in the holy sacrament; but the sacrilegious priest not only does not tremble, but, as St. John Chrysostom says, he audaciously tramples on the Son of God in his own person.[2] In the sacrilegious priest are verified the words of the Apostle: *How much more do you think he deserveth worse punishments who hath trodden under foot the Son of God, and hath esteemed the blood of the testament unclean by which he was sanctified?*[3] Then, in the presence of that God at whose beck *the pillars of heaven tremble, and the whole earth and all things in it are moved*,[4] a worm of the earth dares to trample on the blood of the Son of God!

But, alas! what greater calamity can befall a priest than to change redemption into perdition; sacrifice into sacrilege, and life into death? Great, indeed, was the impiety of the Jews who drew blood from the side of Jesus Christ; but far greater is the impiety of the priest who receives from the chalice the same blood and insults it. Such is the thought of Peter de Blois; he adds, while borrowing the words of St. Jerome: " Shame on the perfidious Jew; shame on the perfidious Christian : the Jew caused the blood to flow from the side of Christ; the Christian, the priest, causes the same blood to flow from the chalice in order to profane it."[5] Of such priests our Lord complained one day to St. Bridget, saying,

[1] *Life*, ch. 38.

[2] "Quando qui particeps est cum ipso in mysteriis, peccatum committit, non eum conculcat."—*In Heb.* hom. 20.

[3] "Quanto majus putatis deteriora mereri supplicia, qui Filium Dei conculcaverit, et sanguinem testamenti pollutum duxerit, in quo sanctificatus est?"—*Heb.* x. 20.

[4] "Columnæ cœli contremiscunt."—*Job*, xxvi. 11.

[5] "Quam perditus ergo est, qui redemptionem in perditionem, qui sacrificium in sacrilegium, qui vitam convertit in mortem! Verbum beati Hieronymi est: ' Perfidus Judæus, perfidus Christianus, ille de latere, iste de calice, sanguinem Christi fudit!'"—*Epist.* 123.

"They crucify my body more cruelly than the Jews did."[1] A learned author says that the priest who celebrates in the state of sin is guilty, as it were, of murdering before the eyes of the eternal Father his own Son.[2]

Oh! what an impious treason. Behold how Jesus Christ complains, by the mouth of David, of the sacrilegious priest: *For if My enemy had reviled Me I would verily have borne with it,* . . . *but thou, a man of one mind, and My familiar, who didst take sweetmeats together with Me*.[3] Behold an exact description of a priest who offers Mass in the state of sin. If my enemy, said the Lord, had insulted me, I would have borne the offence with less pain; but you whom I have made my familiar, my minister, a prince among my people, to whom I have so often given my flesh for food—you have sold me to the devil for the indulgence of passion, for a beastly gratification, for a little earth. Of this sacrilegious treason the Lord complained to St. Bridget: "Such priests," he said, "are not my priests, but real traitors; for, like Judas, they sell and betray me."[4] St. Bernardine of Sienna teaches that such priests are even worse than Judas; because Judas betrayed the Saviour to the Jews, but they deliver him up to devils by receiving him into their sacrilegious breasts, which are ruled by devils.[5]

[1] "Corpus meum amarius crucifigunt, quam Judæi."—*Rev.* l. 4, c. 133.

[2] "Ne, si peccatis obnoxii offerunt, eorum oblatio sit quasi qui victimat Filium in conspectu Patris."—*Durant. De Rit. Eccl.* l. 2, c. 42, § 4.

[3] "Quoniam, si inimicus meus maledixisset mihi, sustinuissem utique; . . . tu vero, homo unanimis, dux meus et notus meus, qui simul mecum dulces capiebas cibos!"—*Ps.* liv. 13.

[4] "Tales Sacerdotes non sunt mei Sacerdotes, sed veri proditores ipsi enim et me vendunt quasi Judas."—*Rev.* l. 1, c. 47.

[5] "Juda traditore deteriores effecti, eo quod, sicut ille tradidit Jesum Judæis, sic isti tradunt diabolis, eo quod illum ponunt in loco sub potestate diaboli constituto."—T. II. s. 55, a. 1, c. 3.

Peter Comestor observes that when a sacrilegious priest begins the prayer *Aufer a nobis iniquitates nostras*, etc. ("Take away from us our iniquities, etc."), and kisses the altar, Jesus appears to reproach him, and say: Judas, do you betray me with a kiss?[1] And when the priest, says St. Gregory, extends his arm to communicate, I think I hear the Redeemer say what he said to Judas,' 'Behold the hand that betrays me is with me on the altar."[2] Hence, according to St. Isidore of Pelusium, the sacrilegious priest is, like Judas, entirely possessed by the devil.[3]

Ah! the blood of Jesus Christ, so much insulted, cries more powerfully for vengeance against the sacrilegious priest than the blood of Abel did against Cain. This Jesus himself declared to St. Bridget. Oh! what horror must God and his angels feel at the sight of a sacrilegious Mass! This horror the Lord made known in the following manner, in the year 1688, to his servant Sister Mary Crucified, of Palma, in Sicily. At first she heard a doleful trumpet, which uttered, in a tone of thunder, audible over the entire earth, the following words: *Ultio, pœna, dolor* (vengeance, punishment, pain). She then saw several sacrilegious ecclesiastics singing psalms with discordant voices, and in a confused and irregular manner. She next saw one of them rise up to go to the altar and say Mass. While he was putting on the sacred vestments, the church was covered with darkness and mourning. He approaches the altar, and, in saying the *Introibo ad altare Dei*, the trumpet sounds

---

[1] "Nonne Christus potest stare, et dicere: Juda! tradis osculo Filium hominis!"—*Serm.* 42.

[2] "Qui Christi corpus indigne conficit, Christum tradit, ut Christus, dum traditur dicat; Ecce manus tradentis me mecum est in mensa." —*P. de Blois, Epist.* 123.

[3] "In eis qui peccant, nec sancta mysteria contingere verentur, totus dæmon se insinuat; quod etiam in proditore quoque fecit."—*Epist.* l. 3, ep. 364.

CHAP. VII.] *The Sacrilegious Mass.* 133

again and repeats, *ultio, pœna, dolor*. In an instant the altar appeared to be surrounded by flames of fire, which denoted the just fury of the Lord against the unworthy celebrant; and at the same time a great multitude of angels were seen with swords in their hands as if to execute vengeance on him for the sacrilegious Mass which he was going to offer. When the monster came near the consecration, a crowd of vipers sprung from the midst of the flames to drive him away from the altar; these vipers represented his fears and stings of conscience. But they were all useless; the impious wretch preferred his own reputation to all these stings of remorse. Finally he pronounced the words of consecration; and instantly the servant of God felt a universal earthquake, which caused heaven, earth, and hell to tremble. She saw angels around the altar bathed in tears; but the divine mother wept still more bitterly at the death of her innocent son, and at the loss of a sinful child. After a vision so tremendous and dismal, the servant of God was so overpowered with fear and sorrow that she could do nothing but weep. The author of her life remarks that it was in the same year the earthquake happened which produced such havoc in the city of Naples and in the surrounding country. Hence we may infer that this earthquake was a punishment for the sacrilegious Mass at which Sister Mary was present.

But, exclaims St. Augustine, what more horrid impiety can be conceived than that the tongue that calls down the Son of God from heaven should be, at the very same moment, employed in outraging his majesty? or that the hands that are bathed in the blood of Jesus Christ should be, at the same time, polluted with the blood of sin.[1] To the sacrilegious priest St. Bernard says: O

[1] "Ne lingua, quæ vocat de cœlo Filium Dei, contra Dominum loquatur; et manus, quæ intinguntur sanguine Christi, polluantur sanguine peccati."—*Molina, Instr. Sacr.* tr. 1, c. 5, § 2.

unworthy wretch! if you wish to commit the enormous crime of celebrating Mass in the state of sin, at least procure another tongue, and do not employ that which is washed in the blood of Jesus Christ; procure hands different from those which you stretch out to touch his sacred flesh.¹ Oh! let the priest who wishes to live at enmity with God at least abstain from sacrilegiously offering sacrifice on his altar! But, no! says St. Bonaventure: he will, for the sake of the miserable stipend that he receives, continue to commit a sin of such horrible enormity.² Perhaps he expects that the sacred flesh of Jesus Christ which he offers in sacrifice will deliver him from his iniquities? *Shall the holy flesh*, says the prophet Jeremias, *take away from thee thy crimes in which thou hast boasted?*³ No: the contact of that sacred body, as long as you remain in the state of sin, shall render you more guilty and more deserving of chastisement. He, says St. Peter Chrysologus, who commits a crime in the presence of his judge can advance no grounds of defence.⁴

What chastisement does not the priest deserve who, instead of carrying with him to the altar flames of divine charity, brings the fetid fire of unchaste love! Speaking of the punishment inflicted on the sons of Aaron for having offered strange fire, St. Peter Damian says: "Let us take care not to mingle unholy fire, that is, the flames of lust with the salutary sacrifices."⁵

---

¹ "Quando ergo peccare volueris, quære aliam linguam quam eam quæ rubescit sanguine Christi, alias manus præter eas quæ Christum suscipiunt."

² "Accedunt, non vocati a Deo, sed impulsi ab avaritia."—*De Præp. ad M.* c. 8.

³ "Numquid carnes sanctæ auferent a te malitias tuas, in quibus gloriata es?"—*Jer.* xi. 15.

⁴ "Excusatione caret, qui facinus, ipso judice teste, committit."
—*Serm.* 26.

⁵ "Cavendum est ne alienum ignem, hoc est, libidinis flammam, inter salutares hostias deferamus."—*Opusc.* 26, c. 1. *Levit.* x.

Whosoever, adds the saint, shall dare to carry the flame of lust to the altar, shall certainly be consumed by the fire of God's vengeance.[1] May the Lord, then, says the holy Doctor in another place, preserve us from ever adoring on the altar the idol of impurity, and from placing the Son of the Virgin in the Temple of Venus, that is, in an unchaste heart![2] If the man that came to the feast without the nuptial garment was cast into darkness, how much greater vengeance shall fall on him who approaches the divine table not only not clothed with a decent garment, but exhaling the stench of his impurities? says the same St. Peter Damian.[3] Woe, exclaimed St. Bernard, to him that separates himself from God; but still greater woe to the priest who approaches the altar with a guilty conscience.[4] Speaking one day to St. Bridget of a priest who had sacrilegiously celebrated Mass, the Lord said that he entered into the soul of that priest as a spouse for his sanctification, and that he was obliged to depart from it as a judge, to inflict the punishment merited by the sacrilegious reception of his body.[5]

If the sacrilegious priest will not abstain from celebrating the divine mysteries in the state of sin, through horror of the insult, or rather of so many insults, offered to God by sacrilegious Masses, he ought at least to

[1] "Quisquis carnalis concupiscentiæ flamma æstuat, et sacris assistere mysteriis non formidat, ille, procul dubio, divinæ ultionis igne consumitur."—*Opusc.* 27, c. 3.

[2] "Absit ut aliquis huic idolo substernatur, ut Filium Virginis in Veneris templo suscipiat."—*Serm.* 60.

[3] "Quid illi sperandum, qui, cœlestibus tricliniis intromissus, non modo non est spiritualis indumenti decore conspicuus, sed ultro etiam fætet sordentis luxuriæ squalore perfusus."—*Opusc.* 18, d. 1, c. 4.

[4] "Væ ei qui se alienum fecerit ab eo: et multum væ ei qui immundus accesserit."—*De Ord. vitæ.* c. 2.

[5] "Ingredior ad Sacerdotem istum ut sponsus; egredior ut Judex, judicaturus contemptus a sumente."—*Rev.* l. 4, c. 62.

tremble at the awful chastisement prepared for him. St. Thomas of Villanova teaches that no punishment is sufficient to avenge a crime so enormous as a sacrilegious Mass. "Woe," he says, "to the sacrilegious hands! woe to the unclean breast of the impious priest! Every punishment is inadequate to the sin by which Christ is despised in this sacrifice."[1] Our Lord once said to St. Bridget that such priests are cursed by all creatures in heaven and on earth.[2] A priest, as we have said in another place, is a vessel consecrated to God; and as Balthasar was chastised for having profaned the vessels of the Temple, so says, Peter de Blois, shall the priest be punished who unworthily offers sacrifice: "We see priests abusing vessels consecrated to God, but near them is that hand and that terrible writing: *Mane, Thecel, Phares*—numbered, weighed, divided."[3] *Thou art numbered:* a single sacrilege is sufficient to put an end to the number of divine graces. *Thou art weighed:* such a crime is enough to make the balance of divine justice descend to the eternal perdition of the sacrilegious priest. *Divided:* enraged at such an enormity, the Lord shall banish and separate you from himself for eternity. Thus, then, shall be verified the words of David: *Let their table become as a snare before them.*[4] The altar shall become for the sacrilegious priest the place of his punishment, where, remaining obstinate in sin, he shall be bound in the chains of hell, and shall be made the perpetual slave of Satan. For, according to St.

---

[1] "Væ sacrilegis manibus, væ immundis pectoribus impiorum Sacerdotum! omne supplicium minus est flagitio quo Christus contemnitur in hoc sacrificio."—*De Sacram. alt.* conc. 3.

[2] "Maledicti sunt a cœlo et terra, et ab hominibus creaturis, quæ ipsæ obediunt Deo, et isti spreverunt."—*Rev.* l. 1, c. 47.

[3] "Videmus Sacerdotes abutentes vasis Deo consecratis; sed prope est manus illa et scriptura terribilis: *Mane, Thecel, Phares:* Numeratum, Appensum, Divisum."—*Serm.* 56.

[4] "Fiat mensa eorum coram ipsis in laqueum."—*Ps.* lxviii. 23.

CHAP. VII.] *The Sacrilegious Mass.* 137

Laurence Justinian, they that communicate in mortal sin adhere with greater pertinacity to sin.[1] This is conformable to the doctrine of the apostle, that *he that eateth and drinketh unworthily eateth and drinketh judgment to himself.*[2] Hence St. Peter Damian exclaims: O priest of God, who offer to the eternal Father his own Son in sacrifice do not beforehand immolate yourself as a victim to the devil.[3]

[1] "Sumentes indigne, præ cæteris delicta graviora committunt, et pertinaciores in malo sunt."—*S. de Euchar.*

[2] "Qui enim manducat et bibit indigne, judicium sibi manducat et bibit."—1 *Cor.* xi. 29.

[3] "Cur, o Sacerdos, qui sacrificium Deo debes offerre, temetipsum prius maligno spiritui non vereris victimam immolare?"—*Opusc.* 17, c. 3.

CHAPTER VIII.

THE SIN OF SCANDAL.

THE devil first procured the invention of deities addicted to vice, he then sought to induce the Gentiles to worship them, that thus men might consider it lawful to sin as often as they pleased, and that they might even lose all horror for the vices with which they saw their gods clothed. This, Seneca, who was a Gentile, confessed: " Since we have such gods the horror of vice should disappear from among men."[1] " To attribute vices to the gods—what is it but to inflame passion in the hearts of men, at the same time legalizing all the disorders through the example of the divinity?"[2] Hence, as we read in the works of the same Seneca, the unhappy Gentiles would say: " Why should that be forbidden to me what the gods have a right to do?"[3] But what the devil obtained from the Gentiles by means of these pretended deities, whom he proposed as models for imitation, he now obtains from Christians by means of the scandalous priest, who by his bad example persuades poor seculars into a belief that what they see in their pastor is lawful, or at least not a great evil in worldlings. " Seculars think," says St. Gregory, " that all is allowed them what they see their pastors do, so that

---

[1] " Quibus nihil aliud actum est, quam ut pudor hominibus peccandi demeretur."—*De Vita beata*, c. 26.
[2] " Quid aliud est vitia incendere, quam auctores illis inscribere deos, dare morbo, exemplo divinitatis, excusatam licentiam?"—*De Brevit. vitæ*, c. 16.
[3] " Quod divos decuit, cur mihi turpe putem?"

CHAP. VIII.] *The Sin of Scandal.* 139

they imitate them the more ardently."[1] God has placed priests in the world that they may be a model to others, as our Saviour himself was sent by his Father to be an example to the world: *As the Father hath sent me, I also send you.*[2] Hence St. Jerome wrote to a bishop to guard against actions by the imitation of which others might be drawn, as it were, by force into sin.[3]

The sin of scandal consists not only in directly advising others to do evil, but also in inducing them indirectly by acts to the commission of sin. Scandal is thus defined by St. Thomas and other theologians: "Every word or action, more or less inordinate, that constitutes for the neighbor an occasion of falling into sin."[4] To understand the grievousness of the sin of scandal, it is enough to know, that according to St. Paul he who offends against a brother by leading him into sin, offends against Jesus Christ: *When you sin against the brethren, and wound their weak conscience, you sin against Christ.*[5] St Bernard assigns the reason, saying, that the author of scandal robs Jesus Christ of the souls redeemed by his blood. The saint goes so far as to say that Jesus Christ suffers more from those that scandalize others than he did from his crucifiers. "If our Lord," he says, "has given his blood to redeem souls, do you not think that of these two persecutions, the one in which scandal robs him of souls purchased by his blood, the other in which

---

[1] "Persuadent sibi id licere, quod a suis pastoribus fieri conspiciunt, et ardentius perpetrant."

[2] "Sicut misit me Pater, et ego mitto vos."—*John*, xx. 21.

[3] "Cave ne committas quod, qui volunt imitari, coguntur delinquere."—*Ep. ad Heliod.*

[4] "Dictum vel factum minus rectum, præbens occasionem ruinæ."—2, 2, q. 43, a. 1.

[5] "Peccantes autem in fratres, et percutientes conscientiam eorum infirmam, in Christum peccatis."—1 *Cor.* viii. 12.

the Jews shed his blood, the first is much more cruel to his heart?"[1]

But if in all, even in seculars, the sin of scandal is so detestable, how much greater must be its malice in a priest, whom God has placed on earth to save souls and to conduct them to heaven! The priest is called the salt of the earth and the light of the world.[2] The office of salt is to preserve soundness and prevent putrefaction, and the office of the priest is to preserve souls in the grace of God. What, says St. Augustine, shall become of the people if the priest does not perform the office of salt.[3] Then the saint proceeds to say, this salt shall be fit only to be cast away by the Church, and to be trodden by all.[4] But what, if, instead of being a preservative, this salt be employed in producing and promoting corruption? If instead of bringing souls to God, a priest is occupied in leading them to perdition, whast punishment shall he deserve?

The priest is also the light of the world.[5] Hence, says St. John Chrysostom, he should shine with the splendor of his sanctity so as to enlighten all others to imitate his virtues.[6] But should this light be changed into darkness, what must become of the world? Shall it not

---

[1] "Si (Dominus) proprium sanguinem dedit in pretium redemptionis animarum, non tibi videtur graviorem sustinere persecutionem ab illo qui, scandali occasione avertit ab eo animas quas redemit, quam a Judæo, qui sanguinem suum fudit?"—*In Conv. S. Pauli*, s. 1.

[2] "Vos estis sal terræ?"—*Matt.* v. 13.

[3] "Itaque, si sal infatuatum fuerit, in quo salietur? Qui erunt homines per quos a vobis error auferatur, cum vos elegerit Deus, per quos errorem auferat cæterorum?"

[4] "Ergo ad nihilum valet sal infatuatum, nisi ut mittatur foras, et calcetur ab hominibus."—*De Serm. Dom. in monte*, l. 1, c. 6.

[5] "Vos estis lux mundi."—*Matt.* v. 14.

[6] "Splendore vitæ totum illuminantis orbem splendere debet animus Sacerdotis."—*De Sacerd.* l. 6.

CHAP. VIII.] *The Sin of Scandal.* 141

be brought to ruin? says St. Gregory.[1] The saint has written the same to the bishops of France, whom he exhorted to chastise the priest who is guilty of scandal.[2] This is conformable to the words of the Prophet Osee: *And there shall be like people like priest.*[3] By the mouth of Jeremias the Lord has said, *And I will fill the soul of the priest with fatness: and My people shall be filled with good things.*[4] Hence St. Charles Borromeo says that if the priests be fat and rich in virtue, the people, too, shall be rich; but if the priests be poor, the people shall be in still greater poverty.[5]

Thomas de Cantimpré writes that in Paris a devil told an ecclesiastic to preach to the clergy of that city, and to say that the princes of hell saluted and thanked some of them for having caused the damnation of an immense multitude of souls.[6] Of this the Lord complained by the Prophet Jeremias: *My people hath been a lost flock; their shepherds have caused them to go astray.*[7] There is no alternative, says St. Gregory; when the priest walks into the precipice, the people, too, are dashed to ruin.[8] The bad example of the priest necessarily produces im-

---

[1] "Laqueus ruinæ populi mei, Sacerdotes mali."—*Past.* p. 1, c, 2.
[2] "Ne paucorum facinus multorum possit esse perditio; nam causa sunt ruinæ populi Sacerdotes mali."—*Epist.* l. 9, ep. 64.
[3] "Et erit, sicut populus, sic Sacerdos."—*Os.* iv. 9.
[4] "Et inebriabo animam Sacerdotum pinguedine, et populus meus bonis meis adimplebitur."—*Jer.* xxxi. 14.
[5] "Si pingues sint Sacerdotes, erunt itidem populi pingues; et secus, si illi inanes erunt, magnum populis imminebit paupertatis periculum."—*In Synod. diœc.* 11, orat. 1.
[6] "Principes tenebrarum principes Ecclesiæ salutant. Læti omnes nos gratias eisdem referimus, quia, per eorum negligentiam, ad nos devolvitur totus fere mundus."—*De Apib.* l. 1, c. 20.
[7] "Grex perditus factus est populus meus; pastores eorum seduxerunt eos."—*Jer.* l. 6.
[8] "Unde fit ut, cum pastor per abrupta graditur, ad præcipitium grex sequatur."—*Past.* p. 1, c. 2.

morality among his people, says St. Bernard.[1] Should a secular mistake the way, he alone is lost; but when a priest errs, he shall cause the perdition of many, particularly of those that are under his care, says the same St. Bernard.[2] The Lord ordained in Leviticus that for the sin of a single priest a calf should be offered, as well as for the sins of the entire people. From this Innocent III. concludes that the sin of a priest is as grievous as the sins of the whole people. The reason is, says the Pontiff, that by his sin the priest leads the entire people into sin.[3] And, long before, the Lord himself said the same: *If the priest that is anointed shall sin, he maketh the people to offend.*[4] Hence, St. Augustine, addressing priests, says, " Do not close heaven: but this you do if you give to others a bad example to lead a wicked life."[5] Our Lord said one day to St. Bridget, that when sinners see the bad example of the priest, they are encouraged to commit sin, and even begin to glory in the vices of which they were before ashamed.[6] Hence our Lord added that worse maledictions shall fall on the priest than on others, because by his sinful life he brings himself and others to perdition.[7]

[1] " Misera eorum conversatio plebis subversio est."—*In Conv. S. Pauli*, s. 1.

[2] " Si quis de populo deviat, solus perit; verum principis error multos involvit, et tantis obest, quantis præest ipse."—*Epist.* 127.

[3] " Unde conjicitur quod peccatum Sacerdotis totius multitudinis peccato coæquatur, quia Sacerdos in suo peccato totam fecit delinquere multitudinem."—*In Consecr. Pont.* s. 1.

[4] " Si Sacerdos qui unctus est, peccaverit, delinquere faciens populum."—*Lev.* iv. 3.

[5] " Nolite eis cœlum claudere; clauditis, dum male vivere ostenditis."—*Ad Fratr. in er.* s. 36.

[6] " Viso exemplo pravo Sacerdotum, peccator fiduciam peccandi sumit, et incipit de peccato, quod prius reputabat erubescibile, gloriari."

[7] " Ideo ipsis erit amplior maledictio præ aliis, quia se vita sua perdunt et alios."—*Rev.* l. 4. c. 132.

The author of the *Imperfect Work* says that all that see a tree covered with pale and withered leaves immediately infer that its roots have been injured; and when we see a people immoral, we may justly conclude, without danger of rash judgment, that the priest is a man without virtue.[1] Yes, says St. John Chrysostom, the life of the priest is the root from which the people, who are the branches, receive nutriment. St. Ambrose[2] also says that priests are the head from which virtue flows to the members, that is, to seculars. *The whole head is sick*, says the Prophet Isaias; . . . *from the sole of the foot unto the top of the head there is no soundness therein*.[3] St. Isidore explains this passage in the following words: "This languishing head is the priest that commits sin, and that communicates his sin to the whole body."[4] St. Leo weeps over this evil, saying, How can health be found in the body if the head be not sound?[5] Who, says St. Bernard, shall seek in a sink the limpid water of the spring? Shall I, adds the saint, seek counsel from the man that knows not how to give counsel to himself?[6] Speaking of the bad example of princes, Plutarch[7] says, that it poisons not a single cup, but the public fountain; and thus, because all draw from the

[1] "Vidit arborem pallentibus foliis marcidam, et intellexit agricola quia læsuram in radicibus habet; ita, cum videris populum irreligiosum, sine dubio cognoscis quia Sacerdotium ejus non est sanum."—*Hom.* 38.

[2] *De Dignit. sac.* c. 5.

[3] "Omne caput languidum. . . . A planta pedis usque ad verticem, non est in eo sanitas."—*Is.* i. 5.

[4] "Caput enim languidum doctor est agens peccatum, cujus malum ad corpus pervenit."—*Sent.* l. 3, c. 38.

[5] "Totius familiæ Domini status et ordo nutabit, si, quod requiritur in corpore, non inveniatur in capite."—*Epist.* 87.

[6] "Quis enim in cœno fontem requirat? . . . An vero idoneum eum putabo, qui mihi det consilium, quod non dat sibi?"—*Officior.* l. 2, c. 12.

[7] *Opusc. Max. cum princip. philos.*

fountain, all are poisoned. This may be said with greater truth of the bad example of priests; hence Eugene III. has said that bad Superiors are the principal causes of the sins of inferiors.[1]

Priests are called by St. Gregory[2] *Patres Christianorum* —The Fathers of Christians. Thus also are they called by St. John Chrysostom, who says that a priest as the representative of God is bound to take care of all men, because he is the Father of the whole world.[3] As a parent, then, sins doubly when he gives bad example to his children, so a priest is also guilty of a double sin when he gives bad example to seculars, says Peter de Blois.[4] St. Jerome made the same remark in a letter to a certain bishop: " Whatever you do, all will think they may also do."[5] When they sin at the sight of the bad example of a priest, seculars, as Cesarius has observed, say, " Do not also priests do such things?"[6] St. Augustine puts the following words into the mouth of a secular: "Why do you reproach me? are not priests doing the same? and you wish to force me not to do so?"[7] St. Gregory says that when, instead of edifying the people, a priest gives scandal, he renders sin, in a certain manner, honorable rather than an object of horror.[8]

[1] " Inferiorum culpæ ad nullos magis referendæ sunt, quam ad desides rectores."—*S. Bernard. De Consid.* 1. 3, c. 5.

[2] *In Evang.* hom. 17.

[3] "Quasi totius orbis pater Sacerdos est; dignum igitur est ut omnium curam agat, sicut ut Deus, cujus fungitur vice."—*In* 1 *Tim.* hom. 6.

[4] " Quid faciet laicus, nisi quod patrem suum spiritualem viderit facientem."—*Serm.* 57.

[5] " Quidquid feceris, id sibi omnes faciendum putant."—*Ep. ad Heliod.*

[6] " Numquid talia clerici, etiam majoris ordinis, faciunt?"—*Serm.* 15.

[7] " Quid mihi loqueris? Ipsi clerici non illud faciunt, et me cogis ut faciam?"—*Serm.* 137, *E. B.*

[8] "In exemplum culpa vehementer extenditur, quando, pro reverentia Ordinis, peccator honoratur."—*Past.* p. 1, c. 2.

Such a priest, then, is at the same time a parent and a parricide; for, as St. Gregory says, he is the cause of the death of his spiritual children. "You see," says the saint, "what blows daily are given to the people, and whose fault is it but the fault of priests? We are the cause of the death of the people, while we should be their leaders to eternal life."[1] Some one that has lost the divine light may say I must give an account of my own sins, but what have I to do with the sins of others? He may say what he pleases, but I exhort him to listen to the words of St. Jerome: "If you say I have enough to do with my own conscience; what do I care for people's talk? listen to the words of the Apostle: *Providing good things, not only in the sight of God, but also in the sight of all men.*"[2] St. Bernard says that the scandalous priest kills others at the same time that he murders his own soul.[3] And in another place the saint writes that there is no plague more noxious to the people than ignorance in a priest united with irregularity of life.[4] In another place the same saint says that in their sermons many priests are orthodox, but in their conduct they are heretics; because by their bad example they inflict a deeper wound on religion than heretics do by teaching false doctrines, because acts have more force than words.[5]

[1] "Quibus quotidie percussionibus intereat populus videtis; cujus hoc, nisi nostro præcipue, peccato agitur? Nos pereunti populo auctores mortis existimus, qui esse debuimus duces ad vitam."—*In Evang.* hom. 17.

[2] "Si dixeris: Et mihi sufficit conscientia mea; non curo quid loquantur homines;—audi Apostolum scribentem: 'Providentes bona, non tantum coram Deo, sed etiam coram omnibus hominibus.'"—*Rom.* xii. 17.

[3] "Non parcunt suis, qui non parcunt sibi, perimentes pariter et pereuntes."—*In Cant.* s. 77.

[4] "Post indoctos prælatos malosque, in Ecclesia, nulla pestis ad nocendum infirmis valentior invenitur."—*De Ord. vitæ.* c. 1.

[5] "Multi sunt catholici prædicando, qui hæretici sunt operando:

Seneca says that the way of instruction is a long and tedious way of learning vice or virtue; but the way of example is short and efficacious.[1] Hence, speaking particularly of the chastity of priests, St. Augustine has written: "To all chastity is very necessary, but especially to the ministers of Christ, whose lives should be to others a sermon unto salvation."[2] How can the slave of lust preach chastity? says St. Peter Damian.[3] St. Jerome says that the very state and dress of an ecclesiastic call for and demand chastity.[4] What a source of scandal, then, to the Church to see a man with the name and rank of a saint give examples of vice? "No one," says St. Gregory, "injures the Church more than he that bears the name and the Order of sanctity."[5] And must it not, adds St. Isidore of Pelusium, be a still more disastrous evil to see a priest avail himself of his dignity as the arms with which he commits sin?[6] According to the words of Ezechiel, such a priest renders the exalted dignity of his state an object of abomination: *Thou hast made thy beauty to be abominable.*[7] St. Bernard says that the priest that does not give good example is an ob-

---

quod hæretici faciebant per prava dogmata, hoc faciunt plures hodie per mala exempla; et tanto graviores sunt hæreticis, quanto prævalent opera verbis."—*S. ad Past. in Syn.*

[1] "Longum iter est per præcepta, breve et efficax per exempla."—*Epist.* 6.

[2] "Omnibus castitas pernecessaria est, sed maxime ministris Christi altaris, quorum vita aliorum debet esse assidua salutis prædicatio."—*Serm.* 291, E. B. app.

[3] "Qui prædicator constitutus es castitatis, non te pudet servum esse libidinis?"—*Opusc.* 17, c. 3.

[4] "Clamat vestis clericalis, clamat status professi animi sanctitatem."

[5] "Nemo amplius in Ecclesia nocet, quam qui, perverse agens, nomen vel ordinem sanctitatis habet."—*Past.* p. 1, c. 2.

[6] "Sacerdotii dignitate velut armis ad vitium abuti."—*Epist.* l. 2, ep. 162.

[7] "Abominabilem fecisti decorem tuum."—*Ezech.* xvi. 25.

ject of scorn to the entire people.[1] It is not in order to see a priest live like worldlings; but what a scandal to see his conduct worse than that of seculars? says the author of the *Imperfect Work*.[2] And what example, says St. Ambrose, can the people take from you, if in you, who are esteemed holy, they witness actions of which they themselves are ashamed?[3]

Hear ye this, O priests, says the prophet Osee, . . . *for there is a judgment against you, because you have been a snare to them whom you should have watched over, and a net spread upon Thabor.*[4] The sportsman employs decoys, that is, birds that are bound so that they cannot fly away, and the devil employs the authors of scandal in order to catch souls in his net. Says St. Ephrem: "When the soul is once caught it becomes as a snare for catching others."[5] Of these authors of scandal God complains by the prophet Jeremias, saying, *For among My people are found wicked men, that lie in wait as fowlers, setting snares and traps to catch.*[6] But, says Cæsar of Arles, the devil seeks in a special manner to employ for his decoys scandalous priests; hence this author calls them decoy birds whom the devils usually incite to catch others.[7]

[1] "Aut cæteris honestiores, aut fabula omnibus sunt."—*De Consid.* l. 4, c. 6.

[2] "Quomodo non sit confusio esse Sacerdotes inferiores laicis, quos etiam esse æquales magna confusio est?"—*Hom.* 40.

[3] "Si, quæ in se erubescit, in te, quem reverendum arbitratur, offendat?"—*Epist.* 6.

[4] "Audite hoc, Sacerdotes; . . . quia vobis judicium est, quoniam laqueus facti estis speculationi, et rete expansum."—*Os.* v. 1.

[5] "Cum primum capta fuerit anima, ad alias decipiendas fit laqueus."—*De recta viv. rat.* c. 22.

[6] "Quia inventi sunt in populo meo impii insidiantes quasi aucupes, laqueos ponentes et pedicas ad capiendos viros."—*Jer.* v. 26.

[7] "Quomodo aucupes facere solent, qui columbas, quas prius ceperint, excæcant et surdas faciunt, ut, dum ad illas reliquæ columbæ convenerint, præparatis retibus capiantur."—*Hom.* 35.

A certain author attests that in ancient times when a simple ecclesiastic passed by the way all rose up and besought him to recommend them to God. Is this done at the present day? Alas! Jeremias weeps, and says: *How is the gold become dim, the finest color is changed, the stones of the sanctuary are scattered in the top of every street ?*[1] The gold, according to the exposition of Cardinal Hugo, signifies ecclesiastics, in some of whom it has lost its beautiful color: it has ceased to be ruddy with holy charity; it has grown dim, and no longer shines with the splendor of brilliant examples. The stones of the sanctuary, that is, says St. Jerome, many of the priests, are scattered through the streets, and serve only to precipitate poor seculars into vice. This passage is thus explained also by St. Gregory: " The gold is obscured, for the priests dishonor their lives by the baseness of their works. It has lost its beautiful color, since their shameful actions have covered with reproach the sacerdotal dignity. The stones of the sanctuary are scattered through the streets, because recollection and the holy exercises have given way to dissipation and worldly occupations, so that one finds really no secular enterprise to which the priest has not consecrated his energy."[2]

The sons of My mother have fought against Me.[3] Origen applies this passage to the disorderly priest, who, he says, arms himself by his scandals against his own mother, the Church. St. Jerome says that the Church

---

[1] "Quomodo obscuratum est aurum, mutatus est color optimus, dispersi sunt lapides sanctuarii in capite omnium platearum!"—*Lam.* iv. 1.

[2] "Aurum quippe obscuratum est, quia Sacerdotum vita, per actiones infirmas, ostenditur reproba; color optimus est mutatus, quia ille sanctitatis habitus, per abjecta opera, ad ignominiam despectionis venit; dispersi sunt lapides sanctuarii in capite omnium platearum, quia hi qui, per vitam et orationem, intus semper esse debuerant, foris vacant. Ecce jam pene nulla est sæculi actio, quam non Sacerdotes administrat."—*In Evang.* hom. 17.

[3] "Filii matris meæ pugnaverunt contra me."—*Cant.* i. 5.

is laid waste by the scandalous lives of some of her priests.[1] Hence on the words of Ezechias, *Behold in peace is My bitterness most bitter*,[2] St. Bernard, speaking in the name of the Church, said: "Now we have peace from pagans, peace from heretics, not, however, from our own children."[3] At present, says the holy Church, I am not persecuted by the pagans, for the tyrants have ceased, nor by the heretics, because there are no new heresies; but I am persecuted by the ecclesiastic, who by his scandals robs me of so many souls. "I think," says St. Gregory, "that no one injures the interests of God as the priests do whom he has himself charged with the duty of drawing souls from vice, and who by their bad example precipitate them into it."[4]

By his bad example the scandalous priest brings disgrace even on his own ministry, that is, on his sermons, Masses, and all his functions. Against this the Apostle has warned priests: *Giving no offence to any man, that our ministry be not blamed, but in all things let us exhibit ourselves as the ministers of God*.[5] Salvian says that through certain priests the law of Jesus Christ is dishonored.[6] St. Bernardine of Sienna writes that many, seeing the bad example of the scandalous ecclesiastic, begin even to waver in faith, and thus abandon themselves to vice, despising the sacraments, hell, and heaven.[7]

[1] "Propter vitia Sacerdotum Dei, sanctuarium destitutum est."—*Ep. ad Sabinianum.*
[2] "Ecce in pace amaritudo mea amarissima."—*Is.* xxxviii. 17.
[3] "Pax a paganis, pax ab hæreticis, sed non profecto a filiis."—*In Cant.* s. 33.
[4] "Nullum puto ab aliis majus præjudicium, quam a Sacerdotibus, tolerat Deus, quando eos, quos ad aliorum correctionem posuit, dare de se exempla pravitatis cernit."—*In Evang.* hom. 17.
[5] "Nemini dantes ullam offensionem, ut non vituperetur ministerium nostrum; sed in omnibus exhibeamus nosmetipsos sicut Dei ministros."—2 *Cor.* vi. 3.
[6] "In nobis lex christiana maledicitur."
[7] "Plurimi, considerantes cleri sceleratam vitam, ex hoc vacillantes,

St. John Chrysostom writes that the infidels, seeing the vices of certain priests, would say that the God of the Christians either was not the true God, or that he was not a God of sanctity. For, said they, were he holy, how could he tolerate the sins of his priests?[1] In the instruction on the Mass we shall relate more at length the fact of a heretic who had resolved to abjure his errors, but being afterwards present at a Mass celebrated in a scandalous manner, he determined to remain in his heresy, and said that even the Pope did not believe in the Mass, for if he did he would condemn such priests to be burnt alive. St. Jerome said that among those that had infected the Church and perverted the people, he found in history the names only of priests.[2] And Peter de Blois says: "On account of the negligence of priests heresies came into existence."[3] In another place he says: "On account of the sins of priests the holy Church of God has been covered with opprobrium and trodden in the dust."[4] St. Bernard was of opinion that greater injury is done to the Church by scandalous priests than even by the heretics; because we may guard against heretics, but how can we guard against the priest of whose ministry we must necessarily avail ourselves? "See," says the holy Doctor, "what poison is now ravaging the whole body of the Church! The more it extends the less it can be checked, and the greater the

imo multoties deficientes in fide, sacramenta despiciunt, vitia non evitant, non horrent inferos, cœlestia minime concupiscunt."—T. I. s. 19, a. 2, c. 1.

[1] "Qualis est eorum Deus, qui talia agunt? numquid sustineret eos talia facientes, nisi consentiret eorum operibus?"—*Hom.* 10.

[2] "Veteres scrutans historias, invenire non possum scidisse Ecclesiam, et populos seduxisse, præter eos qui Sacerdotes a Deo positi fuerunt."—*In Oseam*, c. 9.

[3] "Propter negligentiam Sacerdotum, hæreses pullularunt."

[4] "Propter peccata nostra (Sacerdotum), data est in conculcationem et opprobrium Sanctæ Ecclesia Christi."—*Serm.* 60.

danger of becoming more hidden. Let a heretic preach impious doctrines, and he will be expelled; let him have recourse to violence, and we shall flee from him. But now how can we reject or expel priests? We need them, and all are our enemies."[1]

Oh! how great the punishment which is reserved for the scandalous priest! If against every secular that gives scandal vengeance has been threatened, *Woe to that man by whom the scandal cometh*,[2] how much more tremendous the scourge that shall fall on the scandalous priest whom God has chosen from among all men for his own minister! *He chose him out of all flesh*.[3] Jesus Christ has chosen him to bring forth fruit by saving souls. *I have chosen you, and have appointed you, that you should go, and should bring forth fruit.*[4] And by bad example he robs Jesus Christ of souls redeemed with his blood. St. Gregory says that such a priest merits as many deaths as he gives examples of vice.[5] Speaking especially of priests, our Lord said to St. Bridget: "Upon them greater malediction will come, because by their conduct they damn not only themselves, but also others."[6] To them is intrusted the care of cultivating the vineyard of the Lord; but he casts out of his vineyard the scandalous priest, and places in his stead others that will bring forth good fruit: *He will bring those evil men to an evil end: and will let*

---

[1] "Serpit hodie putida tabes per omne corpus Ecclesiæ, et, quo latius, eo desperatius, eoque periculosius quo interius: nam, si insurgeret apertus inimicus hæreticus, mitteretur foras; si violentus inimicus, absconderet se ab eo; nunc vero, quem ejiciet, aut a quo abscondet se? omnes necessarii, et omnes adversarii."—*In Cant.* s. 33.

[2] "Væ homini illi per quem scandalum venit."—*Matt.* xviii. 7.

[3] "Elegit eum ex omni carne !"—*Ecclus.* xlv. 4.

[4] "Elegi vos et posui vos, ut eatis et fructum afferatis."—*John*, xv. 16.

[5] "Si perversa perpetrant, tot mortibus digni sunt, quot ad subditos suos perditionis exempla transmittunt."—*Past.* p. 3, c. 1, adm. 5.

[6] "Ipsis erit amplior maledictio, quia se vita sua perdunt, et alios."—*Rev.* l. 4, c. 132.

out His vineyard to other husbandmen, that shall render Him the fruit in due season.[1] Alas! what shall become of the scandalous priest on the day of judgment? *I will,* says the Lord, *meet them as the bear that is robbed of her whelps.*[2] With what rage does the bear rush on the sportsman that has killed or stolen her whelps! It is thus God has declared that he will meet on the day of judgment the priest that has destroyed instead of saving souls. And if, says St. Augustine, we shall scarcely be able to give an account of ourselves, what shall become of the priest that shall have to render an account of the souls he has sent to hell?[3] And St. John Chrysostom says, "If priests sin, all the people are led to sin. Hence every one must render an account of his own sins; but the priests are also responsible for the sins of others."[4] Oh! how many seculars, how many peasants, how many weak and tender women, shall cover the priest with shame and confusion in the valley of Josaphat! "The layman," says St. John Chrysostom, "will on the day of judgment receive the priestly stole, but the sinful priest, stripped of his dignity, will have to take his place among infidels and heretics."[5]

Let us, then, dearly beloved priests, guard against bringing to hell by our bad example the souls for whose salvation God has placed us in the world. And for this

---

[1] "Malos male perdet, et vineam suam locabit aliis agricolis, qui reddant ei fructum temporibus suis."—*Matt.* xxi. 41.

[2] "Occurram eis quasi ursa, raptis catulis."—*Os.* xiii. 8.

[3] "Si pro se unusquisque vix poterit in die judicii rationem reddere, quid de Sacerdotibus futurum est, a quibus sunt omnium animæ requirendæ?"—*Serm.* 287, *E. B. app.*

[4] "Si Sacerdotes fuerint in peccatis, totus populus convertitur ad peccandum; ideo, unusquisque pro suo peccato reddet rationem, Sacerdotes autem pro omnium peccatis."—*Hom.* 38.

[5] "Laicus, in die judicii, stolam sacerdotalem accipiet; Sacerdos autem peccator spoliabitur sacerdotii dignitate quam habuit, et erit inter infideles et hypocritas."—*Hom.* 40.

purpose we must avoid not only actions that are in themselves unlawful, but also those that have the appearance of evil. *From all appearance of evil refrain yourselves.*[1] The Council of Agatha ordains "that servant maids be removed from the houses of priests."[2] To keep young servant maids, though they were not an occasion of evil (which is impossible), has at least the appearance of evil, and may give scandal to others. Hence the Apostle has written that we should sometimes abstain from what is lawful, lest it *become a stumbling-block to the weak.*[3] It is also necessary to abstain with great care from giving expression to certain worldly maxims; such as, we must not allow others to take precedence; we must enjoy the present life; happy the man that abounds in riches; God is full of mercy and has pity on us, even on sinners that persist in sin. But how scandalous would it be to praise persons for sinful conduct! For example, for resenting an injury, or for maintaining a dangerous friendship. "It is worse," says St. John Chrysostom, "to praise those that do wrong, than to do wrong ourselves."[4] He that has hitherto had the misfortune of giving scandal, or of being the occasion of scandal, is bound under pain of grievous sin to repair it by external good example.

[1] "Ab omni specie mala abstinete vos."—1 *Thess.* v. 22.
[2] "Ut ancillæ a mansione, in qua clericus manet, removeantur."—*Conc. Agath.* c. 11.
[3] "Ne forte, . . . offendiculum fiat infirmis."—1 *Cor.* viii. 9.
[4] "Longe pejus est, collaudare delinquentes, quam delinquere."—*De Saul et David,* hom. 2.

CHAPTER IX.

THE ZEAL OF THE PRIEST.

(In giving the spiritual exercises to the clergy, the sermon on zeal is the most necessary, and may be the most useful of all; for if one of the priests who assist at the exercises resolves (as we ought to hope through the divine grace) to employ himself in procuring the salvation of souls, God will gain not one but a hundred and a thousand souls, who will be saved through the labors of that priest.)

WE shall speak in this chapter:
1. Of the obligation of priests to labor for the salvation of souls.
2. Of the pleasure that a priest who seeks the salvation of souls gives to God.
3. Of the eternal glory and the great reward that a priest who labors for the salvation of souls may expect from God.

I.

The Obligation of Every Priest to Labor for the Salvation of Souls.

" In the world there are at the same time many and few priests—many in name, but few in reality,"[1] says the author of the " Imperfect Work." The world is filled with priests, but few of them labor to be priests; that is, to fulfil the duty and obligations of a priest, or to save souls.

The dignity of priests is great, because they are the coadjutors of God. " We are God's coadjutors."[2] And

---
[1] "Multi Sacerdotes, et pauci Sacerdotes: multi nomine, pauci opere."—*Hom.* 43.
[2] " Dei enim sumus adjutores."—1 *Cor.* iii. 9.

CHAP. IX.] *The Zeal of the Priest.* 155

what greater dignity, says the Apostle, than that of cooperating with Jesus Christ in saving the souls which he has redeemed? Hence St. Denis the Areopagite calls the dignity of the priest a divine dignity, and even the most divine of all divine things.[1] For, as St. Augustine says, it requires more power to sanctify a sinner than to create heaven and earth.[2]

St. Jerome used to call priests the saviours of the world.[3] St. Prosper calls them the administrators of the royal house of God.[4] And, long before, Jeremias called them the fishers and sportsmen of the Lord: *Behold, I will send many fishers, saith the Lord, and after this I will send many hunters, and they shall hunt them from every mountain and from every hill, and out of the holes of the rocks.*[5] St. Ambrose[6] explains this passage of priests who gain to God the most abandoned sinners, and deliver them from all their vices. The *mountain* signifies pride; the *hill*, pusillanimity; and the *holes* of the rocks, bad habits, which bring with them darkness of understanding and coldness of heart. Peter de Blois says that in the work of creation God had no one to assist him, but in the mystery of redemption he wished to have coadjutors.[7] Who on this earth is superior to the priest? "To the king are intrusted earthly things; to me, a priest, heavenly things,"[8] says St. Chrysostom.

[1] See page 46.
[2] See page 35.
[3] "Sacerdotes Dominus mundi esse voluit salvatores."—*In Abdiam*, 21.
[4] "Dispensatores regiæ domus."—*De vita cont.* l. 2, c. 2.
[5] "Ecce ego mittam piscatores multos, dicit Dominus, et piscabuntur eos; et post hæc, mittam eis multos venatores, et venabuntur eos de omni monte, et de omni colle, et de cavernis petrarum."—*Jer.* xvi. 16.
[6] *In Ps.* 118, s. 6.
[7] "In opere creationis, non fuit qui adjuvaret; in mysterio vero redemptionis, voluit habere coadjutores."—*Serm.* 47.
[8] "Regi. quæ hic sunt, commissa sunt; mihi cœlestia, mihi Sacerdoti."—*De Verbis Is. hom.* 4.

And Innocent III. adds: "Although the dignity of the Blessed Virgin was greater than that of the apostles, yet to these, and not to her, were given the keys of the kingdom of heaven."[1]

St. Peter Damian calls the priest the leader of the people of God.[2] St. Bernard styles him the guardian of the Church, which is the spouse of Jesus Christ.[3] St. Clement, an earthly god.[4] For by the ministry of priests the saints are formed on earth. St. Flavian says that all the hope and salvation of men is placed in the hands of priests.[5] And St. John Chrysostom writes, "Our parents generate us for the present life, priests for life eternal."[6] Without priests, says St. Ignatius Martyr, there would be no saints on this earth.[7] And, long before, holy Judith said that on priests depends the salvation of the people. *You are the ancients among the people of God, and their very soul resteth upon you.*[8] The priest is the author of holiness of life in seculars, and on him depends their salvation. Hence St. Clement has said: "Honor priests as those that effect good conduct in others."[9]

Great, then, beyond measure, is the dignity and office of priests, but great also is their obligation to labor for

[1] "Licet Beatissima Virgo excellentior fuerit Apostolis, non tamen illi, sed istis Dominus claves regni cœlorum commisit."—*Cap. Nova quædam, de Pœn. et Rem.*

[2] "Sacerdos, dux exercitus Domini."—*Opusc.* 25, c. 2.

[3] "Sponsæ Custodem."—*In Cant.* s. 77.

[4] "Post Deum. terrenus deus."—*Const. Apost.* l. 2, c. 26.

[5] "Nihil honorabilius Sacerdotibus; omnis enim spes atque salus in iis est."—*Ep. ad S. Leon.*

[6] "Parentes in præsentem, Sacerdotes in vitam æternam nos generant."—*De Sacerd.* l. 3.

[7] "Absque Sacerdotibus, nulla sanctorum congregatio."—*Ep. ad Trall.*

[8] "Vos estis presbyteri in populo Dei, et ex vobis pendet anima illorum."—*Judith*, viii. 21.

[9] "Honorate Sacerdotes, ut bene vivendi auctores."

the salvation of souls. *For*, says the apostle, *every high-priest taken from among men, in the things that appertain to God, that he may offer up gifts and sacrifices for sins.*[1] He afterwards proceeds to say: *Who can have compassion on them that are ignorant.*[2] The priest, then, is appointed by God as well to honor him by sacrifices, as also to save souls by instructing and converting sinners.

A kingly priesthood, . . . a purchased people.[3] The order of ecclesiastics differs altogether from that of seculars. The latter attend to the things of the world and to themselves, but the former are a purchased people; a people whose business it is to gain not the goods of this earth, but the souls of men, says St. Ambrose.[4] St. Antonine says that the very name of the priest explains the nature of his office, for *sacerdos* signifies "he that teaches holy things."[5] And St. Thomas says, "He that distributes holy things."[6] Honorius of Autun says, *presbyter* signifies "he that shows the way from exile to our country."[7] St. Ambrose calls priests the "leaders of the flock of Christ."[8] Hence the saint says in another place: "May the name and the works agree, so that the name may not remain a vain title and may not become the cause of terrible crime."[9] If, then, the meaning of the words *sacerdos* and *presbyter* is to assist souls in order to save

[1] "Omnis namque Pontifex ex hominibus assumptus, pro hominibus constituitur in iis quæ sunt ad Deum, ut offerat dona et sacrificia pro peccatis."—*Heb.* v. 1.
[2] "Qui condolere possit iis qui ignorant et errant."—*Ibid.* v. 2.
[3] "Regale sacerdotium, . . . populus acquisitionis."—1 *Pet.* ii. 9.
[4] "Clericatus officium est quæstus, non pecuniarum, sed animarum." —*Serm.* 78.
[5] "Sacerdos, id est, sacra docens."—*Summ.* p. 3, tit. 14, c. 7, § 1.
[6] "Sacerdos, quasi sacra dans."—P. 3, q. 22, a. 1.
[7] "Presbyter dicitur præbens iter populo de exsilio ad patriam."— *Gemma. an.* l. 1, c. 181.
[8] "Duces et Rectores gregis Christi."—*De Dignit. sac.* c. 2.
[9] "Nomen congruat actioni, ne sit nomen inane, crimen immane." *-Ibid.* c. 3.

and conduct them to heaven, let the name and conduct, says St. Ambrose, correspond; that the name may not be empty, and that the honor of the office may not become a source of guilt. "The misery of the flock is the shame of the shepherd,"[1] adds the same holy Doctor.

If, then, says St. Jerome, you wish to perform the office of a priest, let the salvation of others be the gain of your soul.[2] And St. Anselm holds that the proper office of a priest is to preserve souls from the corruption of the world, and to lead them to God.[3] Hence the Lord has separated priests from the rest of mankind, that they may save themselves and others.[4] Zeal, as St. Augustine says,[5] springs from love. Hence, as charity obliges us to love God and our neighbor, so zeal obliges us first to procure the glory and to prevent the dishonor of God, and afterwards to seek the welfare and to avert the injury of our neighbor.

It is useless to say, I am a simple priest; I have not the care of souls; it is enough for me to attend to myself. No: every priest is bound to attend, in the way in which he can, to the salvation of souls, according to their necessity. And in a district in which souls are in grievous spiritual necessity for want of confessors a simple priest is, as we have proved in our Moral Theology,[6] bound to hear confessions; and if he has not the necessary qualifications, he is obliged to qualify himself for the office of confessor. This is the opinion that the learned Father Pavone of the Society of Jesus has held

[1] "Detrimentum pecoris pastoris ignominia est."—*Reg. Monach. de Laude vit.*

[2] "Si officium vis exercere presbyteri, aliorum salutem fac lucrum animæ tuæ."—*Ep. ad Paulin.*

[3] "Sacerdotis proprium est, animas e mundo rapere, et dare Deo."

[4] "De medio populi segregantur, ut, non solum seipsos, verum et populum tueantur."—*De Dignit. cler.* c. 2.

[5] *In Ps.* 118, s. 30.

[6] *Theolog. Moral.* l. 6, n. 625.

in his works, and not without reason; for as God has sent Jesus Christ to save the world, so Jesus Christ has appointed priests to convert sinners. *As the Father hath sent me, I also send you.*[1] Hence the Council of Trent ordains that they that wish to receive priesthood should prove themselves fit for the administration of the sacraments.[2] For this end, says the angelic Doctor, God has constituted the order of priests, that they may sanctify others by the administration of the sacraments.[3] And priests are specially appointed to administer the sacrament of penance. For immediately after the words: *As the Father hath sent me, etc.*,[4] St. John has added: *When He had said this, He breathed on them; and He said to them: Receive ye the Holy Ghost.*[5] Since, then, it is the office of a priest to absolve from sins, one of his principal obligations is to qualify himself for that office, at least when there is necessity, that he may not receive the reproach contained in the words of St. Paul to his companions in the priesthood: *And we helping to exhort you, that you receive not the grace of God in vain.*[6]

Priests, as Venerable Bede writes, are destined by God to be the salt of the earth, that they may preserve souls from the corruption of sins.[7] But if salt do not perform the office of salt, it is fit only to be cast out of the house of the Lord, and to be trodden by all.[8]

[1] "Sicut misit me Pater, et ego mitto vos."—*John*, xx. 21.

[2] "Ad ministranda Sacramenta idonei comprobentur."—*Sess.* 23, cap. 14, *de Ref.*

[3] "Ideo posuit Ordinem in eo, ut quidam aliis Sacramenta traderent."—*Suppl.* q. 34, a. 1.

[4] "Sicut misit me Pater, et ego mitto vos."—*John*, xx. 21.

[5] "Hæc cum dixisset, insufflavit, et dixit eis: Accipite Spiritum Sanctum; quorum remiseritis peccata, remittuntur eis."—*Ibid.* xx. 22.

[6] "Adjuvantes autem, exhortamur ne in vacuum gratiam Dei recipiatis."—2 *Cor.* vi. 1.

[7] "Ut sales, condiant animos ad corruptionis sanitatem."

[8] "Vos estis sal terræ. Quod si sal evanuerit, in quo salietur? ad nihilum valet ultra, nisi ut mittatur foras, et conculcetur ab hominibus."—*Matt.* v. 13.

Every priest, says St. John Chrysostom, is, as it were, the father of the whole world, and therefore should have care of all the souls to whose salvation he can co-operate by his labors.[1] Besides, priests are appointed by God as physicians to cure every soul that is infirm; thus Origen has called them "Physicians of souls,"[2] and St. Jerome, "Spiritual physicians."[3] Hence St. Bonaventure says, "If the physician flees from the sick, who will cure them?"[4]

Priests are also called the walls of the Church: "The Church has her walls," says St. Ambrose, "that is, her apostolic men."[5] And the author of the "Imperfect Work" says, "Her walls are the priests."[6] They are also called the stones that support the Church of God,[7] and by St. Eucherius they are called the pillars that sustain the tottering world.[8] Finally, they are called by St. Bernard the very house of God. Hence we may say with St. John Chrysostom, that if a part of the house fall, the injury may be easily repaired;[9] but if the walls fall, if the foundations and the pillars that sustain the edifice give way; finally, if the whole house tumbles to the ground,—how can the loss be ever repaired? Moreover, priests are called by the same St. John Chrysostom, the husbandmen of the vineyard of the Lord.[10] But, O

---

[1] "Quasi totius orbis pater Sacerdos est; dignum igitur est ut omnium curam agat, sicut et Deus, cujus fungitur vice."—*In* 1 *Tim. hom.* 6.
[2] "Medicos animarum."
[3] "Medicos spirituales."
[4] "Si medicus fugit ægrotos, quis curabit?"—*De Sex Alis Ser.* c. 5.
[5] "Habet et Ecclesia muros suos."—*In Ps.* 118, s. 22.
[6] "Muri illius sunt Sacerdotes."—*Hom.* 10.
[7] "Lapides sanctuarii."—*Lam.* iv, 1.
[8] "Columnæ sanctorum, merita Sacerdotum sunt, qui nutantis mundi statum orationibus sustinent."—*Hom. de Dedic. eccl.*
[9] "Si pars domus fuerit corrupta, facilis est reparatio."—*Hom.* 47.
[10] "Coloni populum, quasi vineam, colentes."—*Hom.* 40.

CHAP. IX.] *The Zeal of the Priest.* 161

God! exclaims St. Bernard with tears, the husbandmen sweat and labor the whole day in the cultivation of their own vineyards.[1] But what are the occupations of priests whom God has appointed to cultivate his vineyard? They are, continues the saint, always corrupted with idleness and worldly pleasures[2]

The harvest is indeed great, but the laborers are few.[3] No: the bishops and parish priests are not sufficient for the spiritual wants of the people. If God had not destined other priests to assist souls, he should not have sufficiently provided for his Church. St. Thomas[4] says that the twelve apostles destined by Jesus Christ for the conversion of the world represented the bishops, and the seventy-two disciples represented all priests ordained for the salvation of souls, the fruit which the Redeemer demands of his priests: *I have chosen you that you should go, and should bring forth fruit.*[5] Hence St. Augustine calls priests the administrators of the interests of God.[6] To priests has been intrusted the duty of extirpating vice and pernicious maxims from the minds of the people, and of infusing into them the virtues of the Gospel and the maxims of eternity. On the day God raises a man to the priesthood he says to him what he said to Jeremiah: *Lo, I have set thee thus over the nations, and over kingdoms, to root up and pull down, and to waste and to destroy, and to build and to plant.*[7]

I do not know how a priest can be excused from sin, who sees the people of the district in grievous neces-

[1] "Sudant agricolæ, putant et fodiunt vinitores."
[2] "Torpent otio, madent deliciis."—*Declam.* n. 10, 11.
[3] "Messis quidem multa, operarii autem pauci."—*Matt.* ix. 37.
[4] 2. 2, q. 184, a. 6.
[5] "Posui vos, ut eatis et fructum afferatis."—*John*, xv. 16.
[6] "Eorum quæ Dei sunt negotiatores."—*Ad Frat. in er.* s. 36.
[7] "Ecce constitui te hodie super gentes et super regna, ut evellas, et destruas, et disperdas, et dissipes, et ædifices, et plantes."—*Jer.* i. 10.

11

sity, and is able to assist them by teaching the truths of faith, or by preaching the divine word, and even by hearing confessions, and through sloth neglects to give them spiritual aid? I know not, I say, how he can escape on the day of judgment the reproof and chastisement threatened against the slothful servant who hid the talent given to him, that he might *trade with it*. The master gave him that talent that he might trade with it, but he hid it; and when the master demanded an account of the profit he had received from it, he answered: *I hid thy talent in the earth ; behold, here thou hast that which is thine.*[1] But for hiding the talent the master reproved him, saying: What! I have given you a talent that you might trade with it; this is the talent, but where are the profits? He then took the talent from him, commanded it to be given to another, and ordered him to be cast into exterior darkness: *Take ye away therefore the talent from him, and give it him that hath ten talents; . . . and the unprofitable servant cast ye out into the exterior darkness.*[2] To be cast into exterior darkness means, according to the commentators, to be sent into the fire of hell, which gives no light, and to be excluded from heaven.

This passage is applied by St. Ambrose,[3] Calmet, Cornelius à Lapide, and Tirinus to those that can procure the salvation of souls, and neglect to do it, either through negligence or through a vain fear of commiting sin. "This," says Father Cornelius, "is advice to those who through indifference or a vain fear of sinning do not devote to the salvation of their neighbor the lights, the talents that they receive from God; no doubt Christ will ask of them an account on the day of

---

[1] "Abscondi talentum tuum in terra; ecce habes quod tuum est."— *Matt.* xxv. 25.

[2] "Tollite itaque ab eo talentum, et date ei qui habet decem talenta; . . . et inutilem servum ejicite in tenebras exteriores."

[3] *De Dignit. sac.* c. 1.

judgment."[1] And St. Gregory says: "Hear! whoever does not wish to employ his talents will be cast out by a sentence of damnation."[2] Peter de Blois writes: "Whoever employs God's gifts for the good of others deserves to have a greater measure of what he already possesses; but from him who hides the Lord's talent will be taken what he seems to possess."[3] St. John Chrysostom says that he cannot conceive how a priest can be saved who does nothing for the salvation of his neighbor.[4] After having mentioned the parable of the talent, he says that for a priest the neglect of having employed the talent given to him is criminal, and shall be the cause of his damnation.[5] Addressing those who say, "I am satisfied if only I save my soul,"[6] St. Augustine says, "Do you not recall to mind the servant who buried his talent?"

St. Prosper says that to save his own soul it will not be enough for a priest to lead a holy life, for he shall be damned with those that are lost through his fault.[7] In one of the apostolical canons we read the following words:

---

[1] "Notent hoc qui ingenio, doctrina, aliisque dotibus sibi a Deo datis, non utuntur ad suam aliorumque salutem, ob desidiam vel metum peccandi; ab his enim rationem exposcet Christus in die judicii." —*In Matt.* 25, 18.

[2] "Audiant quod talentum qui erogare noluit, cum sententia damnationis amisit."—*Past.* p. 3, c. 1. adm. 26.

[3] "Qui Dei donum in utilitatem alienam communicat, plenius meretur habere quod habet; qui autem talentum Domini abscondit, quod videtur habere, auferetur ab eo."—*De Inst. Episc.*

[4] "Neque id mihi persuasi, salvum fieri quemquam posse, qui pro proximi sui salute nihil laboris impenderit."

[5] "Neque juvabit talentum sibi traditum non imminuisse; immo hoc ille nomine periit, quod non auxisset et duplicasset."—*De Sacerd.* l. 6.

[6] "Sufficit mihi anima mea. Eia, non tibi venit in mentem servus ille qui abscondit talentum."—*In Jos.* tr. 10.

[7] "Ille cui dispensatio verbi commissa est, etiam si sancte vivat, et tamen perdite viventes arguere, aut erubescat aut metuat, cum omnibus qui eo tacente perierunt, perit; et quid ei proderit non puniri suo, qui puniendus est alieno peccato!"—*De Vit. cont.* l. 1, c. 20.

"The priest that does not take care of the clerics or of the people should be punished, and if he perseveres in his carelessness, let him be deposed."[1] Why, says St. Leo, should you take the honor of the priesthood if you will not labor for the salvation of souls?[2] The Council of Cologne declared that if a person take the Order of priesthood without the intention of performing the office of vicar of Jesus Christ, or of saving souls, a great and certain chastisement is reserved for him, as for a wolf and a robber, which he is called in the Gospel.[3]

St. Isidore does not hesitate to charge with mortal sin the priest that neglects to instruct the ignorant and to convert sinners.[4] And St. John Chrysostom says, "Not on account of their own, but on account of the sins of others that they did not prevent, priests are often condemned to hell."[5] St. Thomas, speaking of a simple priest, says that the priest that fails either through negligence or ignorance to assist souls, renders himself accountable to God for all the souls that are lost through his fault.[6] St. John Chrysostom says the same: "If priests take care only of their own souls, and

---

[1] "Presbyter qui cleri vel populi curam non gerit, segregatur; et si in secordia perseveret, deponatur."—*Can.* 57.

[2] "Qua conscientia honorem sibi debitum vendicant, qui pro animabus sibi creditis non laborant."—*Ep. ad Turrib.* c. 16.

[3] "Sacerdotio initiandus non alio affectu accedere debet, quam ad submittendos humeros publico muneri vice Christi in Ecclesia. Qui alio affectu sacros Ordines ambiunt, hos Scriptura lupos et latrones appellat. . . . Quod ingens ultio tandem certo subsequetur."

[4] "Sacerdotes pro populorum iniquitate damnantur, si eos aut ignorantes non erudiant aut peccantes non arguant."—*Sent.* l. 3, c. 46.

[5] "Sæpe non damnantur propriis peccatis, sed alienis quæ non coercuerunt."

[6] "Si enim Sacerdos, ex ignorantia vel negligentia, non exponat populo viam salutis, reus erit apud Deum animarum illarum quæ sub ipso perierunt."—*De Officio Sac.*

neglect the souls of others, they will be condemned to hell with the damned."[1]

A certain priest in Rome felt great fears at death for his eternal salvation, although he had led a life of retirement and piety. Being asked why he was so much afraid, he answered: "I am afraid, because I have not labored for the salvation of souls." He had reason to tremble, since the Lord employs priests to save souls, and to rescue them from vice. Hence, if a priest do not fulfil this duty, he must render to God an account of all the souls that are lost through his fault: *If when I say to the wicked, Thou shalt surely die; thou declare it not to him, nor speak to him, that he may be converted from his wicked way and live; the same wicked man shall die in his iniquity, but I will require his blood at thy hand.*[2] Thus, says St. Gregory, speaking of idle priests, they shall be accountable before God for the souls whom they could assist, and who are lost through their negligence.[3]

Jesus Christ has redeemed souls with the price of his blood: *For you are bought with a great price.*[4] But these souls the Redeemer has intrusted to the care of priests. Unhappy me, said St. Bernard, when he saw himself a priest, if I be negligent in taking care of this deposit; that is, of the souls whom the Redeemer considered to be more precious than his own blood.[5] Seculars have to render an account of their own sins, but priests must

[1] "Si Sacerdos suam tantum disposuerit salvare animam, et alienas neglexerit, cum impiis detrudetur in gehennam."

[2] "Si, dicente me ad impium: Morte morieris;—non annuntiaveris ei, neque locutus fueris ut avertatur a via sua impia, et vivat, ipse impius in iniquitate sua morietur, sanguinem autem ejus de manu tua requiram."—*Ezech.* iii. 18.

[3] "Ex tantis procul dubio rei sunt, quantis, venientes ad publicum, prodesse potuerunt."—*Past.* p. 1. c. 5.

[4] "Empti enim estis pretio magno."—1 *Cor.* vi. 20.

[5] "Si depositum, quod sibi Christus sanguine proprio pretiosius judicavit, contigerit negligentius custodire."—*In Adv. Dom.* s. 3.

render an account of the sins of all, says the author of the *Imperfect Work*.[1] And before him the apostle said: *For they watch as being to render an account of your souls.*[2] Thus the sins of others are imputed to the priest that neglects to prevent them, says St. John Chrysostom.[3] Hence St. Augustine has said: "If on the day of judgment one can scarcely render an account of one's own soul, how will the priest fare if he has to render an account of all sins?"[4] Speaking of those that become priests not to save souls, but to secure a more comfortable means of living, St. Bernard says, Oh, how much better would it have been for them to labor in the field, or to beg, than to have taken to the priesthood! On the day of judgment they shall hear complaints against them from so many souls that have been damned through their sloth.[5]

II.

The Pleasure that a Priest who Labors for the Salvation of Souls gives to God.

To understand how ardently God desires the salvation of souls, it is enough to consider what he has done in the work of the redemption of man. Jesus Christ clearly expressed this desire when he said: *I have a baptism, wherewith I am to be baptized; and how am I straitened until it be accomplished.*[6] He said that he felt as if swooning

[1] "Unusquisque pro suo peccato reddet rationem; Sacerdotes, pro omnium peccatis."—*Hom.* 38.

[2] "Ipsi enim pervigilant, quasi rationem pro animabus vestris reddituri."—*Heb.* xiii. 17.

[3] "Quod alii peccant, illi imputatur."—*In Act.* hom. 3.

[4] "Si pro se unusquisque vix poterit, in die judicii, rationem reddere, quid de Sacerdotibus futurum est, a quibus sunt omnium animæ requirendæ?"—*Serm.* 287, E. B. *app.*

[5] "Bonum erat magis fodere, aut etiam mendicare, Venient, venient ante tribunal Christi; audietur populorum querela, quorum vixere stipendiis, nec diluerunt peccata!"—*Declam.* n. 19.

[6] "Baptismo autem habeo baptizari; et quomodo coarctor usquedum perficiatur?"—*Luke,* xii. 50.

away through the ardor with which he wished to see the work of redemption accomplished, that men might be saved. From this St. John Chrysostom justly infers, that there is nothing more acceptable to God than the salvation of souls.¹ And before him St. Justin said: "Nothing is so pleasing to God as to labor to make others better."² Our Lord once said to Bernard Colnado, a priest who had labored much for the conversion of sinners: "Labor for the salvation of sinners, for this is what is most pleasing to me."³ This is so dear to God, adds Clement of Alexandria, that the salvation of men appears to be his sole concern.⁴ Hence, addressing a priest, St. Laurence Justinian said: "If you wish to honor God, you can do no better than labor in behalf of the salvation of souls."⁵

St. Bernard says that in the eyes of God a soul is more valuable than the whole world.⁶ Hence, according to St. John Chrysostom, a person pleases God more by converting a single soul than by giving all his goods, to the poor.⁷ Tertullian asserts that to God the salvation of a single sheep that has strayed away, is as dear as the salvation of the entire flock.⁸ Hence the Apostle

¹ "Nihil ita gratum Deo, et ita curæ, ut animarum salus."—*In Gen.* hom. 3.
² "Nihil tam Deo gratum, quam operam dare ut omnes reddantur meliores."
³ "Labora pro salute peccatorum; hoc enim præ omnibus est mihi carissimum."
⁴ "Nihil aliud est Domino curæ, præterquam hoc solum opus, ut homo salvus fiat."—*Orat. ad Gentes.*
⁵ "Si Deum honorare conaris, non aliter melius, quam in hominis salute, poteris actitare."—*De Compunct.* p. 2.
⁶ "Totus iste mundus ad unius animæ pretium æstimari non potest."—*Medit.* c. 3.
⁷ "Etsi ingentes erogaveris pecunias, plus efficieris, si unam converteris animam."—*In* 1 *Cor.* hom. 3.
⁸ "Erat una pastoris ovicula; sed grex una carior non erat."—*De Pœnit.*

said: *I live in the faith of the Son of God, who loved me and delivered Himself up for me.*[1] By these words he signified that Jesus Christ would have died as soon for a single soul as for the salvation of all men, says St. John Chrysostom in his comment on this passage.[2] This our Redeemer gave us to understand by the parable of the groat that had been lost. On this parable St. Thomas writes: "He calls together all the angels, not that all men, but that he himself may be congratulated on account of the groat that was found, as if man were God's God, as if his salvation depended on man's finding him, and as if God could not be happy without him."[3]

It is related by several authors * of St. Carpus, Bishop, that he had a vision in which he seemed to see a scandalous sinner who had induced an innocent person to commit sin, and that he felt himself impelled by zeal to throw him into a precipice on the brink of which he stood, but Jesus Christ appeared to support the sinner with his hand, and said to St. Carpus: "Strike me, for I am ready again to die for sinners."[4] As if he said: Hold, strike me rather than this sinner; for I have given my life for him, and am ready to give it again to save him from perdition.

The ecclesiastical spirit, says Louis Habert,[5] consists

[1] "Dilexit me, et tradidit semetipsum pro me."—*Gal.* ii. 20.

[2] "Neque enim recusaturus esset vel ob unum hominem tantam exhibere dispensationem."

[3] "Omnes Angelos convocat ad congratulandum non homini, sed sibi, quasi homo Dei Deus esset, et tota salus divina ab ipsius inventione dependeret, et quasi sine ipso beatus esse non posset."—*De Beat.* c. 7.

[4] "Percute me, quia iterum pro peccatoribus mori paratus sum."

[5] "Essentialiter consistit in ardenti studio promovendi gloriam Dei et salutem proximi."—*De Sacr. Ord.* p. 3, c. 5.

---

* The first of these authors is St. Denis the Areopagite (*Ep. ad Demoph.*), and it is believed that St. Carpus, who had this vision, is the one of whom St. Paul speaks in 2 Tim. iv. 13.—ED.

precisely in an ardent zeal for promoting the glory of God, and the salvation of our neighbor. Hence, according to Natalis Alexander, they that wish to attend only to themselves, and not to others, should not be admitted to the priesthood.[1] The Lord commanded[2] that the priests of the Old Law should wear vestments covered all over with certain circles, which resembled eyes, to show, as a certain author says, that the priest should be all eyes to attend to the sanctification of the people. St. Augustine says that zeal for the salvation of souls and for the promotion of divine love in all men springs from love. Then, adds the saint, he that has not zeal, shows that he does not love God; and he that does not love God is lost.[3] He that watches over his own soul pleases God; but he that watches over the souls of his neighbors, pleases him still more, says St. Bernard.[4]

God, says St. John Chrysostom, has no better proof of the fidelity and affection of a soul than in seeing her zealous for the welfare of her neighbor.[5] The Saviour three times asked St. Peter if he loved him: *Simon, son of John, lovest thou Me?*[6] When assured of Peter's love, Jesus Christ asked him to do nothing else in proof of his love than to take care of souls: *He said to him: Feed My sheep.*[7] On this passage St. John Chrysostom says: "The Lord might have said, If you love me, cast away

---

[1] "Quis ferat presbyterum ordinari, ut sibi tantum vacet, et non aliis?"—*De Ord.* c. 3, a. 5, reg. 22.

[2] *Exod.* xxviii.

[3] "Zelus est effectus amoris; ergo, qui non zelat, non amat; qui non amat, manet in morte."

[4] "Tu quidem, in tui custodia vigilans, bene facis; sed, qui juvat multos, melius facit."—*In Cant.* s. 12.

[5] "Nihil adeo declarat quis sit fidelis et amans Christi, quam si fratrum curam agat; hoc maximum amicitiæ argumentum est."—*Serm. de B. Philog.*

[6] "Simon Joannis, amas me?"—*John*, xxi. 17.

[7] "Pasce oves meas."

money, practise strict fast, sleep on the hard floor, and macerate yourself by hard labor. But no; he says, Feed my sheep."[1] On the word *my*, St. Augustine remarks that our Lord wished to say: " Feed them as my sheep, not as thine; seek in them my glory, not thine; my profit, not thine."[2] In these words the saint has taught that he that desires to labor for the salvation of souls should seek neither his own glory nor his own gain, but only the advancement of the divine glory.

After reading the lives of the holy martyrs, and of the holy workmen in God's vineyard, St. Teresa[3] said that she envied the latter more than the former, on account of the great glory which they that labor for the conversion of sinners give to God. St. Catharine of Sienna used to kiss the ground that had been trodden by priests employed in saving souls. Such was her zeal for the salvation of sinners, that she desired to be placed at the mouth of hell, that no soul might enter into that land of torment. And what do we, who are priests, say? What do we do? We see so many souls perish, and shall we remain idle spectators of their perdition?

St. Paul said that to obtain the salvation of his neighbors he would have consented to be separated from Jesus Christ, that is, according to commentators, for a time: *For I wished myself to be an anathema from Christ, for my brethren.*[4] St. John Chrysostom desired to be blind, provided the souls under his care were converted.[5] St.

---

[1] "Poterat dicere: Si amas me, abjice pecunias, jejunia exerce, macera te laboribus. Nunc vero ait: ' Pasce oves meas.' "—*Serm. de B. Philog.*

[2] " Sicut meas pasce, non sicut tuas; gloriam meam in eis quære, non tuam; lucra mea, non tua."—*In Jo.* tr. 123.

[3] *Found.* ch. 1.

[4] "Optabam enim ego ipse anathema esse a Christo pro fratribus meis."—*Rom.* ix. 3.

[5] " Millies optarem ipse exsecrabilis esse, si per hoc liceret animas vestras convertere."—*In Act.* hom. 3.

CHAP. IX.] *The Zeal of the Priest.* 171

Bonaventure declared that he would have accepted as many deaths as there are sinners in the world, that all might be saved.¹ During a winter which he spent among the heretics of Chablais, St. Francis de Sales used to creep over a river on a beam of ice, with great risk and inconvenience to himself, in order to preach to them. Being in Naples during the great revolution of 1647 and seeing the great loss of souls which it caused, St. Cajetan felt so intense a sorrow that he died of grief. St. Ignatius used to say that he would rather live uncertain of his eternal lot than die with a certainty of salvation, provided he could continue to assist souls. Behold the zeal for souls which animated priests that loved God! And still, in order to avoid a trifling inconvenience, or through fear of illness, some even among those that are charged with the care of souls withhold the aid of their ministry. St. Charles Borromeo used to say, that a pastor of souls, who wishes to have every convenience, and to take all the precautions that may be useful to health, will never be able to fulfil his duties. Hence he would add, that a parish priest should not go to bed till after the third paroxysm of fever.

He that truly loves God, says St. Augustine,² does everything in his power to draw all to his love, and can say with David: *O magnify the Lord with me; and let us extol His name together.*³ He goes in every direction: exhorting in the pulpit and in the confessional, in the public places and in private houses, saying, Brethren, let us love God, let us praise his name, in words and works.

¹ *Stim. div. am.* p. 2, c. 11.
² " Si amatis Deum, rapite omnes ad amorem Dei."—*In Ps.* 53, en. 2.
³ "Magnificate Dominum mecum, et exaltemus nomen ejus in idipsum."—*Ps.* xxxiii. 4.

III.

How Secure the Priest who Labors for the Salvation of Souls Renders his own Salvation, and how Great the Reward that he shall receive in Heaven.

The priest who has labored for the salvation of souls can hardly die a bad death. *When thou shalt pour out,* says the prophet Isaias, *thy soul to the hungry, and shalt satisfy the afflicted soul, then shall thy light rise up in darkness. . . . And the Lord will give thee rest continually, and will fill thy soul with brightness, and deliver thy bones.*[1] If you have spent your life in assisting a soul in need, and have consoled her in her afflictions, in the darkness of your temporal death, the Lord shall fill you with light, and shall deliver you from eternal death. This was the doctrine of St. Augustine: "In saving a soul thou hast predestined your own," says the holy Doctor.[2] And, long before, the apostle St. James said: *He must know, that he who causeth a sinner to be converted from the error of his way, shall save his soul* (that is, his own soul, as appears from the Greek text) *from death, and shall cover a multitude of sins.*[3]

A priest of the Society of Jesus, who during life devoted a great deal of time to the conversion of sinners, died with joy and confidence of salvation; this some considered to be excessive. Hence he was told that at death we should entertain sentiments of fear as well as of confidence. He answered: Have I served Mahomet? I have served a God who is so grateful and faithful; why, then, should I fear? When St. Ignatius of Loyola declared

---

[1] "Cum effuderis animam tuam, et animam afflictam repleveris, orietur in tenebris lux tua; . . . et requiem tibi dabit Dominus semper, et implebit splendoribus animam tuam, et ossa tua liberabit."—*Is.* lviii. 10.

[2] "Animam salvasti, animam tuam prædestinasti."

[3] "Qui converti fecerit peccatorem ab errore viæ suæ, salvabit animam ejus a morte, et operiet multitudinem peccatorum."—*James,* v. 20.

that in order to assist souls he would remain on earth in an uncertainty about his salvation, though he was certain that by dying he should be saved, a person said: "But, Father, it is not prudent to expose your own soul to danger for the salvation of others." The saint replied, "Is God a tyrant, who, after seeing me risk my salvation in order to gain souls, would send me to hell?"

After having saved the Jews from the hands of the Philistines, by the victory that he won with so much personal danger, Jonathan was condemned to death by Saul for having, contrary to his orders, eaten a little honey But the people cried out, *Shall Jonathan then die, who hath wrought this great salvation in Israel?*[1] Why, O king, said they, should Jonathan be put to death after having saved us all from destruction? Thus they obtained his pardon. The priest who has saved souls may well expect a similar reward on the day of his death. These souls shall come and say to Jesus Christ: Wilt Thou, O Lord, send to hell the priest who has delivered us from eternal misery? And if Saul remitted the punishment of death at the prayers of the people, surely God will not refuse to pardon such a priest for the prayers of the souls that are his friends in heaven. Priests who have labored for the salvation of souls shall hear from God himself the announcement of eternal rest: *From henceforth now, saith the Spirit, that they may rest from their labors.*[2] Oh! what consolation and confidence shall the remembrance of having gained a soul to Jesus Christ infuse at the hour of death! As repose is sweet to him who is oppressed with fatigue,—*Sleep is sweet to a laboring man,*[3]—so death is sweet to a priest who has labored for God.

[1] "Ergone Jonathas morietur, qui fecit salutem hanc magnam in Israel?"—1 *Kings*, xiv. 45.

[2] "Amodo jam dicit spiritus, ut requiescant a laboribus suis; opera enim illorum sequuntur illos."—*Apoc.* xiv. 13.

[3] "Dulcis est somnus operanti."—*Eccles.* v. 11.

St. Gregory says that the more souls a sinner shall have converted from their sins, the sooner he shall be absolved from his own transgressions.[1] He that has the good fortune of being employed in converting sinners has a great mark of predestination, and of being written in the book of life. This the Apostle insinuated when, in speaking of those that assisted him in the conversion of nations, he said: *I entreat thee also, my sincere companion, help those women that have labored with me in the Gospel with Clement and the rest of my fellow-laborers, whose names are* (mark these words) *in the book of life.*[2]

With regard to the great reward that priests who labor for souls shall receive, Daniel said: *They shall shine . . . as the brightness of the firmament: and they that instruct many to justice, as stars for all eternity.*[3] As we now see the stars shine in the firmament, so the priest who converts souls to God shall shine among the blessed in the empyreal heaven with a brilliant light of glory. If, says St. Gregory, he that rescues a man from temporal death deserves a great reward, how much greater shall be the recompense of a priest who delivers a soul from eternal death, and brings her to eternal life![4] And before him our Saviour said: *But he that shall do and teach, he shall be called great in the kingdom of heaven.*[5] How great shall be the chastisement in hell of a damned

---

[1] "Tanto celerius quisque a suis peccatis absolvitur, quanto, per ejus vitam et linguam, aliorum animæ solvuntur."

[2] "Etiam rogo et te, germane compar: adjuva illas quæ mecum laboraverunt in Evangelio, cum Clemente et cæteris adjutoribus meis, quorum nomina sunt in Libro vitæ."—*Phil.* iv. 3.

[3] "Fulgebunt, . . . qui ad justitiam erudiunt multos, quasi stellæ in perpetuas æternitates."—*Dan.* xii. 3.

[4] "Si magnæ mercedis est a morte eripere carnem quandoque morituram, quanti est meriti a morte animam liberare sine fine victuram!"— *Mor.* l. 19, c. 16.

[5] "Qui autem fecerit et docuerit, hic magnus vocabitur in regno cœlorum."—*Matt.* v. 19.

priest who by his scandals has perverted many souls! On the other hand, will not God, whose liberality in rewarding virtue surpasses his severity in punishing vice, give great glory in heaven to the good priest who by his labors shall have gained many souls?

St. Paul placed the hope of his eternal crown in the salvation of those whom he had converted to God, and trusted that they should procure for him a great recompense for eternity: *For what is our hope, or joy, or crown of glory? Are not you in the presence of our Lord Jesus Christ at His coming?*[1] St. Gregory says that a priest who works in the Lord's vineyard obtains as many crowns as he gains souls to God.[2] We read in the Canticles, *Come from Libanus, My spouse, come from Libanus, come: thou shalt be crowned.*[3] Behold the promise of the Lord to him who is employed in the conversion of sinners—the souls that were once wild beasts and monsters of hell, but were afterwards converted and became dear to God, shall be so many gems adorning the crown of the priest who has brought them back to the path of virtue. A priest who is damned does not go to hell alone, and the priest that is saved is certainly not saved alone. When St. Philip Neri died and went to heaven, the Lord sent to meet him all the souls that he had saved. The same is related of that great servant of God, Brother Cherubim of Spoleto. He was seen entering heaven accompanied by many thousands of souls that had been saved by his labors. It is also related of the Venerable Father Louis la Nuza, that he was seen in heaven sitting on a lofty throne, at the foot of which were seated all the souls that he had converted.

[1] "Quæ enim nostra spes, aut gaudium, aut corona gloriæ? Nonne vos ante Dominum nostrum Jesum Christum estis in adventu ejus?"—1 *Thess.* ii. 19.

[2] "Tot coronas sibi multiplicat, quot Deo animas lucrifacit."

[3] "Veni de Libano, sponsa mea, veni de Libano, veni; coronaberis . . . de cubilibus leonum, de montibus pardorum."—*Cant.* iv. 8.

The poor husbandman suffers toils and sweats in sowing and cultivating the ground, and in reaping the crop; but all his labors are superabundantly compensated by the joy of the harvest. *Going, they went and wept, casting their seeds; but coming, they shall come with joyfulness, carrying their sheaves.*[1] It is true that in the work of bringing souls to God many pains and labors are endured; but the laborer shall be recompensed with immense superabundance by the joy that he shall feel in presenting to Jesus Christ in the valley of Josaphat all the souls he had saved.

Nor should the priest who labors without success to bring souls to God be disheartened, nor turned away from so noble a work. Beloved priest, says St. Bernard, be not discouraged by your want of success, but rest secure of the reward that awaits you. God does not require of you to save souls: labor for their salvation, and he will reward you, not in proportion to your success, but according to the toils you have endured.[2] St. Bonaventure confirms this doctrine, and says that a priest shall not merit less for those that draw little or no profit from his labors, than from the souls that reap great benefit from them.[3] The same saint adds, that the husbandman who cultivates the barren and rocky soil merits a greater reward though he reaps less fruit.[4] He

[1] "Euntes ibant et flebant, mittentes semina sua; venientes autem venient cum exsultatione, portantes manipulos suos."—*Ps.* cxxv. 6.

[2] "Noli diffidere; curam exigeris, non curationem. Denique audisti· 'Curam illius habe' (*Luke*, x. 35); et non: Cura, vel Sana illum;—quia unusquisque secundum suum laborem accipiet (1 *Cor.* iii. 8), et non secundum proventum; reddet Deus mercedem laborum (*Wisd.* x. 17) sanctorum suorum."—*De Cons.* l. 4, c. 2.

[3] "Non minus meretur in illis qui deficiunt vel modicum proficiunt, quam in his qui maxime proficiunt; non enim dixit Apostolus (1 *Cor.* iii. 8): Unusquisque propriam mercedem accipiet secundum suum profectum; sed, secundum suum laborem."

[4] "In terra sterili et saxosa, etsi fructus paucior, sed pretium majus."
—*De Sex Alis Ser.* c. 5.

meant to say, that a priest who endeavors, though without success, to bring back an obstinate sinner to God shall have a greater reward, because his labor is greater.

IV.

The End, the Means, and the Labors of the Priest who has Zeal.

1. THE END TO BE PROPOSED.

If we wish to receive from God the reward of our labors for the salvation of souls, we must do all not through human respect, nor for our own honor or temporal gain, but only for God and for his glory; otherwise, instead of a reward we shall receive punishment. Great should be our folly, says St. Joseph Calasanctius, were we to seek from men a temporal remuneration for our labors. The office of saving souls, says St. Bernard, is in itself very dangerous, since we shall have once to render an account of the actions of others.[1] And St. Gregory writes: "The priest possesses as many souls as he is instructing subjects."[2] With the divine aid we shall be able to avoid sin and merit a reward in the work of saving others; but he who performs this work for any other end than to please God, shall be abandoned by God; and without the divine assistance, how shall he be able to avoid sin? And how, says St. Bonaventure, shall they avoid sin who "receive holy Orders, seeking not the salvation of souls, but temporal gain,"[3] or whose motive, as St. Prosper says, is not to become better, but

---

[1] "Maximum periculum de factis alterius rationem reddere."—*In Heb.* c. 13, lect. 3.

[2] "Quot regendis subditis præest, reddendæ apud eum (Christum Judicem) rationis tempore, ut ita dicam, tot solus animas habet."—*Mor.* l. 24, c. 30.

[3] "Ad sacros Ordines accedunt, non salutem animarum, sed quæstum pecuniarum quærentes."—*De Præp. ad M.* c. 8.

richer: not more holy, but more honored?[1] When, says Peter de Blois, there is question of obtaining a benefice, do persons ask how many souls may be gained, or do they not inquire rather about the amount of its revenues?[2] *Many*, says the Apostle, *seek the things that are their own, not the things that are Jesus Christ's*.[3] O execrable abuse, says Father John d'Avila, to make heaven subordinate to earth! St. Bernard observes that when our Lord intrusted his sheep to St. Peter he said: "Feed my sheep; do not milk nor shear them."[4] The author of the *Imperfect Work* says: "We have been hired as day-laborers; and just as no one hires a day-laborer only for the purpose of eating, so Jesus Christ has not called us to labor only for our own profit, but for God's glory."[5] Hence St. Gregory says of priests, "Priests should not rejoice that they precede others but that they can be useful to them."[6]

The glory of God, then, must be the sole end of the priest who labors for souls.

2. MEANS TO BE EMPLOYED.

With regard to the means that a priest should adopt in order to gain souls to the Lord:

I. The priest must above all attend to the perfection of his own soul. The sanctity of the priest is the prin-

[1] "Non ut meliores, sed ut ditiores: nec ut sanctiores, sed ut honoratiores sint?"—*De Vita cont.* l. 1, c. 21.

[2] "Hodie, in promotione quorumdam, prima quæstio est, quæ sit summa reddituum, non quæ sit conversatio subjectorum."—*Epist.* 15.

[3] "Quæ sua sunt, quærunt, non quæ sunt Jesu Christi."—*Phil.* ii. 21.

[4] "'Pasce oves meas;' nec Mulge, seu Tonde."—*Declam.* n. 12.

[5] "Mercenarii sumus conducti; sicut ergo nemo conducit mercenarium ut solum manducet, sic et nos, non ideo vocati sumus a Christo ut solum operemur quæ ad nostrum pertinent usum, sed ad gloriam Dei."—*Hom.* 34.

[6] "Nec præesse se hominibus gaudeant, sed prodesse."—*Past.* p. 2, c. 6.

cipal means of converting sinners. St. Eucherius says that priests by the power of their sanctity sustain the world.[1] The priest, as mediator, is charged with the office of making peace between God and men, says St. Thomas.[2] But he who is a mediator must not be hateful to the person before whom he has to intercede; otherwise, he will increase his wrath, says St. Gregory.[3] Hence the saint adds, " Pure must be the hand of the one that wishes to cleanse others of their stains."[1] Hence St. Bernard concludes that a priest, in order to be fit to convert sinners, must first purify his own conscience and afterwards the conscience of others.[5] St. Philip Neri used to say, give me ten zealous priests and I will convert the whole world. What did not a solitary St. Francis Xavier do in the East? It is related that he alone converted ten millions of pagans to the faith. What did not a St. Patrick, a St. Vincent Ferrer, do in Europe? A single priest of moderate learning, who loves God ardently, will convert more souls to God than a hundred priests of great learning and little zeal.

II. He who wishes to reap an abundant harvest of souls must devote a good deal of time to mental prayer. In prayer he must first receive from God sentiments of piety, and afterwards communicate them to others: *That which you hear in the ear, preach ye upon the housetops.*[6] It is necessary, says St. Bernard, to be first a

[1] " Hi onus totius orbis portant humeris sanctitatis."—*Hom. de Dedic. eccl.*

[2] " Ad mediatoris officium proprie pertinet conjungere eos inter quos est mediator."—P. 3, q. 26, a. 1.

[3] "Cum is qui displicet, ad intercedendum mittitur, irati animus ad deteriora provocatur."—*Past.* p. 1, c. 11.

[4] " Necesse est ut esse munda studeat manus, quæ diluere aliorum sordes curat."—*Past.* p. 2, c. 2.

[5] " Rectus ordo postulat ut prius propriam, deinde alienas curare studeas conscientias."—*Epist.* 8.

[6] " Quod in aure auditis, prædicate super tecta."—*Matt.* x. 27.

reservoir and then a canal.'¹ The saints have converted more souls by their prayers than by their labors.

3. WORKS OF A ZEALOUS PRIEST.

The works in which a zealous priest should be employed are:

I. The correction of sinners. Priests who see insults offered to God and remain silent are called by Isaias *mute dogs*.² But to these mute dogs shall be imputed all the sins that they could have but have not prevented. "Do not be silent," says Alcuin, "lest the sins of the people be ascribed to you."³ Some priests abstain from reproving sinners because they do not wish to disturb their peace of mind; but, says St. Gregory, for this peace that they desire, they shall miserably lose peace with God.⁴ An animal falls, exclaims St. Bernard, and many are found to lift it; a souls falls, and no one is found to raise her up.⁵ Yes, sinners are not converted, although, according to St. Gregory, priests are specially appointed by God to point out the path of virtue to those who go astray.⁶ Hence St. Leo adds: "The priest who does not withdraw another from error proves that he is himself involved in it."⁷ St. Gregory writes that we kill as many souls as we see committing sin without endeavoring to apply a remedy.⁸

¹ "Concham te exhibebis, non canalem. Canales hodie in Ecclesia multos habemus, conchas vero perpaucas."—*In Cant.* s. 18.

² "Canes muti, non valentes latrare."—*Is.* lvi. 10.

³ "Nolite tacere, ne populi peccata vobis imputentur."—*Epist.* 28.

⁴ "Dum pacem desiderant, pravos mores nequaquam redarguunt; et consentiendo perversis, ab Auctoris sui se pace disjungunt."—*Past.* p. 3, c. 1, adm. 23.

⁵ "Cadit asina, et est qui sublevet eam; perit anima, et nemo est qui reputet."—*De Cons.* l. 4, c. 6.

⁶ "Eligitur viam erranti demonstrare."—*Epist.* l. 7, ind. 2, ep. 110.

⁷ "Sacerdos qui alium ab errore non revocat, seipsum errare demonstrat."—*Ep. ad Turrib.* c. 15,

⁸ "Nos qui Sacerdotes vocamur, tot occidimus, quot ad mortem ire quotidie tepide videmus."—*In Ezech.* hom. 11.

II. A zealous priest ought to be employed in preaching. By preaching, the world has been, as the Apostle says, converted to the faith of Jesus Christ: *Faith cometh by hearing; and hearing by the word of Christ.*[1] And by preaching, the faith and the fear of God are preserved in the hearts of the faithful. Priests who feel themselves unable to preach should at least endeavor as often as possible, in their conversation with friends or relatives, to edify by words of edification, by relating examples of virtues practised by the saints, by inculcating some maxim of eternity, by impressing on them the vanity of the world, the importance of salvation, the certainty of death, the peace enjoyed by those who are in the grace of God, or some similar truths.

III. The priest should be occupied in assisting the dying, which is a work of charity most dear to God, and most conducive to the salvation of souls; for the dying are more strongly tempted by the devils, and are less able to assist themselves. St. Philip Neri frequently saw angels suggesting words to priests who were attending dying persons. For parish priests this work is an obligation of justice, but for every priest it is a duty of charity. It may be performed with advantage by every priest, even by those who have not talent for preaching. In attending the sick, a priest may be of great service to their friends and relatives. That is the fittest time for spiritual discourses. On such an occasion it is even unbecoming in a priest to speak of anything but of God and of spiritual things. But let it be remembered that he who performs this office must use great caution, that he may not be an occasion of ruin to himself or others. Moreover, he who cannot preach should at least labor in teaching the Christian doctrine to the children and the poor, many of whom in the rural districts, in conse-

---

[1] " Fides ex auditu; auditus autem per verbum Christi."—*Rom.* x. 17.

quence of not being able to go often to the church, live in ignorance of even the principal mysteries of faith.

IV. Lastly, it is necessary to be persuaded that the work which is most conducive to the salvation of souls is the administration of the sacrament of penance. The Venerable Louis Fiorillo, of the Order of St. Dominic, used to say, that by preaching the priest casts out the net, but by hearing confessions he draws it ashore and takes the fish. But some may say this is a very perilous office. There is no doubt, dearly beloved priest, says St. Bernard, that to become the judge of consciences is attended with much danger; but you shall fall into greater danger if through sloth or excessive fear you neglect to fulfil this office when God calls you to it. "Woe to you," says the same saint, "if you are a Superior! But a greater woe to you if through fear of commanding you shrink from doing good."[1] We have already spoken[2] of the obligation of every priest to employ the talent that God has given him that he may save souls; and we have already said that at his ordination a priest is destined in a special manner for the administration of the sacrament of penance. But you may say that you are not qualified for this office, because you have not studied theology. But do you not know that a priest is bound to study? *The lips of the priest shall keep knowledge, and they shall seek the law at his mouth.*[3] If you did not intend to study in order to be able to assist your neighbor, why did you become a priest? Who, says the Lord, asked you to take holy Orders? *Who required these things at your hands that you should walk in My courts?*[4]

[1] "Væ tibi, si præes; sed væ gravius, si, quia præesse metuis, prodesse refugis!"—*Epist.* 86.

[2] Page 158.

[3] "Labia enim Sacerdotis custodient scientiam, et legem requirent ex ore ejus."—*Mal.* ii. 7.

[4] "Quis quæsivit hæc de manibus vestris, ut ambularetis in atriis meis?"—*Is.* i. 12.

Who, asks St. John Chrysostom, has forced you to become a priest?[1] Before your ordination, adds the saint, you ought to have examined your fitness for this duty; but now that you are a priest you must work and not examine; and if you are not fit for the work, you must qualify yourself for it.[2] To excuse yourself now on the ground of ignorance, continues the holy Doctor, is to excuse one sin by another.[3] Some priests read many useless books, and neglect to study the science that may enable them to save souls. St. Prosper says that such priests violate justice.[4]

In fine, it is necessary to be persuaded that the priest should seek nothing but the glory of God and salvation of souls. Hence St. Sylvester ordained that with regard to ecclesiastics the days of the week should be called by no other name than that of *Feriæ*, or vacant days.[5] The Gentiles themselves used to say that priests should attend only to the things of God, and therefore they forbade their priests to exercise the office of magistrates, that they might be entirely devoted to the worship of their gods. After he had been appointed by God to promote his honor, and the observance of his law, Moses spent a good deal of his time in settling disputes. Jethro justly reproved him, saying: *Thou art spent with foolish labor. . . . Be thou to the people in those things that*

[1] " Quisnam ad id te coegit?"—*De Sacerd.* 1. 4.
[2] " Tempus nunc agendi, non consultandi."
[3] " Neque licet ad ignorantiam confugere, quandoquidem qui delegatus est ut aliorum emendet ignorantiam, is ignorantiam prætendere minime poterit: hoc nomine supplicium nulla excusatione poterit depellere, quamvis unius dumtaxat animæ jactura acciderit."—*De Sacerd.* 1. 6.
[4] " Contra justitiam faciunt, qui otiosum studium fructuosæ utilitati regendæ multitudinis anteponunt."—*De Vita cont.* l. 3, c. 28.
[5] " Quotidie clericos, abjecta cæterarum rerum cura, uni Deo prorsus vacare debere."—*Breviar.* 31 Dec.

pertain to God.[1] Before you were ordained priest, says St. Athanasius, you might devote yourself to any occupation you wished, but now that you are a priest, you must be employed in the fulfilment of the office for which you are destined.[2] And what is the nature of this office? One of its principal duties is, as we have shown, to labor for the salvation of souls. This doctrine is confirmed by St. Prosper, who says: " To priests properly belong the care of saving souls."[3]

[1] "Stulto labore consumeris. . . . Esto tu populo in his quæ ad Deum pertinent."—*Exod.* xviii. 18.
[2] " Id scire oportet, te, priusquam ordinabaris, tibi vixisse; ordinatum autem, illis quibus ordinatus est."—*Ep. ad Dracont.*
[3] " Sacerdotibus proprie animarum curandarum sollicitudo commissa est."—*De Vita cont.* l. 2, c. 2.

CHAPTER X.

THE VOCATION TO THE PRIESTHOOD.

1.

Necessity of a Divine Vocation to take Holy Orders.

To enter any state of life, a divine vocation is necessary; for without such a vocation it is, if not impossible, at least most difficult to fulfil the obligations of our state, and obtain salvation. But if for all states a vocation is necessary, it is necessary in a particular manner for the ecclesiastical state. *He that entereth not by the door into the sheepfold, but climbeth up another way, the same is a thief and a robber.*[1] Hence he who takes holy orders without a call from God is convicted of theft, in taking by force a dignity which God does not wish to bestow upon him.[2] And before him St. Paul said the same thing: *Neither doth any man take the honor to himself, but he that is called by God, as Aaron was. So Christ also did not glorify Himself: that He might be made a high priest; but he that said unto Him: Thou art My Son; this day I have begotten Thee.*[3]

No one, then, however learned, prudent, and holy he may be, can thrust himself into the sanctuary unless he is first called and introduced by God. Jesus Christ himself, who among all men was certainly the most learned

---

[1] "Qui non intrat per ostium in ovile ovium, sed ascendit aliunde, ille fur est et latro."—*John*, x. 1.

[2] "Latrones et fures appellat eos qui se ultro, ad non sibi datam desuper gratiam, obtrudunt."—*In Jo.* x. 10.

[3] "Nec quisquam sumit sibi honorem, sed qui vocatur a Deo tamquam Aaron. Sic et Christus non semetipsum clarificavit ut pontifex fieret; sed qui locutus est ad eum. Filius meus es tu."—*Heb.* v. 4, 5.

and the most holy, *full of grace and truth,*[1] *in whom are hid all the treasures of wisdom and knowledge,*[2]—Jesus Christ, I say, required a divine call in order to assume the dignity of the priesthood.

In entering the sanctuary, even after God himself had called them to it, the saints trembled. When his bishop ordered St. Augustine to receive ordination, the saint through humility regarded the command as a chastisement of his sins.[3] To escape the priesthood St. Ephrem of Syria feigned madness; and St. Ambrose pretended to be a man of a cruel disposition.

To avoid the priesthood, St. Ammonius the Monk cut off his ears, and threatened to pluck out his tongue, if the persons who pressed him to take holy orders should continue to molest him. In a word, St. Cyril of Alexandria says, " The saints have dreaded the dignity of the priesthood as a burden of enormous weight."[4] Can any one, then, says St. Cyprian, be so daring as to attempt of himself, and without a divine call, to assume the priesthood?[5]

As a vassal who would of himself take the office of minister should violate the authority of his sovereign, so he who intrudes himself into the sanctuary without a vocation violates the authority of God. How great should be the temerity of the subject who, without the appointment, and even in opposition to the will of the monarch, should attempt to administer the royal patrimony, to decide lawsuits, to command the army, and to assume the viceregal authority ! " Among you," asks

[1] " Plenum gratiæ et veritatis."—*John,* i. 14.
[2] " In quo sunt omnes thesauri sapientiæ et scientiæ absconditi."— *Col.* ii. 3.
[3] " Vis mihi facta est merito peccatorum meorum."—*Epist.* 21, *E. B.*
[4] " Omnes sanctos reperio divini ministerii ingentem veluti molem formidantes."—*De Fest. pasch. hom.* 1.
[5] " Ita est aliquis sacrilegæ temeritatis, ac perditæ mentis, ut putet sine Dei judicio fieri sacerdotem ?'—*Epist.* 55.

CHAP. X.] *The Vocation to the Priesthood.* 187

St. Bernard in speaking to clerics, "is there any one so insolent as, without orders and contrary to the will of the pettiest monarch, to assume the direction of his affairs?"[1] And are not priests, as St. Prosper says, the administrators of the royal house?[2] Are they not, according to St. Ambrose, the "leaders and rectors of the flock of Christ"?[3] according to St. Chrysostom, the "interpreters of the divine judgments,"[4] and according to St. Denis, the "vicars of Christ"?[5] Will any one who knows all this dare to become the minister of God without a divine call?

To think of exercising royal authority is, according to St. Peter Chrysologus, criminal in a subject.[6] To intrude into the house of a private individual, in order to dispose of his goods and to manage his business, would be considered temerity; for even a private individual has the right of appointing the administrators of his affairs. And will you, says St. Bernard, without being called or introduced by God, intrude into his house to take charge of his interests and to dispose of his goods?[7]

The Council of Trent has declared that the Church regards not as her minister, but as a robber, the man who audaciously assumes the priesthood without a vocation.[8] Such priests may labor and toil, but their labors

---

[1] " Auderetne aliquis vestrum terreni cujuslibet regni, non præcipiente aut etiam prohibente eo, occupare ministeria, negotia dispensare ?"—*De Conv. ad cler.* c. 19.

[2] " Dispensatores regiæ domus."—*De Vita cont.* l. 2, c. 2.

[3] " Duces et rectores gregis Christi."—*De Dign. sac.* c. 2.

[4] " Interpretes divinorum judiciorum."

[5] " Vicarii Christi."—*Hom.* 17.

[6] " Regnum velle servum, crimen est."—*Serm.* 23.

[7] "Quid istud temeritatis, imo quid insaniæ est? tu irreverenter irruis, nec vocatus, nec introductus."—*De Vita cler.* c. 5.

[8] " Decernit sancta Synodus eos qui ea (ministeria) propria temeritate sibi sumunt, omnes, non Ecclesiæ ministros, sed fures et latrones per ostium non ingressos habendos esse."—*Sess.* 23, *cap.* 4.

shall profit them little before God. On the contrary, the works that are meritorious in others shall deserve chastisement for them. Should a servant who is commanded by his master to take care of the house, through his own caprice labor in cultivating the vineyard, he may toil and sweat, but instead of being rewarded he shall be chastised by his master. Thus, in the first place, because they are not conformable to the divine will, the Lord shall not accept the toils of the man who, without a vocation, intrudes himself into the priesthood. *I have no pleasure in you*, saith the Lord of Hosts, *and I will not receive a gift of your hand.*[1] In the end God will not reward, but will punish the works of the priest who has entered the sanctuary without a vocation. *What stranger soever cometh to it (the tabernacle) shall be slain.*[2]

Whosoever, then, aspires to holy Orders must, in the first place, carefully examine whether his vocation is from God. "For," says St. John Chrysostom, "since this dignity is great, it must be approved by a divine sentence, so that only the one that is worthy may be admitted thereto."[3] Now to know whether his call is from God, he should examine the marks of a divine vocation. He, says St. Luke, who wishes to build a tower first computes the necessary expenses, in order to know if he has the means of completing the edifice.[4]

[1] "Non est mihi voluntas in vobis, dicit Dominus exercituum, et munus non suscipiam de manu vestra."—*Mal.* i. 10.
[2] "Quisquis externorum accesserit (ad tabernaculum) occidetur."—*Num.* i. 51.
[3] "Quoniam dignitas magna est, et revera divina sententia comprobanda."—*In* 1 *Tim.* hom. 5.
[4] "Quis enim ex vobis, volens turrim ædificare, non prius sedens computat sumptus qui necessarii sunt, si habeat ad perficiendum?"—*Luke*, xiv. 28.

II.

Marks of a Divine Vocation to the Sacerdotal State.

Let us now see what are the marks of a divine vocation to the sacerdotal state.

Nobility is not a mark of a divine vocation. To know, says St. Jerome, whether a person should become the guide of the people in what regards their eternal salvation, we must consider not nobility of blood, but sanctity of life.[1] St. Gregory says the same: "By one's conduct, not by one's high birth, is one's vocation to be proved."[2]

Nor is the will of parents a mark of a divine vocation. In inducing a child to take priesthood they seek not his spiritual welfare, but their own interest, and the advancement of the family. "How many mothers," says St. John Chrysostom, or the author of the *Imperfect Work*, "have eyes only for the bodies of their children and disdain their souls! To see them happy here below is all that they desire; as for the punishments that perhaps their children are to endure in the next life, they do not even think of them."[3] We must be persuaded, as Jesus Christ has said, that with regard to the choice of a state of life we have no enemies more dangerous than our own relatives. *And a man's enemies shall be they of his own household.*[4] Hence the Redeemer adds: *He that loveth father*

---

[1] "Principatum in populos, non sanguini deferendum, sed vitæ."—*In Tit.* I.

[2] "Quos dignos divina probet electio, secundum vitæ, non generis meritum."

[3] "Matres corpora natorum amant, animas contemnunt; desiderant illos valere in sæculo isto, et non curant quid sint passuri in alio."—*Hom.* 35.

[4] "Et inimici hominis, domestici ejus."—*Matt.* x. 36.

or mother more than Me is not worthy of Me.[1] Oh! how many priests shall we see condemned on the day of judgment for having taken holy Orders to please their relatives.

When a young man, in obedience to the call of God, wishes to become a religious, what efforts do not his parents make, either through passion or for the interest of the family, to dissuade him from following his vocation! It is necessary to know that, according to the common opinion of theologians, this cannot be excused from mortal sin. See what I have written on this subject in my Moral Theology. Parents who act in this manner are guilty of a double sin. They sin first against charity, because they are the cause of a grievous evil to the child whom God has called to religion. A person who dissuades even a stranger from following a religious vocation is guilty of a grievous sin. They sin, secondly, against piety; for by their obligation to educate a child they are bound to promote his greater spiritual welfare. Some ignorant confessors tell their penitents who wish to become religious, that in this they should obey their parents, and abandon their vocation if their parents object to their entering religion. These confessors adopt the opinion of Luther, who taught that a person sins by entering religion without the consent of his parents. But the doctrine of Luther was rejected by the holy Fathers, and by the Tenth Council of Toledo, in which it was decreed that children who had attained their fourteenth year may lawfully enter religion even against the will of their parents. A child is bound to obey his parents in what regards his education and the government of the house; but with regard to the choice of a state of life, he should obey God by embracing the state to which God calls him. When

[1] "Qui amat patrem aut matrem plus quam me, non est me dignus." —*Matt.* x. 37.

parents seek to be obeyed in this matter we must answer them in the words of the apostles to the princes of the Jews: *If it be just in the sight of God to hear you rather than God, judge ye.*[1]

St. Thomas expressly teaches that in the choice of a state of life children are not obliged to obey their parents. And the saint says that when there is question of a vocation to religion, a person is not bound even to consult his relatives; for on such occasions self-interest changes relatives into enemies.[2] Parents are, as St. Bernard says, content to see their children damned with them, rather than see them saved by entering religion and separating from the family.[3] But when a person wishes to enter the sacerdotal state, in which he may be able to serve the family, what efforts do not his parents make to procure his ordination, either by lawful or unlawful means, whether he is called or not called to the priesthood! And with what severity do they not treat him if, through remorse of conscience, he refuse to take holy orders! Barbarous fathers! Let us, with St. Bernard, call them not parents, but murderers![4] Unhappy fathers! miserable children! I say again. How many shall we see condemned in the valley of Josaphat for having interfered with the vocation of others, or for not having attended to their own! For, as we shall hereafter demonstrate, the salvation of each individual depends on following the divine call.

But let us return to our subject. Neither nobility of birth nor the will of parents are marks of a vocation to

[1] "Si justum est, in conspectu Dei, vos potius audire quam Deum, judicate."—*Acts*, iv. 19.

[2] "Propinqui autem carnis, in hoc proposito, amici non sunt, sed potius inimici, juxta sententiam Domini: 'Inimici hominis, domestici ejus.'"—*Contra retr. a. rel.* c. 9.

[3] "O durum patrem, o sævam matrem, quorum consolatio mors filii est; qui me malunt perire cum eis, quam regnare sine eis!"—*Epist* 111.

[4] "Non parentes, sed peremptores."

the priesthood; nor is talent or fitness for the offices of a priest a sign of vocation, for along with talent a holy life and a divine call are necessary.

What, then, are the marks of a divine vocation to the ecclesiastical state? There are three principal marks:

1. PURITY OF INTENTION.

The first is a good intention. It is necessary to enter the sanctuary by the door, but there is no other door than Jesus Christ: *I am the door of the sheep. . . . If any man enter in, he shall be saved.*[1] To enter, then, by the door is to become a priest not to please relatives, nor to advance the family, nor for the sake of self-interest or self-esteem, but to serve God, to propagate his glory, and to save souls. "If any one," says a wise theologian, the learned continuator of Tourvely, "presents himself for holy Orders without any vicious affection, and with the sole desire to be employed in the service of God and in the salvation of his neighbor, he, we may believe, is called by God."[2] Another author asserts that he who is impelled by ambition, interest, or a motive of his own glory, is called not by God, but by the devil.[3] "But," adds St. Anselm, "he who enters the priesthood through so unworthy motives shall receive not a blessing but a malediction from God.[4]

---

[1] "Ego sum ostium ovium. . . . Per me si quis introierit, salvabitur."—*John*, x. 7.

[2] "Si enim aliquis, liber ab omni vitioso affectu, ad clerum, Deo deserviendi causa et salutis populi gratia solum, se conferat, vocari a Deo præsumitur."—*De Ord.* q. 4, a. 4.

[3] "Ambitione duceris, vel avaritia? inhias honori? Non te vocat Deus, sed diabolus tentat."—*Hall,* p 1, s. 3, c. 2, § 4.

[4] "Qui enim se ingerit et propriam gloriam quærit, gratiæ Dei rapinam facit; et ideo non accipit benedictionem, sed maledictionem."—*In Heb.* 5.

2. SCIENCE AND TALENTS.

The second mark is the talent and learning necessary for the fulfilment of the duties of a priest. Priests must be masters to teach the people the law of God. *For the lips of the priest shall keep knowledge, and they shall seek the law at his mouth.*[1] Sidonius Apollinarius used to say: "Ignorant physicians are the cause of many deaths."[2] An ignorant priest, particularly a confessor, who teaches false doctrines and gives bad counsels will be the ruin of many souls; because, in consequence of being a priest, his errors are easily believed. Hence Ivone Carnotensis has written: "No one should be admitted to holy Orders unless he has given sufficient proofs of good conduct and learning."[3]

A priest must not only have a competent knowledge of all the rubrics necessary for the celebration of Mass, but must be also acquainted with the principal things that regard the sacrament of penance. It is true, as we have said in the preceding chapter of this work, that every priest is not obliged to hear confessions, unless there is great necessity for his assistance in the district in which he lives; however, every priest is bound to be acquainted with what a priest must ordinarily know in order to be able to hear the confessions of dying persons; that is, he is bound to know when he has faculties to absolve, when and how he ought to give absolution to the sick, whether conditionally or absolutely; what obligation he ought to impose on them, if they are under any censure. He should also know at least the general principles of Moral Theology.

[1] "Labia enim Sacerdotis custodient scientiam, et legem requirent ex ore ejus."—*Mal.* ii. 7.
[2] "Medici parum docti multos occidunt."—*Lib.* 2, ep. 12.
[3] "Nulli ad sacros Ordines sunt promovendi, nisi quos vita et doctrina idoneos probat."

3. POSITIVE GOODNESS OF CHARACTER.

The third mark of an ecclesiastical vocation is positive virtue.

Hence, in the first place, the person who is to be ordained should be a man of innocent life, and should not be contaminated by sins. The Apostle requires that they who are to be ordained priests should be free from every crime. In ancient times a person who had committed a single mortal sin could never be ordained, as we learn from the First Council of Nice.[1] And St. Jerome says that it was not enough for a person to be free from sin at the time of his ordination, but that it was, moreover, necessary that he should not have fallen into mortal sin since the time of his baptism.[2] It is true that this rigorous discipline has ceased in the Church, but it has been always at least required that he who had fallen into grievous sins should purify his conscience for a considerable time before his ordination. This we may infer from a letter to the Archbishop of Rheims, in which Alexander III. commanded that a deacon who had wounded another deacon, if he sincerely repented of his sin, might, after being absolved, and after performing the penance enjoined, be permitted again to exercise his Order; and that if he afterwards led a perfect life, he might be promoted to priesthood.[3] He, then, who finds himself bound by a habit of any vice cannot take any holy Order without incurring the guilt of mortal sin. "I am horrified," says St. Bernard,[4] "when I think

[1] "Qui confessi sunt peccata, canon (ecclesiasticus ordo) non admittit."—*Can.* 9.

[2] "Ex eo tempore quo in Christo renatus est, nulla peccáti conscientia remordeatur."—*In Tit.* 1.

[3] "Et si perfectæ vitæ et conversationis fuerit, eum in presbyterum (poteris) ordinare."—*Cap.* 1, *De diacono. Qui cler.*

[4] "Horreo considerans unde, quo vocaris, præsertim cum nullum intercurrerit pœnitentiæ tempus. Et quidem rectus ordo requirit ut prius propriam, deinde alienas curare studeas conscientias."—*Epist.* 8.

whence thou comest, whither thou goest, and what a short penance thou hast put between thy sins and thy ordination. However, it is indispensable that thou do not undertake to purify the conscience of others before thou purifiest thy own." Of those daring sinners who, though full of bad habits, take priesthood, an ancient author, Gildas, says, "It is not to the priesthood that they should be admitted, but they should be dragged to the pillory."[1] They, then, says St. Isidore, who are still subject to the habit of any sin should not be promoted to holy Orders.[2]

But he who intends to ascend the altar must not only be free from sin, but must have also begun to walk in the path of perfection, and have acquired a habit of virtue. In our Moral Theology[3] we have shown in a distinct dissertation (and this is the common opinion) that if a person in the habit of any vice wish to be ordained, it is not enough for him to have the dispositions necessary for the sacrament of penance, but that he must also have the dispositions required for receiving the sacrament of order; otherwise he is unfit for both: and should he receive absolution with the intention of taking Orders without the necessary dispositions, he and the confessor who absolves him shall be guilty of a grievous sin. For it is not enough for those who wish to take holy Orders to have left the state of sin: they must also, according to the words of Alexander III. (*si perfectæ vitæ et conversionis fuerit*), cited in the preceding paragraph, have the positive virtue necessary for the ecclesiastical state. From the words of the Pontiff we learn that a person who has done penance may exercise

---

[1] "Multi digniores erant ad catastam pœnalem, quam ad Sacerdotium trahi."—*Cast. in eccl. ord.*

[2] "Non sunt promovendi ad regimen Ecclesiæ, qui adhuc vitiis subjacent."—*Sent.* l. 3, c. 34.

[3] *Theol. moral.* l. 6, n. 63, et s.

an order already received, but he who has only done penance cannot take a higher order. The angelic Doctor teaches the same doctrine: "Sanctity is required for the reception of holy Orders, and we must place the sublime burden of the priesthood only upon walls already dried by sanctity; that is, freed from the malignant humor of sin."[1] This is conformable to what St. Denis wrote long before: "Let no one be so bold as to propose himself to others as their guide in the things of God, if he has not first, with all his power, transformed himself into God to the point of perfect resemblance to him."[2] For this St. Thomas adduces two reasons: the first is, that as he who takes orders is raised above seculars in dignity, so he should be superior to them in sanctity.[3] The second reason is, that by his ordination a priest is appointed to exercise the most sublime ministry on the altar, for which greater sanctity is required than for the religious state.[4]

Hence the Apostle forbade Timothy to ordain neophytes; that is, according to St. Thomas, neophytes in perfection as well as neophytes in age.[5] Hence the

[1] "Ordines sacri præexigunt sanctitatem; unde pondus Ordinum imponendum est parietibus jam per sanctitatem desiccatis, id est, ab humore vitiorum."—2, 2, q. 189, a. 1.

[2] "In divino omni non audendum aliis ducem fieri, nisi secundum omnem habitum suum factus sit deiformissimus et Deo simillimus."—*De Eccl. Hier.* c. 3.

[3] "Ad idoneam executionem Ordinum, non sufficit bonitas qualiscumque, sed requiritur bonitas excellens, ut, sicut illi, qui Ordinem suscipiunt, super plebem constituuntur gradu Ordinis, ita et superiores sint merito sanctitatis; et ideo præexigitur gratia quæ sufficiat ad hoc quod digne connumerentur in plebe Christi."—*Suppl.* q. 35, a. 1.

[4] "Quia per sacrum Ordinem aliquis deputatur ad dignissima ministeria, quibus ipsi Christo servitur in Sacramento altaris; ad quod requiritur major sanctitas interior, quam requirat etiam religionis status."—2, 2, q. 184, a. 8.

[5] "Qui non solum ætate neophyti, sed et qui neophyti sunt perfectione."

CHAP. X.] *The Vocation to the Priesthood.* 197

Council of Trent, in reference to the words of Scripture, *And a spotless life in old age,*[1] prescribes to the bishops to admit to ordination only those who show themselves worthy by a conduct full of wise maturity.[2] And of this positive virtue it is necessary, according to St. Thomas, to have not a doubtful but a certain knowledge.[3] This, according to St. Gregory, is particularly necessary with regard to the virtue of chastity: "No one should be admitted to the ministry of the altar unless an assurance has been given of his perfect chastity."[4] With regard to chastity, the holy Pontiff required a proof of many years.[5]

From this we may infer that God will demand a terrible account of the parish priest who gives to persons aspiring to the priesthood a testimony of their having frequented the sacraments and led exemplary lives, though they had neglected the frequentation of the sacraments, and had given scandal rather than good example. Such parish priests by these false attestations, given not through charity, as they pretend, but against the charity due to God and the Church, render themselves guilty of all the sins that shall be afterwards committed by the bad priests who were ordained in consequence of these testimonials. For in this matter bishops trust to the testimony of parish priests, and are deceived. Nor should a parish priest in giving such attestations trust the testimony of others: he cannot give them unless he is certain that what he attests is

[1] "Ætas senectutis, vita immaculata."—*Wisd.* iv. 9.
[2] "Sciant episcopi debere ad hos (sacros) Ordines assumi dignos dumtaxat, et quorum probata vita senectus sit."—*Sess.* 23, *cap.* 12.
[3] "Sed etiam habeatur certitudo de qualitate promovendorum."— *Suppl.* q. 36, a. 4.
[4] "Nullus debet ad ministerium altaris accedere, nisi cujus castitas ante susceptum ministerium fuerit approbata."—*Lib.* 1, ep. 42.
[5] "Ne unquam ii qui ordinati sunt, pereant, prius aspiciatur si vita eorum continens ab annis plurimis fuit."—*Lib.* 3, *cp.* 26.

true, namely, that the ecclesiastic has really led an exemplary life, and has frequented the sacraments. And as a bishop cannot ordain any person unless he be a man of approved chastity, so a confessor cannot permit an incontinent penitent to receive ordination without having a moral certainty that he is free from the bad habit which he had contracted, and that he had acquired a habit of the virtue of chastity.*

III.

To what Dangers one Exposes One's Self by taking Holy Orders without a Vocation.

From what has been said, it follows that he who takes holy Orders without the marks of a vocation cannot be excused from the guilt of grievous sin. This is the doctrine of many theologians,—of Habert, of Natalis Alexander, of Juenin, and of the continuator of Tournely. And before them St. Augustine taught the same. Speaking of the chastisement inflicted on Core, Dathan, and Abiron, who, without being called, attempted to exercise the sacerdotal functions, the holy Doctor said: "God struck them that they might serve as an example, and thus to warn off him who would dare to assume a sacred charge. Indeed, this is the chastisement reserved for those who would thrust themselves into the office of bishop, priest, or deacon."[1] And the reason is, first, because he who thrusts himself into the sanctuary without a divine call cannot be excused from grievous presump-

[1] "Condemnati sunt ut daretur exemplum, ne quis non sibi a Deo datum munus pontificatus invaderet. . . . Hoc patiuntur quicumque se in episcopatus, aut presbyteratus, aut diaconatus, officium conantur ingerere."—*Serm.* 30, *E. B. app.*

* We may also see other useful reflections on the virtue required to be admitted to holy Orders, in the "Practice of the Love of Jesus Christ," Chapter VII, vol. vi. page 382.—ED.

tion; secondly, because he shall be deprived of the congruous and abundant helps, without which, as Habert writes, he shall be absolutely unable to comply with the obligations of his state, but shall fulfil them only with great difficulty. He will be like a dislocated member, which can be used only with difficulty, and which causes deformity.'

Hence Bishop Abelly writes: "He who of himself, without inquiring whether he has a vocation or not, thrusts himself into the priesthood will no doubt expose himself to the great danger of losing his soul; for he commits against the Holy Spirit that sin for which, as the Gospel says, there is hardly or very rarely any pardon."[2]

The Lord has declared that his wrath is provoked against those who wish to rule in his Church without being called by him. On this passage St. Gregory says, "It is by themselves and not by the will of the Supreme Head that they reign."[3] Divine vocation is entirely wanting to them, and they have followed only the ardor of vile cupidity, not certainly to accept, but to usurp this sublime dignity.[4] How many intrigues, adulations, entreaties, and other means do certain persons employ in order to procure ordination, not in obedience to the call of God, but through earthly motives! But woe to such

---

[1] "Manebitque in corpore Ecclesiæ velut membrum in corpore humano suis sedibus motum, quod servire potest, sed ægre admodum et cum deformitate."—*De Ord.* p. 3, c. 1, § 2.

[2] "Qui sciens et volens, nulla divinæ vocationis habita ratione, sese in sacerdotium intruderet, haud dubie seipsum in apertissimum salutis discrimen injiceret, peccando scilicet in Spiritum Sanctum, quod quidem peccatum vix aut rarissime dimitti ex Evangelio discimus."—*Sac. chr.* p. 1, c. 4.

[3] "Ipsi regnaverunt, et non ex me, . . . iratus est furor meus in eos."—*Os.* viii. 4.

[4] "Ex se, et non ex arbitrio summi Rectoris, regnant: nequaquam divinitus vocati, sed sua cupidine accensi, culmen regiminis rapiunt potius quam assequuntur."—*Past.* p. 1, c. 1.

men, says the Lord by the prophet Isaias: *Woe to you, apostate children, . . . that you would take counsel, and not of me.*[1] On the day of judgment they shall claim a reward, but Jesus Christ shall cast them off. *Many will say to Me in that day, have we not prophesied in Thy name* (by preaching and teaching), *and cast out devils in Thy name* (by absolving penitent sinners), *and done many miracles in Thy name* (by correcting the wicked, by settling disputes, by converting sinners). *And then will I profess unto them: I never knew you; depart from Me, you that work iniquity.*[2] Priests who have not been called are indeed workmen and ministers of God, because they have received the sacerdotal character; but they are ministers of iniquity and rapine, because they have of their own will, and without vocation, intruded themselves into the sheepfold. They have not, as St. Bernard says,[3] received the keys, but have taken them by force. They toil, but God will not accept; he will, on the contrary, punish their works and labors, because they have not entered the sanctuary by the straight path. *The labor of fools shall afflict them that know not how to go to the city.*[4] The Church, says St. Leo, receives only those whom the Lord chooses, and by his election makes fit to be his ministers.[5] But, on the other hand, the Church rejects those

[1] " Væ filii desertores, dicit Dominus, ut faccretis consilium, et non ex me !"—*Isa.* xxx. 1.

[2] " Multi dicent mihi in illa die. Domine, Domine, nonne in nomine tuo prophetavimus (prædicando, docendo), et in nomine tuo dæmonia ejecimus (absolvendo pœnitentes), et in nomine tuo virtutes multas fecimus (corrigendo, lites componendo, errantes reducendo)?—Et tunc confitebor illis: Quia nunquam novi vos: discedite a me, qui operamini iniquitatem."—*Matt.* vii. 22.

[3] " Tollitis, non accipitis claves; de quibus Dominus queritur: 'Ipsi regnaverunt, et non ex me.' "—*De Conv. ad cler.* c. 19.

[4] " Labor stultorum affliget eos, qui nesciunt in urbem pergere."—*Eccles.* x. 15.

[5] " Eos Ecclesia accipit, quos Spiritus Sanctus præparavit, . . . et dignatio cœlestis gratiæ gignit."—*In die ass. suæ,* s. 2.

whom, as St. Peter Damian has written, God has not called; for instead of promoting her welfare, they commit havoc among her members; and instead of edifying, they contaminate and destroy her children.[1]

Whom He (the Lord) *shall choose, they shall approach to Him*.[2] God will gladly admit into his presence all whom he has called to the priesthood, and will cast off the priest whom he has not chosen. St. Ephrem regards as lost the man who is so daring as to take the order of priesthood without a vocation. "I am astonished," he says, "at that which those fools dare to do, who, without the grace of vocation through Christ, full of boldness, seek to insinuate themselves into the office of the priesthood. Miserable beings, that know not that they are preparing for themselves an eternal fire."[3] And Peter de Blois has written: "What ruin does not the bold man prepare for himself who of the sacrifice makes a sacrilege, and of life an instrument of death!"[4] He who errs in his vocation exposes himself to greater danger than if he transgressed particular precepts; for if he violates a particular command, he may rise from his fall, and begin again to walk in the right path, but he who errs in his vocation mistakes the way itself. Hence the longer he travels in it, the more distant he is from his home. To him we may justly apply the words of St. Augustine: "You run well, but on the wrong road."[5]

It is necessary to be persuaded of the truth of what St. Gregory says, that our eternal salvation depends

[1] "Nemo deterius Ecclesiam lædit."—*Cont. cler. aul.* c. 3.
[2] "Quos elegerit (Dominus). appropinquabunt ei."—*Num.* xvi. 5.
[3] "Obstupesco ad ea quæ soliti sunt quidam insipientium audere, qui temere se conantur ingerere ad munus Sacerdotii assumendum, licet non adsciti a gratia Christi: ignorantes, miseri, quod ignem et mortem sibi accumulant."—*Or. de Sacerd.*
[4] "Quam perditus est, qui sacrificium in sacrilegium, qui vitam convertit in mortem."—*Ep. ad rich. lond.*
[5] "Bene curris, sed extra viam."

principally on embracing the state to which God has called us.[1] The reason is evident: for it is God that destines, according to the order of his Providence, his state of life for each individual, and according to the state to which he calls him, prepares for him abundant graces and suitable helps. "In the distribution of graces," says St. Cyprian, "the Holy Spirit takes into consideration his own plan and not our caprices."[2] And according to the Apostle: *And whom He predestinated, them He also called. And whom He called, them He also justified.*[3] Thus to vocation succeeds justification, and to justification, glory; that is, the attainment of eternal life. He, then, who does not obey the call of God shall neither be justified nor glorified. Father Granada justly said that vocation is the main wheel of our entire life. As in a clock, if the main wheel be spoiled the entire clock is injured, so, says St. Gregory Nazianzen, if a person err in his vocation his whole life will be full of errors; for in the state to which God has not called him he will be deprived of the helps by which he can with facility lead a good life.

Every one, says St. Paul, *hath his proper gift from God; one after this manner, and another after that.*[4] The meaning of this passage, according to St. Thomas and other commentators, is, that the Lord gives to each one graces to fulfil with ease the obligations of the state to which he calls him. "God," says the angelic Doctor, "gives to every man not only certain aptitudes, but also all that is necessary to exercise them."[5] And in another place

[1] "A vocatione pendet æternitas."

[2] "Ordine suo, non nostro arbitrio, Sancti Spiritus virtus ministratur."—*De Sing. cler.*

[3] "Quos prædestinavit, hos et vocavit; et quos vocavit, hos et justificavit; quos autem justificavit, illos et glorificavit."—*Rom.* viii. 30.

[4] "Unusquisque proprium donum habet ex Deo: alius quidem sic, alius vero sic."—I *Cor.* vii. 7.

[5] "Cuicumque datur potentia aliqua divinitus, dantur etiam ea per quæ executio illius potentiæ possit congrue fieri."—*Suppl.* q. 35, a. I.

he writes: "God does not destine men to such or such a vocation without favoring them with gifts at the same time, and preparing them in such a way as to render them capable of fulfilling the duties of their vocation; for, says St. Paul: *Our sufficiency is from God, who also hath made us fit ministers of the New Testament.*[1] As each person, then, will be able to discharge with facility the office to which God elects him, so he will be unfit for the fulfilment of the office to which God does not call him. The foot, which is given to enable us to walk, cannot see; the eye, which is given to see, is incapable of hearing; and how shall he who is not chosen by God to the priesthood be able to discharge its obligations?

It belongs to the Lord to choose the workmen who are to cultivate his vineyard: *I have chosen you, . . . and have appointed you that you should go; and should bring forth fruit.*[2] Hence the Redeemer did not say, Beg of men to go and gather the harvest; but he tells us to ask the master of the crop to send workmen to collect it.[3] Hence he also said: *As the Father hath sent Me, I also send you.*[4] When God calls, he himself, says St. Leo, gives the necessary helps.[5] This is what Jesus Christ has said: *I am the door. By Me if any man enter in he shall be saved, and he shall go in, and go out, and shall find pastures.*[6] "He shall go in:"[7]

---

[1] "Illos quos Deus ad aliquid eligit, ita præparat et disponit, ut ad id ad quod eliguntur, inveniantur idonei, secundum illud: 'Idoneos nos fecit ministros Novi Testamenti.'"—(2 *Cor.* iii. 5.)—P. 3, q. 27, a. 4.

[2] "Ego elegi vos, et posui vos, ut eatis et fructum afferatis."—*John*, xv. 16.

[3] "Rogate ergo dominum messis, ut mittat operarios in messem suam."—*Luke*, x. 2.

[4] "Sicut misit me Pater, et ego mitto vos."—*John*, xx. 21.

[5] "Qui mihi honoris est auctor, ipse mihi fiet administrationum adjutor; dabit virtutem, qui contulit dignitatem."—*In die ass. suæ*, s. 1.

[6] "Ego sum ostium. Per me si quis introierit, salvabitur; et ingredietur, et egredietur, et pascua inveniet."—*John*, x. 9.

[7] "Ingredietur."

what the priest called by God undertakes, he shall easily accomplish without sin, and with merit. *And shall go out:*[1] he shall be in the midst of perils and occasions of sin, but with the divine aid he shall readily escape injury. *And shall find pastures:*[2] finally, in consequence of being in the state in which God has placed him, he will be assisted in all the duties of his ministry by special graces, which will make him advance in perfection. Hence he will be able to say with confidence, *The Lord ruleth me: and I shall want nothing. He hath set me in a place of pasture.*[3]

But priests whom God has not sent to work in his Church he shall abandon to eternal ignominy and destruction. *I did not send prophets,* says the Lord by the prophet Jeremiah, *yet they ran.* He afterwards adds: *Therefore I will take you away, carrying you, and will forsake you;* . . . *and I will bring an everlasting reproach upon you, and a perpetual shame which shall never be forgotten.*[4]

In order to be raised to the sublimity of the priesthood, it is necessary, as St. Thomas says, for a man " to be exalted and elevated by divine power above the natural order of things,"[5] because he is appointed the sanctifier of the people, and the vicar of Jesus Christ. But in him who raises himself to so great a dignity shall be verified the words of the Wise Man: *There is that hath appeared a fool after he was lifted up on high.*[6] Had he remained in

[1] "Et egredietur."
[2] "Et pascua inveniet."
[3] "Dominus regit me, et nihil mihi deerit; in loco pascuæ ibi me collocavit."—*Ps.* xxii. 1.
[4] "Non mittebam prophetas, et ipsi currebant.—Propterea ecce ego tollam vos portans, et derelinquam vos; . . . et dabo vos in opprobrium sempiternum, et in ignominiam æternam, quæ nunquam oblivione delebitur."—*Jer.* xxiii. 21-39.
[5] "Ut divina virtute evehatur, et transmittatur supra naturalem rerum ordinem."—*Habert, de Ord.* p. 3, c. 1, § 2.
[6] "Stultus apparuit, postquam elevatus est in sublime."—*Prov.* xxx. 32.

the world, he should perhaps have been a virtuous layman; but having become a priest without a vocation, he will be a bad priest, and instead of promoting the interest of religion, he will do great injury to the Church. Of such priests the Roman Catechism says: "Such ministers are for the Church of God the gravest embarrassment and the most terrible scourge."[1] And what good can be expected from the priest who has entered the sanctuary without a vocation? "It is impossible," says St. Leo, "that a work so badly begun should finish well."[2] St. Laurence Justinian has written: "What fruit, I ask, can come from a corrupted root?"[3] Our Saviour has said, *Every plant which My heavenly Father hath not planted shall be rooted up.*[4] Hence Peter de Blois writes that when God permits a person to be ordained without a vocation, the permission is not a grace, but a chastisement. For a tree which has not taken deep root, when exposed to the tempest shall soon fall and be cast into the fire.[5] And St. Bernard says that he who has not lawfully entered the sanctuary shall continue to be unfaithful; and instead of procuring the salvation of souls, he shall be the cause of their death and perdition.[6] This is conformable to the doctrine of Jesus Christ: *He*

---

[1] "Hujusmodi hominum genere nihil infelicius, nihil Ecclesiæ Dei calamitosius esse potest."—P. 2, c. 7, q. 3.

[2] "Difficile est ut bono peragantur exitu, quæ malo sunt inchoata principio."—*Epist.* 87.

[3] "Qualem, oro, potest fructum producere corrupta radix?"—*De Compunct.*

[4] "Omnis plantatio, quam non plantavit Pater meus cœlestis, eradicabitur."—*Matt.* xv. 13.

[5] "Ira est, non gratia, cum quis ponitur super ventum, nullas habens radices in soliditate virtutum."—*De inst. ep.* c. 3.

[6] "Qui non fideliter introivit, quidni infideliter agat et contra Christum? faciet ad quod venit, ut mactet utique et disperdat."—*De Vita cler.* c. 7.

that entereth not by the door into the sheepfold, . . . the same is a thief and a robber.[1]

Some may say, if they only were admitted to orders who have the marks of vocation which have been laid down as indispensable, there should be but few priests in the Church, and the people should be left without the necessary helps. But to this the Fourth Council of Lateran has answered: "It is much better to confer the priesthood on a small number of virtuous clerics than to have a large number of bad priests."[2] And St. Thomas says that God never abandons his Church so as to leave her in want of fit ministers to provide for the necessity of the people.[3] St. Leo justly says that to provide for the wants of the people by bad priests would be not to save but to destroy them.[4]

If, then, a priest has been ordained without a vocation, what must he do?[5] Must he look on himself as lost? must he abandon himself to despair? No. St. Gregory has asked the same question. He answers: "He must lament."[6] Behold what such a priest must do if he wish to save his soul: "He must lament;"[6] he must weep, and seek to appease the anger of God by tears and by repentance, and to move him to pardon the great sin that he committed in thrusting himself into the sanctuary without a divine call. He must, as St. Bernard exhorts, endeavor to attain after his ordination the sanctity of life which ought to precede it.[7] He must

---

[1] "Qui non intrat per ostium, . . . ille fur est et latro.—Fur non venit nisi ut furetur, et mactet, et perdat."—*John*, x. 1-10.
[2] "Satius est maxime in ordinatione sacerdotum paucos bonos quam multos malos habere."—*Cap.* 27.
[3] "Deus nunquam ita deserit Ecclesiam suam, quin inveniantur idonei ministri sufficientes ad necessitatem plebis."—*Suppl.* q. 36, a. 4.
[4] "Non est hoc consulere populis, sed nocere."—*Epist.* 87.
[5] "Sacerdos sum non vocatus; quid faciendum?"
[6] "Ingemiscendum."
[7] "Si vitæ sanctitas non præcessit, sequatur saltem."

change his conduct, his conversation and pursuits. "Let all be holy—your life and your works,"[1] continues the saint. If he is ignorant, he must study; if he has spent his time in worldly conversations and amusements, he must change them into meditations, spiritual reading, and visits to the churches. But to do this he must use violence to himself; for, as has been already said, since he has entered the sanctuary without a vocation, he is but a dislocated member, and therefore he must work out his salvation with great difficulty and great labor. But if in consequence of having become a priest without a divine call, he is, as has been shown, bereft of the helps necessary to enable him to discharge with facility the obligations of the priesthood, how shall he without these helps fulfil the sacerdotal duties? Habert,[2] and the continuator of Tournely,[3] say, let him pray, and by his prayers he shall obtain that assistance which he does not deserve.[4] This is conformable to the doctrine of the Council of Trent: "God commands not impossibilities, but, by commanding, both admonishes thee to do what thou art able, and to pray for what thou art not able (to do), and aids thee that thou mayest be able."[5]

[1] "Bonas fac de cætero vias tuas et studia tua."—*Epist.* 27.
[2] *De Ord.* p. 3, c. 1, § 2.
[3] *De Oblig. cler.* c. 1, a. 1, concl. 3.
[4] "Deus tunc ex misericordia ea homini largitur auxilia, quæ legitime vocatis ex qualicumque justitia debet."
[5] "Deus impossibilia non jubet; sed jubendo monet, et facere quod possis, et petere quod non possis; et adjuvat ut possis."—*Sess.* 6, cap. 11.

PART II.
MATERIAL FOR INSTRUCTIONS.

INSTRUCTION I.

THE CELEBRATION OF MASS.

I.

Importance of the Holy Sacrifice and what it Exacts of the Priest.

For every high-priest taken from among men is ordained for men in the things that appertain to God, that he may offer up gifts and sacrifices for sins.[1] The priest, then, is placed by God in the Church in order to offer sacrifice. This office is peculiar to the priests of the Law of grace, to whom has been given the power of offering the great sacrifice of the body and blood of the Son of God—a sacrifice sublime and perfect in comparison with the ancient sacrifices, the entire perfection of which consisted in being the shadow and figure of our sacrifice. They were sacrifices of calves and oxen, but ours is the sacrifice of the eternal Word made Man. Of themselves they had no efficacy, and were therefore called by St. Paul *weak and needy elements.*[2] But ours has power to obtain the remission of the temporal penalties due to sins,

---

[1] "Omnis namque Pontifex, ex hominibus assumptus, pro hominibus constituitur in iis quæ sunt ad Deum, ut offerat dona et sacrificia pro peccatis."—*Heb.* v. 1.

[2] "Infirma et egena elementa."—*Gal.* iv. 9.

and to procure an augmentation of grace, and more abundant helps for those in whose behalf it is offered.

The priest who has not a just idea of the Mass shall never offer that holy sacrifice as he ought. Jesus Christ performed no action on earth greater than the celebration of Mass. In a word, of all actions that can be performed, the Mass is the most holy and dear to God; as well on account of the oblation presented to God, that is, Jesus Christ, a victim of infinite dignity, as on account of the first offerer, Jesus Christ, who offers himself on the altar by the hand of the priest. "The same now offering," says the Council of Trent, "by the ministry of priests, who then offered himself on the cross."[1] St. John Chrysostom said: "When you see a priest offering, do not believe that this is done by the hand of a priest; the offering is made rather by the hand of God invisibly stretched out."[2]

All the honors that the angels by their homages, and men by their virtues, penances, and martyrdoms, and other holy works, have ever given to God could not give him as much glory as a single Mass. For all the honors of creatures are finite honors, but the honor given to God in the sacrifice of the altar, because it proceeds from a divine person, is an infinite honor. Hence we must confess that of all actions the Mass, as the Council of Trent says, is the most holy and divine: "We must needs confess that no other work can be performed by the faithful so holy and divine as this tremendous mystery itself."[3] It is, then, as we have seen, an action the

[1] "Idem nunc offerens, Sacerdotum ministerio, qui seipsum tunc in cruce obtulit."—*Sess.* 22, cap. 2.

[2] "Cum videris Sacerdotem offerentem, ne ut Sacerdotem esse, putes, sed Christi manum invisibiliter extensam."—*Ad pop. Ant.* hom. 60.

[3] "Necessario fatemur nullum aliud opus adeo sanctum ac divinum a Christi fidelibus tractari posse, quam hoc tremendum mysterium." —*Sess.* 22, *Decr. de obs. in cel. M.*

most holy and dear to God—an action that appeases most efficaciously the anger of God against sinners, that beats down most effectually the powers of hell, that brings to men on earth the greatest benefits, and that affords to the souls in purgatory the greatest relief. It is, in fine, an action in which, as St. Udone, Abbot of Cluni, has written, consists the entire salvation of the world: "Of all the favors granted to me this is the greatest: it is truly by the most generous ardor of his love that God instituted this mystery, without which there would be no salvation in this world."[1] And speaking of the Mass, Timothy of Jerusalem said that by it the world is preserved.[2] But for the Mass the earth should have long since perished on account of the sins of men.

St. Bonaventure says that in each Mass God bestows on the world a benefit not inferior to that which he conferred by his incarnation.[3] This is conformable to the celebrated words of St. Augustine: "O venerable dignity of the priests, in whose hands, as in the womb of the Virgin, the Son of God became incarnate!"[4] Moreover, St. Thomas teaches that since the sacrifice of the altar is nothing else than the application and renewal of the sacrifice of the cross, a single Mass brings to men the same benefits and salvation that were produced by the

---

[1] "Hoc beneficium majus est inter omnia bona quæ hominibus concessa sunt, et hoc est quod Deus majori charitate mortalibus indulsit, quia in hoc mysterio salus mundi tota consistit."—*Collat.* l. 2, c. 28.

[2] "Per quam orbis terræ consistit."—*Or. de proph. Sim.*

[3] "Non minus videtur facere Deus in hoc quod quotidie dignatur descendere de cœlo super altare, quam cum naturam humani generis assumpsit."—*De Inst. Novit.* p. 1, c. 11.

[4] "O veneranda Sacerdotum dignitas, in quorum manibus, velut in utero Virginis, Filius Dei incarnatur."—*Molina, Instr. Sac.* tr. 1, c. 5, § 2.

sacrifice of the cross.[1] St. John Chrysostom says: "The celebration of a Mass has the same value as the death of Christ on the cross."[2] And of this we are still more assured by the holy Church in the Collect for the Sunday after Pentecost: "As many times as this commemorative sacrifice is celebrated, so often is the work of our redemption performed."[3] The same Redeemer who once offered himself on the cross is immolated on the altar by the ministry of his priests. "For the victim is one and the same," says the Council of Trent: "the same now offering by the ministry of priests, who then offered Himself on the cross, the manner alone of offering being different."[4]

In a word, the Mass is, according to the prediction of the prophet, "the good and the beautiful thing" of the Church: *For what is the good thing of him, and what is his beautiful thing, but the corn of the elect and wine springing forth virgins?*[5] In the Mass, Jesus Christ gives himself to us by means of the most holy sacrament of the altar, which is the end and object of all the other sacraments, says the angelic Doctor.[6] Justly, then, has St. Bonaventure called the Mass a compendium of all God's love and of all his benefits to men.[7] Hence the devil has

[1] "In qualibet Missa invenitur omnis fructus quem Christus operatus est in cruce."—*J. Herolt, De Sanct.* s. 48. "Quidquid est effectus Dominicæ passionis, est effectus hujus Sacramenti."—*In Jo.* 6, lect. 6.

[2] "Tantum valet celebratio Missæ, quantum mors Christi in cruce."—*J. Herolt, De Sanct.* s. 48.

[3] "Quoties hujus Hostiæ commemoratio celebratur, opus nostræ redemptionis exercetur."—*Miss. Dom.* 9 *p. Pent.*

[4] "Una enim eademque est Hostia, idem nunc offerens Sacerdotum ministerio, qui seipsum tunc in cruce obtulit, sola offerendi ratione diversa."—*Sess.* 22, cap. 2.

[5] "Quid enim bonum ejus est, et quid pulchrum ejus, nisi frumentum electorum, et vinum germinans virgines?"—*Zach.* ix. 17.

[6] "Sacramenta in Eucharistia consummantur."—*P.* 3, q. 65, a. 3.

[7] "Et ideo hoc est memoriale totius dilectionis suæ, et quasi compendium quoddam omnium beneficiorum suorum."—*De Inst. Novit* p. 1, c. 11.

always sought to deprive the world of the Mass by means of the heretics, constituting them precursors of Antichrist, whose first efforts shall be to abolish the holy sacrifice of the altar, and, according to the prophet Daniel, in punishment of the sins of men, his efforts shall be successful: *And strength was given him against the continual sacrifice because of sins.*[1]

Most justly, then, does the holy Council of Trent require of priests to be most careful to celebrate Mass with the greatest possible devotion and purity of conscience: "It is sufficiently clear that all industry and diligence is to be applied to this end, that it (the mystery) be performed with the greatest possible inward cleanness and purity of heart."[2] And in the same place the Council justly remarks, that on priests who celebrate this great sacrifice negligently, and without devotion, shall fall the malediction threatened by the prophet Jeremiah: *Cursed be he that doth the work of the Lord negligently.*[3] And St. Bonaventure says that he who approaches the altar without reverence and consideration, celebrates or communicates unworthily.[4] In order, then, to avoid this malediction, let us see what the priest must do before Mass, during Mass, and after Mass. Before Mass preparation is necessary, during the celebration of Mass reverence and devotion are necessary, after Mass thanksgiving is necessary. A servant of God used to say that the life of a priest should be nothing else than preparation and thanksgiving for Mass.

[1] "Robur autem datum est ei contra juge Sacrificium propter peccata."—*Dan.* viii. 12.

[2] "Satis apparet omnem operam et diligentiam in eo ponendam esse, ut quanta maxima fieri potest interiori cordis munditia peragatur."—*Sess.* 22, *Decr. de obs. in cel. M.*

[3] "Maledictus, qui facit opus Domini fraudulenter."—*Jer.* xlviii. 10.

[4] "Cave ne nimis tepidus accedas; quia indigne sumis, si non accedis reverenter et considerate."—*De Præp. ad M.* c. 5.

II.
The Preparation for Mass.

In the first place, then, the priest must make his preparation before Mass. Before we come to practice, I ask how does it happen that there are so many priests in the world and so few holy priests? St. Francis de Sales[1] called the Mass a mystery which comprises the entire abyss of divine love. St. John Chrysostom used to say that the most holy sacrament of the altar is the treasure of all God's benignity.[2] There is no doubt that the Holy Eucharist has been instituted for all the faithful, but it is a gift bestowed in a special manner on priests. *Give not*, says our Lord, addressing priests, *that which is holy to dogs; neither cast ye your pearls before swine.*[3] Mark the words *your pearls*. In the Greek the consecrated particles are called *pearls;* but these pearls are called, as it were, the property of priests: *your pearls.* Hence, as St. John Chrysostom says, every priest should leave the altar all inflamed with divine love, so as to strike terror into the powers of hell: " Like lions breathing forth fire should we leave that table, so that we may become terrible to the devil."[4] But this is not the case. The greater number depart from the altar always more tepid, more impatient, proud, jealous, and more attached to self-esteem, to self-interest, and to earthly pleasures. " The defect is not in the food,"[5] says Cardinal Bona. The defect

---
[1] *Introd.* p. 2, ch. 14.
[2] "Dicendo Eucharistiam, omnem benignitatis Dei thesaurum aperio."—*In* 1 *Cor.* hom. 24.
[3] " Nolite dare sanctum canibus, neque mittatis margaritas vestras ante porcos."—*Matt.* vii. 6.
[4] " Tamquam leones ignem spirantes ab illa mensa recedamus, facti diabolo terribiles."—*Ad pop. Ant.* hom. 61.
[5] "Defectus non in cibo est, sed in edentis dispositione."—*De Sacr. M.* c. 6, § 6.

does not arise from the food that they take on the altar; for, as St. Mary Magdalene de Pazzi used to say, that food taken once would be sufficient to make them saints, but it arises from the little preparation that they make for the celebration of Mass.

Preparation for Mass is twofold: remote and proximate.

The *remote* preparation consists in the pure and virtuous life that a priest should lead in order to celebrate worthily. If God required purity in the priests of the Old Law because they had to carry the sacred vessels, *Be ye clean, you that carry the vessels of the Lord*,[1] how much greater should be the purity and sanctity of the priest who has to carry in his hands and in his body the Incarnate Word, says Peter de Blois![2] But to be pure and holy it is not enough for the priest to be exempt from mortal sins: he must be also free from venial sins that are fully deliberate; otherwise he shall have no part with Jesus Christ. "Let no one," says St. Bernard, "disregard little faults, for thus it was said to Peter, that unless Christ purifies of them, we shall have no part in Christ."[3] Hence all the actions and words of the priest who wishes to celebrate Mass must be holy, and serve to prepare him for the worthy celebration of the sacred mysteries.

For the *immediate* preparation, mental prayer is, in the first place, necessary. How can the priest celebrate Mass with devotion without having first made mental prayer? The Venerable John d'Avila used to say that a priest should make mental prayer for an hour or, at least, half an hour, before Mass. I would be content

---

[1] "Mundamini, qui fertis vasa Domini."—*Is.* lii. 11.

[2] "Quanto mundiores esse oportet, qui in manibus et in corpore portant Christum."—*Epist.* 123.

[3] "Hæc nemo contemnat, quoniam ut audivit Petrus nisi laverit ea Christus, non habebimus partem cum eo."—*S. in Cœna Dom.*

with half an hour, or, and for some, with even a quarter of an hour; but a quarter is too little. There are so many beautiful books containing meditations preparatory to Mass, but who makes use of them? It is through neglect of meditation that we see so many Masses said without devotion and with irreverence. The Mass is a representation of the Passion of Jesus Christ. Hence Pope Alexander I. justly said that in the Mass we should always commemorate the Passion of our Lord.[1] And before him the Apostle said: *For as often as you shall eat this bread and drink the chalice, you shall show the death of the Lord until He come.*[2] According to St. Thomas,[3] the Redeemer has instituted the most holy sacrament that we might always have a lively remembrance of the love that he has shown us, and of the great benefits that he obtained for us by offering himself in sacrifice on the cross. But if all should continually remember the Passion of Jesus Christ, how much more should the priest reflect on it when he goes to renew on the altar, though in a different manner, the same sacrifice which the Son of God offered on the cross!

Moreover, even though he had made his meditation, the priest should before he begins Mass always recollect himself at least for a short time, and consider what he is going to do. The Council of Milan, in the time of St. Charles, ordained that all priests should do so.[4] In entering the sacristy to celebrate Mass the priest should take leave of all worldly thoughts, and say with St. Bernard: " Ye cares, solicitudes, earthly troubles, remain

[1] "Inter Missarum solemnia, semper passio Domini miscenda est, ut ejus, cujus corpus et sanguis conficitur, passio celebretur."—*Epist.* 1.

[2] "Quotiescumque enim manducabitis Panem hunc, et Calicem bibetis, mortem Domini annuntiabitis."—1 *Cor.* xi. 26.

[3] *Offic. Corp. Chr.*

[4] "Antequam celebrent, se colligant, et orantes mentem in tanti ministerii cogitatione defigant."—*Const.* p. 2, n. 5.

here: let me go freely to my God, with all my intelligence and with all my heart, and when we have adored we shall return to you; we shall return, alas! and we shall return too soon."[1] In a letter to St. Jane Chantal, St. Francis de Sales said: When I turn to the altar to begin Mass, I lose sight of everything on this earth. Hence, during the celebration of Mass, the priest should take leave of all worldly thoughts, and should think only of the great action that he is going to perform, and of the heavenly bread he is going to eat at the divine table. *When thou shalt sit to eat with a prince*, says Solomon, *consider diligently what is set before thy face*.[2] Let him consider that he is going to call from heaven to earth the Incarnate Word; to treat with him familiarly on the altar; to offer him again to the eternal Father; and finally to partake of his sacred flesh. In preparing to celebrate, Father John d'Avila would endeavor to excite his fervor by saying: "I am now going to consecrate the Son of God, to hold him in my hands, to converse and treat with him, and to receive him into my heart."

The priest should also consider that he ascends the altar to perform the office of intercessor for all sinners, says St. Laurence Justinian.[3] Thus the priest on the altar stands between God and men, presents their petitions, and obtains for them the divine graces, says St. Chrysostom.[4] It is for this reason, says St. Thomas,

---

[1] "Curæ, sollicitudines, servitutes, exspectate me hic, donec ego cum puero, ratio cum intelligentia, usque illuc properantes, postquam adoraverimus, revertamur ad vos; revertemur enim, et, heu! revertemur quam citissime."—*De Amore Dei*, c. 1.

[2] "Quando sederis ut comedas cum principe, diligenter attende quæ apposita sunt ante faciem tuam."—*Prov.* xxiii. 1.

[3] "Mediatoris gerit officium; propterea delinquentium omnium debet esse precator."—*Serm. de Euchar.*

[4] "Medius stat Sacerdos inter Deum et naturam humanam, illinc venientia beneficia ad nos deferens."—*In Isaiam*, hom. 5.

that the sacrifice of the altar is called the Mass: "On this account it is called Mass, because the priest sends his prayers to God through the angel, and the people send them through the priest."[1] In the Old Law the priest was permitted to enter *the holy of holies* only once in the year; but now every priest is allowed to immolate every day the Lamb of God, in order to obtain the divine graces for himself and the entire people, says St. Laurence Justinian.[2] Hence, according to St. Bonaventure, in going to celebrate, a priest should propose to himself three ends: to honor God, to commemorate the Passion of Jesus Christ, and to obtain graces for the whole Church.[3]

III.

The Reverence and the Devotion with which the Priest should Celebrate Mass.

Secondly, it is necessary to celebrate Mass with reverence and devotion. It is well known that the maniple was introduced for the purpose of wiping away the tears of devotion that flowed from the eyes of the priest; for in former times priests wept continually during the celebration of Mass. It has been already said that a priest on the altar represents the very person of Jesus Christ, says St. Cyprian.[4] There he says in the person of Jesus Christ, *hoc est corpus meum: hic est calix sanguinis*

---

[1] " Propter hoc Missa nominatur, quia per Angelum Sacerdos preces ad Deum mittit, sicut populus ad Sacerdotem."—P. 3, q. 83, a. 4.

[2] " Ipsis profecto Sacerdotibus licet, non tantum semel in anno, ut olim, sed diebus singulis introire Sancta Sanctorum, et tam pro ipsis quam pro populi reconciliatione, offerre Hostiam."—*De Inst. præl.* c. 10.

[3] " Tria sunt, quæ celebraturus intendere debet, scilicet: Deum colere, Christi mortem memorari, et totam Ecclesiam juvare."—*De Præp. ad M.* c. 9.

[4] " Sacerdos vice Christi vere fungitur."—*Epist. ad Cæcil.*

mei. But, O God! it would be necessary to weep, and even to shed tears of blood, at the manner in which many priests celebrate Mass. It excites compassion to see the contempt with which some priests and religious, and even priests of the reformed Orders, treat Jesus Christ on the altar. Observe with what kind of attention certain priests celebrate Mass. I hope their number is small. Of them we may well say what Clement of Alexandria said of the pagan priests, that they turned heaven into a stage, and God into the subject of the comedy.[1] But why do I say a comedy? Oh! how great would be their attention if they had to recite a part in a comedy! But with what sort of attention do they celebrate Mass? Mutilated words; genuflexions that appear to be acts of contempt rather than of reverence; benedictions which I know not what to call. They move and turn on the altar in a disrespectful manner; they confound the words with the ceremonies which they perform before the time prescribed by the rubrics, although these rubrics are, according to the true opinion, all preceptive. For St. Pius V. in the Bull inserted in the Missal commands us " strictly, by virtue of holy obedience,"[2] to celebrate Mass according to the rubrics of the Missal: "According to the rite, mode, and norm prescribed in the Missal."[3] Hence he who violates the rubrics cannot be excused from sin, and he who is guilty of a grievous neglect of them cannot be excused from mortal sin.

. All arises from an anxiety to have the Mass soon finished. Some say Mass with as much haste as if the walls were about to fall, or as if they expected to be

---

[1] "O impietatem! scenam cœlum fecistis, et Deus vobis factus est actus."—*Or. ad Gent.*

[2] " Districte, in virtute sanctæ obedientiæ."

[3] " Juxta ritum, modum, ac normam, quæ per Missale hoc a nobis nunc traditur."

attacked by pirates without getting time to fly away. Some priests spend two hours in useless conversation, or in treating of worldly affairs, and are all haste in celebrating Mass. As they begin the Mass without reverence, so they proceed to consecrate, to take Jesus Christ in their hands, and to communicate with as much irreverence as if the holy sacrament were common bread. They should be told what the Venerable John d'Avila said one day to a priest who celebrated with haste and irreverence: " For God's sake treat him better, for he is the Son of a good Father."

The Lord commanded the priests of the Old Law to tremble through reverence in approaching his sanctuary: *Reverence My sanctuary.*[1] And still we see scandalous irreverence in priests of the New Law while they stand at the altar in the presence of Jesus Christ; while they converse with him, take him in their hands, offer him in sacrifice, and eat his flesh. In the Old Law the Lord threatened several maledictions against priests who neglected the ceremonies of sacrifices, which were but figures of our sacrifice. *But if Thou wilt not hear the voice of the Lord thy God, to keep . . . all His ceremonies, ... all these curses shall come upon thee; . . . . cursed shalt thou be in the city, cursed in the field.*[2] St. Teresa used to say: " I would give my life for a ceremony of the Church."[3] And will a priest despise the ceremonies of the holy Mass? Suarez[4] teaches that the omission of any ceremony prescribed in the Mass cannot be excused from sin; and it is the opinion of many theologians, that a notable neglect of the ceremonies may be a mortal sin.

---

[1] " Pavete ad Sanctuarium meum."—*Lev.* xxvi. 2.
[2] " Quod si audire nolueris vocem Domini Dei tui, ut custodias . . . cæremonias, . . . venient super te omnes maledictiones istæ. . . . Maledictus eris in civitate, maledictus in agro."—*Deut.* xxviii. 15.
[3] *Life*, ch. 33.
[4] *De Sacram.* d. 84, s. 2.

In my Moral Theology[1] I have shown, by the authority of many theologians, that to celebrate Mass in less than a quarter of an hour cannot be excused from grievous sin. This doctrine rests on two reasons: first, the irreverence that in so short a Mass is offered to the holy sacrifice; secondly, the scandal that is given to the people.

As to the reverence due to the sacrifice, we have adduced the words of the Council of Trent, commanding priests to celebrate Mass with the greatest possible devotion: "All industry and diligence are to be applied that it be performed with the greatest possible outward show of devotion and piety."[2] The Council adds, that to neglect even this external devotion due to the sacrifice is a species of impiety: "Irreverence that can hardly be separated from impiety."[3] As the due performance of the ceremonies constitutes reverence, so to perform them badly is an irreverence which, when grievous, is a mortal sin. And to perform the ceremonies with the reverence due to so great a sacrifice, it is not enough to go through them; for some who are very quick in their articulation and motions may be able to perform the ceremonies in less than a quarter of an hour, but it is necessary to perform them with becoming gravity, which belongs intrinsically to the reverence due to the Mass.

To celebrate Mass in so short a time is also a grievous sin on account of the scandal given to the people who are present. And here it is necessary to consider what the same Council of Trent says in another place, that the ceremonies have been instituted by the Church in order

---

[1] *Theol. mor.* l. 6, n. 400.

[2] "Omnem operam ponendam esse, ut quanta maxima fieri potest exteriori devotionis ac pietatis specie peragatur."—*Decr. de obs. in M.*

[3] "Irreverentia, quæ ab impietate vix sejuncta esse potest."—*Sess.* 22.

to excite in the faithful the veneration and esteem due to so great a sacrifice, and to the most sublime mysteries that it contains. "The Church," says the holy Council, "has employed ceremonies, whereby both the majesty of so great a sacrifice might be recommended and the minds of the faithful be excited, by those visible signs of religion and piety, to the contemplation of those most sublime things which are hidden in this sacrifice."[1] But instead of inspiring reverence, these ceremonies, when performed with great haste, diminish and destroy the veneration of the people for so holy a mystery. Peter de Blois says that the irreverence with which Mass is celebrated makes people think little of the most holy sacrament.[2] This scandal cannot be excused from mortal sin. Hence in the year 1583 the Council of Tours ordained that priests should be well instructed in the ceremonies of the Mass: "For fear that the people intrusted to their care, far from entertaining veneration for our divine mysteries, might regard them only with indifference."[3]

How can priests expect by Masses said with such irreverence to obtain graces from God, when during the oblation of these Masses they offend and dishonor him more than they honor him? Should a priest not believe in the most holy sacrament of the altar, he would offend God; but it is a still greater offence to believe in it, and to celebrate Mass without due reverence, and thus make the people who are present lose their veneration for the

[1] "Ecclesia cæremonias adhibuit, quo et majestas tanti Sacrificii commendaretur, et mentes fidelium, per hæc visibilia religionis signa, ad rerum altissimarum, quæ in hoc Sacrificio latent, contemplationem excitarentur."—*Sess.* 22, *De Sacrif. M.* c. 5.

[2] "Ex inordinata et indisciplinata multitudine Sacerdotum, hodie datur ostentui nostræ redemptionis venerabile Sacramentum."—*Epist.* 123.

[3] "Ne populum sibi commissum a devotione potius revocent, quam ad sacrorum mysteriorum venerationem invitent."

holy sacrament. In the beginning the Jews respected Jesus Christ, but when they saw him despised by their priests they lost their esteem for him, and in the end joined in the cry of the priests: "Away with this man; crucify him!"[1] And in like manner, seculars, seeing a priest treat the Mass with such irreverence, lose their respect and veneration for it. A Mass said with reverence excites devotion in all who are present at it; but, on the other hand, a Mass celebrated with irreverence destroys devotion and even faith in those that are present. A religious of high reputation told me that a certain heretic had resolved to renounce his errors, but having been afterwards present at a Mass said without reverence, he went to the bishop and said that he no longer intended to abjure his heresy, because he felt convinced that priests who celebrated Mass in such a manner did not sincerely believe in the truth of the Catholic Church; and added: "If I were Pope, and knew that a priest said Mass with irreverence, I would command him to be burned alive." After these words he withdrew, resolved to continue in his heresy.

But some priests say that seculars complain when the Mass is long. Then I ask: Shall the want of devotion in seculars be the rule for the respect due to the Mass? Besides, if all priests said Mass with becoming reverence and gravity, seculars would feel the veneration due to so great a sacrifice, and would not complain of being obliged to spend half an hour in attending Mass. But because Masses are frequently so short, and so little calculated to excite devotion, seculars, after the example of priests, attend Mass with indevotion and with little faith; and when they find that it lasts longer than half an hour, they, on account of the bad habit that they have contracted, grow weary and begin to complain; and though they spend without tediousness several

[1] "Tolle, tolle, crucifige eum!"

hours at play, or in the street, to pass the time, they feel it tedious and fatiguing to spend half an hour in hearing Mass. Of this evil, priests are the cause. *To you, O priests, that despise My name, and have said: Wherein have we despised Thy name ? . . . In that you say: The table of the Lord is contemptible.*[1] The want of reverence with which many priests celebrate Mass is the cause that it is treated with contempt by others.

Poor priests! Having heard that a priest died after celebrating his first Mass, the Venerable Father John d'Avila said: "Oh what a terrible account shall he have to render to God for his first Mass!" But what should Father d'Avila say of priests who have for thirty or forty years said Mass with haste and irreverence, so as to scandalize all that were present at it? And how, I ask again, can such priests propitiate the Lord and obtain his graces, when by celebrating in such a manner they insult rather than honor him? " Since every sin," says Pope Julius, " is wiped out by the holy sacrifice, what would be offered to the Lord in atonement of sin if in offering the sacrifice sin is committed ?"[2] Miserable priests! and miserable the bishop who permits such priests to celebrate. For, as the Council of Trent prescribes, bishops are bound to prevent all irreverences in the celebration of Mass: " The holy synod decrees that the ordinary bishops of places shall take diligent care and be bound to prohibit irreverence, which can hardly be separated from impiety."[3] Mark

[1] " Ad vos, o Sacerdotes, qui despicitis nomen meum, et dixistis: In quo despeximus nomen tuum ? . . . In eo quod dicitis: Mensa Domini despecta est."—*Mal.* i. 6.

[2] " Cum omne crimen sacrificiis deleatur, quid pro delictorum expiatione Domino dabitur, quando in ipsa sacrificii oblatione erratur?"— *Cap. Cum omne, de Consecr.* dist. 2.

[3] " Decernit sancta synodus, ut Ordinarii locorum ea omnia prohibere sedulo curent ac teneantur, quæ irreverentia (quæ ab impietate vix sejuncta esse potest) induxit."—*Sess.* 22, *Decr. de obs. in M.*

the words, *shall take diligent care and be bound;* they are bound to suspend the priest who celebrates without due reverence. And this they are obliged to do even with regard to regulars; for in this every bishop is constituted a delegate of the Apostolic See, and is therefore bound to seek for information regarding the manner in which Mass is celebrated in his diocese.

And let us, dearly beloved priests, endeavor to amend, if we have hitherto offered this great sacrifice with a want of reverence and devotion. Let us, at least from this day forward, repair the evil we have done. Let us, in preparing for Mass, reflect on the nature of the action that we are going to perform: in celebrating Mass we perform an action the most sublime and holy that man can perform. Ah, what blessings does a Mass, said with devotion, bring on him who offers it, and on those that hear it! With regard to the priest who offers it, the Disciple writes: "Prayer is more quickly heard when recited in the presence of a priest saying Mass."[1]* Now, if God hears more speedily the prayers which a secular offers in the presence of a priest celebrating Mass, how much more readily will he hear the prayers of the priest himself if he celebrates with devotion! He who offers the holy Mass every day with devotion shall always receive new lights and new strength from God. Jesus

---

[1] "Oratio citius exauditur in ecclesia in præsentia Sacerdotis celebrantis."

---

* Such is the citation given by our author, but here is what we read in the sermon mentioned as of John Herold, called The Disciple, speaking of the fruits of Mass granted to him that hears it: "Oratio tua citius exauditur in ecclesia in præsentia Dei, et etiam oratio Sacerdotis celebrantis; quia quilibet Sacerdos in qualibet Missa tenetur orare pro circumstantibus."—*De Sanctis*, s. 48. (Prayer, as well as the prayer of the priest celebrating, is more quickly heard in the church in the presence of God; because every priest is obliged at every Mass to pray for those that are present.)—ED.

Christ will always infuse increased knowledge and consolation; he will encourage him, and grant him the graces that he desires. A priest may feel assured, particularly after the consecration, that he shall receive from Jesus Christ all the graces he asks. The Venerable Father D. Anthony de Colellis, of the Congregation of the Pious Workers, used to say: "When I celebrate and hold Jesus Christ in my hands I obtain whatsoever I wish for." With regard to him who celebrates, and to those that hear Mass, it is related in the life of St. Peter of Alcantara that the Mass that he so devoutly celebrated produced more fruit than all the sermons preached in the province in which he lived. The Council of Rhodes commanded priests to show their faith and devotion towards Jesus Christ by pronouncing the words with piety, and performing the ceremonies with reverence and devotion towards Jesus Christ, who is present in the Mass.[1] The external deportment, says St. Bonaventure, is what shows the interior dispositions of the celebrant.[2] And here let us call to mind, in passing, the command of Innocent III.: "We also command that the oratories, vases, corporals, and vestments should be kept clean; for it seems to be absurd to neglect in so holy actions what would be unbecoming in profane actions."[3] O God! the Pontiff has too much reason to speak in this manner; for some priests have no repugnance to celebrate with corporals, purificators, and chalices which they could not bear to use at table.

[1] "Actio et pronuntiatio ostendat fidem et intentionem quam (Sacerdos) habere debet de Christi et Angelorum in Sacrificio præsentia."

[2] "Intrinsecos motus gestus exterior attestatur. —*Spec. disc.* p. 2, c. 1.

[3] "Præcipimus quoque ut oratoria, vasa, corporalia, et vestimenta, munda, et nitida conserventur; nimis enim videtur absurdum in sacris sordes negligere, quæ dedecerent etiam in profanis."—*Tit.* 44, *can.* 1, *Relinqui.*

IV.
Thanksgiving after Mass.

In the third place, after Mass thanksgiving is necessary. The thanksgiving should terminate only with the day. St. John Chrysostom says that for every trifling favor that they confer upon us men expect that we should show our gratitude by making some return. How much more grateful should we be to God, who expects no recompense for his gifts, but wishes us to thank him solely for our welfare![1] If, continues the saint, we are not able to thank the Lord as much as he deserves, let us at least thank him as much as we can. But what a misery to see so many priests who, after Mass, say a few short prayers in the sacristy, without attention or devotion, and then begin to speak on useless subjects or on worldly business, or perhaps leave the church immediately after Mass, and carry Jesus Christ into the street! They should be treated in the manner in which Father John d'Avila once acted toward a priest who left the church immediately after celebrating Mass. He sent two ecclesiastics with lighted torches to accompany him; when asked by the priest why they followed him, they answered: "We accompany the most Holy Sacrament which you carry in your breast." To such priests we may well apply the words of St. Bernard to the Archdeacon Fulcone: "How is it possible that you so quickly grow tired of Christ?"[2] O God! how can you become so soon weary of the company of Jesus Christ, who is within you?

So many books of devotion exhort thanksgiving after

---

[1] "Si homines parvum beneficium præstiterint, exspectant a nobis gratitudinem; quanto magis id nobis faciendum in iis quæ a Deo accepimus, qui hoc solum ob nostrum utilitatem vult fieri?"—*In Gen.* hom. 26.

[2] "Heu! quomodo Christum tam cito fastidis?"—*Epist.* 2.

Mass; but how many priests make it? It is easy to point to those who practise it. Some make mental prayer, recite many vocal prayers, but spend little or no time with Jesus Christ after Mass. They might at least continue in prayer as long as the consecrated species remain within their breast. Father John d'Avila used to say that we ought to set great value on the time after Mass; he ordinarily spent two hours in recollection with God after celebrating Mass.

After Communion the Lord dispenses his graces most abundantly. St. Teresa said that then Jesus Christ remains in the soul as on a throne of grace, and says to her: "What do you wish that I should do for you?"[1] Besides, it is necessary to know that, according to the opinion of Suarez,[2] Gonet,[3] and many other theologians, the more the soul disposes herself by good acts, while the consecrated species remain, the greater the fruit she derives from the holy Communion. For, as the Council of Florence[4] teaches, this sacrament has been instituted in the form of food, and therefore as the longer earthly food remains in the stomach the more nutriment it gives to the body so the longer this heavenly food continues in the body the more it nourishes the soul with grace, provided there be corresponding dispositions in the communicant. This increase of grace is the more confidently to be expected, because during that time every good act has greater value and merit; for the soul is then united with Jesus Christ, as he himself has said: *He that eateth My flesh, and drinketh My blood, abideth in Me, and I in him.*[5] And according to St. John Chrysos-

[1] "Quid vis ut tibi faciam?"
[2] *De Sacram. disp.* 63, sect. 7.
[3] *Man. Thom.* p. 3, tr. 4, c. 9.
[4] *Decr. ad Arm.*
[5] "Qui manducat meam carnem, et bibit meum sanguinem, in me manet, et ego in illo."—*John*, vi. 57.

tom, the soul is then made one thing with Jesus Christ.' Hence, good acts are then more meritorious, because they are performed by the soul while she is united with Jesus Christ.

But, on the other hand, St. Bernard tells us that the Lord will not lose his graces by giving them to the ungrateful.[2] Let us then remain, at least for half an hour, with Jesus Christ after Mass ; or at least for a quarter. But, O God! a quarter of an hour is too little. We should remember that from the day of his ordination the priest belongs no longer to himself, but to God, says St. Ambrose.[3] And before him God himself said the same: *They offer the burnt-offering of the Lord, and the bread of their God, and therefore they shall be holy.*'

V.

The Priest who Abstains from saying Mass.

Some abstain through humility from the celebration of Mass. A word on this subject. To abstain from saying Mass through humility is a good act, but it is not the most perfect: acts of humility give God a finite honor, but the Mass gives him infinite honor, because this honor is offered by a divine person. Attend to the words of Venerable Bede. "A priest who without an important reason omits to say Mass robs the Blessed Trinity of glory, the angels of joy, sinners of pardon, the just of divine assistance, the souls in purgatory of refreshment, the Church of a benefit, and himself of a medicine."[5] St. Cajetan, while in Naples, heard that a

---

[1] " Ipsa re nos suum efficit corpus."—*Ad pop. Ant.* hom. 60.

[2] "Numquid non perit, quod donatur ingrato?"—*In Cant.* s. 51.

[3] "Verus minister altaris, Deo, non sibi, natus est."—*In Ps.* 118, s. 8.

[4] " Incensum enim Domini et panes Dei sui offerunt, et ideo sancti erunt."—*Lev.* xxi. 6.

[5] " Cum Sacerdos, non habens legitimum impedimentum, celebrare omittit, quantum in se est, privat Trinitatem gloria, Angelos lætitia,

Cardinal in Rome, a particular friend, who was accustomed to say Mass every day, had begun to omit it on account of his occupations. The saint resolved to go, and actually went to Rome, in the burning heat of summer, at the risk of his life, in order to persuade his friend to resume his former custom.

The Venerable John d'Avila, as we read in his life, going one day to say Mass in a hermitage, felt himself so feeble that he began to despair of being able to reach the place, which was at a distance, and intended to omit Mass; but Jesus Christ appeared to him in the form of a pilgrim, uncovered his breast, showed him his wounds, and particularly the wound in his side, and said to him. "When I was wounded, I felt more fatigued and feeble than you are." He then disappeared: Father d'Avila took courage, went to the oratory, and celebrated Mass

peccatores venia, justos subsidio, in purgatorio existentes refrigeria Ecclesiam beneficio, et seipsum medicina."—*De Præp. ad M.* c. 5.

INSTRUCTION II.

THE GOOD EXAMPLE THAT THE PRIEST SHOULD GIVE.

JESUS CHRIST has instituted two orders in his church: one, of the simple faithful; the other, of ecclesiastics: but with this difference, that the former are disciples and sheep, the latter are masters and shepherds. To the laity St. Paul says: *Obey your prelates, and be subject to them. For they watch as being to render an account of your souls.*[1] And to ecclesiastics St. Peter has said: *Feed the flock of God which is among you.*[2] And in another place we read: *Take heed to yourselves, and to the whole flock wherein the Holy Ghost hath placed you bishops, to rule the church of God.*[3]

Hence St. Augustine has well said, that "there is nothing more difficult, nothing more dangerous, than the office of priest."[4] The difficulty and danger of the office of a priest arise precisely from his obligation to lead a holy life, not only by interior, but also by exterior sanctity, that others may learn from him, holiness of life. "If the one that is over thee is good, he will be thy nurse; if bad, he will be thy tempter," writes the same saint.[5] The Scripture says that in Jerusalem the people lived in holiness *because of the godliness of Onias the high-*

---

[1] "Obedite præpositis vestris, et subjacete eis; ipsi enim pervigilant, quasi rationem pro animabus vestris reddituri."—*Heb.* xiii. 17.

[2] "Pascite, qui in vobis est, gregem Dei."—1 *Pet.* v. 2.

[3] "Attendite vobis et universo gregi, in quo vos Spiritus Sanctus posuit episcopus, regere Ecclesiam Dei."—*Acts,* xx. 28.

[4] *Epist.* 21, E. B.

[5] "Bonus si fuerit, qui tibi præest, nutritor tuus est; malus si fuerit, tentator tuus est."—*Serm.* 12, E. B.

*priest.*¹ And according to the Council of Trent, "The integrity of those who govern is the safety of the governed."² But, on the other hand, how great the havoc, how strong the temptations, caused by the bad example of a priest! *My people*, says the Lord, by the mouth of the prophet Jeremias, *have been a lost flock; their shepherds have caused them to go astray.*³ "God," writes St. Gregory, "suffers from no one more than from priests whom he has appointed for the salvation of others, and whom he sees giving bad example."⁴ St. Bernard says "that seculars, seeing the sinful life of the priest, think no more of amending their conduct, but begin to despise the sacraments, and the rewards and punishments of the next life." "Very many," writes the holy Doctor, "beholding the wicked life of an ecclesiastic, indulge in vices, despise the sacraments, feel no horror of hell, nor the smallest desire of heavenly things."⁵ For, like the man of whom St. Augustine writes, they say: "Why do you correct me? Do not ecclesiastics do what I do? And do you compel me to abstain from it?"⁶ Our Lord said to St. Bridget: "At the sight of the bad example of the priest the sinner assumes confidence in sinning, and begins to boast of sins which he before regarded as shameful."⁷ "Priests in the Church," says St. Gregory,

¹ "Propter Oniæ pontificis pietatem."—2 *Mach*. iii. 1.
² "Integritas præsidentium salus est subditorum."—*Sess.* 6, *de Ref.* c. 1.
³ "Grex perditus factus est populus meus; pastores eorum seduxerunt eos."—*Jer*. l. 6.
⁴ "Nullum majus præjudicium, quam a Sacerdotibus, tolerat Deus, quando eos, quos ad aliorum correctionem posuit, dare de se exempla pravitatis cernit."—*In Evang*. hom. 17.
⁵ "Plurimi, considerantes cleri sceleratam vitam, Sacramenta despiciunt, vitia non evitant, non horrent inferos, cœlestia minime concupiscunt."—T. I. s. 19, a. 2, c. 1.
⁶ "Quid mihi loqueris? Ipsi clerici non illud faciunt, et me cogis ut faciam?"—*Serm*. 137, *E. B.*
⁷ "Viso exemplo pravo Sacerdotum, peccator fiduciam peccandi su-

"are the foundations of the Church."[1] When the foundations give way the whole edifice falls. Hence, in the ordination of priests, the holy Church prays for them in the following words: "May they shine before others by showing an example of justice, constancy, mercy, and other virtues."[2] Priests ought not only to be holy, but they should also show forth sanctity in their lives: for, says St. Augustine, as a good conscience is necessary for a priest to save his own soul, so he requires a good reputation in order to save his neighbor; otherwise, though he might be merciful and attentive to himself, he would be cruel towards others, and thus should bring himself and them to perdition.[3] God has selected priests from among men, not only that they may offer sacrifices, but also that by the good odor of their virtues they may edify the rest of the Church. *He chose him out of all men living, to offer sacrifice to God, incense, and a good savor.*[4]

Priests are the salt of the earth.[5] "Then," says the Gloss, "priests should give a savor to others, and render them grateful to God, instructing them in the practice of virtue, not only by preaching, but still more by the example of a holy life."[6]

Priests are also the light of the world.[7] The priest, then, as our divine Master proceeds to say, should shine refulgent among the people by the splendor of his

---

mit, et incipit de peccato, quod prius putabat erubescibile, gloriari."—*Rev.* l. 4, c. 132.

[1] "Sacerdotes in Ecclesia, bases in templo."—*In Evang.* hom. 17.

[2] "Justitiam, constantiam, misericordiam, fortitudinem, cæterasque virtutes, in se ostendant; exemplo præeant."

[3] "Conscientia tibi, fama proximo tuo; qui, fidens conscientiæ tuæ, negligit famam suam, crudelis est."—*Serm.* 355, *E. B.*

[4] "Ipsum elegit ab omni vivente, offerre sacrificium Deo, incensum, et bonum odorem."—*Ecclus.* xlv. 20.

[5] "Vos estis sal terræ."—*Matt.* v. 14.

[6] "Condientes alios doctrina et vitæ exemplo."

[7] "Vos estis lux mundi."—*Matt.* v 13.

virtues, and thus give glory to that God who has conferred on him an honor so singular and sublime. *So*, said the Redeemer, *let your light shine before men, that they may see your good works, and glorify your Father who is in heaven.*[1] Of this obligation St. John Chrysostom reminds priests. "Therefore," says the saint, "has God chosen us that we may be luminaries."[2] Pope Nicholas has written the same, saying that priests are the stars that enlighten the people on every side.[3] "They are," said the Pontiff, according to the words of Daniel, *they that instruct many to justice shall shine as stars for all eternity*, "stars shedding light on their neighbors, far and wide."[4] But, to be a luminary, it is not enough for the priest to enlighten by his words: he must also give light by his good example. "For the life of a priest," as St. Charles Borromeo used to say, "is precisely the beacon on which seculars, navigating in the midst of the ocean and darkness of the world, keep their eyes fixed in order to escape destruction." And before him St. John Chrysostom said: "The priest ought to lead a life of order, that all may look to him as to an excellent model; for God has chosen us, that we might be, as it were, luminaries and teachers to others."[5] The life of the priest is the light that is placed on the candlestick to give light to all. *Neither do men light a candle and put it under a bushel, but on a candlestick, that it may shine to all that are in the*

---

[1] "Sic luceat lux vestra coram hominibus, ut videant opera vestra bona, et glorificent Patrem vestrum, qui in cœlis est."—*Matt.* v. 16.

[2] "Idcirco nos elegit, ut simus quasi luminaria."—*In* 1 *Tim.* hom. 10.

[3] "Stellæ longe lateque proximos illuminantes."—*Ep. ad Syned. Silvan.*

[4] "Fulgebunt . . . qui ad justitiam erudiunt multos, quasi stellæ in perpetuas æternitates."—*Dan.* xii. 3.

[5] "Sacerdos debet vitam habere compositam, ut omnes in illum veluti in exemplar excellens intueantur; idcirco enim Deus nos elegit, ut simus quasi luminaria et magistri cæterorum."—*In* 1 *Tim.* hom. 10.

house.¹ Hence the Council of Bordeaux said: "The life of clerics is so exposed to the eyes of all, that all will be inspired by them to lead either a good or a bad life."² The priest, then, is the light of the world; but if the light be changed into darkness, what must become of the world?

Priests are also, as St. Jerome calls them, the fathers of Christians.³ "If then," adds St. John Chrysostom, "priests are the fathers of all, it is their duty to attend to all their spiritual children, edifying them first by a holy life, and afterwards by salutary instructions."⁴ If he give bad example, his spiritual children will imitate him. "What," says Peter de Blois, "will a layman do but what he has seen done by his spiritual father?"⁵

Priests are also the teachers and models of virtue. Our Saviour said to his disciples: *As the Father hath sent Me, I also send you.*⁶ As the eternal Father, then, sent Jesus Christ into the world to be a model for imitation, so Jesus Christ has placed priests in the world to be patterns of all virtues. This the very words *sacerdos* and *presbyter* signify. *Sacerdos*, says Peter de Blois, "means one that gives what is holy, for he gives what is holy of God, that is the sacrament; he gives what is holy for God, that is a good example."⁷ Another author

---

¹ " Neque accendunt lucernam, et ponunt eam sub modio, sed super candelabrum, ut luceat omnibus qui in domo sunt."

² " Clerici vita omnium oculis sic exposita est, ut inde bene vel male vivendi exempla duci soleant."—*Anno* 1583, c. 21.

³ " Patres christianorum."

⁴ " Quasi totius orbis pater Sacerdos est; dignum igitur est ut omnium curam agat."—*In* I *Tim.* hom. 6.

⁵ " Quid faciet laicus, nisi quod patrem suum spiritualem viderit facientem?"—*Serm.* 57.

⁶ " Sicut misit me Pater, et ego mitto vos."—*John*, xx. 21.

⁷ " Sacerdos dicitur quasi sacrum dans: dat enim sacrum de Deo, id est, prædicationem; sacrum Deo, orationem; sacrum Dei, carnem et sanguinem; sacrum pro Deo, vivendi exemplum."—*Serm.* 38.

says that the word *presbyter* signifies "one who shows to the people (by word and example) the way from exile to the kingdom of heaven."[1] This, the Apostle has taught: *In all things show thyself an example, . . . that he who is on the contrary part may be afraid, having no evil to say of us.*[2] St. Peter Damian says that the Lord has separated priests from the laity that they may observe a rule of life different from that which the people follow.[3] And from this rule seculars learn to lead a life of virtue. Hence St. Peter Chrysologus calls the priest "the form of virtues."[4] And, addressing a priest, St. John Chrysostom has said: "Let the splendor of your life be the common school and model of virtues."[5] This, as St. Bernard writes, the sacerdotal ministry itself demands.[6] In order to see the people sanctified, David prayed to the Lord in the following words: *Let Thy priests be clothed with justice, and let Thy saints rejoice.*[7] To be clothed with justice, the priest must give an example of every virtue, of zeal, of humility, of charity, of modesty, etc. In a word, St. Paul says, that we priests should, by holiness of life, show ourselves to be true ministers of the God of holiness. *But in all things let us exhibit ourselves as the ministers of God, . . . in chastity, in knowledge, in long-suffering,* etc.[8] And before him Jesus Christ taught the same: *If*

[1] "Presbyter. dicitur præbens iter, scilicet populo, de exsilio hujus mundi ad patriam cœlestis regni."—*Gemma an.* l. 1, c. 181.

[2] "In omnibus teipsum præbe exemplum, . . . ut is qui ex adverso est, vereatur, nihil habens malum dicere de nobis."—*Tit.* ii. 8.

[3] "Ut quid enim a populo (Sacerdotes) segregantur, nisi ut divisam a populo vivendi regulam teneant?"—*Opusc.* 18, d. 2, c. 2.

[4] "Forma virtutem."—*Serm.* 26.

[5] "Sit communis omnibus schola exemplarque virtutum vitæ tuæ splendor."—*In Tit.* hom. 4.

[6] "Cathedram sanctitatis exigit ministerium hoc."

[7] "Sacerdotes tui induantur justitiam, et sancti tui exsultent."—*Ps.* cxxxi. 9.

[8] "In omnibus exhibeamus nosmetipsos sicut Dei ministros, . . . in castitate, in scientia, in longanimitate . . ."—*2 Cor.* vi. 4.

any man minister to Me, let him follow Me.[1] Hence priests should copy in their life the example of Jesus Christ, so that, as St. Ambrose says, they may give such edification that every one that beholds them may bear testimony to their sanctity, and venerate that God who has such ministers.[2] Hence Minutius Felix writes, that we priests should make ourselves known as priests, not by splendor of dress nor by ornaments of the head, but by modesty and innocence of life.[3] Priests are placed in the world to wash away the stains of others. Hence, says St. Gregory, they must be holy, and appear holy.[4]

The priest is the leader of the people[5] says St. Peter Damian. But, according to St Denis, no one should dare to become a guide to others in what relates to God, unless he himself be made in all things like to God.[6] And Philip the Abbot said: "The life of ecclesiastics is the form of the laity; the former should go before as leaders, and the latter follow as flocks."[7] St. Augustine calls priests, the rulers of the earth.[8] "He, then, who is placed over others for their correction must be irreprehensible," says Pope Hormisdas.[9] And

---

[1] "Si quis mihi ministrat, me sequatur."—*John*, xii. 26.

[2] "Docet actuum nostrorum testem esse publicam existimationem, ut, qui videt ministrum congruis ornatum virtutibus Dominum veneretur, qui tales servulos habeat."—*De Offic.* l. 1, c. 50.

[3] "Nos, non notaculo corporis, sed innocentiæ ac modestiæ signo facile dignoscimus."—*Octav.* c. 9.

[4] "Necesse est ut esse munda studeat manus, quæ diluere aliorum sordes curat."—*Past.* p. 2, c. 2.

[5] "Sacerdos, dux exercitus Domini."—*Opusc.* 25, c. 2.

[6] "In divino omni non audendum aliis ducem fieri, nisi secundum omnem habitum suum factus sit deiformissimus et Deo simillimus."—*De Eccl. Hier.* c. 3.—*S. Thomas, Suppl.* q. 36, a. 1.

[7] "Vita clericorum forma est laicorum, ut illi tamquam duces progrediantur, isti vero tamquam greges sequantur."—*De Dignit. cler.* c. 2.

[8] "Rectores terræ."

[9] "Irreprehensibiles esse convenit, quos præesse necesse est corrigendis."—*Ep. ad Episc. Hispan.*

according to the Council of Pisa, "as ecclesiastics enjoy an exalted dignity, so they ought to shine with the light of virtues, and profess a kind of life which may excite others to sanctity."[1] For, as St. Leo has written, "The integrity of those that preside is the salvation of the subjects."[2]

St. Gregory of Nyssa calls the priest a teacher of sanctity.[3] But if the master exhibit pride, how can he teach humility? If he be vindictive, how can he inculcate meekness? "He," says St. Isidore, "who is appointed to instruct the people must be holy in all things."[4] And if our Lord has said to all: *Be you therefore perfect, as also your heavenly Father is perfect,*[5] how much more, says Salvian, will he demand perfection from priests, who are to teach all the people?[6] How can he inflame others with the love of God unless he shows by his works that his own heart burns with that holy fire? "He," says Gregory, "who does not burn, does not inflame?"[7] and St. Bernard writes, that to him who loves not, the language of love is a strange and barbarous tongue.[8] Hence St. Gregory says that the priest who does not give good example will bring con-

---

[1] "Ecclesiastici, quemadmodum eminent gradu, sic lumine virtutum prælucere debent, et profiteri genus vivendi, quod alios excitet ad sanctitatem."

[2] "Integritas præsidentium salus est subditorum."—*Ep. ad Episc. Afr.* c. 1.

[3] "Doctor pietatis."—*In Baptism. Chr.*

[4] "Qui in erudiendis atque instituendis ad virtutem populis præerit, necesse est ut in omnibus sanctus sit."—*De Off. Eccl.* l. 2, c. 5.

[5] "Estote ergo vos perfecti, sicut et Pater vester cœlestis perfectus est."—*Matt.* v. 48.

[6] "Si viris in plebe positis tam perfectam Deus vivendi regulam dedit, quanto esse illos perfectiores jubet, a quibus omnes docendi sunt ut possint esse perfecti!"—*Ad Eccl. Cathol.* l. 2.

[7] "Lucerna quæ non ardet, non accendit."—*In Ezech.* hom. 11.

[8] "Lingua amoris, ei qui non amat, barbara est."—*In Cant.* s. 79.

tempt on his preaching,¹ and on all his spiritual functions, says St. Thomas.² The Council of Trent ordains that they only are to be admitted to the priesthood who are "conspicuous for piety and chasteness of morals, as that a shining example of good works and a lesson how to live may be expected from them."³ But observe, that good example should be first expected, and afterwards salutary instructions; the Council calls good example a perpetual kind of preaching.⁴ Priests, then, should preach, first by example, and afterwards by words. "Their life," says St. Augustine, "must be a sermon of salvation to others."⁵ And St. John Chrysostom writes: "Good example gives forth a louder sound than trumpets, . . . for people pay more attention to our deeds than to our words."⁶ Hence St. Jerome said to Nepotianus: "Let not works confound your preaching, lest when you speak in the church every one should tacitly answer, Why, then, do you yourself not practise what you preach?"⁷ St. Bernard has written: "You will give power to your voice when people see that you have previously taken the advice yourself before you have given it to others; for action is more

---

¹ "Cujus vita despicitur, restat ut ejus prædicatio contemnatur."—*In Evang.* hom. 12.
² "Et eadem ratione, omnia spiritualia exhibita."—*Suppl.* q. 36, a. 4.
³ "Ita pietate ac castis moribus conspicui, ut præclarum bonorum operum exemplum et vitæ monita ab eis possint expectari."—*Sess.* 23, *de Ref.* c. 14.
⁴ "Est perpetuum prædicandi genus."
⁵ "Quorum vita aliorum debet esse salutis prædicatio."—*Serm.* 291, E. B. *app*.
⁶ "Bona exempla voces edunt omni tuba clariores."—*In Matt.* hom. 15.
⁷ "Non confundant opera tua sermonem tuum, ne, cum in ecclesia loqueris, tacitus quilibet respondeat: Cur ergo hæc, quæ dicis, ipse non facis?"—*Ep. ad Nepotian.*

powerful than speaking."[1] To persuade others, the preacher must show that he himself is convinced of the truth of his doctrine; but how can he evince such a conviction when his conduct is in opposition to his preaching? "He," says the author of the *Imperfect Work*, "who neglects to practise what he teaches, teaches not others, but condemns himself."[2] The sermon, says St. Gregory, which is commended by the life of the preacher persuades and moves.[3] Men believe the eyes sooner than the ears, that is, they are convinced more easily by the examples that they see than by the words that they hear. "Since," says an ancient Council, "men believe the eyes rather than the ears, it is necessary for a priest to give good example, as well in dress as in all his actions."[4]

— Priests are, as the Council of Trent says, the mirrors of the world, in which all look at themselves, and from which they take examples for the regulation of their life: "Others fix their eyes upon them as upon a mirror, and derive from them what they are to imitate."[5] And long before the holy Council, St. Gregory said the same: "The priest should shine before others by good example, for the people see in him, as in a mirror, what they must do, what they must avoid."[6] And the Apostle writes: *We*

[1] "Dabis voci tuæ vocem virtutis, si, quod suades, prius tibi illud cognosceris persuasisse. Validior operis quam oris vox."—*In Cant.* s. 59.

[2] "Qui non facit quod docet, non alium docet, sed semetipsum condemnat."—*Hom.* 10.

[3] "Illa vox libentius auditorum corda penetrat, quam dicentis vita commendat."—*Past.* p. 2, c. 3.

[4] "Quoniam magis oculis quam auribus credunt homines, necesse est ut Sacerdos bonum præbeat exemplum, tam in vestitu quam in reliquis actionibus."

[5] "In eos tamquam in speculum reliqui oculos conjiciunt, ex iisque sumunt quod imitentur."—*Sess.* 22, *de Ref.* c. 1.

[6] "Decet Sacerdotem moribus clarescere, quatenus in eo, tamquam in vitæ suæ speculo, plebs, et eligere quod sequatur, et videre possit quod corrigat."—*Epist.* l. 7, ind. 1, ep. 32.

are made a spectacle to the world, and to angels, and to men.[1]
Everything belonging to the priest demands sanctity.
" The clerical dress," says St. Jerome, " the state of life,
require of him sanctity of life."[2] According to St. Eucherius, priests bear the weight of the whole world, that
is, they are bound by their obligations to save all souls.
But how are they to save them? By the power of their
sanctity and holy example.[3] Hence the Council of Valen-
tia said: " By the gravity of his dress, by his looks and
words, the priest should show that he is a model of discipline and modesty."[4] The priest should then, in the
first place, exhibit gravity in his dress: but can priests
give an example of modesty, if, instead of wearing the
clerical costume, they display vanity and extravagance
in their apparel? Secondly, the priest should exhibit
gravity in his countenance: in order to set an example
of modesty, he must keep his eyes cast down, not only
when he is on the altar and in the church, but also in
all places in which there are women. Thirdly, to exhibit gravity in his words, he must carefully abstain
from uttering certain worldly maxims, and certain jests
that are contrary to modesty. The Fourth Council of
Carthage ordained that the ecclesiastic who indulges in
immodest jests should be suspended from his office.[5]
But you may ask, What harm is there in such jests ?
" Words," says St. Bernard, that are jests among seculars are in the mouth of a priest blasphemies which

---

[1] " Spectaculum facti sumus mundo, et Angelis et hominibus."—1 *Cor.* iv. 9.

[2] " Clamat vestis clericalis, clamat status professi animi sanctitatem."

[3] " Hi onus totius orbis portant humeris sanctitatis."—*Hom. de Dedic. eccl.*

[4] " Sacerdos de religione sua, in habitus, vultus, ac sermonis gravitate, talem se exhibere studeat, ut se formam disciplinæ ac modestiæ infundat."—*Anno* 855, can. 15.

[5] " Clericus verbis turpibus jocularis ab officio removendus."—*Cap.* 60.

excite horror.¹ The saint adds: "You have dedicated your mouth to the Gospel; but to open it for such things is not allowed: to accustomed one's self to doing so would be a sacrilege."² St. Jerome writes: "All that does not edify the hearers is dangerous to those that say it."³ Some things that are trifling in seculars are criminal in a priest; for every bad example by which he leads others into sin is in him a grievous transgression. "What is for the people only a venial sin," says Peter de Blois, "is criminal in the priest, because every fault of the shepherd becomes mortal by the scandal that accompanies it."⁴

St. Gregory Nazianzen writes: "Spots on a garment are more visible, the more beautiful the garment."⁵ In a splendid garment stains are most conspicuous, and produce great deformity.

It is also necessary for the priest to abstain from every species of detraction. St. Jerome says that some renounce other vices, but they appear to think it impossible to give up the sin of detraction.⁶ It is also necessary to avoid familiar intercourse with seculars. The conversations of seculars breathe an infectious air, which, as St. Basil says, gradually destroys the health of the soul.⁷ Finally, the priest must abstain from certain secular amusements, at which the presence of an

¹ "Inter sæculares, nugæ sunt; in ore Sacerdotis, blasphemiæ."
² "Consecrasti os tuum Evangelio; talibus aperire, illicitum; assuescere, sacrilegum."—*De Cons.* l. 2, c. 13.
³ "Omne quod non ædificat, in periculum vertitur loquentium."
⁴ "Quod veniale est plebi, criminale est Sacerdoti. Quod erroneum est ovi, peremptorium est pastori."—*Ad Past. in syn.* s. 3.
⁵ "Splendidæ vestis manifestiores sunt maculæ."—*Orat.* 31.
⁶ "Qui ab aliis vitiis recesserunt, in istud tamen, quasi in extremum diaboli laqueum, incidunt."—*Ep. ad Celant.*
⁷ "Sicut in pestilentibus locis sensim attractus aer morbum injicit, sic in prava conversatione mala hauriuntur, etiamsi statim incommodum non sentiatur."—*Hom. Quod D. non sit auct. mal.*

ecclesiastic does not give edification, such as profane comedies, balls and parties where women are present. But, on the other hand, the priest ought to be seen at prayer in the church, making thanksgiving after Mass, and visiting the Blessed Sacrament, and the images of the divine mother. Some perform these devotions in private, lest they might be seen by others; but it is better for priests to perform them in public, not to seek praise, but to give good example, and thereby induce others to praise God. *That they may see your good works, and glorify your Father who is in heaven.*[1]

[1] "Videant opera vestra bona, et glorificent Patrem vestrum, qui in cœlis est."—*Matt.* v. 16.

INSTRUCTION III.

THE CHASTITY OF THE PRIEST.

I.

The Merit of this Virtue, and its Necessity for the Priest.

No price is worthy of a continent soul.[1] In comparison with a chaste soul, all the riches, all the titles and dignities of the earth are contemptible. Chastity is called by St. Ephrem the life of the spirit;[2] by St. Peter Damian, the queen of virtues;[3] and by St. Cyprian, the acquisition of triumphs.[4] He who conquers the vice opposed to chastity, easily subdues all other vices; and, on the other hand, the man who submits to the tyranny of impurity, easily falls into many other vices, into hatred, injustice, sacrilege, etc.

Chastity, says St. Ephrem, changes a man into an angel.[5] St. Bernard says, "Chastity makes an angel of man."[6] And according to St. Ambrose, "he who has preserved chastity is an angel: he who has lost it is a devil."[7] The chaste, who live at a distance from all carnal pleasures, are justly assimilated to the angels: *They shall be as the angels of God in heaven.*[8] The angels are pure by nature, but the chaste are pure by virtue.

---

[1] "Omnis autem ponderatio non est digna continentis animæ."—*Ecclus.* xxvi. 20.
[2] "Vita spiritus."
[3] "Regina virtutum."
[4] "Acquisitio triumphorum."
[5] "O castitas, quæ homines Angelis similes reddis!"—*De Castit.*
[6] "Castitas angelum de homine facit."—*De Mor. et Off. Ep.* c. 3.
[7] "Castitas angelos facit: qui eam servavit, angelus est; qui perdidit, diabolus."—*De Virg.* l. 1.
[8] "Et erunt sicut Angeli Dei."—*Matt.* xxii. 30.

"Through the merit of this virtue," says Cassian, "men are like unto angels."[1] And St. Bernard asserts that a chaste man differs from an angel only in felicity, not in virtue; and although the chastity of the angel is more blissful, that of man is stronger.[2] St. Basil adds, that chastity renders man like to God, who is a pure spirit.[3]

Chastity is not more excellent than it is necessary for the attainment of salvation. But for priests it is specially necessary. For the priests of the Old Law the Lord ordered so many white vestments and ornaments, and so many external purifications, as symbols of bodily purity, merely because they were to touch the sacred vessels, and because they were a figure of the priests of the New Law, who were to handle and to immolate the most sacred flesh of the Incarnate Word. Hence St. Ambrose has written: "If of the figure such chastity was asked, how much more will it be asked of the reality?"[4] On the other hand, God ordained that the priests who were habitually infected with eruptions on the skin, the symbols of impurity, should be cast off from the altar: *Neither shall he approach to minister to Him, . . . if he have a pearl in his eye, or a continual scab.*[5] "But

---

[1] "Hujus virtutis merito, homines Angelis æquantur."—*De Cœnob. Inst.* l. 6, c. 6.

[2] "Differunt quidem inter se Angelus et homo pudicus, sed felicitate, non virtute; sed, etsi illius castitas felicior, hujus tamen fortior esse cognoscitur."—*De Mor. et Off. Ep.* c. 3.*

[3] "Pudicitia hominem Deo simillimum facit."—*De Vera Virginit.*

[4] "Si in figura tanta observantia, quanta in veritate?"—*De Offic.* l. 1, c. 50.

[5] "Nec accedet ad ministerium ejus, . . . si albuginem habens in oculo, si jugem scabiem."—*Lev.* xxi. 18.

---

* St. John Chrysostom admirably develops this comparison between chaste souls and angels, as may be seen in the breviary, June 21, the 3d nocturn.—Ed.

this evil," says St. Gregory, "he has that is controlled by the concupiscence of the flesh."[1]

Even the pagans, as Plutarch writes, required purity in the priests of their false gods; because they thought that whatsoever related to the divine honor should be clean.[2] And of the Athenian priests Plato says, that for the more effectual preservation of chastity they lived apart from the rest of the people.[3] Hence St. Augustine exclaims: "O great misery among Christians! the pagans have become the teachers of the faithful."[4] Speaking of priests of the true God, Clement of Alexandria says that they only that lead a life of chastity are, or should be, called true priests.[5] "Let the priest be humble and pious," said St. Thomas of Villanova; "if he is not chaste, he is nothing."[6] Chastity is necessary for all, but principally for priests. "To all," says St. Augustine, "chastity is most necessary, but especially to the ministers of the altar."[7] Priests have to treat on the altar with the immaculate Lamb of God, who is called the *Lily of the valleys,*[8] *and feeds only among the lilies.*[9] Hence Jesus Christ would have no other mother than a virgin —no other guardian or precursor than a virgin. And St. Jerome says that Jesus loved John above the other

---

[1] "Jugem habet scabiem, cui carnis petulantia dominatur."—*Past.* p. I, c. II.

[2] "Diis omnia munda."

[3] "Ne contagione aliqua eorum castitas labefactetur."

[4] "O grandis christianorum miseria! ecce pagani doctores fid.lium facti sunt."—*Ad Fr. in er.* s. 37.

[5] "Soli qui puram agunt vitam, sunt Dei Sacerdotes."—*Strom.* l. 4.

[6] Sit humilis Sacerdos, sit devotus; si non est castus, nihil est."— *De D. Ang. conc.* 3.

[7] "Omnibus castitas pernecessaria est, sed maxime ministris Christi altaris."—*Serm.* 291, *E. B. app.*

[8] "Lilium convallium."

[9] "Qui pascitur inter lilia."—*Cant.* ii. 1-16.

disciples on account of the prerogative of chastity.[1] And Jesus intrusted his mother to John on account of his purity, as he consigns to the priest his Church and himself. Hence Origen says: "Above all should the priest who assists at the altar of God be girt about with chastity."[2] And according to St. John Chrysostom, a priest should have purity which would entitle him to stand among the angels.[3] Should none, then, but virgins be promoted to the priesthood? St. Bernard answers: "Long continuance in chastity is regarded as virginity."[4]

Hence the holy Church guards nothing with so much jealousy as the purity of her priests. How many councils and canons enforce it? "Let no one," says Innocent III., "be admitted to holy orders unless he be a virgin, or a man of approved chastity;"[5] and he ordained that "they who are in holy Orders, if they lead not a chaste life, are to be excluded from every dignity: *ab omni gradum dignitate.*[6] St. Gregory says: "No one should approach the ministry of the altar unless his chastity has been proved."[7] St. Paul assigns the reason why the ministers of the altar are obliged to lead a life of celibacy: *He that is without a wife is solicitous for the things that belong to the Lord, how he may please God; but*

[1] "Præ cæteris discipulis diligebat Jesus Joannem, propter prærogativam castitatis."

[2] "Ante omnia, Sacerdos, qui divinis assistit altaribus, castitate debet accingi."—*In Lev.* hom. 4.

[3] "Necesse est Sacerdotem sic esse purum, ut, si in ipsis cœlis esset collocatus, inter cœlestes illas Virtutes medius staret."—*De Sacerd.* l. 3.

[4] "Longa castitas pro virginitate reputatur."—*De Modo b. viv.* c. 22.

[5] "Nemo ad sacrum Ordinem permittatur accedere, nisi aut virgo aut probatæ castitatis exsistat."

[6] "Eos qui in sacris Ordinibus sunt positi, si caste non vixerint, excludendos ab omni graduum dignitate."—*Cap. A multis, de æt. et quol. Ord.*

[7] "Nullus debet ad ministerium altaris accedere, nisi cujus castitas ante susceptum ministerium fuerit approbata."—*Epist.* l. 1, ep. 42.

he that is with a wife, is solicitous for the things of the world, how he may please his wife.[1] He who is free from the conjugal bonds belongs entirely to God; for he has to think of nothing but of pleasing God. But he who is bound to the married state has to think of his wife, of his children, and of the world. Thus his heart is divided, and cannot belong wholly to God. St. Athanasius, then, had reason to call chastity the house of the Holy Ghost, the life of angels, and the crown of saints.[2] And St. Jerome has justly called it the honor of the Church and the glory of priests.[3] Yes: for, as St. Ignatius, Martyr, says, the priest as the house of God, the temple of Jesus Christ, and the organ of the Holy Ghost, by which souls are sanctified, ought to practise chastity.[4]

II.

Means of Preserving Chastity.

Great, then, is the excellence of chastity; but terrible indeed is the war that the flesh wages against men in order to rob them of that precious virtue. The flesh is the most powerful weapon that the devil employs in order to make us his slaves. *His strength is in his loins.*[5] Hence but few gain the victory in this warfare. "Among all combats," says St. Augustine, "the combat for chastity is the most violent, because it is a daily combat, and

---

[1] "Qui sine uxore est, sollicitus est quæ Domini sunt, quomodo placeat Deo; qui autem cum uxore est, sollicitus est quæ sunt mundi, quomodo placeat uxori, et divisus est."—1 *Cor.* vii. 32.

[2] "O pudicitia, domicilium Spiritus Sancti, Angelorum vita, Sanctorum corona!"—*De Virginit.*

[3] "Ornamentum Ecclesiæ Dei, corona illustrior Sacerdotum."

[4] "Teipsum castum custodi, ut domum Dei, templum Christi, organum Spiritus Sancti."—*Ep. ad Heron.*

[5] "Fortitudo ejus in lumbis ejus."—*Job*, xl. 11.

because victory is very rare."[1] How many miserable men, exclaims St. Laurence Justinian with tears, after many years spent in the solitude of a desert, in meditations, fasting, and penitential austerities, have, for the sake of sensual indulgence, left the desert and have lost chastity and God?[2] Priests, then, who are bound to perpetual chastity, must take great care to preserve it. You shall never practise chastity, said St. Charles Borromeo to an ecclesiastic, unless you are careful to watch over yourself with great diligence; for chastity is easily lost by the negligent.[3]

This care and attention consist in taking the means of preserving chastity. These means are, to avoid certain incentives to impurity, and to adopt certain remedies against temptations.

1. Flight of the Occasion.

The first means is to avoid the occasions of sins against purity. "We must," says St. Jerome, "be far from those whose presence may entice us to evil."[4] St. Philip Neri used to say that in this warfare cowards, that is, they that fly from the occasions, are victorious. "Concupiscence," says Peter de Blois, "is overcome by nothing more easily than by flight."[5]

The grace of God is a great treasure, but this treasure we carry in vessels that are frail and easily broken. *We have this treasure in earthen vessels.*[6] Man cannot of

[1] "Inter omnia certamina, sola durio,a sunt prælia castitatis, ubi quotidiana est pugna, et rara victoria."—*Serm.* 293, *E. B. app.*

[2] "Quanti, post frequentes orationes, diutissimam eremi habitationem, cibi potusque parcitatem, seducti spiritu fornicationis, deserta relinquentes, duplici interitu, perierunt!"—*De spir. an. Int.* l. 1.

[3] "Mirum est quam facile ab iis deperdatur, qui ad ejus conservationem non invigilant."

[4] "Primum hujus vitii remedium est longe fieri ab eis quorum præsentia alliciat ad malum."

[5] "Nunquam luxuria facilius vincitur, quam fugiendo."—*Serm.* 45.

[6] "Habemus autem thesaurum istum in vasis fictilibus."—2 *Cor.* iv. 7.

himself acquire the virtue of chastity: God alone can give it. *I knew*, said Solomon, *that I could not otherwise be continent except God gave it.*[1] We have not strength to practise any virtue, but particularly the virtue of chastity; for we have by nature a strong propensity to the opposite vice. The divine aid alone can enable a man to preserve chastity; but this aid God gives not to those that voluntarily expose themselves to the occasion of sin, or remain in it. *He that loveth danger shall perish in it.*[2]

Hence St. Augustine gives the following advice: "To repel the attacks of lust, take flight if you wish to obtain the victory."[3] Oh! how many, said St. Jerome at the hour of death to his disciples (as we read in the epistle of Eusebius to Pope Damasus), how many have been cast into the putrid mire of impurity through a presumptuous security that they should not fall.[4] No one, then, adds the saint, should consider himself secure against this vice: though you were a saint, you are always in danger of failing.[5]

It is not possible, says the Wise Man, for a man to walk on red-hot coals and not be burned. *Can a man walk upon hot coals, and his feet not be burnt?*[6] On this subject St. John Chrysostom writes: "Are you perhaps of stone or of iron? no, you are a man subject to the common weakness of nature. Do you think that you will not be burnt if you take fire into your hand? How

---

[1] "Scivi quoniam aliter non possem esse continens, nisi Deus det.' — *Wisd.* viii. 21.

[2] "Qui amat periculum, in illo peribit."—*Ecclus.* iii. 27.

[3] "Contra libidinis impetum, apprehende fugam, si vis obtinere victoriam."—*Serm.* 293, E. B. *app.*

[4] "Plurimi sanctissimi ceciderunt hoc vitio propter suam securitatem; nullus in hoc confidat."

[5] "Si sanctus es, nec tamen securus es."—*Euseb. Ep. ad Dam. de morte Hier.*

[6] "Numquid potest homo ... ambulare super prunas, ut non comburantur plantæ ejus?"—*Prov.* vi. 27.

else could this be? Put a burning light into the hay, and then say that there will be no blaze! Like hay is this nature of ours."[1] Hence it is not possible for a man to expose himself voluntarily to the occasions of sins against chastity and not fall into a precipice. We should fly from sin as from the face of a serpent. *Flee from sin as from the face of a serpent.*[2] We fly not only from the bite of a serpent, but also from contact with it and proximity to it. We must also avoid the company and conversation of persons who may be to us an occasion of yielding to any sin against purity. St. Ambrose remarks that the chaste Joseph would not stop to hear the first words of Putiphar's wife, but instantly fled away, considering that there was great danger in waiting to listen to her.[3] But some one may say: I know my duty; but let him attend to the words of St. Francis of Assisi: "I know what I ought to do, but I know not what I would do were I to remain in the occasion of sin."

— I. Let us examine the principal occasions that the priest should carefully avoid in order to preserve chastity. It is necessary, above all things, to abstain from looking at dangerous objects. *Death is come up through our windows*,[4] says the Prophet Jeremias. *Through the windows*: that is, through the eyes, as St. Jerome, St. Gregory, and others say in their comments on this passage. For as to defend a fortification it is not enough to lock the gates if the enemy be allowed to enter by the windows; so to preserve chastity all other

---

[1] "Num tu saxeus es, num ferreus? Homo es, communi naturæ imbecillitati obnoxius; ignem capis, nec ureris? Lucernam in feno pone, ac tum aude negare quod fenum uratur. Quod fenum est, hoc natura nostra est."—*In Ps.* 50, hom. 1.

[2] "Quasi a facie colubri, fuge peccata."—*Eccles.* xxi. 2.

[3] "Ne ipsa quidem verba diu passus est; contagium enim judicavit, si diutius moraretur."—*De S. Jos.* c. 5.

[4] "Ascendit mors per fenestras."—*Jer.* ix. 21.

means shall be unprofitable unless we carefully watch over the eyes. Tertullian[1] relates that a certain pagan philosopher plucked out his eyes in order to preserve chastity. This is not lawful for us. But if we wish to avoid sins against purity we must abstain from looking at women, and still more from looking at them a second time. To look at dangerous objects, says St. Francis de Sales, is not so hurtful to us as to repeat the look. And St. John Chrysostom adds, that it is necessary to turn away the eyes not only from women whose dress or manner is immodest, but even from those whose demeanor is full of modesty.[2] Hence holy Job made a compact with his eyes not to look at any woman, even at a chaste virgin; because he knew from looks evil thoughts arise: *I made a covenant with my eyes that I would not so much as think upon a virgin.*[3] Ecclesiasticus advises us to imitate the example of Job. *Gaze not upon a maiden, lest her beauty be a stumbling-block to thee.*[4] St. Augustine says: From looks spring evil thoughts; the thoughts produce a certain carnal delectation, though indeliberate. To this indeliberate delectation succeeds the consent of the will;[5] and, behold, the soul is lost. Cardinal Hugo remarks that the Apostle commanded women to keep their heads veiled in the church *because of the angels*,[6] that is, because of priests, lest looking at their faces they should be tempted to lust.[7] Even while

[1] *Apolog.* c. 46.
[2] "Animus feritur et commovetur, non impudicæ tantum intuitu, sed etiam pudicæ."—*De Sacerd.* l. 6.
[3] "Pepigi fœdus cum oculis meis, ut ne cogitarem quidem de virgine."—*Job*, xxxi. 1.
[4] "Virginem ne conspicias, ne forte scandalizeris in decore illius."—*Ecclus.* ix. 5.
[5] "Visum sequitur cogitatio, cogitationem delectatio, delectationem consensus."
[6] "Propter Angelos."
[7] "'Propter Angelos,' id est, Sacerdotes, ne, in ejus faciem inspicientes, moverentur ad libidinem."—*In* 1 *Cor.* xi. 10.

he lived in a cave at Bethlehem, in constant prayer and penitential austerities, St. Jerome was tormented by the remembrance of the ladies whom he had long before seen in Rome. Hence he cautioned his friend Nepotianus to abstain not only from looking at women, but from even speaking of their figure.[1] By a single look of curiosity at Bethsebee, David miserably fell into the sins of adultery, homicide, and scandal. "The devil only wishes us to begin,"[2] says the same St. Jerome. The devil only requires that we begin to open the door; he will afterwards open it entirely. A deliberate, fixed look at the countenance of a young woman may be an infernal spark that will cause the ruin of the soul. Speaking of priests, St. Jerome says that they ought to avoid not only every unchaste act, but every glance of the eye.[3]

II. If to preserve chastity we must abstain from looking at women, it is far more necessary to avoid conversation with them. *Tarry not among women*,[4] says the Holy Ghost. The inspired writer subjoins the reason, saying, that as the moth comes from clothes, so the wickedness of men has its origin in conversation with women. *For from garments cometh a moth, and from a woman the iniquity of a man.*[5] And, says Cornelius à Lapide, as the moth comes from a garment in spite of the owner, so from intercourse with women evil desires spring up, even when we will them not.[6] He adds that

[1] "Officii tui est, non solum oculos castos custodire, sed et linguam; numquam de formis mulierum disputes."—*Ep. ad Nepot.*
[2] "Nostris tantum initiis (diabolus) opus habet."
[3] "Pudicitia sacerdotalis non solum ab opere se immundo abstineat, sed etiam a jactu oculi sit libera."—*In Tit.* 1.
[4] "In medio mulierum noli commorari."—*Eccles.* xlii. 12.
[5] "De vestimentis enim procedit tinea, et a muliere iniquitas viri."—*Ibid.*
[6] "Sicut tibi nihil tale volenti nascitur in veste et e veste tinea, ita nihil tale volenti nascitur ex femina desiderium."

as the moth is insensibly generated in and corrodes the garment, so by conversation with women concupiscence is imperceptibly excited, even in men who are spiritual.[1] St. Augustine regards as certain the sudden fall of the man who will not avoid familiarity with dangerous objects.[2] St. Gregory relates[3] of Orsinus, who had separated from his wife, and become a priest with her consent, that forty years after their separation, when he was dying, she put her ear to his mouth to ascertain whether he was still alive; but Orsinus exclaimed: "Withdraw, O woman," said he; "take away the straw; for I have still a small portion of the fire of life which may consume us both."[4]

Every one should be filled with terror by the unhappy example of Solomon, who after being so dear to God, and so familiar with him, after being made, as it were, the pen of the Holy Ghost, was in his old age, by conversation with pagan women, induced to worship idols. *And when he was now old, his heart was turned away by women to follow strange gods.*[5] No wonder; for, as St. Cyprian says, it is impossible to stand in the midst of flames without being burned.[6] And St. Bernard has written, that to be familiar with a woman and to preserve chastity require greater virtue than to raise a dead man to life.[7] If, then, says the Holy Ghost, you

[1] "Tinea insensibiliter in veste nascitur, et eam erodit; sic insensibiliter ex conversatione cum muliere oritur libido, etiam inter religiosos."

[2] "Sine ulla dubitatione, qui familiaritatem non vult vitare suspectam, cito labitur in ruinam."—*Serm.* 293, *E. B. app.*

[3] *Dial.* l. 4, c. 11.

[4] "Recede mulier, adhuc igniculus vivit, paleam tolle."

[5] "Cumque jam esset senex, depravatum est cor ejus per mulieres, ut sequeretur deos alienos."—3 *Kings*, xi. 4.

[6] "Impossibile est flammis circumdari, et non ardere."—*De Singular. Cler.*

[7] "Cum femina semper esse, et non cognoscere feminam, nonne plus est quam mortuum suscitare?"—*In Cant.* s. 65.

wish to be secure, *Remove thy way far from her.*[1] Do not even pass near the door of her whom the devil makes an occasion of temptation to you: pass at a distance from it; and should it be really necessary for you to speak to a woman, your words, says St. Augustine, should be few and reserved.[2] St. Cyprian gives the same advice. He says that our intercourse with women should be passing, and as if we were in flight.[3]

But some one may say, The woman with whom I am familiar is a person of deformed figure; God forbid she should be an occasion of sin to me. But St. Cyprian answers that the devil is a painter who, when concupiscence is excited, makes a deformed countenance appear beautiful.[4]

But she is a relative. St. Jerome answers: "Allow not to stay with you even the person that is your relative."[5] Relationship sometimes serves to take away restraint and to multiply sins by adding the guilt of incest to impurity and sacrilege. "The sin will be only the more criminal," says St. Cyprian, "the more easily one can remove the suspicion of misconduct."[6] St. Charles Borromeo[7] passed a decree that his priests should not without his permission dwell in the same house with women, even with near relatives.

But she is a spiritual soul and a saint: there is no danger. Is there no danger? Yes, says St. Augustine,

---

[1] "Longe fac ab ea viam tuam, et ne appropinques foribus domus ejus."—*Prov.* v. 8.

[2] "Cum feminis, sermo brevis et rigidus."

[3] "Transeunter feminis exhibenda est accessio, quodammodo fugitiva."—*De Singular. cler.*

[4] "Diabolus, pingens, speciosus efficit quidquid horridum fuerit."

[5] "Prohibe tecum morari, etiam quæ de genere tuo sunt."—*Ep. ad Ocean.*

[6] "Magis illicito delinquitur ubi sine suspicione securum potest esse delictum."

[7] *Acta Mediol.* p. 2, syn. 4, *Monit.*

there is danger; and because she is spiritual and a saint you ought the more to fear and fly familiarity with her; for the more spiritual and holy a woman is, the more easily she gains the affections of men.[1] The Venerable Father Sertorius Caputo used to say, as we read in his life, that the devil endeavors first to infuse a love for the virtue of the individual, and thus inspire a security that there is no danger; he then excites sentiments of affection for the person, and afterwards tempts to sin; and thus he causes great havoc. Before him St. Thomas said the same: "Although carnal affection is dangerous to all, it is yet more so for those that associate with persons that seem to be spiritual; for, even though the beginning seems pure, yet frequent familiarity is very dangerous; and the more the familiarity increases, the more the first motive is weakened, and thus purity is defiled."[2] He adds, that the devil knows well how to conceal the danger. In the beginning he sends, not poisoned darts, but only those that inflict slight wounds, and kindle an affection; but in a short time the persons begin to act towards each other not like angels, as in the beginning, but like beings clothed with flesh. The looks are not immodest, but they are frequent and reciprocal; their words appear to be spiritual, but are too affectionate. Each begins frequently to desire the company of the other. "And thus," concludes the saint, "a spiritual devotion is converted into a carnal one."

[1] "Sermo brevis et rigidus cum mulieribus est habendus; nec tamen, quia sanctiores fuerint, ideo minus cavendæ; quo enim sanctiores fuerint, eo magis alliciunt."—*De Modo confit.*

[2] "Licet carnalis affectio sit omnibus periculosa, etiam tamen perniciosa est magis, quando conversantur cum persona quæ spiritualis videtur; nam, quamvis eorum principium videatur esse purum, frequens tamen familiaritas domesticum est periculum; quæ quidem familiaritas quanto plus crescit, tanto plus infirmatur principale motivum, et puritas maculatur."

[3] "Sicque spiritualis devotio convertitur in carnalem."—*De Profectu Rel.* l. 2, c. 27.

St. Bonaventure gives five marks by which we may know when a spiritual affection has become carnal. 1. When there are long and useless conversations (and when they are long they are always useless); 2. When there are mutual looks and mutual praise; 3. When one excuses the faults of the other; 4. When they exhibit certain little jealousies; 5. When the absence of one causes a certain inquietude in the other.

Let us tremble: we are flesh. Blessed Jordan severely reproved one of his religious for having, without any bad motive, once taken a woman by the hand. The religious said in answer that she was a saint. But, replied the holy man: "The rain is good, and the earth also, but mix them together and they become mire." Such a man is a saint, and such a woman, too, is a saint; but because they expose themselves to the occasion of sin, both are lost. *The strong hath stumbled against the strong, and both are fallen together.*[1] Listen to the melancholy fall of a holy woman who, as we read in ecclesiastical history, was accustomed through charity to bury the bodies of the holy martyrs. She found one of them whom she believed to be dead; but finding he was still alive, she brought him to her house and took care of him. He recovered; but what happened? These two saints, by conversing together, lost their chastity and the grace of God.

This has happened, not once, nor a few times: how many Christians, who were saints before, have, by similar attachments, which were at first spiritual, in the end lost their soul and God? St. Augustine attests that he knew some great prelates of the Church of whom he had as high an opinion as of St. Jerome and St. Ambrose, and who, by exposing themselves to such occasions, fell

---

[1] "Fortis impegit in fortem, et ambo pariter conciderunt."—*Jer.* xlvi. 12.

away from sanctity into sin.¹ St. Jerome wrote to Nepotianus: "Do not confide too much in your past chastity; be careful not to sit alone with a woman without a witness,"² that is, do not remain with her. St. Isidore of Pelusium says: "If necessity obliges you to converse with women, keep your eyes cast on the ground; and after you have spoken a few words, go away immediately."³ Father Peter Consolini of the Oratory used to say, that we should practise charity towards women who are even saints as towards the souls in purgatory, that is, from a distance, and without looking at them. This good Father would say, that in temptations against chastity priests would do well to reflect on their dignity; and would add that a certain Cardinal, when molested by thoughts, began to look at his cap, and to think of his cardinalitial dignity, saying: "My cap, I recommend myself to you." Thus he resisted the temptation.

III. It is also necessary to fly from bad company. St. Jerome says that a man becomes like the companions with whom he converses.⁴ We walk in a dark and slippery way;⁵ such is the present life ; *Lubricum in tenebris :* if a wicked companion impels us to the precipice, we are lost. St. Bernardine of Sienna relates⁶ that he knew a person who had preserved her virginity for thirty-

¹ "Magnos prælatos Ecclesiæ sub hac specie cornisse reperi, de quorum casu non magis præsumebam, quam Hieronymi et Ambrosii." —*S. Thomas, De modo confit.*

² "Ne in præterita castitate confidas; solus cum sola, absque teste, non sedeas."

³ "Si cum ipsis conversari necessitas te obstringat, oculos humi dejectos habe; cumque pauca locutus fueris, statim avola."—*Lib.* 2, *ep.* 284.

⁴ "Talis efficitur homo, qualium societate fruitur."—*Eusebius, De Morte Hier.*

⁵ "Lubricum in tenebris."

⁶ *T. III. Serm. extr.* s. 13, n. 6.

eight years, and afterwards, in consequence of having heard an immodest word, fell into such habits of impurity, that, says the saint, the devil himself, if clothed with flesh, could not have been guilty of such filthy abominations.

IV. To preserve chastity, it is also necessary to avoid idleness. *Idleness*, says the Holy Ghost, *hath taught much evil*.[1] Ezechiel says that it was the cause of all the wickedness of the inhabitants of Sodom, and of their total destruction. *Behold! this was the iniquity of Sodom . . . the idleness of her and of her daughters*.[2] This was, as St. Bernard remarks, the cause of the fall of Solomon. The concupiscence of the flesh is repressed by labor, says St. Isidore.[3] Hence St. Jerome exhorted Rusticus to be always occupied, so that the devil, whenever he came to tempt him, should find him employed.[4] According to St. Bonaventure, the man who is employed shall be tempted by a single devil, but the idle shall be frequently assailed by many devils.[5]

2. MORTIFICATION.

We have seen, then, that for the preservation of chastity it is necessary to avoid idleness and the occasions of impurity. Let us now examine what we must do in order to preserve this great virtue.

First, it is necessary to practise the mortification of the senses. If, says St. Jerome, any one wishes to live in the midst of earthly delights, and expects at the same time to be free from the vices that accompany pleasures,

[1] "Multam enim malitiam docuit otiositas."—*Ecclus.* xxxiii. 29.
[2] " Hæc fuit iniquitas Sodomæ . . . otium ipsius."—*Ezech.* xvi 49.
[3] "Cedet libido laboribus, cedet operi."—*De Cont. m. de Lab.*
[4] " Facito aliquid operis, ut te semper diabolus inveniat occupatum." —*Ep. ad Rustic.*
[5] "Occupatus ab uno dæmone impugnatur; otiosus ab innumeris vastatur."—*De Prof. rel.* 1. 1. c. 39.

he deceives himself.[1] When the Apostle was molested with the stings of the flesh he had recourse to bodily mortifications. *I, said he, chastise my body and bring it into subjection.*[2] Unless the flesh be mortified, it will submit to the spirit only with difficulty. *As the lily among the thorns, so is My love among the daughters.*[3] As the lily is preserved among thorns, so chastity is guarded by mortifications.

But for him who wishes to practise this sublime virtue, it is, above all, necessary to avoid intemperance as well in drinking as in eating.

Give not, says the wise man, *wine to kings.*[4] He who takes more wine than is necessary, shall certainly be molested with many carnal motions, and shall scarcely be able to rule the flesh and make it obedient to the law of chastity. "The body that is inflamed with wine will overflow with lust," says St. Jerome.[5] For as the prophet Osee has said, wine deprives man of reason, and reduces him to the level of a brute. *Wine and drunkenness take away the understanding.*[6] Of the Baptist it was foretold. *He shall drink no wine and strong drink, and he shall be filled with the Holy Ghost.*[7] Some will argue in favor of the necessity of wine, because it is a remedy for the weakness of the stomach. But, according to the words of St. Paul to Timothy, a small quantity of wine is suffi-

---

[1] "Si quis existimat posse versari in deliciis, et deliciarum vitiis non teneri, seipsum decipit."—*Adv. Jovin.* l. 2.

[2] "Castigo corpus meum, et in servitutem redigo."—1 *Cor.* ix. 27.

[3] "Sicut lilium inter spinas, sic amica mea inter filias."—*Cant.* ii. 2.

[4] "Noli regibus dare vinum."—*Prov.* xxxi. 4.

[5] "Venter enim mero æstuans despumat in libidinem."—*Reg. Monach. de Abst.*

[6] "Vinum et ebrietas auferunt cor."—*Os.* iv. 11.

[7] "Vinum et siceram non bibet, et Spiritu Sancto replebitur."—*Luke*, i. 15.

cient for that malady. *Use a little wine for thy stomach's sake, and thy frequent infirmities.*[1]

It is also necessary to abstain from superfluity of food. St. Jerome asserts[2] that satiety of the stomach provokes incontinence. And St. Bonaventure says: "Impurity is nourished by eating to excess."[3] But, on the other hand, fasting, as the holy Church teaches, represses vice and produces virtue: "O God, who by corporal fasting dost suppress vice, dost elevate the mind, and dost confer virtues and rewards."[4] St. Thomas has written that when the devil is conquered by those whom he tempts to gluttony, he ceases to tempt them to impurity.[5]

3. HUMILITY.

It is necessary to practise humility. Cassian says that he who is not humble cannot be chaste.[6] It happens, not unfrequently, that God chastises the proud by permitting them to fall into some sin against purity. This, as David himself confessed, was the cause of his fall. *Before I was humbled I offended.*[7] It is by humility that we obtain chastity, says St. Bernard.[8] And St Augustine writes: "Charity is the guardian of virginity, humility is the place of the guardian."[9] Divine love is the guardian of purity, but humility is the house in

[1] "Modico vino utere, propter stomachum tuum et frequentes tuas infirmitates."—1 *Tim.* v. 23.
[2] *Adv. Jovin.* l. 2.
[3] "Luxuria nutritur a ventris ingluvie."—*De Prof. rel.* l. 2, c. 52.
[4] "Deus qui, corporali jejunio, vitia comprimis, mentem elevas, virtutem largiris et præmia."
[5] "Diabolus, victus de gula, non tentat de libidine."
[6] "Castitatem apprehendi non posse, nisi prius humilitatis in corde fundamenta fuerint collocata."—*De Cænob. inst.* l. 6, c. 18.
[7] "Priusquam humiliarer, ego deliqui."—*Ps.* cxviii. 67.
[8] "Ut castitas detur, humilitas meretur."—*De Mor. et Off. Ep.* c. 5.
[9] "Custos virginitatis, charitas; locus hujus custodis, humilitas."—*De S. Virginit.* c. 51.

which this guardian dwells. St. John Climacus used to say, that he who expects to conquer the flesh by continence alone is like a man in the midst of the ocean who wishes to save his life by swimming with a single hand. Therefore it is necessary to unite humility to continence.[1]

4. PRAYER.

But above all, to acquire the virtue of chastity prayer is necessary: it is necessary to pray, and to pray continually. It has been already said that chastity can neither be acquired nor preserved unless God grant his aid to preserve it; but this aid he gives only to those who ask it. Hence the holy Fathers teach that, according to the words of Scripture: *We ought always to pray, and not to faint.*[2] *Ask, and it shall be given you.*[3] The prayer of *petition* is necessary for adults,—*necessitate medii*, —that is, as a means without which salvation is impossible. Hence the angelic Doctor has said: "After baptism, continual prayer is necessary to man."[4] And if to practise any virtue Christians require the divine assistance, they stand in need of still greater help in order to preserve chastity, because they have a strong tendency to the opposite vice. It is impossible, says Cassian, for man, by his own strength, without aid from God, to keep himself chaste; and therefore, in our struggle with the flesh, we must ask the Lord, with all the affection of our soul, for the gift of chastity.[5] "According to the

[1] "Qui sola continentia bellum hoc superare nititur, similis est ei qui, una manu natans, pelago liberari contendit; sit ergo humilitas continentiæ conjuncta."—*Scala spir.* gr. 15.
[2] "Oportet semper orare, et non deficere."—*Luke*, xviii. 1.
[3] "Petite, et dabitur vobis."—*Matt* vii. 7.
[4] "Post baptismum, necessaria est homini jugis oratio."—P. 3, q. 39. a. 5.
[5] "Impossibile est hominem suis pennis ad tam præcelsum cœlestem præmium subvolare, nisi eum gratia Domini de terræ cœna evexerit." —*De Cœnob. inst.* l. 6, c. 6.

advice of the Wise Man," says Abelly, "we should pray to God with our whole heart."[1] Hence St. Cyprian teaches that the first means of obtaining chastity is to ask it of God.[2] And before him Solomon said: *And as I knew that I could not otherwise be continent, except God gave it, and this also was a point of wisdom, to know whose gift it was: I went to the Lord, and besought Him, and said with my whole heart.*[3]

We should then, says St. Cyprian, instantly resist the first carnal solicitations with which the devil assails us, and not permit the serpent, that is, the temptation, to grow strong.[4] St. Jerome gives this same advice: "You must not permit bad thoughts to grow in your mind; no, kill the enemy when he is small."[5] It is easy to kill a lion when he is small, but not when he has grown to his full size.

Let us guard against reasoning with temptations contrary to chastity: let us endeavor instantly to banish them. And, as the spiritual masters teach, the best means of banishing such temptations is not to combat them directly face to face, by making contrary acts of the will, but to get rid of them indirectly by acts of the love of God, or of contrition, or at least by turning the mind to other things.

---

[1] "Idcirco, juxta Sapientis monitum (*Wisd.* viii 21) adeundus est Dominus, et ex totis præcordiis deprecandus."—*Sacerd. Chr.* p. 3, c. 14.

[2] "Inter hæc, imo et ante hæc omnia, de divinis castris auxilium petendum est."—*De Disc. et Bono pudic.*

[3] "Et ut scivi quoniam aliter non possem esse continens, nisi Deus det, et hoc ipsum erat sapientiæ, scire cujus esset hoc donum, adii Dominum, et deprecatus sum illum, et dixi ex totis præcordiis meis."—*Wisd.* viii, 21.

[4] "Primis diaboli titillationibus obviandum est, nec foveri debet coluber donec in draconem formetur."—*De Jej. et Tent. Chr.*

[5] "Nolo sinas cogitationem crescere; dum parvus est hostis, interfice."—*Ep. ad Eustoch.*

But the means in which we should place the greatest confidence is prayer, and recommending ourselves to God. It is useful, as soon as we perceive the first motion of impurity, to renew our purpose to suffer death rather than consent to sin, and immediately after to have recourse to the wounds of Jesus Christ for aid. Thus the saints, who were flesh, and subject to temptations, have acted, and thus they have conquered. "If I am tormented," says St. Augustine, " by any bad thought, I have recourse to the wounds of Jesus; for I find rest in the wounds of our Saviour."[1] Thus, also, St. Thomas of Aquinas repelled the attacks of the woman by whom his chastity was assailed: "Do not permit, O Lord Jesus and O most holy Virgin Mary, that I should offend God!" exclaimed the saint.[2]

It is also very useful to make the sign of the cross on the breast, and to have recourse to our angel guardian and our holy patron. But above all, it is useful to have recourse to Jesus Christ and the divine Mother by instantly invoking their most holy names, and by continuing to invoke them until the temptation is beaten down. Oh! how powerful are the most holy names of Jesus and Mary against the attacks of impurity!

Devotion to the holy Virgin, who is called " the Mother of fair love, and the guardian of virginity,"[3] is a most useful devotion for the preservation of chastity. And to recite, at rising in the morning and going to bed at night, three "Hail Marys," in honor of the purity of Mary, is a devotion that has singular efficacy in obtaining the gift of continence.

Father Segneri[4] relates that a sinner addicted to the

[1] "Cum me pulsat aliqua turpis cogitatio, recurro ad vulnera Christi. Tuta requies in vulneribus Salvatoris."—*Manual.* c. 22, 21.
[2] " Ne sinas, Domine Jesu, et Sanctissima Virgo Maria !"—*Surius*, 7 Mart.
[3] " Mater pulchræ dilectionis et Custos virginitatis."
[4] *Crist. istr.* p. 3, r. 34, § 2.

grossest impurities went one day to confession to Father Nicholas Zucchi, of the Society of Jesus. The Father prescribed as a remedy for his wicked habits that he should recommend himself, morning and evening, to the purity of Mary, by saying three " Hail Marys." After the lapse of several years the sinner returned to Father Zucchi, and by his confession showed that all his vices were perfectly corrected.' The Father asked him how such a change had been wrought. He answered that through the little devotion of saying the three " Hail Marys" he had obtained the grace to change his life.

Father Zucchi, with the permission of the penitent, mentioned the fact from the pulpit. There was a soldier present who was actually in the habit of sins of impurity; he began to say every day the three " Hail Marys," and in a short time, with the aid that the divine Mother obtained for him, he soon renounced the evil habit. Through a false zeal, he went one day to the accomplice of his sins in order to convert her; but when he was on the point of entering her house he was suddenly driven back, and found himself transported to a considerable distance. He then understood that he had been prevented from speaking to the woman by a special grace obtained for him by Mary, for which he thanked her. Had he been placed again in the occasion of sin he would probably have relapsed.*

---

* This double example is related with some other details in the *Glories of Mary*, p. 2, Disc. 4 (Vol. VII. page 379).

INSTRUCTION IV.

PREACHING, AND THE ADMINISTRATION OF THE SACRAMENT OF PENANCE.

IF all preachers and confessors fulfilled the obligations of their office the whole world would be sanctified. Bad preachers and bad confessors are the ruin of the world. By bad preachers and confessors I mean those that do not fulfil their duty as they ought.

We shall treat, first, of the preaching of the divine word, and afterwards of the administration of the sacrament of penance.

I.

Preaching.

By preaching, the faith has been propagated, and by the same means God wishes it to be preserved: *Faith cometh by hearing: and hearing by the word of Christ.*[1] But for a Christian, it is not enough to know what he is obliged to do; it is, moreover, necessary for him, by hearing the divine word from time to time, to be reminded of the importance of eternal salvation, and of the means which he ought to adopt in order to secure it. Hence the following command of St. Paul to Timothy: *Preach the word, be instant in season, out of season; reprove, entreat, rebuke in all patience and doctrine.*[2] And the same command God had long before given to the Prophets Isaias and Jeremias. To the former he said: *Cry, cease*

[1] " Fides ex auditu; auditus autem per verbum Christi."—*Rom.* x. 17.
[2] " Prædica verbum: insta opportune, importune; argue, obsecra, increpa, in omni patientia et doctrina."—2 *Tim.* iv. 2.

not to lift up thy voice like a trumpet, and show My people their wicked doings.[1] To the latter: *Behold, I have given My words in thy mouth: lo, I have set thee this day over the nations, and over kingdoms, to root up and to pull down, . . . to build and to plant.*[2] The same command he has also imposed on his priests; for preaching is one of their principal duties. *Going, therefore, teach ye all nations, . . . to observe all things whatsoever I have commanded you.*[3] And should a sinner be damned through the fault of him who preaches the divine word, God will demand an account of the priest who could have announced the truths of salvation to that lost soul. *If, when I say to the wicked thou shalt surely die, thou declare it not to him; . . . the same wicked man shall die in his iniquity, but I will require his blood at thy hand.*[4]

But, to save souls, it is not enough to preach: it is, as I have already said, necessary to preach in a proper manner. In the first place, in order to preach well learning and study are necessary. He who preaches at random will do more injury than service to religion. In the second place, an exemplary life is necessary. The sermons of the man whose conduct excites contempt shall be despised, says St. Gregory.[5] And St. John Chrysostom writes: "How is it possible for a priest to persuade by his words, when his acts are in opposition

---

[1] "Clama, ne cesses: quasi tuba, exalta vocem tuam, et annuntia populo meo scelera eorum."—*Is.* lviii. 1.

[2] "Ecce dedi verba mea in ore tuo; ecce constitui te hodie super gentes et super regna, ut evellas, et destinas, . . . et ædifices, et plantes."—*Jer.* i. 9.

[3] "Euntes ergo, docete omnes gentes . . . servare omnia quæcumque mandavi vobis."—*Matt.* xxviii. 19.

[4] "Si, dicente me ad impium: Morte morieris; non annuntiaveris ei, . . . ipse impius in iniquitate sua morietur, sanguinem autem ejus de manu tua requiram."—*Ezech.* iii. 18.

[5] "Cujus vita despicitur, restat ut ejus prædicatio contemnatur."—*In Evang.* hom. 12.

to his doctrine."¹ The preaching of such a man shall serve only for his condemnation; for according to St. Paul, he who reproves in others what he does himself, condemns himself: *Thou art inexcusable, O man, whosoever thou art that judgest. For wherein thou judgest another, thou condemnest thyself.*² Justly, then, did Father John d'Avila say to a person who asked what rule he should follow in order to preach well, that the best means of preaching well was to love Jesus Christ ardently. "He," says St. Gregory, "who is not on fire does not inflame."³ The divine love must first burn in the preacher, that he may afterwards kindle it in others. St. Francis de Sales used to say that the heart speaks to the heart.⁴ .He meant, that words alone speak to the ears, but do not enter the soul. He only who speaks from the heart, that is, he who feels and practises what he preaches, shall speak to the heart of others, and shall move them to the love of God. Hence, according to the words of the Redeemer, *that which ye hear in the ear, preach ye on the housetop.*⁵ The preacher must have an affection for mental prayer, in which he may excite the sentiments that he will afterwards communicate to others. Mental prayer is the blessed furnace in which sacred orators are inflamed with divine love. *In my meditation*, says David, *a fire shall flame out.*⁶ Here they form the fiery darts that afterwards wound the hearts of their hearers.

It is necessary to preach with a good intention, that is, not for temporal interest, but for the glory of God; not to attract empty praises, but to procure the salva-

---

¹ "Denegatis in opere, quod videmini profiteri in verbo."—*Hom.* 40.
² "Inexcusabilis es, o homo omnis qui judicas ! in quo enim judicas alterum, teipsum condemnas."—*Rom.* ii. 1.
³ "Lucerna quæ non ardet, non accendit."—*In Ezech.* hom. 11.
⁴ *De la Pred.* ch. 5, a. 1.
⁵ "Quod in aure auditis, prædicate super tecta."—*Matt.* x. 27.
⁶ "In meditatione mea exardescet ignis."—*Ps.* xxxviii. 4.

tion of souls. Hence, as the Council of Trent ordains, it is the duty of preachers to preach in a manner accommodated to the capacity of their hearers: "Archpriests shall, either personally or by others who are competent, feed the people committed to them."[1] Empty words and sounding periods are, says St. Francis de Sales the pest of sermons.[2] First, because God does not coöperate with vain preaching.) Secondly, because the persons who are present at sermons are generally rude and illiterate, and incapable of understanding flowery discourses.] What a pity, sometimes, to see so many of the poor going to the sermon, and afterwards leaving the church afflicted and wearied, without having understood almost any part of the discourse. Justly has Father John d'Avila said, that they who preach in a lofty style, not intelligible to the audience, are traitors to Jesus Christ; and that, though sent by him to procure his glory, they seek only their own exaltation. Justly, too, has Father Caspar Sanzio said, that such preachers are at the present day the greatest persecutors of the Church, because by their sermons they are the cause of the perdition of many souls that would be saved by exhortations composed in a simple and apostolic style. *My preaching*, says the Apostle, *was not in the persuasive words of human wisdom, but in showing of the spirit and power*.[3] In the lives of the saints who were employed in saving souls I find many praised for preaching in simple and popular language, but I have not found one eulogized for having preached in a labored and flowery style.

It will be useful to abridge, in this place, what the

---

[1] "Archipresbyteri, per se vel per alios idoneos, plebes sibi commissas, pro earum capacitate, pascent salutaribus verbis."—*Sess.* 5, de Ref. c. 2.

[2] *De la Predic.* ch. 5, a. 1.

[3] "Prædicatio mea non in persuasibilibus humanæ sapientiæ verbis, sed in ostensione spiritus et virtutis."—1 *Cor.* ii. 4.

learned and celebrated Muratori has written in his golden little treatise entitled *Popular Eloquence*.

There are, he says, two sorts of eloquence: the sublime, and the popular. The *sublime eloquence* directs us in the composition of discourses which treat of lofty subjects, contain ingenious reflections, select language, and turned periods. With the aid of the *popular eloquence* the eternal truths are expounded nakedly, subjects easily understood are explained in a simple and familiar style, so that each person present may understand the entire instruction. In sermons, we address not only the learned, but also the uninstructed, and these ordinarily form the greater part of the audience. Hence it is always expedient to preach in a simple, popular style, not only in the missions and spiritual exercises, but also in all sermons addressed to the people. In the sight of God, the souls of the learned and unlearned are equally precious; and, according to the words of the Apostle: *To the wise and to the unwise I am a debtor*.[1] The preacher is obliged to seek the sanctification of the latter as well as of the former. Besides, even to the learned, sermons composed in a simple and familiar style are more profitable than discourses written in lofty and florid language. For in sublime discourses the mind stops to admire and criticise (and this frequently happens); but the will is left without food, and derives no profit from the sermon. Father Paul Segneri, Junior, by preaching in a popular manner ravished (these are the words of Muratori) the hearts even of the learned. The same was the result of the sermons of St. John Francis Regis.

He who wishes to preach, not for the purpose of acquiring praise, but of gaining souls to God, should not seek to hear others say: Oh, what beautiful thoughts! What a splendid speaker! What a great man! But he

[1] "Sapientibus et insipientibus debitor sum."—*Rom.* i. 14.

should desire to see all going away with their heads bowed down, weeping over their sins, resolved to change their lives, and to give themselves to God. The end of true rhetoric is to persuade and move the audience to practise what is inculcated in the discourse. Even in popular eloquence, preachers avail themselves of the art of rhetoric, of figures, of the arrangement of the arguments, of the language, of the peroration. But all must be done simply and without show of art, in order to reap not applause, but fruit. If in such sermons the audience are not delighted by elegant language and ingenious reflections, they shall certainly be pleased to find themselves enlightened and moved to attend to what alone is important—their eternal salvation.

And what has been said is, according to Muratori, applicable to sermons preached in cities, where the audience consists of the ignorant and the learned; but he adds, that in addressing the common people or the inhabitants of the villages the preacher must adopt the most popular and lowest kind of eloquence, in order to accommodate his instruction to their weak understanding. He must imagine himself to be one of them, and that another is anxious to instruct him in some duty and to persuade him to fulfil it. Hence his language ought to be popular and common, the periods short and unconnected, imitating the very mode of reasoning that such persons usually adopt among themselves. In a word, the whole study of the preacher should be to make the audience understand all he says, and to move his hearers most effectually to do what he exhorts them to practise. And as the preacher should adopt a familiar style, so he should also select subjects easily understood; omitting scholastic points and ingenious interpretations of Scripture, which though intelligible will be unprofitable to the poor and illiterate. The great object should be to explain nakedly and simply the eternal truths, the importance of salvation, and to lay before the people the illusions of the devil, the dangers of perdition, and the means to be adopted in some particular cases that may occur. In this consists the breaking of bread to the little ones, which the Lord demands of preachers, and of the general neglect of which he complains: *The little ones have asked for bread, and there was none to break it unto them.*[1] In speaking to the uninstructed, it is also very useful to ask questions from time to time, and to reply to them. It is useful to bring forward examples of the saints, or examples of punishments inflicted on sinners. But above all, it is useful to inculcate things which are practical, and to repeat them several times, that they may remain impressed on the weak understanding of the poor.

Such the doctrine of Muratori, which I have here abridged in order to show that the sacred orators who preach in a high and florid style to the poor, who generally compose the audiences in our churches, receive even from the learned censure rather than praise.

This is enough on preaching the divine word. I hope hereafter, in treating of the exercises of the mission, to subjoin other reflections on the manner of preaching to be adopted in the missions, and on the method of arranging the sermons. Let us now pass to the administration of the sacrament of penance.

II.
The Administration of the Sacrament of Penance.
1. GRAVE RESPONSIBILITY OF CONFESSORS.

The great Pontiff, St. Pius V., said: "Give us fit confessors, and surely the whole of Christianity will be reformed."[2] He who wishes to be a good confessor must,

[1] "Parvuli petierunt panem, et non erat qui frangeret eis."—*Lam.* iv. 4.

[2] "Dentur idonei confessarii; ecce omnium Christianorum plena reformatio."

in the first place, consider that the office of a confessor is very difficult and dangerous, and that on account of its difficulty and danger the Council of Trent has called it an office to be dreaded even by angels.[1] And what, says St. Laurence Justinian, can be more perilous than to assume the responsibility of rendering to God an account of the life of others?[2] St. Gregory says that no error is more dangerous than that which is committed in the direction of souls.[3] It is certain that if a soul be lost through the fault of her confessor, God will demand of him an account of that soul: *I will require My flock at their hand.*[4] And the Apostle writes: *Obey your prelates, . . . for they watch, as being to render an account of your souls.*[5] Hence, according to St. Gregory, a confessor has to render to God an account of as many souls as he has penitents.[6] And St. John Chrysostom says: " If we already tremble having to render an account of our own sins, what awaits him who has to render an account of so many souls?"[7]

This is not applicable to those good priests who, penetrated with a holy fear, labor to qualify themselves for this great office, and afterwards devote themselves to the exercise of it, through the sole desire of bringing souls to God. It is intended only for those who undertake to hear confessions through worldly motives, or

---

[1] " Onus angelicis humeris formidandum."—*Sess.* 6, *de Ref.* c. 1.

[2] " Periculosa res est, pro peccatoribus se fidejussorem constituere." —*De Inst. Prael.* c. 6.

[3] " Nullibi periculosius erratur."

[4] " Requiram gregem meum de manu eorum."—*Ezech.* xxxiv. 10.

[5] " Obedite præpositis vestris, et subjacete eis; ipsi enim pervigilant. quasi rationem pro animabus vestris reddituri."—*Heb.* xiii. 17.

[6] " Quot regendis subditis præest, reddendæ apud eum rationis tempore, ut ita dicam, tot solus animas habet."—*Moral.* l. 24, c. 30.

[7] "Si horremus, dum peccatorum propriorum rationem reddituri sumus, quid illi expectandum est, qui tam multorum nomine causam sit dicturus?"—*De Sacerd.* l. 3.

temporal interest, or self-esteem, or, as sometimes happens, without the necessary learning.

2. THE KNOWLEDGE REQUIRED TO HEAR CONFESSIONS WELL.

St. Laurence Justinian says: "Many graces and not a little knowledge is needed by him who desires to raise souls to life."[1] He, then, who wishes to hear confessions, stands in need of extensive knowledge. Some imagine the science of Moral Theology to be easy, but Gerson justly says that it is the most difficult of all sciences. And before him St. Gregory said: "The directing of souls is the art of arts."[2] St. Gregory Nazianzen writes: "To direct men seems to me to be the greatest of all sciences."[3] St. Francis de Sales also used to say that the office of confessor is of all offices the most important and the most difficult. It is the most important, because on it depends the eternal salvation of souls, which is the end of all the sciences. It is the most difficult, because the science of Moral Theology requires a knowledge of many other sciences, and embraces an immense variety of matter. It is also most difficult, because different decisions must be given, according to the different circumstances of the cases that occur; for, a principle by which a case involving a certain circumstance may be decided will not answer for the solution of another case containing a different circumstance.

Some disdain to read the works of the moralists, saying that to hear confessions is enough to know the general principles of Moral Theology, by which, they add, the particular cases may be resolved. I answer: It is certain that all cases must be decided by means of principles, but there is great difficulty in applying to par-

---

[1] "Gratia indiget plurima, et sapientia non modica, qui proximorum animas ad vitam resuscitare conatur."—*De Compunct.* p. 2.
[2] "Ars est artium regimen animarum."—*Past.* p. 1, c. 1.
[3] "Scientia scientiarum mihi esse videtur hominem regere."—*Apol.* 1.

18

ticular cases just principles of solution. This the moralists have done. They have labored to explain the principles by which many particular cases may be resolved. Besides, at present there is a great number of positive laws contained in the bulls and decrees of Pontiffs, as well as in the ancient canons, and which a confessor is obliged to know. Of these laws he who neglects to read Moral Theology shall scarcely be able to acquire a competent knowledge. The learned author of *The Instruction for Young Confessors* justly says that many divines are as deficient in Moral Theology as they are profound in the speculative sciences. But, on the other hand, Monsignor Sperelli asserts that it is a great error in some confessors to devote all their time to scholastic theology, considering the study of Moral Theology as lost time. Such confessors, as he says, are afterwards unable to distinguish one sin from another. He then adds: "This is an error that will cause eternal ruin both to the confessor and to the penitents."[1]

We must, then, be persuaded that to hear confessions great science and also great prudence are required; for with knowledge without prudence a confessor shall do but little good, and to some his ministry will be more injurious than beneficial.

3. CHARITY AND FIRMNESS THAT THE CONFESSOR SHOULD HAVE.

Sanctity is still more necessary, on account of the great fortitude which a confessor requires in the exercise of his ministry. "Only he that is a great saint," says St. Laurence Justinian, "can without injury to himself occupy himself with the care of souls."[2]

I. A confessor requires a great fund of *charity* in re-

[1] "Qui error confessarios simul et pœnitentes in æternum interitum trahet."

[2] "Nemo, nisi valde sanctus, absque sui detrimento, proximorum curis occupatur."—*De Casto Conn.* c. 12.

ceiving all—the poor, the ignorant, and the vicious. Some hear the confessions only of pious persons; but when a poor peasant comes with a conscience loaded with sins, they hear him with impatience, and send' him away with reproaches. Hence the miserable man, who must have done great violence to himself in resolving to go to confession, seeing himself dismissed in such a manner, will conceive a horror for the sacrament, and a dread of approaching it any more, and thus, through despair, will abandon himself to a dissolute life. To such confessors the Redeemer (who came to save sinners, and was therefore full of charity) says what he said to his disciples: *You know not of what spirit you are.*[1] But such is not the conduct of confessors who, in obedience to the exhortation of the Apostle, put on the bowels of charity: *Put ye on, therefore, as the elect of God, . . . the bowels of mercy.*[2] When a sinner comes to confession, the more abandoned he is, the more they labor to assist him, and the greater the charity with which they treat him. You are not, says Hugo of St. Victor, appointed judges of crimes, to chastise, but, as it were, judges of maladies to heal."[3] It is indeed necessary to admonish the sinner, in order to make him understand his miserable state, and the danger of damnation to which he is exposed; but he must be always admonished with charity, he must be excited to confidence in the divine mercy, and must be taught the means by which he may amend his life. And though the confessor should be obliged to defer absolution, he ought to dismiss the penitent with sweetness; fixing a day for him to return, and pointing out the remedies that he must

---

[1] " Nescitis cujus spiritus estis."—*Luke*, ix. 55.
[2] " Induite vos ergo, sicut electi Dei, sancti et dilecti, viscera misericordiæ."—*Col.* iii. 12.
[3] " Vos non, quasi judices criminum, ad percutiendum positi estis, sed, quasi judices morborum, ad sanandum."—*Misc.* l. 1, tit. 49.

practise in the mean time, in order to prepare himself for absolution. Sinners are saved in this way, but not by harshness and reproaches, which drive them to despair. St. Francis de Sales used to say: "More flies are caught by a drop of honey than by a pound of aloes." But some will say, if we treat sinners in this manner a great deal of our time will be taken up, and others who are waiting cannot be heard. But in answer I say, that it is better to hear one confession well than to hear a great number imperfectly. But the most appropriate answer is, that the confessor has not to give an account to God of the persons who are waiting, but only of the person whose confession he has begun to hear.

II. The confessor also stands in need of great fortitude, and at first in hearing the confessions of women. How many priests have lost their souls in hearing these confessions! We must treat in the confessional with young girls and young women; we must hear their temptations and often the avowal of their falls; for they also are of flesh and blood. We have a natural affection for persons of the other sex, and this affection increases whenever they confide to us their miseries. But if these persons are pious, devoted to spirituality, says St. Thomas, the danger of an inordinate attachment is yet greater, since this natural affection is still more strongly attracted; but, continues the saint, if mutual affection increases, the attachment will also increase in the same proportion; it will assume at first the appearance of piety, and the devil will easily succeed in making "the spiritual devotion change into carnal devotion."[1]

Great fortitude is necessary in correcting penitents and in refusing absolution to those who have not the requisite dispositions, without any regard to their rank or power, or to the loss or injury which the confessor

---
[1] "Spiritualis devotio convertatur in carnalem."—*De Modo confit.*

may sustain, or to the imputations of indiscretion or of ignorance which may be cast upon him. *Seek not,* says the Holy Ghost, *to be made a judge unless thou hast strength enough to extirpate iniquities, lest thou fear the person of the powerful.*[1] A Father of our Congregation had occasion to hear in the sacristy the confession of a priest, whom he refused to absolve. The priest, rising up in a proud and haughty manner, said to him: "Begone! you are a brute." But there is no remedy: poor confessors must submit to such inconveniences and insults. For it often happens that they are bound to refuse or to defer absolution, either because the penitent will not do what they require of him, or because he is a relapsing sinner, or because he is in the proximate occasion of sin. And here it is necessary to examine how a confessor should treat relapsing sinners, and those who are in the occasion of sin. For, in order to save his penitents, the confessor should attend with the greatest care to relapsing sinners, and to those who are in the occasion of sin.

But, before we enter on this subject, it is necessary to remark, that a confessor exposes himself to as much danger of damnation by treating his penitents with too much rigor as he does by treating them with excessive indulgence.

Too much indulgence, says St. Bonaventure, begets presumption, and too much rigor leads to despair.[2] There is no doubt that many err by being too indulgent: and such persons cause great havoc—and I say even the greatest havoc; for libertines, who are the most numerous class, go in crowds to these lax confessors,

[1] "Noli quærere fieri judex, nisi valeas virtute irrumpere iniquitates, ne forte extimescas faciem potentis."—*Ecclus.* vii. 6.

[2] "Cavenda est conscientia nimis larga, et nimis stricta; nam prima generat præsumptionem, secunda desperationem. Prima sæpe salvat damnandum; secunda, e contra, damnat salvandum."—*Comp. theol.* l. 2, c. 52.

and find in them their own perdition. But it is also certain that confessors who are too rigid cause great evil. *You ruled over them with rigor, and with a high hand. And My sheep were scattered,*[1] etc. Too much rigor, says Gerson, serves only to bring souls to despair, and from despair to the abyss of vice.[2] Hence he says in another place: " The Doctors of theology should not, if they are not certain, be so ready to assert that certain sins are mortal sins."[3] Such also is the doctrine of St. Raymond. " Do not be so prone," says the saint, " to declare mortal sins, unless it be clear from Scripture."[4] St. Antonine teaches the same. " It is very dangerous," he says, " to decide whether or not something is mortal, if this be not clear from the authority of Scripture, of a canon, or of an evident reason."[5] For, as the saint adds, he who, without some of the above-mentioned grounds, pronounces an action to be a mortal sin, exposes souls to the danger of damnation.[6] Speaking of the vain ornaments of women the same holy archbishop says: " From what has been said it seems that we must conclude that if the confessor clearly and undoubtedly sees that one cannot use such an ornament without mortal sin, he cannot give absolution if the penitent does not take the resolu-

[1] " Cum austeritate imperabitis eis, et cum potentia; et dispersæ sunt oves meæ."—*Ezech.* xxxiv. 4.

[2] " Per tales assertiones nimis duras et strictas, præsertim in non certissimis, nequaquam eruuntur homines a luto peccatorum, sed in illud profundius, quia desperatius, immerguntur."

[3] " Doctores theologi ne sint faciles asserere actiones aliquas aut omissiones esse mortalia, præsertim in non certissimis."—*De Vita. sp. lect.* 4, *cor.* 11.

[4] " Non sis nimis pronus judicare mortalia peccata, ubi tibi non constat per certam Scripturam."—*Summ.* l. 3, *de Pœnit.* § 21.

[5] "Quæstio qua quæritur de aliquo actu utrum sit peccatum mortale vel non, nisi ad hoc habeatur auctoritas expressa Scripturæ sacræ, aut canonis, seu determinationis Ecclesiæ, vel evidens ratio, non nisi periculosissime determinatur."—P. 2, tit. 1, c. 11, § 28.

[6] " Ædificat ad gehennam."

tion to avoid such a sin. But if one does not clearly see whether this is a mortal sin, one must not hasten to a decision by either refusing absolution or by representing it to the penitent as a mortal sin. If the penitent should afterwards do the same thing, it would be for him a mortal sin, even if it were in itself no mortal sin; for everything that is against conscience exposes the soul to damnation. And since one should use his power rather to loosen than to bind, and it is better to have to give an account to the Lord for too great mercy than too great rigor, as St. John Chrysostom teaches, it seems to be better to absolve such penitents and to leave them to the divine judgment."[1] Silvester teaches the same doctrine; he says: "I say with St. Antonine, that one may with a good conscience choose an opinion and act according to it, if he has on his side notable teachers, and if it is not opposed to any decision of Scripture, of the Church, etc."[2] And this is also the opinion of John Nider, who, after giving the opinion of Doctor William, quotes the passage of Bernard of Clermont or of Gannat of Auvergne: "If among the masters of sacred

---

[1] "Ex prædictis igitur videtur dicendum quod, ubi in hujusmodi ornatibus confessor inveniat clare et indubitanter mortale, talem non absolvat, nisi proponat abstinere a tali crimine. Si vero non potest clare perspicere utrum sit mortale vel veniale, non videtur tunc præcipitanda sententia (ut dicit Gulielmus specie in quadam simili), ut scilicet deneget propter hoc absolutionem, vel illi faciat conscientiam de mortali; quia, faciendo postea contra illud, etiamsi illud non esset mortale, ei erit mortale, quia omne quod est contra conscientiam, ædificat ad gehennam. Et cum promptiora sint jura ad solvendum quam ad ligandum (*Can. Ponderet, dist.* 1), et melius sit Domino reddere rationem de nimia misericordia quam de nimia severitate, ut dicit Chrysostomus (*Can. Alligant*, 26, q. 7), potius videtur absolvendum et divino examini dimittendum."—P. 2, tit. 4, c. 5, § 8.

[2] "Dico, secundum Archiepiscopum, quod tuta conscientia potest quis eligere unam opinionem, et secundum eam operari, si habeat notabiles doctores, et non sit expresse contra determinationem Scripturæ vel Ecclesiæ, etc."—*Summa, verbo Scrupulus*, 5°.

science some say that there is a mortal sin and others deny that it is, then we must consult some learned and prudent persons in whom we have confidence, and after having taken their advice we must decide whether or not there is a sin. For the moment that the masters discuss among themselves and the Church has not given any decision, one may freely embrace that opinion in favor of which we can cite the testimony of wise and prudent persons."[1] And this is conformable to the teaching of St. Thomas: " He who adopts the opinion of a particular Doctor against a formal text of Scripture or against the universal sentiment of the Church, cannot be excused from culpable error."[2] Then, according to the angelic Doctor, a person is excused from error when the opinion that he holds rests on the foundation of authority, and is not opposed to any clear passage of Scripture or to any definition of the Church. Finally, the same doctrine has been laid down more clearly by Gabriel Biel, who flourished in the year 1480. " The opinion," he says, " that is more probable to me is, that we must never condemn as a mortal sin anything for which we cannot allege either a very evident reason or the formal testimony of Scripture."[3]

[1] "Concordat etiam Bernardus Claramontensis, dicens: Si sunt opiniones inter magnos dicentes quod peccatum est, alii vero dicunt quod non, tunc debet consulere aliquos, de quorum judicio confidit, et secundum consilium discretorum facere, et peccatum reputare vel non reputare; ex quo enim opiniones sunt inter magnos, et Ecclesia non determinavit alteram partem, teneat quam voluerit, dummodo judicium in hoc resideat propter dicta eorum saltem quos reputat peritos."—*Consol. tim. consc.* p. 3, c. 12.

[2] "Qui ergo assentit opinioni alicujus magistri, contra manifestum Scripturæ testimonium, sive contra id quod publice tenetur secundum Ecclesiæ auctoritatem, non potest ab erroris vitio excusari."—*Quodlib.* 3, a. 10.

[3] " Prima opinio videtur probabilior, quia nihil debet damnari tamquam mortale peccatum, de quo non habetur evidens ratio vel manifesta auctoritas Scripturæ."—*In* 4 *Sent.* d. 16, q. 4, *concl.* 5.

4. How to Act in Regard to Those Living in the Occasion of
Sin and Those Who Are Relapsing Sinners.

But let us come to particulars, and examine how a confessor ought to treat persons who are in the proximate occasion of sin, and habitual sinners who relapse into any vice. With regard to those who are in the occasion of sin, it is necessary first to distinguish various kinds of occasions.

I. The occasion may be *remote* or *proximate*. The remote occasion is that in which a person rarely sins or in which men, commonly speaking, seldom fall. The occasion that is itself[1] proximate is that in which men always, or nearly always, fall. The occasion that is proximate by accident,[2] or the respective occasion, is that in which a particular person frequently sins. This is the correct definition of the respective occasion, according to the true and common opinion of theologians, in opposition to those who hold that the proximate occasion is that in which a person always, or nearly always, yields to sin. The occasion of sin is also divided into *voluntary* and *necessary*. The occasion is voluntary when it can be removed; it is necessary when it cannot be avoided without grievous loss or grievous scandal to others.

Many theologians say that he who is in the voluntary proximate occasion may be absolved once or twice, provided he has a firm purpose of removing it as soon as possible. But here it is necessary to distinguish, with St. Charles Borromeo, in his *Instructions to Confessors*, occasions that are *in esse*,—such as when a person keeps a concubine in his house,—from those that are not *in esse*, such as when in gaming or conversation a person falls into blasphemies, quarrels, and the like.

In the occasions that are not *in esse*, St. Charles says

[1] "Per se."   [2] "Per accidens."

that the penitent who sincerely promises to renounce them may be absolved the second or third time, but unless he afterwards gives proof of amendment he should not be absolved until he has actually removed the occasion. In the occasions which are *in esse* the saint says that a promise is not sufficient, and that the penitent cannot be absolved until he has taken away the occasion of sin. Ordinarily speaking, this opinion should certainly be followed; as I have shown in my Moral Theology[1] by the authority of many authors. A penitent who wishes to receive absolution before the removal of such an occasion is not disposed for the sacrament; because he is in the proximate danger of violating his purpose as well as the obligation by which he is bound under pain of mortal sin to remove the occasion. To take away proximate occasions is very painful and difficult, and can be effected only by doing great violence to one's self. But he who has already received absolution will scarcely offer such violence to himself. Freed from the fear of being deprived of absolution, he will flatter himself with the hope of being able to resist temptations without taking away the occasion; and thus remaining in the occasion, he will certainly relapse. This we know by the experience of so many miserable sinners who, after receiving absolution from over-indulgent confessors, neglect to remove the occasion of sin: thus they fall back, and become worse than before. Hence, on account of the danger of violating the purpose that he has made of removing the occasion of sin, the penitent who wishes to be absolved before he takes it away is not disposed for absolution, and therefore the confessor who absolves him is certainly guilty of sin. And here let it be observed, that, generally speaking, the greater the rigor with which the confessor treats his penitents, when there is question of the danger of for-

[1] *Theol. Mor.* l. 6, n. 454.

mal sins, particularly against chastity, the more he will promote their sanctification. But, on the other hand, the greater his indulgence, the greater his cruelty to their souls. St. Thomas of Villanova says that confessors who are too indulgent are impiously merciful.[1] Such charity is contrary to charity.

I have said *ordinarily speaking*; for in some rare cases the confessor may absolve before the occasion is removed. For example, if the penitent had evinced a strong determination to amend his life, along with great compunction, and is unable to take away the occasion for a long time; or if he could not return to the same confessor; or if there should be other extraordinary circumstances which would oblige the confessor to absolve him. But such cases are very rare. Hence persons who are in the proximate occasion of sin can scarcely ever be absolved until they have first removed it; particularly if they promised at other times to take away the occasion, but did not afterwards fulfil their promise. It is useless to say that a penitent who is disposed for the sacrament has, after the confession of his sins, a strict right to receive absolution; for it is the common opinion of theologians that a person who has confessed his sins has not a strict right to be immediately absolved, and that the confessor can and should, as a spiritual physician, defer absolution whenever he knows that by deferring it he will promote the amendment of his penitent.

What has been said applies to voluntary occasions: but if the occasion be *necessary*, generally speaking there is not a strict obligation of removing it; for when the penitent does not wish, but rather suffers and permits it against his will, he may hope for greater help from God to resist the temptation. Hence, ordinarily speaking, he who is in a necessary occasion of sin may be

[1] "Impie pios."

absolved, provided he is determined to adopt all the means necessary to guard against a relapse. There are three principal means to be prescribed in necessary occasions. The first is to fly from the occasion and avoid as much as possible being alone with the accomplice, speaking confidentially with her, or looking at her. The second is prayer and unceasing petition to God and the Blessed Virgin for help to resist the temptation. The third is the frequentation of the sacraments of penance and of the Eucharist, by which strength is obtained to resist temptations.

I have said *generally speaking*; for when, after having used all the means the penitent always relapses, without any amendment, then, according to the more common and true opinion, which is to be followed, he cannot be absolved until he quits the occasion of sin, though it should cost him his life,[1] as the theologians say; for he should prefer eternal to temporal life. I add, that though, according to the rules of Moral Theology, a person who is in the necessary occasion of sin may be absolved whenever he is properly disposed for the sacrament, still, when the occasion leads to sins against purity, it will, ordinarily speaking, be expedient to defer absolution until it appears by the experience of a considerable time, of twenty or thirty days, that the penitent has been faithful in practising the means prescribed, and that he has not relapsed. I also add, that when the confessor knows that it will be useful to defer absolution he is bound to defer it; for he is obliged to adopt the most efficacious remedies for the amendment of his penitent. I say, moreover, that when a person is long habituated to sins of impurity, it will not be enough for him to avoid proximate occasions: it will be also necessary for him to remove certain occasions which of themselves would, perhaps, be remote, but with regard to

[1] "Etiam cum jactura vitæ."

him will be not remote, but proximate. Because by so many relapses he has become weak and strongly inclined to the vice of impurity.

II. With regard to relapsing sinners, it is necessary to distinguish between them and habitual sinners.

Habitual sinners are those who have contracted a habit of any vice, but have never confessed the habit. If they are truly penitent, and firmly resolved to adopt the means of overcoming their evil habit, they may be absolved the first time they confess the habit, or when they confess the sin after having, for a considerable time, retracted the habit. But let it be observed, that when a penitent has contracted a bad habit, particularly if it has become inveterate, the confessor can certainly defer absolution, in order to try by experience how the penitent practised the means prescribed.

But *relapsing* sinners are those who after confession have fallen back into the same habit without any amendment. They cannot be absolved when they show only the ordinary signs of repentance—such as the confession of their sins, along with the declaration that they are penitent, and resolved to amend their lives. For Innocent XI. has justly condemned the following proposition: "The moment that a sinner guilty of infringing a divine law, either positive or natural, or a precept of the Church, even if he gave no hope of amendment, but protests at least that he repents and wishes to amend, one cannot refuse or defer absolution."[1] Because although the confession itself, along with a declaration on the part of the habitual sinner that he is sorry for his sins, and resolved to avoid them for the future, gives a kind of moral certainty that he is disposed for the sacrament,

[1] "Pœnitenti habenti consuetudinem peccandi contra legem Dei, naturæ, aut Ecclesiæ, etsi emendationis nulla spes appareat, nec est neganda nec differenda absolutio, dummodo ore proferat se dolere et proponere emendationem."—*Prop. damn.* 60.

unless there is a presumption in favor of the contrary, still when a habit has been contracted, and when, without any improvement, several relapses have taken place after absolution, there is strong reason to suspect that the sorrow and purpose of amendment of the penitent are not sincere. Hence, such a penitent should not be absolved until he shows by a change of conduct for some time, and by practising the means prescribed, that he has the dispositions necessary for the sacrament.

Remember that this holds not only for those who relapse into mortal sin, but also for those who relapse into venial sins, which many penitents confess through custom, but without sorrow and a purpose of amendment. If they wish to receive absolution, the confessor should make them give certain matter for the sacrament, by the confession of a more grievous sin of their past life, for which they are truly penitent, and which they are firmly resolved to avoid for the future.

Hence, to absolve relapsing sinners, it is necessary for the confessor to try for some time the sincerity of their repentance; or at least to see some extraordinary signs of sorrow, which exclude the conditions of the condemned propositions, and give a well-founded hope of their amendment. These signs are, according to the theologians:

1. Great compunction, manifested by tears or by words, proceeding not from the mouth but from the heart. From expressions of this kind we sometimes get more certainty of a penitent's fitness for absolution than even from tears;

·2. A considerable diminution in the number of sins, though the penitent was exposed to the same occasions and temptations;

3. Greater caution against relapses, by avoiding the occasions, and by practising the means prescribed; or a great struggle made before consenting to sin;

4. When the penitent asks, with a sincere desire of amendment, for new remedies or means of freeing himself from the sin;

5. If he come to confession, not to conform to any pious custom already established, such as the practice of going to the sacraments at Christmas, or any other determinate festival; not by the direction of a parent or master, but through a desire infused by God of recovering the divine grace; particularly if the penitent has put himself to great inconvenience in order to come to confession, by making a long journey; or if he has come after a great struggle, or after doing great violence to himself;

6. If he has been impelled to go to confession by hearing a sermon, by the account of the sudden death or some great calamity of another, or by any other extraordinary spiritual motive;

7. If he confesses sins previously concealed through shame;

8. If the penitent shows that by the admonition of the confessor he has acquired new light, and a new horror for his sins, and a new dread of the danger of being lost;

9. Some theologians place among the extraordinary signs of repentance a firm promise made by the penitent to practise the remedies prescribed by his confessor; but unless there is some other sign, the confessor can seldom trust to such promises. For in order to obtain absolution the more easily, penitents make many promises that they are not firmly resolved to fulfil.

Whenever, then, there are such extraordinary signs, a confessor may absolve a relapsing sinner; but he may also defer absolution for some time, when he knows that delay will be profitable to his penitent. Some maintain that it is not always expedient to defer the absolution of a relapsing sinner who has the necessary dispositions;

others teach that it is better to put off the absolution, unless the delay and privation of Communion should give others grounds of suspicion injurious to the reputation of the penitent. My opinion is, as I have stated in my *Instructions to Confessors*,[1] that where there is no external occasion, and the sins are committed through internal frailty, such as blasphemies, hatred, pollution, morose delectation, etc., it is seldom expedient to defer absolution. For we may always hope for better fruit from the aid of the grace which the penitent receives from the sacrament than from the delay of absolution. But when there is an external occasion, though necessary, I, as has been already said, deem it expedient. and generally speaking necessary, for the amendment of the penitent, who is even disposed for the sacrament, to defer absolution.

[1] *Homo Apost. tr. ult. punct.* 2.

INSTRUCTION V.

MENTAL PRAYER.

I.

Necessity of Mental Prayer for Priests.

IF, as the most learned Suarez[1] has asserted, mental prayer is morally necessary for all the faithful, it is still more necessary for priests. Because priests stand in need of greater help from God, on account of the greater obligations by which they are bound to seek perfection, of the greater sanctity of their state, and on account of the office that they hold, of procuring the salvation of souls. Hence, like mothers, who require more corporal nutriment than others, because they have to support themselves and their children, priests stand in need of a double portion of spiritual nourishment. Hence St. Ambrose says, that to teach us the necessity of mental prayer our Saviour separated from the people, and went up the mountain to pray,[2] although he did not require to go into solitary places in order to pray; for his blessed soul, always enjoying the intuitive vision of God, was employed in all places and in every occupation in the contemplation of the divinity and in praying for us. St. Luke tells us, that he spent entire nights in prayer.[3] On this passage St. Ambrose says, if Jesus Christ has spent nights in prayer for your salvation, how much more ought you to pray in order to save your soul![4]

[1] *De Orat.* l. 2, c. 4.
[2] "Et dimissa turba, ascendit in montem solus orare."—*Matt.* xiv. 23.
[3] "Erat pernoctans in oratione."—*Luke*, vi. 12.
[4] "Quid enim te pro salute tua facere oportet, quando pro te Christus in oratione pernoctat!"

Hence the saint has written in another place: "Priests should always devote themselves to prayer."¹ Father John d'Avila used to say, that the offices which a priest holds of offering sacrifice and of offering incense go together.² Every one knows that incense signifies prayer: *Let my prayer be directed as incense in Thy sight*³ Hence St. John saw the angels *having . . . golden vials full of odors, which are the prayers of the saints.*⁴ Oh, what sweet odor do the prayers of good priests give to God! On account of the necessity of mental prayer for ecclesiastics, St. Charles Borromeo ordained, in the Council of Milan,⁵ that every ecclesiastic, before his ordination, should be interrogated in a special manner whether he knew how to make mental prayer, whether he was in the habit of making it, and what meditations he used. Father John d'Avila once dissuaded a person from taking priesthood because he was not accustomed to make mental prayer.

I do not intend to detail at length the reasons why the practice of mental prayer is morally necessary for every priest. It is enough to say, that without mental prayer a priest has but little light; for without it he will reflect but little on the great affair of salvation, he will scarcely see the obstacles to it, and the obligations that he must fulfil in order to be saved. Hence the Saviour said to his disciples: *Let your loins be girt, and lamps burning in your hands.*⁶ These lamps, says St. Bonaventure,⁷

¹ "(Sacerdotes) die noctuque pro plebe sibi commissa oportet orare." —*In* 1 *Tim.* iii.

² "Incensum enim Domini et panes Dei sui offerunt."—*Levit.* xxi. 6.

³ "Dirigatur oratio mea sicut incensum in conspectu tuo."—*Ps.* cxl. 2.

⁴ "Phialas aureas plenas odoramentorum, quæ sunt orationes sanctorum."—*Apoc.* v. 8.

⁵ *Anno* 1579, *Const.* p. 3, n. 2.

⁶ "Sint lumbi vestri præcincti, et lucernæ ardentes in manibus vestris."—*Luke,* xii. 35.

⁷ *Diæta sal.* t. 2, c. 5.

are holy meditations, in which the Lord enlightens us. *Come ye to Him and be enlightened.*[1] He who does not make mental prayer has but little light and little strength. In the repose of meditation, says St. Bernard, we acquire strength to resist enemies and to practise virtue.[2] He who does not sleep during the night is not able to stand steady, and goes tottering along the road.

Be still and see that I am God.[3] He who neglects to withdraw, at least now and then, from the thoughts of the world, and to retire to converse with God, has but little knowledge or light regarding the things of eternity. Seeing, one day, that his disciples had been greatly occupied in works of fraternal charity, Jesus Christ said to them: *Come apart into a desert place, and rest a little.*[4] Retire into some solitary place and rest a while. Our Lord spoke of the repose, not of the body, but of the spirit, which unless it retire from time to time to converse alone with God, has not strength to persevere in doing good, but easily faints and falls into sin in the occasions that occur. All our strength is in the divine aid: *I can do all things in Him who strengtheneth me.*[5] But this aid God gives only to those who pray for it. He is most desirous of dispensing his graces to us; but, as St. Gregory says, he wishes that we pray to him, and that we, as it were, compel him by our prayers to grant them to us.[6] But he who neglects mental prayer has but little knowledge of his defects, of the dangers of losing the divine grace, of the means of conquering tempta-

---

[1] "Accedite ad eum, et illuminamini."—*Ps.* xxxiii. 6.
[2] "Ex hoc otio vires proveniunt."
[3] "Vacate, et videte quoniam ego sum Deus."—*Ps.* xlv. 11.
[4] "Venite seorsum in desertum locum, et requiescite pusillum."—*Mark*, vi. 31.
[5] "Omnia possum in eo qui me confortat."—*Phil.* iv. 13.
[6] "Vult Deus rogari, vult cogi, vult quadam importunitate vinci."—*In Ps. pœnit.* 6.

tions, and of the need he has of asking God's graces; thus he will neglect to ask them, and neglecting to pray for them, he shall certainly be lost. Hence St. Teresa of Jesus used to say, that he who neglects mental prayer does not stand in need of devils to carry him to hell, but brings himself to that land of woe.[1]

Some say many vocal prayers; but he who does not make mental prayer will scarcely say his vocal prayers with attention: he will say them with distractions, and the Lord will not hear him. "Many cry to God," says St. Augustine, "but not with the voice of the soul, but with the voice of the body;[2] only the cry of the heart, of the soul, reaches God."[3] It is not enough to pray only with the tongue: we must, according to the Apostle, pray also with the heart if we wish to receive God's graces: *Praying at all times in the spirit.*[4] And by experience we see that many persons who recite a great number of vocal prayers, the Office and the Rosary, fall into sin, and continue to live in sin. But he who attends to mental prayer scarcely ever falls into sin, and should he have the misfortune of falling into it, he will hardly continue to live in so miserable a state; he will either give up mental prayer, or renounce sin. Meditation and sin cannot stand together. However abandoned a soul may be, if she perseveres in meditation God will bring her to salvation. All the saints have become saints by mental prayer. "By prayer," says St. Laurence Justinian, "fervor is renewed, and the fire of divine love is increased."[5] St. Ignatius used to say, that to

[1] *Life*, ch. 19.
[2] "Multi clamant, non voce sua, sed corporis. Cogitatio tua clamor est ad Dominum."—*In Ps.* 141.
[3] "Clama intus, ubi Deus audit."—*In Ps.* 30, *en.* 4.
[4] "Orantes omni tempore in spiritu."—*Eph.* vi. 18.—*Life*, ch. 8.
[5] "Ex oratione fugatur tentatio, abscedit tristitia, virtus reparatur, excitatur fervor, et divini amoris flamma succrescit."—*De Casto Conn.* c. 22.—*Ribadeneira*, l. 5, c. 1.

remove the disturbance of mind caused by the greatest calamity that could befall him, a meditation of a quarter of an hour would be sufficient. St. Bernard has written: "Consideration rules the affections, directs the actions, corrects excesses."[1] St. John Chrysostom regards as dead the soul that does not make mental prayer.[2] Ruffinus says that all the progress of the soul depends on meditation.[3] And Gerson goes so far as to assert that he who does not meditate, cannot, without a miracle, lead a Christian life.[4] Speaking of the perfection to which every priest is bound, St Aloysius Gonzaga justly said that without a great zeal for mental prayer a soul will never attain great virtue.[5]

(He who desires more detailed proofs of the moral necessity of mental prayer, is referred to the chapter on meditation in the *True Spouse of Jesus Christ*, Ch. XV)*

II.

Answer to Excuses.

I here omit many other arguments that I could adduce in favor of the necessity of mental prayer; I will only answer three excuses put forward by priests who neglect meditation.

[1] "Consideratio regit affectus, dirigit actus, corrigit excessus."—*De Consid.* l. 1, c. 7.
[2] "Quisquis non orat Deum, nec divino ejus colloquio cupit assidue frui, is mortuus est. . . . Animæ mors est, non provolvi coram Deo." —*De or. Deo*, l. 1.
[3] "Omnis profectus spiritualis ex meditatione procedit."—*In Ps.* 36.
[4] "Absque meditationis exercitio, nullus, secluso miraculo Dei, ad Christianæ religionis normam attingit."—*De Med. cons.* 7.
[5] *Cepari*, l. 2, c 3.

---

* Volume X., page 441. See also Discourse on the same subject at the end of this work, and the complete treatise on mental prayer that has been given in Volume III, page 252.—ED.

I. Some say, " I do not make mental prayer, because I am subject to desolation, to distractions, and to temptations; I have a wandering mind that I cannot confine to the subject of meditation, and therefore I have given up mental prayer."

But to such persons St. Francis de Sales says,[1] that if in their meditations they do nothing else than banish distractions and temptations, the meditation is well made, provided the distraction is not voluntary. The Lord is pleased with a good intention, with a patient endurance, during the whole time prescribed for meditation, and with the pain arising from distractions, and will bestow many graces in return. We ought to go to prayer, not to please ourselves, but to please God. Even holy souls generally suffer aridity in meditation, but because they persevere, God enriches them with his blessings. St. Francis de Sales used to say, an ounce of prayer made amid desolations is of greater value before God than a hundred pounds of it in the midst of consolations. Even statues do honor to a prince by standing in his galleries. Whenever, then, the Lord wishes us to remain as statues in his presence, let us be content to honor him as statues. It will then be enough to say to him: Lord, I remain here to please you.

St. Isidore says that the devil never labors so hard to tempt and distract us as in the time of meditation.[2] And why? because he knows the great fruit that we draw from meditation, and therefore he endeavors to make us give it up. They, then, who abandon mental prayer on account of the tediousness that they feel in it, give great delight to the devil. In the time of aridity the soul should do nothing else than humble herself and ask God's graces. She should humble herself, for

[1] *Lettre* 629.
[2] " Tunc magis diabolus cogitationes curarum sæcularium ingerit, quando orantem aspexerit."—*Sent.* l. 3, c. 7.

there is no better time for understanding our own miseries and insufficiency than when we are desolate in prayer: we then see that of ourselves we can do nothing. Hence we should do nothing else than, uniting ourselves with Jesus, desolate on the cross, humble ourselves and ask mercy, saying and repeating, Lord, assist me: Lord, have mercy on me: my Jesus, mercy. Meditation made in this manner will be the most fruitful of all; for to the humble God opens his hands and dispenses his graces: *God resisteth the proud, and giveth His grace to the humble.*[1] Let us then, more than ever, fervently implore mercy for ourselves and for poor sinners. God requires, in a special manner, of priests that they pray for sinners. *The priests, the Lord's ministers, shall weep, and shall say: Spare, O Lord, spare Thy people.*[2] But in answer to this some may say: It is enough for me to say the divine office. But St. Augustine writes, that the barking of dogs is more pleasing to God than the prayers of bad ecclesiastics. The ecclesiastic who neglects mental prayer soon falls away from virtue, for without meditation he shall scarcely acquire the ecclesiastical spirit.[3]

II. Others say, If I neglect mental prayer, I do not mis-spend my time; I employ it in study

But the Apostle said to Timothy: *Take heed to thyself and to doctrine.*[4] Attend first *to thyself*, that is, to prayer, and then to doctrine, that is, to study, in order to procure the salvation of others. If we are not saints, how can we make others become saints? "Happy he that

---

[1] " Deus superbis resistit, humilibus autem dat gratiam."—*James*, iv. 6.

[2] " Plorabunt Sacerdotes, ministri Domini, et dicent: Parce, Domine, parce populo tuo."—*Joel*, ii. 17.

[3] " Plus placet Deo latratus canum, quam oratio talium clericorum." —*Corn. à Lap. in Levit.* i. 17.

[4] " Attende tibi et doctrinæ."—1 *Tim.* iv. 16.

knows Thee, even if he knows nothing else," says St. Augustine.[1] If we knew all sciences and knew not how to love Jesus Christ, our knowledge shall profit us nothing to eternal life. But if we know how to love Jesus Christ, we shall know all things, and shall be happy for eternity. Happy, then, the man to whom is given the science of the saints, that is, the science of loving God: *She gave him the knowledge of the holy things.*[2] A single word from a priest who truly loves God will produce more fruit in others than a thousand sermons of the learned who love God but little.

But this science of the saints is not acquired by the study of books, but by mental prayer, in which the master who instructs and the book that is read is a crucified God. Being asked one day by St. Thomas from what book he had acquired so much learning, St. Bonaventure pointed to the crucifix, and said that there he had acquired all his knowledge. Sometimes a person learns more in a moment during the time of meditation than he would in ten years spent in the study of books. "In the soul," says St. Bonaventure, "there is left, by the desire of unitive love, incomparably greater knowledge than by study."[3]

Human sciences require a good understanding; in the science of the saints it is enough to have a good will. He who loves God most ardently, knows him best. Love, says St. Gregory,[4] is knowledge; and according to St. Augustine, to love is to see.[5] David exhorts us to taste and see how sweet the Lord is: *O taste and see*

---

[1] " Beatus, qui te scit, etiamsi illa nesciat."—*Conf.* l. 5, c. 4.
[2] " Et dedit illi scientiam sanctorum."—*Wisd.* x. 10.
[3] " In anima incomparabiliter, per amoris unitivi desideria, perfectio amplioris cognitionis relinquitur, quam studendo requiratur."—*Myst. Theol.* c. 3, p. 2.
[4] " Amor ipse notitia est."—*In Evang. hom.* 27.
[5] " Amare, videre est."

that the Lord is sweet.[1] He who tastes God most by loving him, sees him most clearly, and has the most perfect knowledge of the immensity of his goodness. He who tastes honey has a more correct notion of it than all the philosophers who study and explain its properties. "If," said St. Augustine, "God is wisdom, a true philosopher is a lover of God."[2] God is wisdom itself; then the true philosopher (by philosopher is meant a person who loves wisdom) is one who truly loves God.

To learn worldly sciences much time and labor are necessary; but to learn the science of the saints it is enough to wish and ask for it. The wise man says that *Wisdom . . . is easily seen by them that love her, and is found by them that seek her. She preventeth them that covet her, so that she first showeth herself to them.*[3] The divine wisdom is easily found by all that seek and covet her; she is found, even before she is sought. *He that watcheth early to seek her shall not labor, for he shall find her sitting at his door.*[4] He who seeks her with diligence shall not labor to find her, for he shall find her sitting at his door waiting for him. Finally, Solomon concludes: *Now all good things came to me with her*[5] That is, he who finds wisdom, or the love of God, finds all goods.

Oh, how much more did St. Philip Neri learn in the grottoes of St. Sebastian, where he spent entire nights in meditation, than in all the books that he had read! How much more did St. Jerome learn in the cave of

[1] " Gustate, et videte quoniam suavis est Dominus."—*Ps.* xxxiii. 9.

[2] " Si sapientia Deus est, verus philosophus est amator Dei."—*De Civ. Dei.* 1. 8, c. 1.

[3] " Sapientia . . facile videtur ab his qui diligunt eam, et invenitur ab his qui quærunt illam. Præoccupat, qui se concupiscunt, ut illis se prior ostendat."—*Wisd.* vi. 13.

[4] " Qui de luce vigilaverit ad illam, non laborabit; assidentem enim illam foribus suis inveniet."—*Ib.* 15.

[5] " Venerunt autem mihi omnia bona pariter cum illa."—*Ib.* vii. 11.

Bethlehem than in all his studies! Father Suarez used to say that he would rather lose all his knowledge than one hour's mental prayer. "May the wise men of this world," says St. Paulinus, "possess their wisdom, the rich their riches, the kings their kingdoms. Jesus Christ is our wisdom, our riches, our kingdom."[1] Let the learned of the world enjoy their wisdom, let the rich possess their wealth, and kings their kingdoms; but let Jesus Christ be our wisdom, our riches, our kingdom; let us say with St. Francis. "My God and my all."[2] This true wisdom we should in a special manner ask of God, for he will certainly give it to all who pray for it. *If any of you want wisdom*, says St. James, *let him ask of God, who giveth to all men abundantly, and upbraideth not*.[3]

I do not deny that study is useful, and even necessary for priests; but the study of the crucifix is still more necessary. In a letter to Jovius, who devoted a great deal of time to the study of the works of the philosophers, but through pretence of not having time, paid but little attention to the exercises of a spiritual life, the same St. Paulinus writes. "You have time to be a philosopher, but you have no time to be a Christian."[4] Some priests spend so much time in the study of mathematics, geometry, astronomy, and profane history (oh that they would at least study what is better suited to their state), and afterwards say that they have not time to make mental prayer. To them it should be said: "You have time to be a learned man, but you have no

---

[1] "Sibi habeant sapientiam suam philosophi, sibi divitias suas divites, sibi regna sua reges, nobis gloria, et possessio, et regnum, Christus est."—*Ep. ad Aprum*.

[2] "Deus meus, et omnia!"

[3] "Si quis autem vestrum indiget sapientia, postulet a Deo, qui dat omnibus affluenter, et non improperat."—*James*, i. 5.

[4] "Vacat tibi ut philosophus sis; non vacat ut christianus sis?"—*Ep. ad Jovium*.

time to be a priest."[1] Seneca says that we have little time, because we lose a great deal of it.[2] And in another place he says: "We are ignorant of what is necessary, because we learn what is superfluous."[3]

III. Others say I would wish to make mental prayer, but I am so much occupied in hearing confessions and preaching, that I have not a moment to spare.

I answer: I praise you, dearly beloved priest, for seeking the salvation of souls, but I cannot praise you for forgetting yourself in order to assist others. We must attend first to ourselves by making mental prayer, and then to our neighbor. The holy apostles labored more than all others for the salvation of souls, but finding that their exertions for the good of others interfered with prayer, they appointed deacons for the performance of the external works of charity, that thus they themselves might have time for prayer and the preaching of the divine word: *Brethren, may we appoint men over this business. But we will give ourselves continually to prayer, and to the ministry of the word.*[1] But remark, they attended first to prayer, and then to preaching; because without prayer sermons produce but little fruit. This is what St. Teresa wrote to the Bishop of Osma, who paid great attention to the care of his flock, but devoted little time to prayer. "Our Lord," says the saint in a letter to him, "has shown me that you are wanting in what is particularly necessary for you (and when the foundation gives way the edifice falls to ruin); you fail in mental prayer, and do not persevere in it: from this defect arises the aridity which the soul suffers."[5] St.

[1] "Vacat tibi ut eruditus sis; non vacat ut Sacerdos sis?"
[2] "Non exiguum tempus habemus, sed multum perdimus."—*De Brevit V.* c. 1.
[3] "Necessaria ignoramus, quia superflua addiscimus."
[4] "Fratres, viros, . . . constituamus super hoc opus. Nos vero orationi et ministerio verbi instantes erimus."—*Acts*, vi. 3.
[5] *Lettre* 8.

Bernard admonished Pope Eugene not to omit meditation on account of external affairs; and added, that he who gives up mental prayer may fall into hardness of heart, which will destroy all remorse for his faults, so that after having committed them he shall feel no hatred for them.[1]

St. Laurence Justinian says that the works of Martha, without the recollection of Mary, cannot be perfect.[2] He deceives himself, says the saint, who expects, without the aid of prayer, to succeed in the work of saving souls—a work as dangerous as it is sublime; without the reflection of mental prayer, he shall certainly faint on the way.[3] Our Lord commanded his disciples to preach what they heard in prayer: *That which you hear in the ear, preach ye upon the housetops.*[4] By the ear in this place is understood the ear of the heart, to which God promises to speak in the solitude of prayer: *I will lead her into the wilderness, and I will speak to her heart.*[5] In prayer, says St. Paulinus, we conceive the spirit, which we must afterwards communicate to others.[6] Hence, speaking of priests, St. Bernard complained, that though a priest should be first a cistern, that is, full of holy lights and affections collected in prayer, and afterwards a canal to diffuse them among his neighbors, still there are in the Church many canals and few cis-

---

[1] " Timeo tibi, Eugeni, ne multitudo negotiorum, intermissa oratione et consideratione, te ad cor durum perducat; quod scipsum non exhorret, quia nec sentit."—*De Cons.* l. 1, c. 2.

[2] " Marthæ studium, absque Mariæ gustu, non potest esse perfectum."

[3] " Fallitur quisquis opus hoc periculosum, absque orationis præsidio, consummare se posse putat; in via deficit, si ab interna maneat refectione jejunus."—*De Inst. præl.* c. 11.

[4] " Quod in aure auditis, prædicate super tecta."—*Matth.* x. 27.

[5] " Ducam eam in solitudinem, et loquar ad cor ejus."—*Osee,* ii. 14.

[6] " In oratione fit conceptio spiritualis."—*Ep. ad Severium.*

terns.[1] Hence before a priest engages in works of charity to others he should have recourse to prayer, says St. Laurence Justinian.[2] Hence, on the passage of the Canticles, *Draw me; we will run after Thee in the odor of Thy ointments*,[3] St. Bernard has written, that the priest who has zeal for the salvation of souls ought to say to God: "I will run not alone; others shall run with me: we will run after Thee in the odor of Thy ointments; that is, we will hasten after Thee, attracted by Thy example.[4] My God, draw me to Thyself; for drawn by Thee, I will run with Thee, and others also shall run with me: I shall run, drawn by the odor of Thy ointments; that is, by the inspirations and graces that I shall receive in prayer, others shall be drawn by my example.

That a priest may be able to draw many souls to God, he must first prepare himself to be drawn by God. Such has been the conduct of holy workmen in God's vineyard—of St. Dominic, St. Philip Neri, St. Francis Xavier, St. John Francis Regis. They employed the day in laboring for the people, and spent the night in prayer, and persevered in that holy exercise until they were overcome by sleep. A priest of moderate learning and great zeal will bring more souls to God than a great number of tepid though learned priests. St. Jerome says, "A man inflamed with zeal is sufficient to amend an entire people."[5] A single word from a priest inflamed with holy charity will do more good than a

[1] Concham te exhibebis, non canalem. Canales hodie in Ecclesia multos habemus, conchas vero perpaucas."—*In Cant.* s. 18.
[2] "Difficile est proximorum lucris insistere. Priusquam hujusmodi studiis se tradat, orationi intendat."—*De Tr. Chr. Ag.* c. 7.
[3] "Trahe me; post te curremus in odorem unguentorum tuorum."— *Cant.* i. 3.
[4] "Non curram ego sola, current et adolescentulæ mecum; curremus simul, ego odore unguentorum tuorum, illæ meo excitatæ exemplo."— *In Cant.* s. 21.
[5] "Sufficit unus homo zelo succensus totum corrigere populum."

hundred sermons composed by a theologian who has but little love of God. St. Thomas of Villanova used to say that words of fire, which are, as it were, darts of the fire of divine love, are necessary to wound and inflame hearts with the love of God. But how, adds the saint, can these darts of fire issue from a heart of snow? It is meditation that inflames the heart of holy workmen in the vineyard of the Lord, and transforms them from snow into fire. Speaking especially of the love that Jesus Christ has borne us, the Apostle says: *For the charity of Christ presseth us.*[1] He means that it is impossible for any one to meditate on the sorrows and ignominies that our Redeemer has endured for us without being inflamed, and without seeking to inflame others, with his love: *You shall draw waters with joy,* says the Prophet Isaias, *out of the Saviour's fountains.*[2] The fountains of the Saviour are the examples of the life of Jesus Christ, from the consideration of which souls draw sweet waters, lights, and holy affections; and inflamed with these affections, they endeavor to kindle them, also, in others, exhorting them to confess and praise, and love the goodness of our God.

III.

The Recitation of the Divine Office.

(It may be useful to say something here on the recitation of the divine Office.)

By the divine Office God is honored, the fury of the enemy is repelled, and the divine mercies are obtained for sinners. But to attain these ends it is necessary to recite the Office in a proper manner: it is necessary to say it "carefully and devoutly,"[3] as the fifth Council of

---

[1] " Charitas enim Christi urget nos."—2 *Cor.* v. 14.

[2] " Haurietis aquas in gaudio de fontibus Salvatoris; et dicetis in die illa: Confitemini Domino, et invocate nomen ejus."—*Isa.* xii. 3.

[3] " Studiose et devote."

Lateran[1] has taught, in the celebrated Canon *Dolentes. Carefully,* by pronouncing the words distinctly; *devoutly,* that is, with attention, as Cassian teaches: "Let that be considered in the heart which is uttered by the lips."[2] How, asks St. Cyprian, can you expect that God will hear you when you do not hear yourself?[3] Prayer made with attention is the odoriferous incense that is most agreeable to God, and obtains treasures of grace; but prayer made with voluntary distraction is a fetid smoke that provokes the divine wrath, and merits chastisement. Hence, while we recite the Office, the devil labors strenuously to make us say it with distractions and defects. We should, then, take all possible care to recite it in a proper manner. We here give some practical advice:

1. It is necessary to enliven our faith, and to consider that in reciting the divine Office we unite with the angels in praising God. "We begin here upon earth the office of the inhabitants of heaven,"[4] says Tertullian. We then perform on earth the office of the citizens of heaven, who unceasingly praise God, and shall praise him for eternity.[5] Hence, as St. John Chrysostom remarks, before we enter the church or take up the breviary we must leave at the door and dismiss all thoughts of the world.[6]

2. In reciting the divine Office we must take care that our affections accompany the sentiments contained in what we read. It is necessary, says St. Augustine: "We

---

[1] *Cap. Dolentes, de Cel. Missar.*
[2] "Hoc versatur in corde, quod profertur in voce."—*Ep.* 211, *E. B.*
[3] "Quomodo te audiri a Deo postulas, cum te ipse non audias?"—*De Or. Dom.*
[4] "Officium futuræ claritatis ediscimus."—*De Or.*
[5] "In sæcula sæculorum laudabunt te."—*Ps.* lxxxiii. 5.
[6] "Ne quis ingrediatur templum curis onustus mundanis; hæc ante ostium deponamus."—*In Is. hom.* 2.

must pray when the Psalmist prays, sigh when he sighs, hope when he hopes.[1]

3. It is useful to renew our attention from time to time; for example, at the beginning of every psalm.

4. We must be careful not to give occasion to mental distractions. How can he who recites the Office in a public place, or in the midst of persons who are jesting and amusing themselves,—how, I ask, can he say it with piety and devotion?

Oh! what treasures do they lay up who daily recite the divine Office with devout attention! St. John Chrysostom says that they are filled with the Holy Ghost.[2] But, on the other hand, they who say it negligently lose great merits, and have to render a great account to God.*

[1] "Si orat Psalmus, orate; si gemit, gemite; si sperat, sperate."— *In Ps.* xxx. *en.* 4.

[2] " Implentur Spiritu Sancto."—*In Eph. hom.* 19.

* We may see a more extended instruction on the recitation of the Office in the *True Spouse of Jesus Christ*, Ch. 24, Vol. XI., page 189. We may also find a short treatise on the same subject at the end of the next volume (Volume XIII.).—ED.

INSTRUCTION VI.

HUMILITY.

Learn of Me, because I am meek and humble of heart.[1] Humility and meekness were the two beloved virtues of Jesus Christ, in which he wished in a special manner to be imitated by his disciples. We shall speak first of humility, and afterwards of meekness.

I.

Necessity of Humility.

St. Bernard says, "The higher one is placed, the humbler one should be."[2] The more exalted, then, the dignity of the priest, the greater should be his humility; otherwise, if he fall into sin, the greater the height from which he is precipitated, the more disastrous his fall. Hence St. Laurence Justinian says that the priest should regard humility as the most precious jewel that shines forth in his character.[3] And St. Augustine writes: "The highest honor should be united with the greatest humility."[4] And before him, Jesus Christ said, *He that is the greater among you, let him become as the younger.*[5] Humility is truth. Hence the Lord has said, that if we

---
[1] "Discite a me quia mitis sum et humilis corde."—*Matth.* xi. 29.
[2] "Tanto quisque debet esse humilior, quanto est sublimior."—*De 7 Donis Sp. S.*
[3] "Humilitas est Sacerdotum gemma."—*De Inst. præl.* c 21.
[4] "In summo honore summa tibi sit humilitas."—*De Virt. et Vit.* c. 10.
[5] "Qui major est in vobis, fiat sicut minor."—*Luke*, xxii. 26.

know how to separate the precious from the vile, that is, what belongs to God from what belongs to ourselves, we should be like his mouth, which always speaks truth: *If thou wilt separate the precious from the vile, thou shalt be as My mouth.*[1] Hence we must always pray with St. Augustine: " O Lord, may I know Thee, may I know myself!"[2] St. Francis of Assisi, admiring in God his greatness and goodness, and in himself his own unworthiness and misery, used to say continually to the Lord: " Who art Thou, and who am I?" Hence the saints at the sight of the infinite perfections of God humble themselves to the very earth. The more they know God, the better they see their own poverty and defects. The proud, because they are bereft of light, have but little knowledge of their own vileness.

Let us, then, continue to separate what is ours from what belongs to God. Ours is nothing but misery and sin. And what are we but a little fetid dust, infected by sin? How, then, can we be proud? *Why is earth and ashes proud?*[3] Nobility, wealth, talent, ability, and the other gifts of nature, are but a garment placed over a poor mendicant. If you saw a beggar glorying in an embroidered garment thrown over him, would you not pronounce him to be a fool? *What hast thou that thou hast not received? And if thou hast received, why dost thou glory as if thou hadst not received it?*[4] Have we anything that God has not bestowed upon us, or that he cannot take away whenever he pleases? The gifts of grace that God confers upon us also belong to him, and we contaminate them by so many defects, distractions, acts

---

[1] " Si separaveris pretiosum a vili, quasi os meum eris."—*Jer.* xv. 19.
[2] " Noverim me, noverim te."—*Solil.* l. 2, c. 1.
[3] " Quid superbit terra et cinis?"—*Ecclus.* x. 9.
[4] " Quid autem habes, quod non accepisti? Si autem accepisti, quid gloriaris, quasi non acceperis?"—1 *Cor.* iv. 7.

of impatience, and inordinate motives, *All our justices are as the rag of a menstruous woman.*[1] Thus, after having said our Masses, Offices, and prayers, though perhaps we esteem ourselves more enlightened and rich in merits, we deserve from the Lord the reproof which he gave to the bishop in the Apocalypse: *Because thou sayest: I am rich, . . . and knowest not that thou art wretched, and miserable, and poor, and blind, and naked.*[2] St. Bernard writes: "What we need in fervor we should supply by an humble acknowledgment of our misery."[3] If we know that we are poor and full of faults in the sight of God, let us at least humble ourselves and confess our miseries. St. Francis Borgia, while a secular, was advised by a holy man, if he wished to make great progress in virtue, to reflect every day on his own miseries. Hence the saint spent every day the first two hours of prayer in endeavoring to know and despise himself. He thus became a saint, and has left us so many beautiful examples of humility.

St. Augustine says: "God is the supreme being: humble thyself and he will descend to thee; but if thou raisest thyself he will flee from thee."[4] To the humble, God unites himself and gives the treasures of his graces; but from the proud he withdraws and flies away: *Every proud man is an abomination to the Lord.*[5] The proud man is an abomination to the Lord. *God*, says St. James, *resisteth the proud and giveth grace to the humble.*[6] The Lord hears

[1] "Quasi pannus menstruatæ, universæ justitiæ nostræ."—*Isa.* lxiv. 6.
[2] "Dicis: Quod dives sum; et nescis quia tu es miser, et miserabilis, et cæcus, et nudus."—*Apoc.* iii. 17.
[3] "Quidquid minus est in te fervoris, humilitas supplebit confessionis."—*De Int. Domo*, c. 21.
[4] "Altus est Deus. Erigis te, et fugit a te; humilias te, et descendit ad te."—*Serm.* 177, E. B. *app.*
[5] "Abominatio Domini est omnis arrogans."—*Prov.* xvi. 5.
[6] "Deus superbis resistit; humilibus autem dat gratiam."—*James*, iv. 6.

the prayers of the humble. *The prayer of him that humbleth himself shall pierce the clouds, . . . and he will not depart till the Most High behold.*[1] But, on the other hand, he rejects the petitions of the proud: *He resisteth the proud.* He looks at the proud as from a distance. *The Lord . . . looketh on the low, and the high He knoweth afar off.*[2] When we see a person at a distance, we know him not; thus God feigns, as it were, not to know nor to hear the proud when they pray to him. They call upon him, but he answers: *Amen, I say to you, I know you not.*[3] In a word, the proud are hateful to God and to men. *Pride*, says Ecclesiasticus, *is hateful before God and men.*[4] Men are sometimes compelled by necessity to pay external honor to the proud; but in their heart they hate them, and censure them before others. *Where pride is*, said Solomon, *there also shall be reproach.*[5]

Praising the humility of St. Paul, St. Jerome writes: "As the shadow follows him who flies from it, and flies from him who pursues it, so glory follows them who fly from it, and flies from them who seek it."[6] Our Lord says: *Whosoever shall exalt himself shall be humbled, and he that shall humble himself shall be exalted.*[7] A priest, for example, does a good work; he is silent about it, but as soon as it is known, all praise him. But if he goes about proclaiming it to others, in order to receive ap-

[1] "Oratio humiliantis se nubes penetrabit; . . . et non discedet, donec Altissimus aspiciat."—*Ecclus.* xxxv. 21.
[2] "Excelsus Dominus, et humilia respicit; et alta a longe cognoscit." —*Ps.* cxxxvii. 6.
[3] "Amen dico vobis, nescio vos."—*Matth.* xxv. 12.
[4] "Odibilis coram Deo est et hominibus superbia."—*Ecclus.* x. 7.
[5] "Ubi fuerit superbia, ibi erit et contumelia."—*Prov.* xi. 2.
[6] "Fugiendo gloriam, gloriam merebatur, quæ virtutem quasi umbra sequitur, et, appetitores sui deserens, appetit contemptores."—*Ep. ad Eustoch.*
[7] "Qui autem se exaltaverit, humiliabitur; et qui se humiliaverit exaltabitur."—*Matth.* xxiii. 12.

plause, he shall earn reproach instead of praise. What a shame, says St. Gregory, to see the teachers of humility become by their example teachers of pride![1] You may say, I manifest my works to make known the truth, and to procure praise for the Lord; but I answer in the words of Seneca: "He that cannot keep silence about the thing itself will not be silent about the author."[2] Every one who hears a priest speaking of his good works will suppose that he relates them in order to be praised; thus he shall lose the esteem of men and merit before God, who seeing him praised according to his desire, will say to him what he said to the hypocrites in the synagogue: *Amen, I say unto you, they have received their reward.*[3] The Lord has declared that three species of sinners he hates with a special hatred, and that the first is a poor man that is proud. *Three sorts my soul hateth, and I am greatly grieved at their life: a poor man that is proud; a rich man that is a liar; and an old man that is a fool.*[4]

II.
The Practice of Humility.

But let us come to the practice of humility. Let us examine what we must do in order to be humble, not in name, but in reality.

1. To have a Horror of Pride.

In the first place, it is necessary to entertain a great fear of the vice of pride; for, as has been already said, God resists the proud, and deprives them of his graces. A priest, particularly, in order to preserve chastity, stands

---
[1] "Doctores humilium, duces superbiæ!"—*Ep.* l. 4. *ep.* 32.
[2] "Qui rem non tacuerit, non tacebit auctorem."—*Ep.* 105.
[3] "Amen dico vobis, receperunt mercedem suam."—*Matth.* vi. 2.
[4] "Tres species odivit anima mea: . . . pauperem superbum, divitem mendacem, senem fatuum."—*Ecclus.* xxv. 3.

in need of a special aid from God. But how can a proud priest practise that sublime virtue if in punishment of his pride the Lord withholds his assistance? *Pride*, says the Wise Man, *is a sign of approaching ruin. The spirit is lifted up before a fall.*[1] Hence St. Augustine has gone so far as to say that it is in a certain manner useful to the proud to fall into some manifest sin, that thus they may learn humility and a horror of themselves.[2] This is what happened to David, who, as he himself afterwards confessed with tears, fell into adultery because he was not humble: *Before I was humbled, I offended.*[3] St. Gregory calls pride the seminary of impurity; because some, while they are exalted by the spirit of pride, are precipitated into hell by the flesh.[4] The spirit of pride easily brings with it the spirit of impurity. *The spirit of fornication*, says the Prophet Osee, *is in the midst of them, . . . and the pride of Israel shall answer in his face.*[5] Ask certain persons why they always fall back into the same impurities; pride shall answer for them, that it is the cause of their relapses: they are full of self-esteem, and therethe Lord chastises them by permitting them to remain immersed in their abominations,—a chastisement which, as the Apostle says, has already fallen on the wise of the world: *God gave them up to the desires of their heart, unto uncleanness, to dishonor their own bodies among themselves.*[6]

[1] "Contritionem præcedit superbia; et ante ruinam, exaltatur spiritus."—*Prov.* xvi. 18.

[2] "Audeo dicere, superbis esse utile cadere in aliquod apertum peccatum, unde sibi displiceant."—*De Civ. D.* 1. 14, c. 13.

[3] "Priusquam humiliarer, ego deliqui."—*Ps.* cxviii. 67.

[4] "Multis sæpe superbia luxuriæ seminarium fuit; quia, dum eos spiritus quasi in altum erexit, caro in infimis mersit."—*Mor.* 1. 26, c. 12.

[5] "Spiritus fornicationum in medio eorum. . . . Et respondebit arrogantia Israel in facie ejus."—*Osee*, v. 4.

[6] "Propter quod tradidit illos Deus in desideria cordis eorum, in immunditiam, ut contumeliis afficiant corpora sua in semetipsis."—*Rom.* i. 24.

The devil has no fear of the proud. Cesarius relates[1] that a demoniac being once brought to a Cistercian monastery, the prior took with him a young religious who had the reputation of being a man of great virtue, and said to the evil spirit: If this monk shall command you to depart, will you dare to remain? I have no fear of him, replied the enemy, because he is proud. St. Joseph Calasanctius used to say that the devil treats a proud priest as a play-toy; that is, he throws him up and pulls him down as he pleases.

Hence the saints have had a greater dread of pride and vainglory than of any temporal calamity that could befall them. Surius[2] relates of a holy man who was greatly esteemed and honored on account of the miracles that he wrought, that finding himself often assailed by vainglory, he besought the Lord that he might be possessed by an evil spirit; his prayer was heard, and he was possessed for five months. He was then delivered from the infernal spirit, and from the spirit of vanity that molested him. For this purpose the Lord also permits even saints to be tormented by temptations against purity, and after they pray to be freed from them, he leaves them as he left St. Paul, to combat with the temptations. *And lest the greatness of the revelations should exalt me, there was given me a sting of the flesh, an angel of Satan to buffet me. For which thing I thrice besought the Lord, that it might depart from me. And He said to me: My grace is sufficient for thee; for power is made perfect in infirmity.*[3] Thus, according to St. Jerome, a sting of the flesh was given to St. Paul to warn him to be humble: " To remind

---

[1] *Dial.* l. 4, c. 5.
[2] 8 *Jan. V. S. Sever.*
[3] "Et ne magnitudo revelationum extollat me, datus est mihi stimulus carnis meæ, angelus Satanæ, qui me colaphizet. Propter quod ter Dominum rogavi, ut discederet a me; et dixit mihi: Sufficit tibi gratia mea; nam virtus in infirmitate perficitur."—2 *Cor.* xii. 7.

him of human misery, and to make him humble in the sublimity of his revelations."[1] Hence St. Gregory concludes: "To preserve chastity in all its splendor we must place it under the care of humility."[2] Let us here make another reflection. To humble the pride of the people of Egypt, the Lord sent not bears and lions, but frogs to molest them. What do I mean? God permits us to be annoyed by certain little expressions, by certain little aversions, by certain trifles, that we may know our miseries and may humble ourselves.

2. NOT TO GLORY IN THE GOOD THAT WE DO.

Secondly, it is necessary to guard against glorying in any good that we may do, particularly if we are raised to the height of the priesthood. The offices intrusted to us are very great. To us is given the great office of offering to God· the sacrifice of his own Son. To us is confided the care of reconciling sinners with God, by preaching, and by the administration of the sacraments: *He hath given to us the ministry of reconciliation.*[3] We are ambassadors and vicars of Jesus Christ, and are made the tongues of the Holy Ghost: *For Christ therefore we are ambassadors, God as it were exhorting by us.*[4] St. Jerome says that the highest mountains are most violently assailed by the tempest: the more exalted, then, is our dignity, the more we are exposed to the molestation of vainglory. We are esteemed by all, we are respected as men of learning, and as saints. He who stands on a great height is in danger of dizziness.

[1] "Ad revelationum humiliandam superbiam, monitor quidam humanæ imbecillitatis apponitur."—*Ep. ad Paulam*.
[2] "Per humilitatis custodiam servanda est munditia castitatis."—*Mor*. l. 26, c. 11.
[3] "Dedit nobis ministerium reconciliationis."—2 *Cor*. v. 18.
[4] "Pro Christo ergo legatione fungimur, tamquam Deo exhortante per nos."—*Ib*. 20.

How many priests have fallen into precipices because they were not humble! Montanus wrought miracles, and he afterwards through ambition became a heresiarch. Tatian wrote at great length and with great success against the pagans, and through pride he fell into heresy. Brother Justin, a Franciscan, attained the highest degree of contemplation, and he afterwards died an apostate from religion, and was lost. In the life of Palemon we read that a certain monk walked on fire and boasted of it, saying to his companions, Which of you can walk on red-hot coals without being burnt? St. Palemon corrected him, but the unhappy man, being full of himself, fell into sin, and died in that miserable state.

A proud spiritual man is the worst of robbers; because he usurps not earthly goods, but the glory of God. Hence, St. Francis was accustomed to say: Lord! if Thou givest any good, watch over it; otherwise I will steal it from Thee. Thus we priests must pray, and say with St. Paul: *By the grace of God I am what I am.*[1] For of ourselves we are incapable not only of doing good works, but of even having a good thought: *Not that we are sufficient to thinking anything of ourselves.*[2]

Hence the Lord says to us: *When you shall have done all these things that are commanded you, say: We are unprofitable servants: we have done that which we ought to do.*[3] Of what use can all our works be to God? What need can he have of our possessions? *I have said to the Lord*, said David, *Thou art my God, for Thou hast no need of my goods.*[4] And Job said: *If thou do justly, . . . what shall he receive*

---

[1] "Gratia autem Dei sum id quod sum."—1 *Cor.* xv. 10.

[2] "Non quod sufficientes simus cogitare aliquid a nobis."—2 *Cor.* iii. 5.

[3] "Cum feceritis omnia quæ præcepta sunt vobis, dicite: Servi inutiles sumus; quod debuimus facere, fecimus."—*Luke*, xvii. 10.

[4] "Deus meus es tu, quoniam bonorum meorum non eges."—*Ps.* xv. 2.

of Thy hand.[1] What can God receive from you to increase his riches? Moreover, we are useless servants, because however much we do for a God who merits infinite love, and has suffered so much for the love of us, it is all nothing. Hence the Apostle writes: *If I preach the Gospel, it is no glory to me, for a necessity lieth upon me.*[2] To all that we do for God we are bound by our obligations and by gratitude; particularly as all that we do is his work more than it is ours. Who would not laugh at the clouds, if they boasted of the rain that they send down? This is the language of St. Bernard.[3] He then adds, that we ought to praise, not so much the saints for the works that they perform, as God who operates through them.[4] St. Augustine says the same: "Every good thing, large or small, is a gift of God: from ourselves comes what is bad."[5] And in another place, speaking to God, he writes: "Whoever enumerates to Thee Thy merits, does he enumerate to Thee anything but Thy merits?"[6]

Hence, when we do any good, we must say to the Lord: *We have given Thee what we received of Thy hand.*[7] When St. Teresa performed any good work, or saw a good act done by others, she began to praise God for it, saying that it was entirely his work. Hence, St. Augustine remarks, that unless humility go before, pride will steal

[1] "Si juste egeris, quid donabis ei, aut quid de manu tua accipiet?"—*Job*, xxxv. 7.

[2] "Si evangelizavero, non est mihi gloria; necessitas enim mihi incumbit."—1 *Cor*. ix. 16.

[3] "Si glorientur nubes, quod imbres genuerint, quis non irrideat?"—*In Cant.* s. 13.

[4] "Laudo Deum in sanctis suis, qui, in ipsis manens, ipse facit opera."—*Ibid.*

[5] "Si quid boni est, parvum vel magnum, donum tuum est; et nostrum non est nisi malum."—*Solil. an. ad D.* c. 15.

[6] "Quisquis tibi enumerat merita sua, quid tibi enumerat, nisi munera tua?"—*Conf.* l. 9, c. 13.

[7] "Quæ de manu tua accepimus, dedimus tibi."—1 *Par.* xxix. 14.

from us all the good we do.[1] And in another place he says: "Pride lays snares for good works that they may be lost."[2] St. Joseph Calasanctius used to say, that the more God favors a soul by special graces, the more she ought to humble herself that she may not lose all. All is lost by every little consent to self-esteem. He, says St. Gregory, who performs many virtuous actions, but has not humility, is like a man who scatters dust before the wind.[3] Trithemius has written: "Thou hast despised others: thou art become worse than others."[4]

The saints have not only not boasted of any perfection, but have sought to make known to others what redounded to their own contempt. Father Villanova, of the Society of Jesus, felt no repugnance to tell all that his brother was a poor workman. Father Sacchini, also a Jesuit, meeting in a public place his father, who was a poor muleteer, ran to embrace him, and said: "Oh, behold my father!" Let us read the lives of the saints, and pride shall depart from us: there we shall find the great things that they have done, at the sight of which we shall feel ashamed of the little we have done.

3. WE MUST DISTRUST OURSELVES.

Thirdly, it is necessary to live in continual distrust of ourselves. Unless God assists us, we shall not be able to preserve ourselves in his grace: *Unless the Lord keep the city, he watcheth in vain that keepeth it.*[5] If God work not in us, we shall be unable to do any good: *Unless the Lord*

---

[1] "Nisi humilitas præcesserit, totum extorquet de manu superbia."—*Ep.* 118, *E. B.*

[2] "Superbia bonis operibus insidiatur, ut pereant."—*Ib.* 211.

[3] "Qui sine humilitate virtutes congregat, quasi in ventum pulverem portat."—*In Ps. pœnit.* 3.

[4] "Cæteros contempsisti; cæteris pejor factus es."

[5] "Nisi Dominus custodierit civitatem, frustra vigilat, qui custodit eam."—*Ps.* cxxvi. 1.

build the house, they labor in vain that build it.[1] Some saints, with very moderate learning, have converted entire nations. By certain discourses that he preached in Rome, though the language was simple, and even incorrect (for he had but an imperfect knowledge of the Italian tongue), St. Ignatius of Loyola, because his words came from a heart that was humble and enamoured of God, produced such an effect on the hearers that they instantly went to confession, but could scarcely speak on account of the many tears that they shed.[2] But, on the other hand, many learned theologians, with all their science and eloquence, preach without converting a single soul. In them are verified the words of the Prophet Osee: *Give them a womb without children, and dry breasts.*[3] Such preachers, because they are puffed up with their learning, resemble unfruitful mothers. they have the name, but are without children. And should they be intrusted with the child of another, with an infant that stands in need of milk, the little one shall die of hunger, for the paps of the proud are filled with wind and smoke, but give no milk: *Knowledge puffeth up.*[4] To this evil the proud are subject. It is, as Cardinal Bellarmine wrote to one of his nephews, difficult for a man of learning to be humble, not to despise others, not to censure their acts, not to be full of his own opinions; he will hardly submit willingly to the judgment and correction of others.

It is true that we ought not to preach at random, or without consideration and study; but after we have studied the discourse, and after we have delivered it with zeal and success, we ought to say: *We are unprofit-*

---

[1] "Nisi Dominus ædificaverit domum, in vanum laboraverunt, qui ædificant eam."—*Ps.* cxxvi. 1.

[2] *Ribadeneira, Vit.* l. 3, c. 2.

[3] "Da eis vulvam sine liberis et ubera arentia."—*Osee,* ix. 14.

[4] "Scientia inflat."—1 *Cor.* viii. 1.

able servants,[1] and should expect the fruit, not from our own labors, but from the hands of God. And what proportion can there ever be between our words and the conversion of sinners? *Shall the axe boast itself against him that cutteth with it?*[2] Can the axe say to him who fells the tree: This tree I, and not you, have cut down? We are like so many pieces of iron, incapable even of motion, unless God moves us: *Without Me, you can do nothing.*[3] On this passage St. Augustine writes: "The Lord does not say, Without me you can do but little, but he says, Without me you can do nothing."[4] And the Apostle has said: *Not that we are sufficient to think anything of ourselves.*[5] If we are incapable of having even a good thought of ourselves, how much less shall we be able to perform a good action! *Neither he that planteth is anything, nor he that watereth: but God that giveth the increase.*[6] It is neither the preacher, nor the confessor who exhorts them, that makes souls advance in virtue: no, it is God that does all. "Let us," says St. John Chrysostom, "call ourselves useless servants, that we may be made useful."[7] Whenever, then, we are praised, let us instantly give the honor to God, saying: *To the only God be honor and glory.*[8] And when any office or work is given us by obedience, let us not be diffident at the sight of our inability, but let us have confidence in God, who speaks to us by the

---

[1] "Servi inutiles sumus."
[2] "Numquid gloriabitur securis contra eum qui secat in ea?"—*Isa.* x. 15.
[3] "Sine me nihil potestis facere."—*John,* xv. 5.
[4] "Non ait, quia sine me parum potestis facere, sed nihil."—*In Jo. tr.* 81.
[5] "Non quod sufficientes simus cogitare aliquid a nobis."—2 *Cor.* iii. 5.
[6] "Neque qui plantat, est aliquid, neque qui rigat, sed qui incrementum dat, Deus."—1 *Cor.* iii. 7.
[7] "Nos dicamus inutiles, ut utiles efficiamur."—*Ad pop. Ant. hom.* 38.
[8] "Soli Deo honor et gloria."—1 *Tim.* i. 17.

mouth of our Superior, and says to us: *I will be in thy mouth.*[1]

Gladly, says the Apostle, *will I glory in my infirmities, that the power of Christ may dwell in me.*[2] We, too, should say the same: we should glory in the knowledge of our insufficiency, that thus we may acquire the power of Jesus Christ, that is, holy humility. Oh, what great things do the humble effect! "Nothing," says St. Leo, "is difficult to the humble."[3] No, for the humble, trusting in God, act with the strength of the divine arm, and therefore they effect whatsoever they wish. *They that hope in the Lord shall renew their strength.*[4] St. Joseph Calasanctius used to say, that the man who wishes that God should make him do great things must labor to be the most humble of all. The humble man says: *I can do all things in Him who strengtheneth me.*[5] When he finds an undertaking difficult, he does not despair of success, but says: *Through God we shall do mightily.*[6] Jesus Christ did not wish to select men of power and learning for the conversion of the world, but poor ignorant fishermen, because they were humble, and distrustful of their own strength. *The weak things of the world hath God chosen that He may confound the strong. . . . That all flesh should not glory in His sight.*[7]

Even when we see that we are subject to defects we must not be diffident. Though we should relapse into the same faults after many purposes, and many promises

---

[1] "Ego ero in ore tuo."—*Exod.* iv. 15.

[2] "Libenter igitur gloriabor in infirmitatibus meis, ut inhabitet in me virtus Christi."—2 *Cor.* xii. 9.

[3] "Nihil arduum est humilibus."—*De Epiph.* s. 5.

[4] "Qui autem sperant in Domino, mutabunt fortitudinem."—*Isa.* xl. 31.

[5] "Omnia possum in eo, qui me confortat."—*Phil.* iv. 13.

[6] "In Deo faciemus virtutem."—*Ps.* lix. 14.

[7] "Infirma mundi elegit Deus, ut confundat fortia, . . . ut non glorietur omnis caro in conspectu ejus."—1 *Cor.* i. 27.

made to God, we should not abandon ourselves to diffidence, as the devil tempts us to do, in order to precipitate us into greater sins; but we must then, more than ever, trust in God's goodness, making use of our failings to increase our confidence in the divine mercy. Thus we are to understand the words of the Apostle: *All things work together unto good.*[1] The Gloss adds: *Even sins.*[2] Hence our Lord sometimes permits us to fall or to relapse into a defect, that thus we may learn to distrust ourselves, and to confide only in the divine aid. Hence David said: *It is good for me that Thou hast humbled me.*[3] Lord, Thou hast permitted these my faults for my good, that I may learn to be humble.

4. To Accept Humiliations.

Fourthly, to acquire humility, it is, above all, necessary to accept humiliations that come to us from God and from men, and in the time of humiliation to say with Job: *I have sinned, and indeed I have offended, and I have not received what I deserved.*[4] Some, as St. Gregory[5] remarks, say with the tongue that they are sinners, that they are wicked, and deserving of every species of contempt; but they do not believe what they say, for when despised or reproved by others they are disturbed. "Many," says St. Ambrose in a letter to Constance, "have the appearance of humility, but not the virtue of humility."[6] Cassian[7] relates that a certain monk, who used to protest that he was a great sinner, and unworthy of living on earth, was corrected by the abbot Serapion

---

[1] "Omnia cooperantur in bonum."—*Rom.* viii. 28.
[2] "Etiam peccata."
[3] "Bonum mihi quia humiliasti me."—*Ps.* cxviii. 71.
[4] "Peccavi et vere deliqui, et, ut eram dignus, non recepi."—*Job*, xxxiii. 27.
[5] *Mor.* l. 22, c. 14.
[6] "Multi habent humilitatis speciem, virtutem non habent."—*Ep.* 44.
[7] *Collat.* 18, c. 11.

for a considerable fault, which consisted in going about idly to the cells of the other monks instead of remaining in his own, according to his rule. The monk became instantly agitated, so as to manifest externally the disturbed state of his interior. The abbot said to him: "My son, hitherto you have declared that you deserved nothing but opprobrium, and why are you now so indignant at a word of charity that I have said to you?" The same happens to many who would wish to be esteemed humble, but are unwilling to suffer any humiliation. *There is*, says Ecclesiasticus, *one who humbleth himself wickedly, and his interior is full of deceit.*[1] St. Bernard has said that to seek praise from humility is not humility, but the destruction of humility.[2] To seek praise from humility only foments pride by the desire of being reputed humble. He who is truly humble has a low opinion of himself, and wishes others to think of him as he thinks himself. "He is humble," says St. Bernard, "who converts humiliations into humility."[3] The truly humble man, when treated with contempt, humbles himself still more, and acknowledges that he justly deserves the humiliation.

Finally, let us bear in mind that unless we are humble we shall not only do no good, but we shall not be saved. *Unless you . . . become as little children, you shall not enter into the kingdom of heaven.*[4] In order, then, to enter into the kingdom of heaven, we must become children, not in age, but in humility. St. Gregory says that as pride is a sign of reprobation, so humility is a mark of pre-

[1] "Est qui nequiter humiliat se, et interiora ejus plena sunt dolo." —*Ecclus.* xix. 23.

[2] "Appetere de humilitate laudem, humilitatis est, non virtus, sed subversio."—*In Cant.* s. 16.

[3] "Est humilis, qui humiliationem convertit in humilitatem."—*Ib.* s. 34.

[4] "Nisi conversi fueritis, et efficiamini sicut parvuli non intrabitis in regnum cœlorum."—*Matth.* xviii. 3.

destination.¹ And St. James has written, *that God resisteth the proud, and giveth grace to the humble.*² From the proud God withholds his graces, but to the humble he opens his hand and dispenses his favors. Be humble, says Ecclesiasticus, and expect from the hands of God as many graces as you desire. *Humble thyself to God, and wait for His hands.*³ And our Saviour has said: *Amen, amen, I say to you, unless the grain of wheat falling into the ground die, itself remaineth alone. But if it die, it bringeth forth much fruit.*⁴ A priest who dies to self-love shall produce great fruit; but he who dies not to himself, and resents insults or trusts in his own talents, *remaineth alone:* he remains alone, and will produce no fruit for himself or others.

¹ "Reproborum signum superbia est; at contra, humilitas electorum."—*Mor.* l. 34, c. 22.

² "Deus superbis resistit; humilibus autem dat gratiam."—*James*, iv. 6.

³ "Humiliare Deo, exspecta manus ejus."—*Ecclus.* xiii. 9.

⁴ "Amen, amen, dico vobis: nisi granum frumenti cadens in terram, mortuum fuerit, ipsum solum manet; si autem mortuum fuerit, multum fructum affert."—*John*, xii. 24.

INSTRUCTION VII.

MEEKNESS.

Learn of Me, because I am meek and humble of heart.[1] Meekness is the virtue of the lamb: lamb is the name by which Jesus Christ wished to be called: *Behold the Lamb of God.*[2] *Send forth, O Lord, the Lamb, the ruler of the earth.*[3] And like a lamb he conducted himself in his Passion. *He shall be dumb as a lamb before his shearer, and he shall not open his mouth.*[4] *As a meek lamb that is carried to be a victim.*[5] Meekness was the beloved virtue of the Saviour. He showed the extent of his meekness in doing good to the ungrateful, in submitting sweetly to his enemies, and in bearing without complaint all that insulted and maltreated him. *Who, when He was reviled, did not revile: when He suffered, He threatened not, but delivered Himself to him who judged Him unjustly.*[6] After being scourged, crowned with thorns, covered with spittle, nailed to a cross, and saturated with opprobrium, he forgot all, and prayed for those that had thus maltreated him. Hence he has exhorted us, above all things, to learn from his example humility and meekness. *Learn of Me, because I am meek and humble of heart.*[7]

[1] "Discite a me quia mitis sum et humilis corde."—*Matth.* xi. 29.
[2] "Ecce Agnus Dei."—*John,* i. 29.
[3] "Emitte Agnum, Domine, dominatorem terræ."—*Isa.* xvi. 1.
[4] "Quasi agnus coram tondente se, obmutescet, et non aperiet os suum."—*Ib.* liii. 7.
[5] "Quasi agnus mansuetus qui portatur ad victimam."—*Jer.* xi. 19.
[6] "Qui, cum malediceretur, non maledicebat; cum pateretur, non comminabatur."—1 *Pet.* ii. 23.
[7] "Discite a me quia mitis sum et humilis corde."

St. John Chrysóstom says that meekness is, of all virtues, that which renders us most like to God.[1] Yes, for it belongs only to God to render good for evil. Hence the Redeemer has said: *Do good to them that hate you, . . . that you may be the children of your Father who is in heaven.*[2] Hence, according to St. John Chrysostom, Jesus Christ has called the meek imitators of God.[3]

To the meek, paradise is promised. *Blessed are the meek, for they shall possess the land.*[4] St. Francis de Sales says that meekness is the flower of charity.[5] And Ecclesiasticus has said: *That which is agreeable to Him is faith and meekness.*[6] A meek and faithful heart is the delight of God. He knows not how to cast off the meek. *The Lord lifted up the meek.*[7] The prayers of the humble and meek are very pleasing in the sight of God. *The prayer of the humble and the meek hath always pleased Thee.*[8]

The virtue of meekness consists in two things: 1. In restraining the motions of passion against those that provoke us to anger; and, 2d, In bearing insults.

I.

We must Repress Anger.

With regard to the first, St. Ambrose says that the passion of anger ought to be either avoided or restrained.[9]

[1] "Mansuetudo præ cæteris virtutibus nos Deo conformes facit."— *In Rom. hom.* 19.
[2] "Benefacite his qui oderunt vos, . . . ut sitis filii Patris vestri qui in cœlis est, qui solem suum oriri facit super bonos et malos."— *Matth.* v. 44.
[3] "Eos solos qui mansuetudine conspicui sunt, Dei imitatores Christus nominat."—*Serm. de Mansuetud.*
[4] "Beati mites, quoniam ipsi possidebunt terram."—*Matth.* v. 4.
[5] "*Introd.* p. 3, ch. 8.
[6] "Quod beneplacitum est illi, fides et mansuetudo."—*Ecclus.* i. 34.
[7] "Suscipiens mansuetos Dominus."—*Ps.* cxlvi. 6.
[8] "Humilium et mansuetorum semper tibi placuit deprecatio."— *Judith,* ix. 16.
[9] "Caveatur iracundia, aut cohibeatur."—*Offic.* l. 1, c. 21.

He who feels himself prone to the vice of anger should endeavor to avoid the occasions of it; and should he through necessity be exposed to them, he ought to prepare himself beforehand by good resolutions either to be silent, to answer with sweetness, or to pray to God for strength to resist the temptation, and not to yield to passion. Some excuse themselves by saying such a person is very impertinent, his conduct is insufferable. But, according to St. John Chrysostom, the virtue of meekness consists not in being agreeable to the meek, but in treating with sweetness those that know not what meekness is.[1] When a neighbor is enraged there is no better means of appeasing his anger than by answering with sweetness. *A mild answer breaketh wrath.*[2] As water extinguishes fire, so, says St. John Chrysostom, a mild answer softens the anger of a brother, however great may be his excitement.[3] This is conformable to the words of Ecclesiasticus: *A sweet word multiplieth friends and appeaseth enemies.*[4] St. John Chrysostom adds: "We cannot extinguish fire by fire."[5] Even towards sinners the most abandoned, obstinate, and insolent, we priests must exercise all possible meekness in order to draw them to God. Hugh of St. Victor has written: "You must know the faults, not to punish them, but the diseases to heal them."[6] When, on the other hand, we feel ourselves assailed by any motion of

---

[1] "Cum his qui sunt a mansuetudine alienissimi, tunc virtus ostenditur."—*In Ps.* 119.

[2] "Responsio mollis frangit iram."—*Prov.* xv. 1.

[3] "Sicut rogum accensum aqua exstinguit, ita animam ira æstuantem verbum cum mansuetudine prolatum mitigat."—*In Gen. hom.* 58.

[4] "Verbum dulce multiplicat amicos, et mitigat inimicos."—*Ecclus.* vi. 5.

[5] "Igne non potest ignis exstingui, nec furor furore."

[6] "Vos non, quasi judices criminum, ad percutiendum positi estis sed, quasi judices morborum, ad sanandum."—*Misc.* l. 1, *tit.* 49.

anger, the remedy is to be silent, and to ask strength from God not to make a reply. "The best remedy," says Seneca, "is in delay,"[1] for should we speak while we are inflamed with passion, what we say will appear reasonable, but it will be unjust and sinful. For passion is a certain veil that covers the eyes of the soul, and does not permit us to see the unreasonableness of our reply. "The eye disturbed by anger cannot see," says St. Bernard.[2] Sometimes it appears to us just, and even necessary, to repress the boldness of a person who treats us with insolence: for example, of an inferior who acts disrespectfully towards us. It would indeed be right in such circumstances to show moderate displeasure; to be, as the angelic Doctor says, angry according to right reason.[3] This is conformable to the words of David: *Be ye angry, and sin not.*[4] This would be right if in such anger there were no fault on our part; but in this consists the difficulty. To leave one's self in the hand of anger is a very dangerous thing: you might as well mount a furious horse that refuses to obey the bit, and carries you wheresoever he pleases. Hence St. Francis de Sales, in the Devout Life,[5] says that however just the reason of our anger, it is always expedient to restrain it; and that it is better for you to have it said that you are never angry than that you are wisely angry. When, says St. Augustine,[6] anger has entered the soul, it is difficult to expel it. Hence he exhorts us in the beginning to close the gate that anger may not enter. When a person who is corrected sees his Superior in a passion, he will derive but little fruit

---

[1] "Maximum remedium est iræ, mora."—*De Ira.* l. 2, c. 28.

[2] "Turbatus præ ira oculus rectum non videt."—*De Consid.* l. 2, c. 11.

[3] "Secundum rectam rationem irasci."—2. 2, q. 158, a. 1.

[4] "Irascimini, et nolite peccare."—*Ps.* iv. 5.

[5] *Introd.* p. 3, ch. 8.   [6] *Ep.* 38, *E. B.*

from the admonition: he will regard it as the effect of anger rather than of charity. A single admonition given with sweetness and a tranquil countenance will do more good than a thousand reproaches, however just, accompanied with motions or expressions of anger.

But to be meek does not imply that in order to show kindness or to avoid the displeasure of another we should omit to correct him with just rigor, when such correction is necessary. To omit correction in that case would not be virtue, but a culpable and abominable negligence. Wo, says the Prophet, to him who furnishes a pillow to sinners that they may peacefully sleep in their deadly slumber. *Wo to them that sew cushions under every elbow; and make pillows for the heads of persons of every age, to catch souls: . . . you have strengthened the hands of the wicked that he should not return from his evil way and live.*[1] This vicious condescension, says St. Augustine, " is not charity, but carelessness."[2] It is neither charity nor meekness, but it is negligence, and even cruelty, to the poor souls that thus remain in the state of damnation, without being admonished of their miserable condition. St. Cyprian says that when the sick man feels the knife he assails the surgeon; but when he is cured he will thank him.[3] Meekness, then, implies that when it is necessary to correct a brother we should do it with firmness, but at the same time with sweetness. And when it is our duty to correct others, the Apostle exhorts us first to consider our own defects, that we may have compassion for our neighbor

---

[1] " Væ, quæ consuunt pulvillos sub omni cubito manus, et faciunt cervicalia sub capite universæ ætatis, ad capiendas animas! . . . Et confortastis manus impii, ut non reverteretur a via sua mala, et viveret."—*Ezech.* xiii. 18.

[2] " Non est ista charitas, sed languor."—*In* 1 *Jo. tr.* 7.

[3] " Licet conqueratur æger impatiens per dolorem, gratias aget postmodum, cum senserit sanitatem."- *De Lapsis.*

as we have for ourselves. *Brethren, if a man be overtaken in a fault, you who are spiritual instruct such a one in the spirit of meekness, considering thyself lest thou also be tempted.*[1] Peter de Blois says that it is great baseness in a Superior to correct an inferior with anger and asperity.[2] Anger so disfigures the face that it gives to the most beautiful countenance a horrible appearance, says Seneca.[3] In this matter, then, we should always attend to the admonition of St. Gregory: "Be kind, yet without effeminacy; use rigor, but without exasperating; be merciful, without sparing more than is expedient."[4]

Physicians, says St. Basil,[5] should not get angry with a patient, but should only assail his disease in order to restore his health. Cassian relates[6] that a young religious who was violently tempted against chastity sought advice from an aged monk; but instead of assisting and encouraging him, the old man loaded him with reproaches. But what was the result? The Lord permitted the aged monk to be so violently attacked by the spirit of impurity that he ran like a madman through the monastery. Having heard of his indiscretion towards the young man, the abbot went to him, and said: "Brother, know that God has permitted you to be molested by this temptation, that you may learn to take compassion on others."

When, therefore, we witness the weaknesses and faults of others, we ought not to reprove them with a vain conceit of ourselves: but in applying, to the best of our

---

[1] " Fratres, et si præoccupatus fuerit homo in aliquo delicto, vos qui spirituales estis, hujusmodi instruite in spiritu lenitatis, considerans teipsum, ne et tu tenteris."—*Gal.* vi. 1.

[2] " Turpe quidem est in prælato, cum ira et austeritate corripere."—*Ep.* 100.

[3] " Facies turbatior, pulcherrima ora fœdavit."—*De Ira*, l. 2, c. 35.

[4] " Sit amor, sed non emolliens; sit rigor, sed non exasperans; sit pietas, sed non plus, quam expediat, parcens."—*Mor.* l. 20, c. 6.

[5] *Reg. fus. disp. int.* 51.   [6] *Collat.* 2, c. 13.

ability, a remedy to their faults, we should be humble in our own estimation: otherwise God will permit us to fall into the very defects that we condemn in others. The same Cassian [1] relates that a certain abbot, called Machete, confessed that he had miserably fallen into three faults of which he had before judged his brethren. Hence St. Augustine says that compassion for our neighbor, and not indignation, should precede correction.[2] And St. Gregory tells us that the consideration of our own defects will make us pity and excuse the faults of others.[3]

Thus to yield to anger is never profitable to ourselves or to others. If it produce no other evil, it at least robs us of peace. Agrippinus the philosopher having once lost some of his goods, said: "If I have lost my property I will not lose my peace." The disturbance of mind to which we give way on account of the maltreatment we receive from others is more hurtful to us than the injuries offered to us. Seneca has said: "My anger will hurt me more than their insults."[4] He who indulges anger when an affront is offered to him is a cause of pain to himself. "Thou hast decreed, O Lord!" says St. Augustine, "that the soul that is inordinate should be its own torment."[5]

Hence that great master of meekness, St. Francis de Sales,[6] teaches that it is necessary to practise meekness not only to others, but also to ourselves. After yielding to a fault, some are indignant with themselves, and

---

[1] *De Cænob. inst.* l. 5, c. 30.
[2] "Reprehensionem, non odium, sed misericordia præcedat."—*De Serm. D. in monte*, l. 2, c. 19.
[3] "Considerata infirmitas propria, mala nobis excusat aliena."—*Mor.* l. 5, c. 33.
[4] "Plus mihi nocitura est ira, quam injuria."—*De Ira*, l. 3, c. 25.
[5] "Jussisti ut pœna sua sibi sit omnis inordinatus animus."—*Conf.* l. 1, c. 12.
[6] *Introd.* p. 3, ch. 9.

give way to disquietude, and in this state of agitation they commit a thousand faults. In troubled water, says St. Aloysius Gonzaga, the devil always finds fish to catch. It is necessary, then, when we perceive that we have fallen into a defect, not to be disturbed (to give way to disquietude after a fault is the effect of our own pride, and of the high opinion we had of our own virtue), but to humble ourselves peacefully, to detest the sin, and instantly to have recourse to God, hoping to receive from him help to avoid a relapse.

In a word, they who are truly humble and meek live always in peace, and in every occurrence preserve tranquillity of soul. *Learn of Me*, says Jesus Christ, *because I am meek and humble of heart, and you shall find rest to your souls*.[1] And before him, David said: *The meek shall inherit the land, and shall delight in abundance of peace*.[2] "Nothing is able to disturb their serenity,"[3] says St. Leo. No insult, no loss, no misfortune, disturbs the peace of a meek heart.

Should we feel angry on any occasion, we must endeavor (according to the advice of the holy bishop of Geneva) to repress passion without waiting to examine whether it is right or not to subdue it. And after a dispute, which may perhaps have disturbed our peace, let us observe the advice of the 'Apostle: *Let not the sun go down upon your anger. Give not place to the devil*.[4] Let us first put our soul in peace, and then be reconciled to the person by whom we have been offended, lest through that spark the devil should kindle in our souls a deadly flame that may cause our ruin.

[1] "Discite a me quia mitis sum et humilis corde, et invenietis requiem animabus vestris."—*Matth*. xi. 29.
[2] "Mansueti autem hereditabunt terram, et delectabuntur in multitudine pacis."—*Ps*. xxxvi. 11.
[3] "Nihil asperum mitibus."—*De Epiph*. s. 5.
[4] "Sol non occidat super iracundiam vestram; nolite locum dare diabolo."—*Ephes*. iv. 26.

II.

We must Bear Contempt.

Secondly, the virtue of meekness consists still more in bearing insults. Many, says St. Francis of Assisi, place their sanctification in saying many prayers, or in the practice of many corporal mortifications, but afterwards they cannot bear an offensive word. "Not understanding," says the saint, "of what profit it is to bear insults."[1] A soul gains more by peacefully bearing an affront than by fasting for ten days on bread and water.

St. Bernard says that there are three degrees of advancement, to which a soul that wishes to be a saint, ought to aspire. The first is not to wish for authority over others; the second, to wish to be subject to all; the third is to bear insults with peace.[2] You will, for example, see that what is given to others is denied to you: what others say is heard with attention; what you say is received with derision: others are praised, are elected to offices of honor, to transact business of importance; but you are despised: what you do is censured and ridiculed. You will be truly humble, says St. Dorotheus,[3] if you accept in peace all these humiliations, and recommend to God, as your best benefactors, all that treat you in this manner; for they thus cure your pride, which is a most malignant and deadly malady.

In thy humiliation keep patience.[4] Behold, then, what we must do; we must give way neither to anger nor to complaints, but accept insults as due to our sins. He

---

[1] "Non intelligentes, quanto majus sit lucrum in tolerantia injuriarum."

[2] "Primus profectus, nolle dominari; secundus, velle subjici; tertius, injurias æquanimiter pati."--*De Divers.* s. 60.

[3] *Doctr.* 20.

[4] "In humilitate tua patientiam habe."—*Ecclus.* ii. 4.

who has offended God merits very different insults: he deserves to be cast under the feet of the devils. St. Francis Borgia was once obliged on a journey to sleep in the same bed with his companion, Father Bustamente, who labored under asthma, and spent the whole night coughing and casting out phlegm. He thought that he was spitting towards the wall; but frequently the phlegm fell on the face of St. Francis. In the morning the Father was greatly grieved at what he had done; but the saint placidly answered: " Father, be not troubled; for certainly in this room there is no place so fit for the reception of spittle as my face." The proud, because they esteem themselves worthy of all honor, convert the humiliations that they receive into an occasion of pride; but the humble, because they think themselves deserving of all ignominies, convert the insults offered to them into a source of humility. " He is humble," says St. Bernard, " who changes humiliations into humility."[1] Rodriguez says that when reproved the proud imitate the hedgehog, which when touched becomes all thorns; that is, they get into a fury, and instantly break out into complaints, reproaches, and detraction. But, on the other hand, the humble when blamed for their conduct humble themselves still more, confess that they are full of defects, thank the person who corrects them, and preserve tranquillity of soul. He who is disturbed by correction shows that in him pride still reigns. Hence they who are disquieted by correction or admonitions must humble themselves more before God, and entreat him to deliver them from the hands of pride, which still lives in their hearts.

My spikenard sent forth the odor thereof.[2] The spikenard is a small odoriferous plant that sends forth its

---

[1] " Est humilis, qui humiliationem convertit in humilitatem."—*In Cant.* s. 34.

[2] " Nardus mea dedit odorem suum."—*Cant.* i. 11.

odors when bruised and twisted. Oh, what odors of sweetness does an humble soul give to God when she peacefully suffers insults, and delights in seeing herself despised and maltreated! Being asked what must be done in order to acquire true humility, Zachary, a monk, took his cowl, and trampling on it said: "He who delights in seeing himself treated in this manner is truly humble." Father Alvarez used to say that the time of humiliation is the time of getting rid of our miseries, and of acquiring great treasures of merit. God is as liberal of his gifts to the humble as he is sparing to the proud: *God resisteth the proud, and giveth grace to the humble*.[1] St. Augustine says that a guilty conscience is not healed by praise, nor a good conscience wounded by insults.[2] It was this that St. Francis of Assisi meant when he said: "We are what we are before God." It is, then, of little importance to us whether we are praised or censured by men: it is enough for us to merit praise from God. And God will certainly bestow great praise on all that cheerfully bear insults from others for his sake.

The meek are dear to God and to men. St. John Chrysostom says that there is nothing that gives greater edification to others, and draws souls more powerfully to God, than the meekness of the man who, when treated with derision, contempt, and insult, seeks not revenge, but bears all with a peaceful and placid countenance.[3] St. Ambrose writes that Moses was more beloved by the Hebrews on account of the meekness with which he received insults, than on account of the miracles which he wrought.[4] The meek are useful to themselves and to

[1] "Deus superbis resistit; humilibus autem dat gratiam."—*James*, iv. 6.

[2] "Nec malam conscientiam sanat laudantis præconium, nec bonam vulnerat conviciantis opprobrium."—*Contra Petil.* l. 3, c. 7.

[3] "Nihil ita conciliat domino familiares, ut quod illum vident mansuetudine jucundum."—*S. de Mansuet.*

[4] "Ut plus cum pro mansuetudine diligerent, quam pro factis admirarentur."—*Offic.* l. 2, c. 7.

others, says St. John Chrysostom.[1] Father Maffei relates that while a Jesuit was preaching in Japan, an insolent bystander spit in his face; the Father wiped away the spittle, and continued the sermon as if nothing had happened. At the sight of such meekness one of the audience was converted, and said that a religion that teaches such humility must be true and divine. Thus, also, by the meekness and tranquillity with which he bore all the insults heaped upon him by the heretical ministers, St. Francis de Sales converted an immense number of heretics. Meekness is the touchstone of sanctity. St. John Chrysostom says[2] that the surest means of knowing whether a soul has virtue is to observe if she practises meekness under contradictions. In the history of Japan, Crasset relates that a certain Augustinian missionary who, in the time of the persecution, had changed his dress, received a buffet without resenting it. Seeing his meekness, the idolaters instantly supposed him to be a Christian, and laid hold of him; for said they, no one but a Christian could practise such virtue.

Ah! at the sight of Jesus loaded with contempt it is easy to bear all insults. Standing one day before a crucifix, Blessed Mary of the Incarnation said to her religious: "O sisters! can it be possible that we will not bear contempt when we see a God so despised?" On his journey to Rome to receive the crown of martyrdom, St. Ignatius, Martyr, finding himself so maltreated by the soldiers, said: "I now begin to be the servant of Christ."[3] What can be expected from a Christian if he is not able to bear contempt for Jesus Christ? It is indeed very painful to our pride to be despised and insulted, without seeking revenge, or even making a reply.

[1] "Mansuetus, utilis sibi et aliis."—*In Act. hom.* 6.
[2] *In Gen. hom.* 34.
[3] "Nunc incipio esse Christi discipulus."—*Ep. ad Rom.*

But in doing violence to ourselves consists our progress in perfection, says St. Jerome.[1] A holy nun, whenever she received an affront, was accustomed to go to the holy sacrament, and to say: "Lord, I am a poor miserable creature: I have nothing to present to you, but I offer this little gift—this insult that I have received." Oh, how lovingly does Jesus Christ embrace the soul that is despised! Oh, how soon does he console her and enrich her with his graces!

Ah! the soul that truly loves Jesus Christ not only bears insults in peace, but embraces them with pleasure and joy. The holy Apostles *went from the presence of the council rejoicing that they were accounted worthy to suffer reproach for the name of Jesus.*[2] St. Joseph Calasanctius used to say that in many are verified the last words of this passage—they are accounted worthy to suffer reproach for the name of Jesus, but not the first—*they went rejoicing.* But he who wishes to be a saint must at least aspire to this degree of perfection. "He is not humble that does not wish to be despised,"[3] says the same saint. The Venerable Louis da Ponte did not at first understand how a man could rejoice in contempt; but when he afterwards attained higher perfection he easily comprehended it, and experienced joy under insults. It was this that St. Ignatius of Loyola, coming from heaven, taught St. Mary Magdalene de Pazzi: he said to her that true humility consists in attaining such a state of mind as to feel a continual joy in all things which can lead a person to self-contempt.

Worldlings do not rejoice as much in the honors that they receive, as the saints do in seeing themselves de-

---

[1] "Tantum proficies, quantum tibi ipsi vim intuleris."—*De Imit.* l. 1, c. 25.

[2] "Ibant gaudentes a conspectu concilii, quoniam digni habiti sunt pro nomine Jesu contumeliam pati."—*Acts,* v. 41.

[3] "Non est humilis, qui non optat sperni."

spised. Brother Juniper, of the Order of St. Francis, when treated with insult held out his habit as if to receive precious gems. When St. John Francis Regis saw himself made an object of laughter he not only rejoiced at the humiliation, but sought still more to excite derision. To St. John of the Cross the Redeemer once appeared with a cross on his shoulders and a crown of thorns on his head, and said: "John, ask what you desire of me."[1] The saint answered: "O Lord! to suffer and to be despised for Thee."[2] As if he said: Lord, since I see you so afflicted and despised for my sake, what else can I ask but sufferings and contempt?

To conclude: He who wishes to belong entirely to God, and to assimilate himself to Jesus Christ, must love to be unknown and disregarded. "Love to be unknown, and to be regarded as nothing,"[3] was the great lesson of St. Bonaventure, which St. Philip Neri constantly inculcated to his spiritual children. Jesus Christ tells us to esteem ourselves happy, and to exult with joy when we are hated, cast off, and censured by men for his sake. He tells us that the more galling the insults which we accept with joy, the greater the reward will he give us in heaven. *Blessed shall you be when men shall hate you, and when they shall separate you, and shall reproach you, and cast out your name as evil, for the Son of Man's sake. Be glad in that day and rejoice; for, behold, your reward is great in heaven.*[4] And what greater joy can a soul feel than that which arises from seeing herself despised for the love of Jesus Christ? Then, says St. Peter, she obtains the

---

[1] "Joannes, pete quid vis a me."
[2] "Domine, pati et contemni pro te."
[3] "Ama nesciri et pro nihilo reputari."—*Alphab. rel.*
[4] "Beati eritis, cum vos oderint homines, et cum separaverint vos, et exprobraverint, et ejecerint nomen vestrum tanquam malum, propter Filium hominis. Gaudete in illa die, et exsultate; ecce enim merces vestra multa est in cœlo."—*Luke*, vi. 22.

greatest honor that it is possible for her to receive; for God then treats her as he has treated his own very Son. *If you are reproached for the name of Christ, you shall be blessed, for that which is of the honor, glory, and power of God . . . resteth upon you.*[1]

[1] "Si exprobramini in nomine Christi, beati eritis, quoniam quod est honoris, gloriæ, et virtutis Dei, et qui est ejus Spiritus, super vos requiescit."—1 *Pet.* iv. 14.

INSTRUCTION VIII.

MORTIFICATION, AND PARTICULARLY INTERIOR MORTIFICATION.

I.
Necessity of Mortification in General.

MAN was created by God in a state of integrity, so that without a struggle the senses obeyed the spirit, and the spirit obeyed God: *God made man right.*[1] Sin came and deranged the beautiful order that God had established, and the life of man began to be a state of continual warfare: *For the flesh lusteth against the spirit: and the spirit against the flesh.*[2] *But I see,* says the Apostle in a tone of lamentation, *another law in my members, fighting against the law of the mind, and captivating me in the law of sin that is in my members.*[3]

Hence for man there are two kinds of life—the life of the angels, who seek to do the will of God, and the life of beasts, who attend only to the indulgence of the senses. If a man labors to do the will of God he becomes an angel; if he seeks after sensual gratifications he becomes a beast. Hence what the Lord prescribed to Jeremias, *Lo, I have set thee this day . . . to root up and to pull down, . . . to build and to plant,*[4] we ought to do in

[1] "Quod fecerit Deus hominem rectum."—*Eccles.* vii. 30.
[2] "Caro enim concupiscit adversus spiritum, spiritus autem adversus carnem."—*Gal.* v. 17.
[3] "Video autem aliam legem in membris meis. repugnantem legi mentis meæ. et captivantem me in lege peccati."—*Rom.* vii. 23.
[4] "Constitui te . . ut evellas et destruas, . . . ædifices et plantes."—*Jer.* i. 10.

22

ourselves: we should plant virtues, but we should first extirpate noxious weeds. Hence we must always carry in our hand the mattock of mortification, to cut down the evil desires that constantly spring up and bud forth within us from the infected roots of concupiscence; otherwise the soul shall become a forest of vices.

In a word, it is necessary to cleanse the heart, if we wish for light to know God, the sovereign Good: *Blessed are the clean of heart, for they shall see God.*[1] Hence St. Augustine has said: "If you wish to see God take care to purify your heart."[2] Isaias asks: *Whom shall He teach knowledge? . . . Them that are weaned from the milk, that are drawn away from the breasts.*[3] God gives the science of the saints, that is, the science of knowing and loving him, only to them that are weaned and drawn away from the breasts of the world: *But the sensual man perceiveth not these things that are of the Spirit of God.*[4] He who like a brute animal seeks after sensual pleasures is not capable of even understanding the excellence of spiritual goods.

St. Francis de Sales says that as salt preserves flesh from corruption, so mortification preserves the soul from sin. In the soul in which mortification reigns all virtues shall flourish. *Myrrh and stacte and cassia perfume thy garments.*[5] On this passage Guerric the abbot writes: "When myrrh begins to exhale a perfume, soon other aromatical perfumes will be exhaled."[6] This is precisely what the

[1] "Beati mundo corde, quoniam ipsi Deum videbunt."—*Matth.* v. 8.
[2] "Deum videre vis? prius cogita de corde mundando."—*Serm.* 177, E. B. *app.*
[3] "Quem docebit (Deus) scientiam? Ablactatos a lacte, avulsos ab uberibus."—*Isa.* xxviii. 9.
[4] "Animalis autem homo non percipit ea quæ sunt Spiritus Dei."— I. *Cor.* ii. 14.
[5] "Myrrha, et gutta, et casia, a vestimentis tuis."—*Ps.* xliv. 9.
[6] "Si myrrha prima spirare cœperit per mortificationem voluptatum, consequentur et aliæ species aromaticæ."—*De Annunt.* s. 1.

sacred Spouse has said: *I have gathered my myrrh with my aromatical spices.*[1]

All our sanctity and salvation consist in following the examples of Jesus Christ: *For whom He foreknew, He also predestinated to be made conformable to the image of His Son.*[2] But we shall not be able to imitate Jesus Christ unless we deny ourselves, and embrace by mortification the cross that he gives us to carry: *If any man will come after Me, let him deny himself and take up his cross and follow Me.*[3] The life of our Redeemer was all full of sufferings, of sorrows, and ignominies. Hence Isaias said of him, that he was *despised and the most abject of men: a man of sorrows.*[4] As a mother takes nauseous medicine in order to cure the infant to which she gives suck, so our Redeemer, says St. Catharine of Sienna, wished to assume so many pains in order to heal the infirmities of us poor sinners. But since Jesus Christ has endured so much for the love of us, it is but just that we suffer for his sake. We must, then, endeavor to follow the advice of St. Paul: *Always bearing about in your body the mortification of Jesus, that the life also of Jesus may be made manifest in our bodies.*[5] "This we shall do," says St. Anselm in his comment on the preceding text, when, "in imitation of him, we assiduously practise mortification."[6] To this we priests, who celebrate the mysteries of the Passion of our Lord, are bound in a special manner. "Because," says Hugh of St. Victor, "while celebrating the divine mysteries we

---

[1] "Messui myrrham meam cum aromatibus meis."—*Cant.* v. 1.

[2] "Quos præscivit, et prædestinavit conformes fieri imaginis Filii sui."—*Rom.* viii. 29.

[3] "Si quis vult post me venire, abneget semetipsum, et tollat crucem suam, et sequatur me."—*Matt.* xvi. 24.

[4] "Despectum et novissimum virorum, virum dolorum."—*Isa.* liii. 3.

[5] "Semper mortificationem Jesu in corpore nostro circumferentes, ut et vita Jesu manifestetur in corporibus nostris."—2 *Cor.* iv. 10.

[6] "Ad ejus imitationem, assidue carnem mortificemus."

celebrate the Passion of our Lord; we should therefore be careful to reproduce it in our lives."[1]

The principal means of acquiring sanctity are prayer and mortification, represented in the sacred Scripture by incense and myrrh. *Who is this that goeth up by the desert, as a pillar of smoke of aromatical spices, of myrrh and frankincense.*[2] The Holy Ghost adds: *and of all the powders of the perfumer*,[3] to show that prayer and mortification are followed by all virtues.—Prayer, then, and mortification, are necessary to render a soul holy; but mortification must precede prayer: *I will go to the mountain of myrrh and to the hill of frankincense.*[4] Thus our Lord invites us to follow him, first to the mountain of myrrh, and then to the hill of frankincense. St. Francis Borgia used to say, that prayer introduces divine love into the heart; but it is mortification that prepares a place for charity, by removing from the soul the world, which should otherwise prevent the entrance of love. Should a person go to a fountain for water with a vessel full of earth, he shall take back nothing but mire. He must first cast away the earth, and then fill the vessel with water. Father Baltassar Alvarez used to say that prayer without mortification is either an illusion, or will be only of short duration. And St. Ignatius of Loyola has said that a mortified soul unites herself more intimately to God in a quarter of an hour's prayer, than an immortified soul does in several hours. Hence, having once heard a person praised for his great spirit of prayer, the saint said: "It is a sign that he practises great mortification."

[1] "Quia passionis dominicæ mysteria celebramus, debemus imitari quod agimus."

[2] "Quæ est ista quæ ascendit per desertum, sicut virgula fumi ex aromatibus myrrhæ et thuris?"—*Cant*. iii. 6.

[3] "Et universi pulveris pigmentarii."

[4] "Vadam ad montem myrrhæ et ad collem thuris."—*Cant*. iv. 6.

II.

Necessity of Interior Mortification.

We have a soul and a body. External mortification is necessary in order to mortify the disorderly appetites of the body; and interior mortification is necessary in order to mortify the irregular affections of the soul. All this is comprised in the following words of the Saviour: *If any man will come after Me, let him deny himself, and take up his cross, and follow Me.*[1] External mortification is included in the words *let him take up his cross;* this species of mortification is necessary, as we shall see hereafter: but interior mortification is still more important and necessary—*let him deny himself.* This consists in subjecting to reason the disorderly passions of the soul; such as ambition, inordinate anger, self-esteem, attachment to self-interest, to our own opinion, or to self-will. "There are two kinds of crosses," says St. Augustine, "one corporal, the other spiritual. The latter is more sublime, and consists in curbing the inordinate inclinations of the heart."[2] External mortification, then, represses the appetites of the body in order to bring it under subjection to the spirit; the interior mortification restrains the affections of the heart in order to subject them to reason and God; hence it has been called by the Apostle: *The circumcision is that of the heart, in the spirit.*[3] In themselves the passions are indifferent, and not sinful; and when well regulated by reason they are useful, because they contribute to the preservation of our existence. But when opposed to reason, they are the ruin of the soul. Miserable the

---

[1] "Si quis vult post me venire, abneget semetipsum, et tollat crucem suam, et sequatur me."—*Matt.* xvi. 24.

[2] "Duo sunt crucis genera, unum corporale, aliud spirituale. Alterum est sublimius, scilicet, regere motus animi."—*Serm.* 196, *E. B. app.*

[3] "Circumcisio cordis in spiritu."—*Rom.* ii. 29.

soul that God leaves in the hands of her own desires! This is the greatest chastisement which he can inflict upon her. *I let them go according to the desires of their own hearts: they shall walk in their own inventions.*[1] Hence we must always pray to the Lord in the words of Solomon: *Give me not over to a shameful and foolish mind.*[2] My God, do not abandon me into the hands of my passions.

Our principal care, then, should be to conquer ourselves. *Conquer thyself.*[3] St. Ignatius of Loyola appeared not to consider any lesson more important than that which is contained in the words *Conquer thyself:* his familiar discourses were ordinarily on conquering self-love and subduing self-will; and he would say, that out of a hundred persons who practise prayer, more than ninety are attached to their own opinion. He set a greater value on a single act of mortification of self-will than on several hours spent in prayer, in the midst of spiritual consolations. To a Brother who separated from the company of the others in order to get rid of a certain defect the saint said, that he would have gained more by a few acts of mortification in the society of his companions than he would by remaining silent in a cave for an entire year. "It is no small matter," writes Thomas à Kempis, "even in things the most trifling, to relinquish self."[4] On the other hand, St. Peter Damian asserts that unless he leaves himself, it will profit a man nothing to have forsaken all things.[5] Hence, to a person who wished to leave all things in order to give himself to God, St. Bernard said: "Remember that if you have resolved to

---

[1] "Dimisi eos secundum desideria cordis eorum; ibunt in adinventionibus suis."—*Ps.* lxxx. 13.
[2] "Animæ irreverenti et infrunitæ ne tradas me."—*Ecclus.* xxiii. 6.
[3] "Vince teipsum."
[4] "Non est minimum, in minimis seipsum relinquere."—*De Imit.* l. 3, c. 39.
[5] "Nihil prodest, sine seipso cætera reliquisse."—*Hom.* 9.

leave everything, you must count yourself among those things that you must leave."¹ Unless, adds the saint, you deny yourself, you shall never be able to be a follower of Jesus Christ.² Our Redeemer *hath rejoiced as a giant to run the way*.³ But, says the holy Doctor, he who carries the weight of his passions and of earthly affections, and wishes to follow the Saviour, shall not be able to keep within view of Jesus running the way.

It is necessary, above all, to attend to the subjugation of the predominant passion. Some are careful to mortify themselves in many things, but make little effort to conquer the passion to which they are most inclined; such persons can never advance in the way of God. He who allows any irregular passion to rule over him, is in great danger of being lost. But, on the other hand, he who subdues the predominant passion will easily conquer all his other passions. When the strongest enemy is vanquished, it is easy to defeat less powerful foes. The value and merit of the victory is greatest when the greatest valor is required: for example, some are not avaricious of money, but are full of self-esteem; others are not ambitious of honors, but feel a great thirst for riches. Unless the former are careful to practise mortification, when treated with contempt, their disregard for riches will profit them but little. Unless the latter labor to mortify the desire of wealth, their contempt for honors will be but of little advantage to them. In a word, a person gains most merit and makes the greatest progress when he uses the greatest violence to conquer himself. "So much will you advance in virtue," says

¹ "Qui relinquere disponis omnia, te quoque inter relinquenda numerare memento."—*Declam*. n. 3.
² "Sane, nisi abnegaverit semetipsum, sequi eum (Christum) non potest."—*Ib*. n. 48.
³ "Exsultavit ut gigas ad currendam viam" (*Ps*. xviii. 6); "nec sequi poteras oneratus."—*Declam*. n. 2.

St. Jerome, "as you do violence to yourself."[1] St. Ignatius was naturally prone to anger, but by virtue he became so meek that he was considered to be a man of a mild disposition. St. Francis de Sales was also strongly inclined to anger; but by the violence that he offered to himself he became, as we read in his life, an example of patience and sweetness in the many contradictions and insults that he received.

External mortification, without interior self-denial, profits the soul but little. Of what use, says St. Jerome, is it to reduce the body by fasting, and afterwards to swell with pride? or to abstain from wine, and to be inebriated with hatred?[2] The Apostle says that we must put off the old man, that is, attachment to self-love, and clothe ourselves with the new man, that is, Jesus Christ, who never pleased himself. *For*, says St. Paul, *Christ did not please Himself*.[3] Hence St. Bernard pitied certain monks who wore an humble dress, but interiorly cherished their passions: "This humble habit is not a sign of interior holiness, but a cover thrown over inveterate corruption. They have not stripped themselves of the old man, but have only hidden him."[4] They, says the saint, do not put off their vices: they only cover them with the exterior marks of penance. Hence, fasting, watching, hair-shirts, and disciplines are of little or no use to him who is attached to himself, and to what belongs to him.

[1] "Tantum proficies, quantum tibi ipsi vim intuleris."—*De Imit.* l. 1, c. 25.

[2] "Quid prodest tenuari abstinentia, si animus intumescit superbia? Quid vinum non bibere, et odio inebriari?"—*Ep. ad Celant.*

[3] "Etenim Christus non sibi complacuit."—*Rom.* xv. 3.

[4] "Humilis habitus non sanctæ novitatis est meritum, sed priscæ vetustatis operculum. Veterem hominem non exuerunt, sed novo palliant."—*In Cant.* s. 16.

III.

The Practice of Interior Mortification.

They, says St. John Climacus,[1] who wish to belong entirely to God must divest themselves of attachment to four things in particular: to property, to honors, to relatives, and above all, to self-will.

1. PROPERTY.

First, it is necessary to remove attachment to property or to riches. St. Bernard says that riches are a burden to him who possesses them, that they contaminate the man who loves them, and torture him who loses them.[2] The priest ought to remember, that when he entered the sanctuary he declared, in the following words, that he wished for no other possessions than God: *The Lord is the portion of my inheritance; . . . it is Thou that wilt restore my inheritance to me.*[3] The ecclesiastic, then, says St. Peter Damian, who after having chosen God for his portion attends to the acquisition of riches, offers a great insult to his Creator.[4] Yes, for by his conduct he shows that he considers the Lord not sufficient to content his heart. St. Bernard says, and says truly, that among the covetous there is none more avaricious than the ecclesiastic who is attached to money.[5] How many priests are there who, but for the miserable *honorarium* that they receive, would seldom say Mass! Would to God that they never

---
[1] *Scal. par. gr.* 2.
[2] "Possessa onerant, amata inquinant, amissa cruciant."—*Ep.* 103.
[3] "Dominus pars hereditatis meæ et calicis mei; tu es qui restitues hereditatem meam mihi."—*Ps.* xv. 5.
[4] "Si igitur Deus portio ejus est, non levem Creatori suo contumeliam videtur inferre, qui, super hoc singulare talentum, terrenam æstuat pecuniam cumulare."—*Opusc.* 27. *proœm.*
[5] "Quis, obsecro, avidius clericis quærit temporalia?"—*S. ad Past. in syn.*

offered the holy sacrifice! They, as St. Augustine says, belong to that class of men who do not seek for money in order to serve God; but serve God in order to accumulate riches.[1] What a disgrace, exclaims St. Jerome, to see a priest intent on the acquisition of wealth![2]

But let us pass by the disgrace, and examine the great danger of perdition, to which a priest intent on heaping up riches exposes his soul. "Those priests are greatly in peril," says St. Hilary, "who are anxious to amass riches and increase their fortune."[3] This the Apostle has taught, saying that such persons shall not only be molested by many cares which impede their spiriual progress, but shall also fall into temptations and desires which will lead them to ruin. *They that will become rich, fall into temptations, . . . and into many unprofitable and hurtful desires, which draw men into destruction and perdition.*[4] And into what excesses, thefts, injustice, simony, and sacrileges has the desire of money precipitated certain priests! St. Ambrose says: "He who amasses gold loses the grace of God."[5] St. Paul assimilates avarice to idolatry: *A covetous person* (*which is a serving of idols*).[6] And justly, for the covetous man makes money his God, that is, his last end.

"Extirpate the thirst for gold," says St. John Chrysostom, "and you will extirpate all crimes."[7] If, then, we wish to possess God, let us remove all attachment to the

[1] "Non nummum propter Deum impendunt, sed Deum propter nummum colunt."—*De Civ. D.* l. 11, c. 25.

[2] "Ignominia Sacerdotis est studere divitiis."—*Ep. ad Nepot.*

[3] "Ingenti periculo sunt Sacerdotes qui curis pecuniæ, et familiarium rerum incrementis, occupantur."—*In Ps.* 138.

[4] "Qui volunt divites fieri, incidunt in tentationem, et in laqueum diaboli, et desideria multa inutilia et nociva, quæ mergunt homines in interitum et perditionem."—1 *Tim.* vi. 9.

[5] "Qui aurum redigit, gratiam prodigit."—*Serm.* 59.

[6] "Avarus, quod est idolorum servitus."—*Ephes.* v. 5.

[7] "Tolle pecuniarum studium, et omnia mala sublata sunt."—*In* 1 *Tim. hom.* 17.

goods of this world. St. Philip Neri used to say that he who seeks after riches shall never become a saint. The riches of us who are priests should consist not in possessions, but in virtues; these will make us great in heaven, and give us strength on earth against the enemies of our salvation. This is the language of St. Prosper: "Our riches are chastity, piety, humility, meekness: they only will make us great in heaven, and at the same time strong upon earth against the enemies of our salvation."[1] Let us, says the Apostle, be content with moderate food for the support of life, and simple raiment to cover the body: let us labor to become saints; this alone is important to us: *But having food, and wherewith to be covered, with these we are content.*[2] Of what use are earthly goods, which we must one day quit, and which never content the heart? Let us seek to acquire goods which shall accompany us to eternity, and make us happy forever in heaven: *Lay not up to yourselves treasures on earth, where the rust and the moth consume. . . . But lay up treasures in heaven.*[3] Hence, in the Council of Milan the following admonition was given to priests: "Lay up treasures not on earth, but good works and souls for heaven.'[4] The treasures of a priest should consist in good works, and in gaining souls to God.

Hence, in conformity with the words of the Apostle: *No man being a soldier to God entangleth himself with secular business, that he may please Him to Whom he hath engaged*

[1] "Divitiæ nostræ sunt pudicitia, pietas, humilitas, mansuetudo; illæ nobis ambiendæ sunt, quæ nos ornare possint, pariter et munire." —*De Vita cont.* l. 2, c. 13.

[2] "Habentes autem alimenta, et quibus tegamur, his contenti simus."—1 *Tim.* vi. 8.

[3] "Nolite thesaurizare vobis thesauros in terra, ubi ærugo et tinea demolitur. . . . Thesaurizate autem vobis thesauros in cœlo."— *Matth.* vi. 19.

[4] "Thesaurizate, non thesauros in terra, sed bonorum operum et animarum in cœlis."

himself.[1] The holy Church prohibits, with so much rigor, and under pain of censure, ecclesiastics to engage in traffic. The priest is consecrated to God; he therefore should attend to no other business than the advancement of God's glory. The Lord does not accept empty victims from which the marrow has been extracted. *I will offer up to Thee*, said David, *holocausts full of marrow.*[2] The sacrifices, the Masses, Offices, and works that a priest dissipated by the cares of traffic offers to God are, says St. Peter Damian, empty; for he has taken away the marrow, that is, attention and devotion, and presents only the skin or external appearance.[3] What a misery to see a priest, who could save souls and do great things for the glory of God, employed in buying and selling, and engaged in traffic of cattle and corn. "You are consecrated," says Peter de Blois, "to great things; do not occupy yourself with what is trivial."[4] What but a spider's web, says St. Bernard, is earthly traffic?[5] As the spider eviscerates itself, making its web for the purpose of catching a fly, so, O God! certain priests spend themselves, lose their time, and the fruit of their spiritual works, in order to gain a little dust. They submit to labors, to anxiety and disquietude, for emptiness, when they could possess God, who is the Lord of all things. "Why do we trouble ourselves," exclaims St. Bonaventure, "about nothing, while we may possess the Creator of all things?"[6]

[1] "Nemo, militans Deo, implicat se negotiis sæcularibus, ut ei placeat, cui se probavit."—2 *Tim.* ii. 4.

[2] "Holocausta medullata offeram tibi."—*Ps.* lxv. 15.

[3] "Quisquis se per negotiorum sæcularium exercitia delectabiliter fundit, holocausti sui medullas cum visceribus subtrahit, et solam victimæ pellem Deo adolere contendit."—*Opusc.* 12. c. 22.

[4] "Magnis addictus es, noli minimis occupari."—*De Inst. Episc.*

[5] "Fructus horum quid, nisi araneorum telæ?"—*De Cons.* l. 1. c. 2.

[6] "Nescio cur nos affligimus circa nihil, cum possidere Creatorem omnium valeamus!"—*Stim. div. am.* p. 2, c. 2.

Some will say: But I act justly; I attend to this business without any scruple of conscience. I answer, first, that, as has been already said, ecclesiastics are forbidden to engage even in a just traffic: hence if they do not violate justice, they at least sin against the precept of the Church. Besides, St Bernard says: "Wherever the river flows there it hollows out the earth; so the application to earthly affairs injures the conscience."[1] As in their passage the running waters eat away the banks of the river, so the cares of traffic gnaw the conscience, that is, they make us always fail in some duty. If, says St. Gregory, traffic were productive of no other evil, at least the crowd of worldly thoughts that it engenders closes the ear of the heart, and prevents it from hearing the divine inspirations.[2] In a word, St. Isidore writes: "The more priests occupy themselves with the care of earthly affairs, the more they separate themselves from the things of heaven."[3] It is true that some are obliged by charity to attend to the affairs of their family; but, according to St. Gregory, this should be permitted only in cases of strict necessity.[4] Some priests undertake, without necessity, the care of the concerns of their family, and even forbid relatives to interfere in them; but if they wished to attend to the affairs of their family why have they become ministers of the family of God?

The priest who seeks to be employed in the courts of the great also exposes his soul to very imminent danger. Peter de Blois says that as the saints are saved through many tribulations, so they who enter courts are

[1] "Rivus, qua fluit, cavat terram; sic discursus temporalium conscientiam rodit."—*De Cons.* l. 4, c. 6.

[2] "Aurem cordis terrenarum cogitationum turba, dum perstrepit, claudit."—*Mor.* l. 23, c. 20.

[3] "Quanto se rerum studiis occupant, tanto a charitate divina se separant."

[4] "Sæcularia negotia aliquando ex compassione toleranda sunt, nunquam vero ex amore requirenda."—*Past.* p. 2, c. 7.

lost through many tribulations.¹ It is very dangerous for a priest to plead as an advocate in the courts of law. "In the court," says St. Ambrose, "Christ is not found."² What fervor, I ask, can the priest have who pleads in the courts? How can he say the Office and Mass with devotion when the causes he has to defend fill his whole mind and hinder him from thinking of God? The causes that a priest should advocate are the causes of poor sinners; and these he should seek to deliver from the hands of the devil and from eternal death by sermons, by hearing confessions, or at least by admonitions and prayers. A priest should abstain from pleading, not only for others, but also for himself. Every temporal law-suit is a seminary of cares and disquietudes, of rancor and sins. Hence we read in the Gospel: *And if a man will contend with thee in judgment and take away thy coat, let go thy cloak also to him.*³ We know that this is only a counsel; but let us at least avoid suits that are but of trifling importance. You may get rid of temporal misery, you may gain a victory, but you shall suffer a great loss of fervor and peace. "Sacrifice something," says St. Augustine, "in order that you may enjoy God and escape law-suits. Lose your money in order to purchase peace for your soul."⁴ St. Francis de Sales has said that to go to law, and not yield to folly, is scarcely given to the saints. Hence St. John Chrysostom condemned all that engaged in litigation.⁵

¹ "Per multas tribulationes, intrant justi in regnum cœlorum; hi autem, per multas tribulationes, promerentur infernum."—*Ep.* 14.

² "Non in foro Christus reperitur."—*De Virginit.* l. 3.

³ "Ei qui vult tecum judicio contendere, et tunicam tuam tollere, dimitte ei et pallium."—*Matt.* v. 40.

⁴ "Perde aliquid, ut Deo vaces, non litibus. Perde nummos, ut emas tibi quietem."—*Serm.* 167, *E. B.*

⁵ "Hinc jam te condemno, quod judicio contendas."—*In* 1 *Cor. hom.* 16.

What shall we say of gaming? According to the Canons, it is certain that to play frequently and for a long time at games of mere hazard, or for a large sum, at least when it is accompanied with scandal to others, is a mortal sin. With regard to other games, which are called games of amusement, I will not here discuss the question whether they are lawful or unlawful; but I say that such amusements are but little suited to a minister of God, who, if he wishes to fulfil his obligation to himself and his neighbor, has certainly no superfluous time to spend in gaming. I read that St. John Chrysostom says: "It is the devil that has introduced gaming into the world."[1] I find that St. Ambrose writes: "I am of opinion that one should not only avoid frequent plays, but all plays."[2] In the same place he says that recreation is lawful; but not the recreations which derange regularity of life, or which are not suited to one's state. Hence he adds: "Although at times a play may be proper, yet it is not proper for ecclesiastics."[3]

2. HONORS.

Secondly, a priest should divest himself of attachment to worldly honors. Peter de Blois says that the ambition of honors is the ruin of souls.[4] For ambition disturbs regularity of life, and injures charity towards God. Ambition, as the same author says, pretends to resemble charity, and is quite opposed to it. Charity suffers all things, but only for the attainment of eternal goods: ambition bears all things,[5] but only for things

[1] "Diabolus est qui in artem ludos ingessit."—*In Matth. hom.* 6.
[2] "Non solum profusos, sed omnes etiam jocos declinandos arbitror."—*Offic.* l. 1, c. 23.
[3] "Licet interdum honesta joca sint, tamen ab ecclesiastica abhorrent regula."
[4] "Animarum subversio, cupiditas dignitatum."—*Ep.* 23.
[5] "Patitur omnia, sed pro caducis."—*Ep.* 14.

perishable. Charity is all benignity to the poor, but ambition is kind to the rich.[1] Charity bears all[2] in order to please God; ambition submits to all evils for the sake of vanity. Charity believes and hopes for all that appertains to eternal glory; ambition believes all things, hopes for all things, that tend to the glory of this life.[3]

Oh! to how many thorns, fears, censures, refusals, and insults must the ambitious submit in order to attain a dignity, an office of honor! "How many thorns await those that strive after honors!"[4] says St. Augustine. And in the end what do the ambitious gain but a little smoke, which, when enjoyed, does not content the heart, and speedily disappears. *I have seen the wicked highly exalted, and lifted up like the cedars of Lebanon. And I passed by, and lo he was not.*[5] Besides, the Scripture says that to him who seeks it honor becomes an occasion of disgrace. *The promotion of fools is disgrace.*[6] And, according to St. Bernard, the greater the honor the more the unworthy possessor, who has procured it by his own exertions, is despised by others.[7] For the more exalted the dignity, the more clearly the man who is unfit for it shows his unworthiness by seeking to obtain it.[8]

Add to this the great dangers of eternal salvation which arise from offices of honor. Father Vincent Carafa once visited a sick friend who had just been appointed to a situation of great emolument, but also of

---

[1] "Benigna est, sed divitibus."
[2] "Omnia suffert pro vanitate."
[3] "Omnia credit, omnia sperat, sed quæ sunt ad gloriam hujus vitæ."
[4] "In honorum cupiditate, quantæ spinæ!"—*Enarr. in Ps.* 102.
[5] "Vidi impium superexaltatum, et elevatum sicut cedros Libani; et transivi, et ecce non erat."—*Ps.* xxxvi. 35.
[6] "Stultorum exaltatio, ignominia."—*Prov.* iii. 35.
[7] "Eo deformior, quo illustrior."—*De Cons.* l. 2, c. 7.
[8] "Claras suas maculas reddit."—*Variar.* l. 12, n. 2.

great danger. The sick man entreated the Father to obtain from God the restoration of his health; but Carafa answered: No, my friend, God forbid that I should violate the love that I bear you: your sickness is a grace from the Lord, who wishes to save you by sending death now that your soul is in a good state. Perhaps you might not be in such a state hereafter should you enter on the office that has been given you. The friend died, and died full of consolation. We should have a special fear of all offices to which the care of souls is annexed. St. Augustine said that many envied his elevation to the episcopacy, but he was afflicted at it on account of the danger to which his salvation was exposed.[1] St. John Chrysostom when made bishop was so much terrified that, as he afterwards said, he felt as if his soul were separating from the body: he had great doubts about the salvation of a pastor of souls.[2] But if the saints, forced against their will to become prelates, tremble for the account that they must render to God, how should he tremble who intrudes himself into an office to which is annexed the care of souls? " The measure of honor," says St. Ambrose, "must be measured by the strength of him that is to bear it, otherwise if the bearer is too weak the burden will weigh him down and cause his ruin."[3] A weak man who puts on his back a great weight shall not be able to carry it, but shall be oppressed by it.

St. Anselm says that he who wishes to obtain ecclesiastical honors through right and wrong does not re-

[1] "Invident nobis; ibi nos felices putant, ubi periclitamur."—*Serm.* 354, *E. B.*
[2] "Miror, an fieri possit, ut aliquis ex rectoribus salvus fiat."—*In Heb. hom.* 34.
[3] "Mensura oneris, pro mensura debet esse gestantis; alioquin impositi oneris fit ruina, ubi vectoris infirmitas est."—*Lib. de Viduis.*

ceive them, but takes them by force.¹ St. Bernard says the same: "Those whom we see entering of themselves the vineyard of the Lord are not laborers, but robbers."² This is conformable to the words of Osee: *They have reigned, but not by Me.*³ * Hence it happens, as St. Leo says, that the Church, which is governed by such ambitious ministers, is neither served nor honored, but despised and defiled.⁴

Let us, then, attend to the beautiful lesson of Jesus Christ: *Sit down in the lowest place.*⁵ He who sits on the ground is not afraid of falling. We are ashes: "The place of ashes and dust is not in a high place, for they will be scattered by the wind," says the angelic Doctor.⁶ Happy the priest who can say: *I have chosen to be an abject in the house of my God rather than to dwell in the tabernacles of sinners.*⁷

3. RELATIVES.

Thirdly, a priest must divest himself of attachment to relatives. *If any man*, says Jesus Christ, *hate not his father and mother, . . . he cannot be my disciple.*⁸ But how

---

¹ "Qui enim se ingerit, et propriam gloriam quærit; non sumit honorem, sed, gratiæ Dei rapinam faciens, jus alienum usurpat."— *In Heb.* v. 4.

² "Quos videmus vineis·dominicis se ingerere, fures sunt, non cultores."—*In Cant.* s. 30.

³ "Ipse regnaverunt, et non ex me."—*Osee*, viii. 4.

⁴ "Corpus Ecclesiæ ambientium contagione fœdatur."—*Ep.* 1.

⁵ "Recumbe in novissimo loco."—*Luke*, xiv. 10.

⁶ "Cineri non expedit, ut in alto sit, ne dispergatur a vento."—*De Erud. princ.* l. 1, c. 1.

⁷ "Elegi abjectus esse in domo Dei mei, magis quam habitare in tabernaculis peccatorum."—*Ps.* lxxxiii. 11.

⁸ "Si quis . . . non odit patrem suum et matrem, . . . non potest meus esse discipulus."—*Luke*, xiv. 26.

---

* We may also apply here the words of our Lord: "Qui non intrat per ostium in ovile ovium, sed ascendit aliunde, ille fur est et latro." —*John*, x. 1.

are we to hate relatives? We must, says a learned author, (disown them in whatever is opposed to our spiritual advancement:) "If they hinder us from living according to the rules of ecclesiastical discipline, if they ask that we should involve ourselves in secular business, then we must hate and shun them as our opponents."[1] And before him St. Gregory said: "To those that are a hindrance to us on the road to God we must show by hatred and flight that we do not know them."[2] Peter de Blois writes: "No one should be chosen priest who does not say to his father and mother, I know you not."[3] St. Ambrose says that he who wishes to serve God ought to deny his relatives.[4] We should honor parents, but we must first obey God, says St. Augustine.[5] To show great kindness to relatives, and not to obey God, is, according to St. Jerome, not piety, but impiety.[6] Our Redeemer has declared that he came on earth to detach us from relatives. *I came to set a man at variance against his father, and the daughter against her mother*, etc.[7] And why? Because in spiritual concerns relatives are our greatest enemies: *A man's enemies shall be they of his household.*[8] Hence St. Basil exhorts us to avoid, as a temptation of the devil, the care of the property of rela-

[1] " Si prohibeant ne vitam secundum ecclesiasticæ disciplinæ normam instituat, si negotiis sæcularibus eum implicent, tunc eos, tanquam in Dei adversarios, odisse et fugere tenetur."—*Abelly, Sac. chr.* p. 4, c. 6.

[2] "Quos adversarios in via Dei patimur, odiendo et fugiendo nesciamus."—*In Evang. hom.* 37.

[3] " Nec in domo Domini Sacerdos eligitur, nisi qui dixerit patri et matri: Nescio vos."—*Ep.* 102.

[4] " Suis se abneget, qui servire Deo gestit."—*De Esau*, c. 2.

[5] " Honorandus est pater, sed obediendum est Deo."—*Serm.* 100, E. B.

[6] "Grandis in suos pietas, impietas in Deum est."—*Ep. ad Paulam.*

[7] " Veni enim separare hominem adversus patrem suum."—*Matth.* x. 35.

[8] " Et inimici hominis, domestici ejus."—*Ibid.* 36.

tives.[1] What a misery to see a priest who could save numberless souls altogether occupied in transacting the business of his family, and in attending to the management of farms, flocks of sheep, and the like? What! exclaims St. Jerome, must a priest abandon the service of the Father of heaven to please an earthly parent?[2] The saint says that when there is question of serving God, a son (if it be necessary) should trample on his father: "What would you do in the house of your parents, O delicate soldier!" asks the saint, "where is the wall, where the ditch? Yes, even if the father lay across the threshold walk quietly over him, and hasten with unmoistened eyes to the banner of the cross. Filial piety in this case consists in being cruel."[3]

St. Augustine relates that St. Anthony having received a letter from his relatives threw it into the fire, saying: "I burn you lest I be burnt by you."[4] According to St. Gregory, he who wishes to be united with God must detach himself from relatives.[5] Otherwise, as Peter de Blois says, the love of flesh and blood will soon deprive us of the love of God.[6] It is difficult to find Jesus Christ in the midst of relatives. "How shall I," says St. Bonaventure, "find Thee, O Jesus! among my relatives, since Thou wert not found among Thine?"[7] When the divine mother, after having found Jesus in

[1] "Fugiamus illorum curam tamquam diabolicam."—*Const. Mon.* c. 21.

[2] "Propter patrem, militiam Christi deseram?"

[3] "Quid facis in paterna domo, delicate miles? Ubi vallum? ubi fossa? Licet in limine pater jaceat, per calcatum perge patrem, siccis oculis ad vexillum Crucis evola. Solum pietatis genus est in hac re, esse crudelem."—*Ep. ad Heliod.*

[4] "Comburo vos, ne comburar a vobis."—*Ad Fr. in er.* s. 40.

[5] "Extra cognatos quisque debet fieri, si vult Parenti omnium verius jungi."—*Mor.* l. 7, c. 18.

[6] "Carnalis amor extra Dei amorem cito te capiet."—*Ep.* 134.

[7] "Quomodo te, bone Jesu, inter meos cognatos inveniam, qu inter tuos minime es inventus?"—*Spec. Disc.* p. 1, c. 23.

the temple, said to him: *Son, why hast Thou done so to us?*[1] the Redeemer answered: *How is it that you sought Me? did you not know that I must be about My Father's business?*[2] Such should be the answer of a priest to his relatives when they wish to charge him with the care of his family. I am a priest; I can attend only to the things of God; to you who are seculars it belongs to mind the things of the world. It was this our Lord wished to signify to the young man whom he called to follow him, when, in answer to the young man's request to be permitted to bury his father, he said: *Let the dead bury the dead.*[3]

4 SELF-WILL.

It is necessary, above all, to remove attachment to self-will. St. Philip Neri used to say that sanctity consists in the mortification of self-will. Blosius has asserted that he who mortifies self-will does an act more pleasing to God than if he gave life to the dead.[4] Hence many priests and pastors, and even bishops, who led exemplary lives, and devoted their time and labor to the salvation of souls, not content with all this, have entered religion in order to live under obedience to others; believing—what is really the truth—that they could not offer to God a sacrifice more acceptable than the renunciation of their own will. All are not called to the religious state; but he who wishes to walk in the way of perfection (besides the obedience due to his prelate) must submit his will to the direction of at least a spiritual Father, who will guide him in all his spiritual exercises, and also in temporal affairs of importance,

[1] "Fili, quid fecisti nobis sic?"

[2] "Quid est quod me quærebatis? nesciebatis quia, in his quæ Patris mei sunt, oportet me esse?"—*Luke*, ii. 49.

[3] "Dimitte mortuos sepelire mortuos suos."—*Matth.* viii. 22.

[4] "Acceptius obsequium homo præstat Deo, suam voluntatem mortificans, quam si mortuos ad vitam revocaret."—*Sac. an.* p. 1, § 5.

which are connected with the sanctification of his soul. What is done through self-will is of little or no advantage to the soul. *In the day of your fast your own will is found.*¹ Hence St. Bernard has written: "A great evil is self-will, which causes the good that you do not to be good to you."² The greatest enemy we have is self-will. "Let self-will cease," says the same St. Bernard, "and there will be no longer a hell."³ Hell is full of self-will. What but our own will is the cause of our sins? St. Augustine confessed of himself that he was impelled by grace to forsake sin, but he remained in it bound by no other chain than that of his own will.⁴ St. Bernard teaches that self-will is so opposed to God that were his destruction possible it would destroy him.⁵ He, says the same saint, who becomes his own disciple, becomes the disciple of a fool.⁶

It is necessary to understand that all our good consists in a union with the divine will. *And life in his good will.*⁷ But, ordinarily speaking, God makes his will known to us only through our Superiors, that is, through our prelate or director. *He that heareth you*, says Jesus Christ, *heareth Me ;*⁸ and he adds: *despiseth you, despiseth Me.*⁹ Hence in the Scripture not to submit to the

¹ "In die jejunii vestri, invenitur voluntas vestra."—*Isa.* lviii. 3.
² "Grande malum, propria voluntas, qua fit ut bona tua tibi bona non sint."—*In Cant.* s. 71.
³ "Cesset voluntas propria, et infernus non erit."—*In Temp. Pasch.* s. 3.
⁴ "Ligatus, non ferro alieno, sed mea ferrea voluntate."—*Conf.* l. 8, c. 5.
⁵ "Quantum in ipsa est, Deum perimit propria voluntas."—*In Temp. Pasch.* s. 3.
⁶ "Qui se sibi magistrum constituit, stulto se discipulum subdit."—*Ep.* 87.
⁷ "Et vita in voluntate ejus."—*Ps.* xxix. 6.
⁸ "Qui vos audit, me audit."—*Luke*, x. 16.
⁹ "Et qui vos spernit, me spernit."

authority of Superiors is called a species of idolatry. *Because it is like the sin of witchcraft to rebel.*[1] But, on the other hand, St. Bernard assures us that in whatever our spiritual Father directs us, unless it be certainly sinful, we should feel as secure as if God himself had spoken to us.[2]

Happy he who can say at death with the Abbot John: "I have never done my own will, and never taught anything that I did not do myself."[3] Hence Cassian, who relates this fact, has written that by the mortification of self-will all vices are destroyed.[4] And before him the Wise Man said: *An obedient man shall speak of victory.*[5] And in another place: *Obedience is better than sacrifices.*[6] For he who offers to God the sacrifice of alms, fasts, penitential works, sacrifices to him only a part of himself; but he who gives God his will by subjecting it to obedience, gives all that he is able to give, and can say to him: Lord, having given you my will, I have nothing more to give you. Hence St. Laurence Justinian has written that they who offer the sacrifice of self-will to God shall obtain from him whatever they ask.[7] And God himself has promised those who renounce self-will that he will raise them above the earth, and make them celestial men. *If thou turn away thy foot . . . from*

---

[1] "Quasi scelus idololatriæ, nolle acquiescere."—1 *Kings*, xv. 23.

[2] "Quidquid, vice Dei, præcipit homo, quod non sit tamen certum displicere Deo, haud secus omnino accipiendum est, quam si præcipiat Deus."—*De Præc. et Disp.* c. 9.

[3] "Nunquam meam feci voluntatem; nec quemquam docui, quod prius ipse non feci."

[4] "Mortificatione voluntatum marcescunt universa vitia."—*De Cænob. Inst.* l. 4, c. 28-43.

[5] "Vir obediens loquetur victoriam."—*Prov.* xxi. 28.

[6] "Melior est enim obedientia quam victimæ."—1 *Kings*, xv. 22.

[7] "Sicut seipsum Deo tradidit, voluntatem propriam immolando, sic a Deo, omne quod poposcerit, consequetur."—*Lign. v. de Obed.* c. 3.

doing thy own will, ... I will lift thee up above the high places of the earth.[1]

5. MEANS OF CONQUERING SELF-WILL.

The means of conquering self-will and of subduing all irregular passions are the following:

1. Prayer: he who prays, obtains all graces. " Though prayer is but one, it can do all things,"[2] says St. Bonaventure. And before him Jesus Christ said: *You shall ask whatever you will, and it shall be done unto you.*[3]

2. To do violence to self with a determined will. A resolute will surmounts all difficulties.

3. To make our examen on the passion that molests us, and to impose a penance on ourselves as often as we yield to it.

4. To indulge in a multitude of desires. " I," said St. Francis de Sales,[4] " desire but few things, and my desire for them is not strong."

5. To practise mortification in small things, and even in things that are not sinful; for thus we shall acquire a facility of overcoming great difficulties. For example, by abstaining from certain jests, by not indulging curiosity, not pulling a flower, not opening letters for some time after we receive them, by giving up certain undertakings, making a sacrifice of them to God, regardless of the honor that they might procure for us. What advantage do we now derive from so many gratifications? from so many successful undertakings? Had we been mortified on such occasions, how many merits should we now have treasured up before God ! Henceforth let us labor to gain something for eternity. Let

---

[1] " Si averteris . . . facere voluntatem tuam, . . . sustollam te super altitudines terræ."—*Isa*. lviii. 13.

[2] " Oratio, cum sit una, omnia potest."

[3] " Quodcumque volueritis, petetis, et fiet vobis."—*John*, xv. 7.

[4] *Entret*. 21.

us reflect that we are drawing near the grave. The more we mortify ourselves the less we shall suffer in purgatory, and the greater the glory that we shall merit for eternity in heaven. On this earth we are only in passage: we shall soon be in eternity. I conclude with the words of St. Philip Neri: "Foolish is the man who does not become a saint."

INSTRUCTION IX.

EXTERIOR MORTIFICATION.

I.

Necessity of Exterior Mortification.

St. Gregory says that no man is fit to be a minister of God, and to offer the sacrifice of the altar, unless he has first sacrificed himself entirely to God.[1] And St. Ambrose writes: " This is the primitive sacrifice, that every one offers himself first to God, in order afterwards to be able to offer his gift."[2] And long before, the Redeemer said: *Unless the grain of wheat falling into the ground die, itself remaineth alone.*[3] He, then, who wishes to bring forth fruits of eternal life, must die to himself; that is, he must desire nothing for his own satisfaction, and, as St. Gregory has written, he must embrace all that is mortifying to the flesh.[4] He who is dead to himself must, according to Lanspergius, live in the world as if he saw nothing, heard nothing; as if nothing disturbed and as if nothing gave him content but God. *For*, says Jesus Christ, *he that will save his life shall lose it.*[5] Happy

[1] "Nullus Deo et Sacrificio dignus est, nisi qui prius se viventem hostiam exhibuerit."—*Apolog.* 1.

[2] "Hoc est sacrificium primitivum, quando unusquisque se offert hostiam, ut postea munus suum possit offerre."—*De Cain et Ab.* l. 2, c. 6

[3] "Nisi granum frumenti cadens in terram mortuum fuerit, ipsum solum manet; si autem mortuum fuerit, multum fructum affert."—*John.* xii. 24.

[4] "Nihil quod caro blanditur, libeat; nihil quod carnalem vitam trucidat, spiritus perhorrescat."—*In Evang. hom.* 11.

[5] "Qui enim voluerit animam suam salvam facere, perdet eam; qui autem perdiderit animam suam propter me, inveniet eam."—*Matth.* xvi. 25.

loss, exclaims St. Hilary, when everything in this world, and even life itself, is lost in order to follow Jesus Christ and to gain eternal glory.[1] St. Bernard says that were there no other reason for giving ourselves entirely to God, it would be enough to know that God has given himself entirely to us.[2] But to give ourselves to God without reserve, it is necessary to banish from the heart every earthly desire. " Wherever charity is augmented," says St. Augustine, " there cupidity is diminished. Freedom from all cupidity is perfection."[3] He who least desires the goods of the earth, loves God most; he who desires nothing, loves God perfectly.

In the preceding instruction we have spoken of interior mortification: we shall now speak of external mortification, or the mortification of the senses. This species of mortification is also necessary, because on account of sin our flesh wars, as the Apostle said of himself, against reason, and is an enemy to our salvation: *I see another law in my members, fighting against the law of my mind.*[4] " That is," says St. Thomas in his comment on this passage, " the concupiscence of the flesh that is struggling with reason."[5] It is necessary to understand that the soul must bring the body under subjection, or the body will trample on the soul. God has given us senses that we employ them, not as we please, but as he directs; hence we must mortify the desires that are contrary to the divine law.

They that are Christ's have crucified their flesh, with the

---

[1] " Jactura felix! contemptu universorum, Christus sequendus est, et æternitas comparanda."—*In Matth. can.* 16.

[2] " Integrum te da illi, quia ille, ut te salvaret, integrum se tradidit."—*De Modo bene. viv.* c. 8.

[3] " Nutrimentum charitatis est imminutio cupiditatis; perfectio, nulla cupiditas."—*De div. quæst.* q. 36.

[4] " Video autem aliam legem in membris meis, repugnantem legi mentis meæ."—*Rom.* vii. 23.

[5] " Id est concupiscentia carnis contrarians rationi."

vices and concupiscences. Hence the saints have been so careful to macerate the flesh. St. Peter of Alcantara purposed never to give any indulgence to the body, and observed his resolution till death. St. Bernard maltreated his body to such a degree, that at death he asked its pardon. St. Teresa used to say that "it would be silliness to imagine that God admits to his friendship persons who seek their own ease and convenience;"[2] and in another place she says: "Souls that truly love God cannot ask for comforts."[3] And St. Ambrose has written that he who does not cease to indulge the body shall cease to please God.[4] According to St. Augustine, he who subjects reason to the flesh is a monster that walks with his head downwards and his feet upwards.[5] We are born for a more noble end than to be the slaves of the body, said the pagan Seneca.[6] How much more should we say it, who know by faith that we have been created to enjoy God for eternity? St. Gregory says that by gratifying the desires of the flesh we only nourish enemies.[7]

St. Ambrose weeps over the misfortune of Solomon, saying that this unhappy king had the glory of building the temple of God, but that it would have been far better for him to preserve to God the temple of his body, for the gratification of which he lost his body, his soul, and his God.[8] A man mounted on a furious horse must

[1] "Qui autem sunt Christi, carnem suam crucifixerunt cum vitiis et concupiscentiis."—*Gal.* v. 24.

[2] *Way of Perf.* ch. 19. [3] *Foundat.* ch. 5.

[4] "Qui non peregrinatur a corpore, peregrinatur a Domino."—*In Luc.* c. 9.

[5] "Inversis pedibus ambulat."—*Ad Fr. in er.* s. 50.

[6] "Major sum et ad majora genitus, quam ut mancipium sim mei corporis."—*Ep.* 65.

[7] "Dum (carni) parcimus, ad prælium hostem nutrimus."—*Mor.* l. 30, c. 28.

[8] "Salomon templum Deo condidit; sed utinam corporis templum pse servasset!"—*Apol. David.* l. 2.

always keep the reins tight: it is thus we must treat the body. St. Bernard says that we ought to treat the flesh as a physician treats a patient who seeks what is noxious and refuses what is conducive to health. Were a physician, in order to please a sick man, to give him what should cause his death, would he not be guilty of cruelty? And in like manner, let us be persuaded that to indulge the body is not charity, but the greatest act of cruelty we can commit against ourselves; because, for a momentary indulgence of the flesh, we condemn the soul to an eternity of torments. Such is the language of St. Bernard: "Such a charity destroys charity; such mercy is full of cruelty; for in such a manner the body is served, but the soul is destroyed."[1] In a word, we must change our palate, and follow the admonition of our Lord to St. Francis: "If you desire me, take what is bitter as sweets, and what is sweet as bitter."

Let us now attend to the fruits of external mortification.

First, it satisfies for the pains due to the pleasures in which we have indulged: these pains are far milder in this than in the next life. St. Antonine relates that an angel proposed to a sick man the choice of remaining three days in purgatory, or of being confined for two years to his bed by the infirmity under which he labored. The sick man chose the three days in purgatory; but he was scarcely an hour there when he began to complain to the angel that his purgatory, instead of continuing for three days, had lasted for several years. What! replied the angel, your body is still warm on the bed of death, and you speak of years! "If you do not wish to be punished," says St. John Chrysostom, "be your own judge—chastise and amend yourself."[2]

[1] "Ista charitas destruit charitatem; talis misericordia crudelitate plena est, qua ita corpori servitur, ut anima juguletur."—*Apol. ad Guill.* c. 8

[2] "Non vis castigari; sis judex tui ipsius, te reprehende et corrige."

Secondly, mortification detaches the soul from earthly pleasures, and gives her a facility of flying to God, and of uniting herself with him. St. Francis de Sales used to say that "if the flesh is not mortified and depressed, the soul will never be able to raise herself up to God." St. Jerome has said the same: "Only by mortification can the soul rise to heavenly things."[1]

Thirdly, penance merits for us eternal goods, as St. Peter of Alcantara revealed from heaven to St. Teresa, saying: "O happy penance that has merited for me so much glory!"[2]

Hence the saints have endeavored to mortify the flesh continually, and to the best of their ability. St. Francis Borgia said that he would die without consolation on any day on which he had not mortified his body by some penitential work. A life of ease and pleasure on this earth cannot be the life of a Christian.

II.

Practice of Exterior Mortification.

If we have not fervor to mortify the body by great penances, let us at least practise some little mortifications: let us bear with patience the pains that happen to us. For example, let us submit in peace to the inconvenience, the want of sleep, the disagreeable smell that we feel in attending the dying, to the annoyance we experience in going to hear the confessions of persons confined in prison, in hearing the confessions of the poor and the ignorant, and to similar occasions of pain or trouble. Let us at least deprive ourselves from time to time of some lawful pleasure. Clement of Alexandria says: "Whoever does everything that is allowed will soon do what is not allowed."[3] He who

---

[1] "Anima in coelestia non surgit, nisi mortificatione membrorum."

[2] "O felix poenitentia, quæ tantam mihi promeruit gloriam!"

[3] "Cito adducuntur, ut ea faciant quæ non licent, qui faciunt omnia quæ licent."—*Pædag.* l. 2, c. 1.

wishes to indulge in all gratifications that are in themselves lawful, will not abstain long from unlawful pleasures. That great servant of God, Vincent Carafa, of the Society of Jesus, used to say that God has given us earthly goods not only for our delight, but also that we might have a means of showing our gratitude to him by abstaining from pleasures, and giving him back his own gifts in proof of our love; for, as St. Gregory writes,[1] he who is accustomed to renounce lawful gratifications easily abstains from forbidden pleasures.

Let us speak of the mortifications of the senses that we can practise, and especially of the mortifications of the eyes, the taste, and the touch.

1. THE EYES AND THE WHOLE EXTERIOR.

First, it is necessary to mortify the eyes. "Through the eyes," says St. Bernard, "the dart of impure love enters the heart."[2] The first darts that wound, and sometimes kill, the chaste soul, enter through the eyes.[3] By means of the eyes bad thoughts spring up in the mind. "What is not seen," says St. Francis de Sales, "is not desired." Hence the devil first tempts a person to look, then to desire, and afterwards to consent. Thus he acted with the Saviour himself: *He showed Him all the kingdoms of the world.* He then tempted him, saying: *All these will I give Thee, if falling down Thou wilt adore me.*[4] The evil spirit gained nothing by tempting Jesus Christ, but by thus tempting Eve he gained a great deal: *She saw that the tree was good to eat, and fair to the eyes, . . . and she took of the fruit thereof,*[5] etc.

[1] *Dial.* l. 4, c. 11.
[2] "Per oculos intrat ad mentem sagitta amoris."—*De Modo bene viv.* s. 23.
[3] "Oculus meus deprædatus est animam meam."—*Lam.* iii. 51.
[4] "Hæc omnia tibi dabo, si cadens adoraveris me."—*Matth.* iv. 9.
[5] "Vidit igitur mulier quod bonum esset lignum ad vescendum, et pulchrum oculis, aspectuque delectabile; et tulit de fructu illius, et comedit."—*Gen.* iii. 6.

Tertullian says that certain little glances are the beginnings of the greatest iniquities.[1] And St. Jerome compares the eyes to certain hooks, which drag us, as it were, by force to sin.[2] He who wishes not to admit the enemy into the fortress, should lock the gate. The Abbot Pastor was molested by bad thoughts for forty years after having looked at a woman. In consequence of having seen a woman in the world, St. Benedict was afterwards so strongly tempted, that to conquer the flesh he threw himself naked among thorns, and thus overcame the temptations. While he lived in the cave of Bethlehem, St. Jerome was for a long time troubled with bad thoughts on account of having formerly seen certain women in Rome. These saints conquered temptations by the divine aid, by prayers and penitential works; but many others, on account of the eyes, have miserably fallen. On account of the eyes a David fell; on account of the eyes a Solomon fell. Listen to an alarming fact related by St. Augustine of Alipius. He went to the theatre, resolved not to look at any dangerous object, saying, "I will be absent though present;"[3] but being tempted to look, he, says the saint, not only prevaricated, but also made others prevaricate: "He opened his eyes, applauded, became excited, and left the theatre carrying sin with him."[4]

Seneca justly said that blindness is a great help to preserve innocence.[5] It is not lawful to pull out our eyes, but we ought to make ourselves blind by closing the eyes, and by not looking at objects which may impel us to evil: *He . . . that shutteth his eyes that he may*

---

[1] "Exordia sunt maximarum iniquitatum."
[2] "Oculi, quasi quidam raptores ad culpam."—*In Lam.* 3.
[3] "Adero absens."
[4] "Spectavit, clamavit, exarsit; abstulit inde secum insaniam."—*Conf.* l. 6, c. 8.
[5] "Pars innocentiæ, cæcitas."—*De Remed. fort.*

Exterior Mortification. 369

see no evil, he shall dwell on high.[1] Hence Job said that he had made a covenant with his eyes never to look at a woman, lest he should be afterwards molested by bad thoughts: *I made a covenant with my eyes, that I would not so much as think upon a virgin.*[2] St. Aloysius Gonzaga never dared to raise his eyes to look at his mother. St. Peter of Alcantara abstained from looking even at his brothers in religion: he knew them not by the sight, but by the voice.

The Council of Tours tells priests that they should guard against everything that can offend the eyes or the ears.[3] But particular caution is necessary for secular priests, who frequent public places, or the houses of seculars. If they permit the eye to look at every object that is presented to them, they shall scarcely preserve chastity. *Turn away thy face,* says the Holy Ghost, *from a woman dressed up, . . . for many have perished by the beauty of a woman.*[4] And, says St. Augustine, should the eyes happen sometimes to fall on a woman, let us take care never to fix them on her.[5] Hence it is necessary to abstain from going to balls, or profane comedies, which are frequented by men and women; and when through necessity a priest is obliged to go to a place in which there are women, he must pay special attention to modesty of the eyes. Father Alvarez was once present at a public degradation of a priest, but because there were women present, he held in his hand an

---

[1] "Qui claudit oculos suos ne videat malum, iste in excelsis habitabit."—*Isa.* xxxiii. 15.

[2] "Pepigi fœdus cum oculis meis, ut ne cogitarem quidem de virgine."—*Job,* xxxi. 1.

[3] "Ab omnibus quæcunque ad aurium et ad oculorum pertinent illecebras, Dei Sacerdotes abstinere debent."—*Anno* 813, *can.* 7.

[4] "Averte faciem tuam a muliere compta, et ne circumspicias speciem alienam; propter speciem mulieris, multi perierunt."—*Eccles.* ix. 8

[5] "Oculi vestri, etsi jaciuntur in aliquam, figantur in nullam."—*Reg. ad serv. D.* n. 6.

image of the Blessed Virgin, on which he kept his eyes constantly fixed for several hours, lest they might fall on a woman. From the moment we awake in the morning, let us pray with David: *Turn away my eyes, that they may not behold vanity*.[1]

Oh! how profitable is it to us ecclesiastics, and how edifying to others, to keep the eyes cast down! St. Francis once said to his companion, that he wished to go out in order to preach a sermon: he went out and walked through the village with his eyes fixed on the ground. After they had returned, his companion asked when he intended to preach the sermon. The saint replied: We have already preached by the modesty with which we walked before the people. A certain author remarks that the Evangelists, in order to show that he ordinarily kept them cast down, mention in several places that our Redeemer raised his eyes: *Lifting up His eyes on His disciples*.[2] *When Jesus had lifted up His eyes*.[3] Hence St. Paul has praised the modesty of Jesus Christ, saying: *I beseech you by the mildness and modesty of Christ*.[4]

St. Basil says that we should keep the eyes cast down upon the earth and the soul raised up to heaven.[5] And St. Jerome has written, that the countenance is the mirror of the soul, and that chaste eyes indicate a chaste heart.[6] But, on the other hand, St. Augustine says: "The immodesty of the eyes betrays the vices of the heart."[7] St. Ambrose adds, that the motions of the body

---

[1] "Averte oculos meos, ne videant vanitatem."—*Ps*. cxviii. 37.

[2] "Elevatis oculis in discipulos suos."—*Luke*, vi. 20.

[3] "Cum sublevasset ergo oculos Jesus."—*John*, vi. 5.

[4] "Obsecro vos per mansuetudinem et modestiam Christi."—*2 Cor*. x. 1.

[5] "Oportet oculos habere ad terram dejectas, animam vero ad cœlum erectam."—*Serm. de Ascesi*.

[6] "Speculum mentis est facies, et taciti oculi cordis fatentur arcana."—*Ep. ad Furiam*.

[7] "Impudicus oculus impudici cordis est nuntius."—*Reg. ad serv. D*. n. 6.

show the recollection or dissipation of the soul.[1] Hence the saint relates that he foreboded the fall of two men on account of the irregularity of their gait. The prediction was verified; for one fell into impiety, and the other into heresy. Speaking especially of men whose character is sacred, St. Jerome says that their actions, language, and gesture are a lesson for seculars.[2]

The Council of Trent has said: "They ought by all means so to regulate their whole life and conversation, as that in their dress, comportment, gait, discourse, and all things else, nothing appear but what is grave, regulated, and replete with religiousness."[3] And St. John Chrysostom has written: "The mind of the priest should be resplendent with virtues, that it may enlighten those that look up to him."[4] Thus the priest ought to give to all an example of modesty in all things: modesty in looks, modesty in his gait, modesty in his conversation, particularly by saying little, and by speaking as a priest ought to speak. By saying little.—He who speaks much to men, shows that he converses but little with God. Men of prayer are men of few words. When the mouth of the furnace is opened, the heat rushes out. "In silence," says Thomas à Kempis, "the soul maketh progress."[5] And St. Peter Damian calls silence the guardian of justice.[6] We read in Isaias: *In silence and in hope shall your strength be.*[7] In silence consists our strength,

[1] "Vox quædam est animi, corporis motus."—*Offic.* l. 1, c. 18.
[2] "Quorum habitus, sermo, vultus, incessus, doctrina virtutum est."—*Ep. ad Rusticum.*
[3] "Sic decet omnino clericos vitam moresque suos componere, ut habitu, gestu, incessu, nil nisi grave ac religione plenum præ se ferant."—*Sess.* 22, *de Ref.* c. 1.
[4] "Sacerdotis animum splendescere oportet, ut illustrare possit, qui oculos in eum conjiciunt."—*De Sacerd.* l. 3.
[5] "In silentio proficit anima."—*De Imit.* l. 1, c. 20.
[6] "Custos justitiæ, silentium."—*Ep.* l. 7, ep. 6.
[7] "In silentio et in spe erit fortitudo vestra."—*Isa.* xxx. 15.

for in speaking much there is always some defect.) *In the multitude of words there shall not want sin*, says Solomon.[1] By speaking as a priest ought to speak, St. Anselm says, " Thy mouth must be the mouth of Christ: and thou shouldst not only not open it for calumnies or lies, but not even for idle discourse."[2] He who loves God seeks to speak always of God. He who loves a fellow-man can scarcely speak of anything else than of him. "Forget not," says Gilbert, "that thy mouth is consecrated only to heavenly sayings, and look upon it as sacrilegious if something comes forth from it that is not divine."[3] It is, according to St. Ambrose, a violation of modesty to speak in a very loud tone.[4] It belongs to modesty to abstain, not only from immodest words, but also from listening to them: *Hedge in thy ears with thorns, hear not a wicked tongue.*[5] A priest should be modest also in his dress. St. Augustine says that in order to appear well dressed exteriorly, some strip themselves of interior modesty.[6] Vanity and costliness of dress in a priest show that there is but little virtue in the soul. St. Bernard writes: " The poor cry out to thee: To us belongs what you waste; from our necessities is withdrawn what you bestow upon vanities."[7] In the 16th Canon of the second Council of Nice we

---

[1] " In multiloquio non deerit peccatum."—*Prov.* x. 19.

[2] " Os tuum, os Christi; non debes, non dico, ad detractiones, ad mendacia, sed nec ad otiosos sermones os aperire."—*Medit.* 1, § 5.

[3] " Memento, os tuum cœlestibus oraculis consecratum; sacrilegium puta, si quid non divinum sonet."—*In Cant.* s. 18.

[4] " Vocis sonum libret modestia, ne cujusquam offendat aurem vox fortior."—*Offic.* l. 1, c. 18.

[5] " Sepi aures tuas spinis, linguam nequam noli audire."—*Ecclus.* xxviii. 28.

[6] " Ut foris vestiaris, intus exspoliaris."—*Serm.* 60, E. B.

[7] " Clamant nudi, et dicunt: Nostrum est, quod effunditis; nostris necessitatibus detrahitur, quidquid accedit vanitatibus vestris."—*De Mor. et Off. Ep.* c. 2.

read: "A priest should wear simple garments, for what goes beyond what is necessary is luxury, and this vanity will be imputed to him as a crime."[1] The priest ought to be modest in his hair. Pope Martin ordained that ecclesiastics should not minister in the church unless their head was shorn so that the ears would be visible.[2] What shall we say of those whom Clement of Alexandria calls "illiberales tonsos,"[3] that is, persons who are so much attached to their hair that they allow it to be cut only sparingly. What a shame, says St. Cyprian, for an ecclesiastic to appear with his head decked out like the head of a woman.[4] And before him the Apostle, in his epistle to the Corinthians, said, that to nourish the hair is as disgraceful in a man as it is becoming in a woman: *A man indeed if he nourish his hair, it is a shame unto him.*[5] And this he said of all, even of seculars. What, then, must we think of the ecclesiastic who curls his hair and arranges it in a worldly fashion?

Minutius Felix says that we ought to show ourselves to be ecclesiastics, not by the ornaments of the body, but by examples of modesty.[6] St. Ambrose has written, that the deportment of a priest should be such that all who behold him may be inspired with reverence for God, whose priest and minister he is.[7] But, on the

[1] "Virum sacerdotalem cum moderato indumento versari debere; et quidquid, non propter usum, sed ostentatorium ornatum, assumitur, in nequitiæ reprehensionem incurrere."—*Can.* 16.

[2] "Nisi attonso capite, patentibus auribus."

[3] "Illiberali tonsu se tondentes."—*Pædag.* l. 3, c. 3.

[4] "Capillis muliebribus se in feminas transfigurant."—*De Jej. et Tent. Christi.*

[5] "Vir quidem, si comam nutriat, ignominia est illi."—1 *Cor.* xi. 14.

[6] "Nos, non notaculo corporis, sed innocentiæ ac modestiæ signo, facile dignoscimus."—*Octav.* c. 9.

[7] "Decet actuum nostrorum esse publicam æstimationem, ut, qui videt ministrum altaris congruis ornatum virtutibus, Dominum veneretur, qui tales servulos habeat."—*Offic.* l. 1, c. 50.

other hand, a priest who violates modesty excites irreverence towards God.

2. THE TASTE OR APPETITE.

We shall now speak on the mortification of the taste or of the appetite. In his treatise entitled *The One Thing Necessary*, Father Rogacci says, that the principal part of external mortification consists in the mortification of the appetite. Hence St. Andrew Avellino used to say, that he who wishes to walk in the way of perfection must begin to mortify the taste. St. Leo asserts that this has been the practice of the saints.[1] To a penitent who practised but little mortification St. Philip Neri said, "My son, unless you mortify the appetite you shall never become a saint."[2] St. Francis Xavier used to eat nothing but a few grains of toasted rice. St. John Francis Regis took only a little coarse flower boiled in water. St. Francis Borgia, even when a secular, and viceroy of Catalonia, was content with bread and herbs. The food of St. Peter of Alcantara was nothing more than a small quantity of broth.

St. Francis de Sales says that we ought to eat in order to support life, and not live for the purpose of eating. Some appear to live for the sole purpose of eating, making, as the Apostle said, the belly their God: *They are enemies of the cross of Christ; whose end is destruction, whose God is their belly.*[3] Tertullian says that the vice of gluttony kills, or at least inflicts a deep wound, on all other virtues.[4] The sin of gluttony has caused the ruin

---

[1] "Tyrocinium militiæ christianæ sanctis jejuniis inchoarunt."—*De Jejun. Pent.* s. 1.

[2] *Bacci*, l. 2, ch. 14.

[3] "Inimicos crucis Christi, quorum finis interitus, quorum deus venter est."—*Phil.* iii. 18.

[4] "Omnem disciplinam victus aut occidit aut vulnerat."—*De Jeiunio*.

of the world: for the sake of eating an apple, Adam brought death on himself and the entire human race.

But priests, who are bound by a vow of chastity, should pay special attention to the mortification of the appetite. St. Bonaventure says that excess in eating nourishes impurity.[1] And St. Augustine has written: "If the soul is weighed down by too much food, the mind becomes torpid, and there will spring up thorns of wicked desires."[2] Hence in the forty-second Canon of the Apostles we read: "Those priests are to be deposed that are given excessively to good cheer."[3] The Wise Man has said, that he who accustoms servants to delicate food shall not find them obedient to his commands: *He that nourishes a servant delicately from his childhood, afterwards shall find him stubborn.*[4] St. Augustine exhorts us not to give the flesh strength to fight against the soul.[5] Palladius relates that a certain monk being asked why he treated his body so badly, said: "I trouble him that troubles me."[6] St. Paul has done and said the same. *I chastise my body, and bring it into subjection.*[7] If the flesh is not mortified, it obeys reason only with difficulty. But, on the other hand, according to St. Thomas, the devil, when vanquished in his temptations to the indulgence of the appetite, ceases to tempt to impurity.[8] Cornelius à Lapide says that when intemperance is

---

[1] "Luxuria nutritur a ventris ingluvie."—*De Prof. rel.* l. 2, c. 52.

[2] "Si ciborum nimietate anima obruatur, illico mens torpescit, et corporis nostri terra spinas libidinum germinabit."—*Serm.* 141, *E. B. app.*

[3] "Sacerdotes qui intemperanter ingurgitant, deponendi sunt."

[4] "Qui delicate a pueritia nutrit servum suum, postea sentiet eum contumacem."—*Prov.* xxix. 21.

[5] "Ne præbeamus vires corpori, ne committat bellum adversus spiritum."—*De Sal. docum.* c. 35.

[6] "Vexo eum qui vexat me"—*Vit. S. M.* c. 7.

[7] "Castigo corpus meum, et in servitutem redigo."—1 *Cor.* ix. 27.

[8] "Diabolus, victus de gula, non tentat de libidine."

overcome, all other vices are easily conquered.¹ Blosius remarks that many find it easier to conquer other vices than the vice of intemperance.²

But some may say God has purposely created the various kinds of food that we may enjoy them. I answer, God has created them that they may serve for the support of life, but not to be abused by intemperance. There are some delicious meats that are not necessary for the support of life; these God has created, that by sometimes abstaining from them we may practise mortification. God created the apple that he forbade Adam to eat, that Adam might abstain from it. Let us at least practise temperance in the use of delicacies.

To practise temperance, St. Bonaventure says that we must avoid four things: first, eating out of the time of meals, as animals do; secondly, eating with too much avidity, like famished dogs; thirdly, eating too large a quantity, of food; and fourthly, we must avoid too much delicacy.³ What a shame to see a priest seeking a variety of meats, dressed in various ways, and giving trouble and annoyance to servants, and to the whole house, when everything is not prepared so as to please his taste. Fervent priests are satisfied with what is placed before them.

Reflect on the words of St. Jerome: "The cleric cannot easily escape contempt if he frequently accepts invitations to dinner."⁴ Hence exemplary priests fly

¹ "Gula debellata, christianus facilius cætera vitia profligabit."—*In* 1 *Cor.* ix. 27.

² "Ingluvies a plerisque superari difficilius solet, quam cætera vitia."—*Enchir. parv.* l. 1, doc. 11.

³ "1. Ante debitum tempus, vel sæpius quam deceat, comedere, præter necessitatem, more pecudum. 2. Cum nimia aviditate, sicut canes famelici. 3. Nimis se implere ex delectatione. 4. Nimis exquisita quærere."—*De Prof. rel.* l. 1, c. 36.

⁴ "Facile contemnitur clericus qui, sæpe vocatus ad prandium, ire non recusat."—*Ep. ad Nepot.*

from banquets, in which, ordinarily speaking, there is a want of modesty and of temperance. "Lay people," adds the holy Doctor, " would rather enjoy our consolations in their trials than our presence at their banquets."[1]

3. THE TOUCH.

Thirdly, with regard to the sense of touch, it is necessary, in the first place, to abstain from familiarity with persons of the opposite sex, even though they are relatives. You will say: They are my sisters, my nieces; yes, but they are women.

With regard to this sense (which is very dangerous for priests), they must use all possible caution and modesty with themselves. *Every one of you*, says St. Paul, *should know how to possess his vessel in sanctification and honor, . . . not in the passion of lust.*[2]

Holy priests are accustomed to practise some painful penitential works, such as the discipline, or the use of little chains. Some despise these things, saying that sanctity consists in the mortification of the will. But I find that all the saints have thirsted after penitential austerities, and have sought to macerate the flesh to the utmost of their power. St. Peter of Alcantara wore a hair-shirt of punched iron, which kept his shoulders constantly lacerated. St. John of the Cross wore a waistcoat armed with iron points, and an iron chain, which could not be removed after his death without taking with it a piece of the flesh. This saint used to say that a person who should teach lax doctrine regarding the mortification of the flesh ought not to be believed, even though he confirmed it by miracles.[3]

[1] "Consolatores nos potius (laici) in mœroribus suis, quam convivas in prosperis, noverint."
[2] "Sciat unusquisque vestrum vas suum possidere in sanctificatione et honore, non in passione desiderii."—1 *Thess.* iv. 4.
[3] *Sent.* 72.

It is true that interior mortification is the most necessary; but exterior mortification is also indispensable. To a person who wished to dissuade him from macerating his body, by saying that sanctity consists in conquering self-will, St. Aloysius Gonzaga replied, in the words of the Gospel: *These things you ought to have done, and not leave those undone.*[1] To Mother Mary of Jesus, of the Order of St. Teresa, our Lord said the world is destroyed not by penitential works, but by pleasures.

"Mortify your body and you will conquer the devil says St. Augustine.[2] The remedy of the saints, particularly in temptations against purity, was the maceration of the flesh. In temptations contrary to chastity, St. Benedict and St. Francis rolled themselves among thorns. Father Rodriguez says, "If a person had entwined round him a serpent, which by its poisoned bites would seek to kill him, surely if he could not take away its life he would at least endeavor to draw its blood and diminish its strength, in order to render it less able to injure him."

Job tells us that wisdom is not found among earthly delights: *Man knoweth not the price thereof, neither is it found in the land of them that live in delights.*[3] In one place the Spouse in the Canticles said that he dwells on the mountain of myrrh: *I will go to the mountain of myrrh;*[4] and in another, that he feeds among the lilies: *Who feedeth among the lilies.*[5] In reconciling these two passages, Philibert says that on the mountain of myrrh, where the flesh is mortified, the lilies of purity spring

---

[1] " Hæc oportuit facere, et illa non omittere."—*Matth.* xxiii. 23.
[2] " Mortifica corpus tuum, et diabolum vinces."
[3] " Nescit homo pretium ejus, nec invenitur in terra suaviter viventium."—*Job,* xxviii. 13.
[4] " Vadam ad montem myrrhæ."—*Cant.* iv. 6.
[5] " Qui pascitur inter lilia."—*Cant.* ii. 16.

up and flourish.¹ Should a person have ever violated chastity, reason requires that he should afterwards chastise the flesh: *For as you have yielded your members to serve uncleanness and iniquity unto iniquity, so now yield your members to serve justice unto sanctification.*²

4. INVOLUNTARY MORTIFICATIONS.

If we have not courage to mortify the flesh by works of penance, let us at least endeavor to accept with patience the mortifications arising from the infirmities, the heat and cold, that God sends us. St. Francis Borgia once arrived late at a college of the Order, and was obliged to remain all night in the open air, exposed to the cold and snow. In the morning the Fathers of the college were afflicted at what had happened; but the saint said he was greatly consoled by thinking that God had sent the wind, the frost, and snow. "Hasten, O Lord," says St. Bonaventure, "hasten to wound Thy servants with Thy sacred wounds, lest they be wounded by deadly wounds of vice."³ This we, too, should say when we are afflicted with sickness and pains: Lord, chastise me with these healing wounds, that I may be freed from the deadly wounds of the flesh; or let us say with St. Bernard: "It is just that he should be bowed down and become sad who has despised Thee, O Lord!"⁴ Yes, my God, it is just that I who have insulted you should suffer affliction: I have been con-

---

¹ "Lilia hæc oriuntur in monte myrrhæ, et nusquam magis illæsa servantur: ubi carnis mortificantur affectus, ibi lilia castimoniæ nascuntur et florent."—*In Cant.* s. 28.

² "Sicut enim exhibuistis membra vestra servire immunditiæ et iniquitati ad iniquitatem, ita nunc exhibete membra vestra servire justitiæ in sanctificationem."—*Rom.* vi. 19.

³ "Curre, Domine, curre, et vulnera servos tuos vulneribus sacris, ne vulnerentur vulneribus mortis."

⁴ "Conteratur contemptor Dei; si recte sentis, dices: Reus est mortis, crucifigatur."—*Medit.* c. 15.

demned to eternal death; let me, then, be crucified in this life, that I may not be tormented for eternity in the next.

Let us at least bear the pains that God sends us. A certain author well observes, that a person who does not embrace voluntary pains will scarcely bear involuntary sufferings with perfect patience. And, on the other hand, St. Anselm says: "God will cease to chastise the sinner who voluntarily punishes himself for his sins."[1]

III.
The Good that is derived from a Mortified Life.

Some imagine that a life of mortification is an unhappy life. No: the life of the man who practises mortification is not unhappy; but the life of him who indulges his senses so as to offend God is truly miserable: *Who hath resisted Him, and hath had peace?*[2] A soul in sin is a sea agitated by the tempest: *The wicked are like the raging sea, which cannot rest.*[3] St. Augustine says that the man who is not in peace with God is an enemy that wages war against himself.[4] The gratifications that we give the body fight against us, and make us unhappy: *From whence are wars and contentions amongst you? Are they not hence from your concupiscences, which war in your members?*[5]

On the other hand, the Lord says: *To him that overcometh, I will give the hidden manna.*[6] To them who prac-

[1] "Cessat vindicta divina, si conversio præcurrat humana."—*In* 1 Cor. 11.
[2] "Quis restitit ei, et pacem habuit?"—*Job*, ix. 4.
[3] "Impii autem, quasi mare fervens, quod quiescere non potest."—*Isa.* lvii. 20.
[4] "Ipse sibi est bellum, qui pacem noluit habere cum Deo."—*Enarr. in Ps.* 75.
[5] "Unde bella et lites in vobis? nonne hinc, ex concupiscentiis vestris, quæ militant in membris vestris?"—*James*, iv. 1.
[6] "Vincenti dabo manna absconditum."—*Apoc.* ii. 17.

tise mortification God gives that sweetness and peace that are hidden from the unmortified, and that surpass all sensual pleasures: *The peace of God, which surpasseth all underst nding.*[1] Hence they who live dead to earthly delights are pronounced happy: *Blessed are the dead who die in the Lord.*[2] Worldlings regard as miserable the life of those who live at a distance from sensual gratifications. *They see the Cross, but not its interior unction,*[3] says St. Bernard; they see the mortifications of the saints, but not the interior consolations with which God caresses them, even in this life. The promises of God cannot fail: *Take up My yoke upon you, . . and you shall find rest to your souls.*[4] Ah! the soul that loves God suffers not in her mortifications. He who loves, finds nothing difficult, says St. Augustine.[5] "Love," says a certain author, "blushes at the word *difficulty*."[6] As nothing resists death, so nothing resists love: *Love is as strong as death.*[7]

If we wish to acquire eternal delights, we must deprive ourselves of temporal pleasures: *He that will save his life shall lose it.*[8] Hence St. Augustine says: "Beware of enjoying yourself in this life, lest you suffer eternally."[9] St. John saw all the saints with palms in their hands.[10] To be saved, we must all be martyrs, either by the sword of the tyrant or by voluntary mortification. Let us reflect that all we suffer is nothing

[1] "Pax Dei, quæ exsuperat omnem sensum."—*Phil.* iv. 7.
[2] "Beati mortui, qui in Domino moriuntur."—*Apoc.* xiv. 13.
[3] "Crucem videntes, sed non etiam unctionem."—*In Dedic.* s. 1.
[4] "Tollite jugum meum super vos, . . . et invenietis requiem animabus vestris."—*Matth.* xi. 29.
[5] "Qui amat, non laborat."—*In Jo. tr.* 48.
[6] "Amor, difficultatis nomen erubescit."—*Lign. v. de Char.* c. 4.
[7] "Fortis est ut mors dilectio."—*Cant.* viii. 6.
[8] "Qui enim voluerit animam salvam facere, perdet eam."—*Matth.* xvi. 25.
[9] "Noli amare in hac vita, ne perdas in æterna vita."—*In Jo. tr.* 51.
[10] "Stantes ante thronum, . . . et palmæ in manibus eorum."—*Apoc.* vii. 9.

compared with the eternal glory which awaits us: *The sufferings of this time are not worthy to be compared with the glory to come, that shall be revealed in us.*[1] The transitory pains of this life shall merit for us eternal beatitude: *For that which is at present momentary and light of our tribulation, worketh for us above measure exceedingly an eternal weight of glory.*[2] Hence Philo the Jew has written: "The pleasures which we give the body to the detriment of the soul are thefts of the glory of heaven, which we commit against ourselves."[3] On the other hand, St. John Chrysostom says that when God gives us an occasion of suffering, he bestows a greater grace than if he gave us power to restore life to the dead.[4] He assigns the reason, saying: "For the miracles I am a debtor to God, and by suffering with patience I have Christ as my debtor."[5] The saints are the living stones that compose the heavenly Jerusalem: *As living stones built up, a spiritual house.*[6] But these must be first polished by the chisel of mortification, as is sung by the Church:

" Many a blow and biting sculpture
Polished well those stones elect,
In their places now compacted
By the heavenly Architect."[7]

[1] "Non sunt condignæ passiones hujus temporis ad futuram gloriam quæ revelabitur in nobis."—*Rom.* viii. 18.

[2] "Id enim quod in præsenti est momentaneum et leve tribulationis nostræ, supra modum in sublimitate æternum gloriæ pondus operatur in nobis."—2 *Cor.* iv. 17.

[3] "Oblectamenta præsentis vitæ, quid sunt, nisi furta vitæ futuræ?"

[4] "Quando Deus dat alicui ut mortuos resuscitet, minus dat, quam cum dat occasionem patiendi."

[5] "Pro miraculis enim, debitor sum Deo; ut pro patientia, debitorem habes Christum."—*In Phil. hom.* 4.

[6] "Tamquam lapides vivi superædificamini, domus spiritualis."—1 *Pet.* ii. 5.

[7] "Scalpri salubris ictibus,
Et tunsione plurima,
Fabri polita malleo,
Hanc saxa molem construunt."—*Off. Dedic. Eccl. Hymn.*

Hence every act of mortification is a work for heaven. This thought will sweeten all the bitterness we shall feel in mortification: *The just man liveth by faith.*[1] To live well, and obtain salvation, we must live by faith, that is, in view of the eternity which awaits us: *Man shall go into the house of his eternity.*[2] Let us consider, says St. Augustine, that at the very time when the Lord exhorts us to combat against temptations, he assists us, and prepares a crown for us.[3] Speaking of wrestlers, the Apostle said, that they abstain from everything that can be an obstacle to their winning a miserable temporal crown; how much more ought we to die to all things in order to acquire an infinite and eternal crown: *Every one that striveth for the mastery refraineth himself from all things; and they indeed that they may receive a corruptible crown, but we an incorruptible one.*[4]

[1] " Justus autem ex fide vivit."—*Rom.* i. 17.

[2] " Quoniam ibit homo in domum æternitatis suæ."—*Eccles.* xii. 5.

[3] " Deus hortatur ut pugnes, et deficientem sublevat, et vincentem coronat."—*In Ps.* 32, *enarr.* 2.

[4] " Omnis autem qui in agone contendit, ab omnibus se abstinet; et illi quidem ut corruptibilem coronam accipiant, nos autem incorruptam." —1 *Cor.* ix. 25.

INSTRUCTION X.

THE LOVE OF GOD.

I.

Special Obligation for the Priest to belong Entirely to God.

PETER DE BLOIS says that a priest without divine love "may be called a priest but is not a priest."[1] From the day of his ordination a priest is no longer his own, but belongs to God. St. Ambrose has said: "A true minister of the altar is in the world for God and not for himself."[2] And before him God himself said: *They offer the burnt-offering of the Lord, and the bread of their God, and therefore they shall be holy.*[3] Origen has called a priest "a being consecrated to God."[4] From his very entrance into the ecclesiastical state the priest declared that he wished for no other portion than God.[5] If, then, adds St. Ambrose, God is the portion of the priest, he should live only for God.[6] Hence the Apostle has said, that he who is devoted to the service of the divine majesty should not engage in worldly affairs, but should seek only to please him to whom he has given himself: *No man being a soldier to God, entangleth himself with secular business; that he may please Him to Whom he*

---

[1] "Sacerdos dici potes, esse non potes."—*Serm.* 41.
[2] "Verus minister altaris Deo, non sibi, natus est."—*In Ps.* 118, s. 3.
[3] "Incensum enim Domini et panes Dei sui offerunt, et ideo sancti erunt."—*Levit.* xxi. 6.
[4] "Mens consecrata Deo."—*In Lev. hom.* 15.
[5] "Dominus pars hereditatis meæ."
[6] "Cui Deus portio est, nihil debet curare, nisi Deum."—*De Esau*, c. 2.

hath engaged himself.[1] Jesus Christ forbade the young man who wished to become one of his disciples to return home for the purpose of burying his father: *Follow Me, and let the dead bury the dead.*[2] This lesson was, as the same St. Ambrose writes, directed to all ecclesiastics, to teach them that it is their duty to prefer the concerns of the divine glory to all human affairs, which may be an obstacle to their belonging entirely to God.[3]

Even in the Old Law, God declared to the priests that he had chosen them from among the people that they might be his without reserve. Hence he told them that they should have no possession, no portion among seculars, because he himself wished to be their portion and inheritance: *You shall possess nothing in their land, neither shall you have a portion among them: I am thy portion and inheritance in the midst of the children of Israel.*[4] On this passage Oleaster writes: "O priest! understand what great happiness God has conferred upon thee by wishing to have thee as his inheritance. And what can be wanting to thee if thou possessest God?"[5] The priest, then, should say with St. Augustine: "Let others choose for their portion temporal things; God is my portion."[6]

---

[1] "Nemo, militans Deo, implicat se negotiis sæcularibus, ut ei placeat. cui se probavit."—2 *Tim.* ii. 4.

[2] "Sequere me, et dimitte mortuos sepelire mortuos suos."—*Matth.* viii. 22.

[3] "Hic paterni funeris sepultura prohibetur, ut intelligas humana posthabenda divinis."—*In Luc.* c. 9.

[4] "In terra eorum nihil possidebitis, nec habebitis partem inter eos; ego pars et hereditas tua in medio filiorum Israel."—*Num.* xviii. 20.

[5] "Magna dignatio Domini, si eam, Sacerdos, cognoscas: quod velit Deus esse pars tua. Quid non habebis, si Deum habeas?"

[6] "Eligant sibi alii partes, quibus fruantur, terrenas et temporales; portio sanctorum, Dominus æternus est. Bibant alii mortiferas voluptates; portio calicis mei, Dominus est."—*Enarr. in Ps.* 15.

And, says St. Anselm, if we love not God, what shall we love?[1] The Emperor Diocletian placed before St. Clement gold, silver, and precious stones, in order to induce him to deny the faith: seeing his God put in comparison with a little dust, the saint heaved a sigh of sorrow: *But one thing is necessary.*[2] He who possesses all things without God, has nothing; but he who possesses God without anything else, has all things. Hence, St. Francis had reason to say, and to repeat, as he did for an entire night, *My God, and my all.* Happy, then, is he who can say with David: *For what have I in heaven? and besides Thee what do I desire upon earth? . . . God is my portion forever.*[3] My God, neither in heaven nor on earth do I wish for anything but Thee. Thou art, and shall be always, the Lord of my heart, and my only riches.

God deserves to be loved for his own sake, because he is an object worthy of infinite love: but we should love him, at least, through gratitude for the infinite love he has shown in the benefit of redemption. What more could God do for us, than become man and die for us? *Greater love than this no man hath, that a man lay down his life for his friends.*[4] Before redemption, men could doubt if God loved them with a tender love; but how can they doubt it after having seen him dead on a cross for the love of them. This has been, as it was called by Moses and Elias on Mount Thabor, an excess of love: *And they spoke of His decease* [excess] *that He should accomplish in Jerusalem.*[5] An excess that all the

---

[1] " Si non amavero te, quid amabo?"—*Medit.* 13.

[2] " Unum est necessarium."—*Luke,* x. 42.

[3] "Quid enim mihi est in cœlo? et a te quid volui super terram? . . . Deus cordis mei, et pars mea Deus in æternum."—*Ps.* lxxii. 25.

[4] " Majorem hac dilectionem nemo habet, ut animam suam ponat quis pro amicis suis."—*John,* xv. 13.

[5] " Dicebant excessum ejus, quem completurus erat in Jerusalem."— *Luke,* ix. 31.

angels shall not be able to comprehend for all eternity. Who among men, says St. Anselm, could deserve that a God should die for him?[1] But it is certain that this Son of God has died for each of us: *Christ died for all*.[2] The Apostle writes, that when the death of our Saviour was preached to the Gentiles it appeared to them foolishness: *We preach Christ crucified, unto the Jews indeed a stumbling-block, and unto the Gentiles foolishness*.[3] It was neither foolishness nor a lie, but a truth of faith,— a truth which, as St. Laurence Justinian says, makes a God appear to us foolish through love for man.[4] O God, if Jesus Christ wished to show his love for his eternal Father, could he give him a more convincing proof than by dying on a cross, as he has died, for each of us? I say more: If a servant had died for us, could we but love him? But where is our love and gratitude towards Jesus Christ?

Let us at least frequently remember what our Redeemer has done and suffered for us. They who frequently remember his Passion give great pleasure to Jesus Christ. If a person submitted to insults, wounds, and imprisonment for the sake of a friend, how great should his gratification be at hearing that the friend frequently remembered and thought of his sufferings. Ah! the soul that frequently thinks on the Passion of Jesus Christ, and on the love that that enamoured God has shown us in his pains and humiliations, cannot but feel herself chained to his love: *The charity of Christ presseth us*.[5] But if all should burn with love for Jesus

[1] "Quis dignus erat ut Filius Dei mortem pro eo pateretur?"—*De Mensura Cruc*. c. 2.

[2] " Pro omnibus mortuus est Christus."—2 *Cor*. v. 15.

[3] "Prædicamus Christum crucifixum, Judæris quidem scandalum, Gentibus autem stultitiam."—1 *Cor*. i. 23.

[4] " Vidimus Sapientiam amoris nimietate infatuatam."—*Serm. de Nat. D*.

[5] " Charitas enim Christi urget nos."—2 *Cor*. v. 14.

Christ, we priests should love him with a special love; for Jesus Christ has died in a special manner to make us priests: for, as has been said in Chapter I., without the death of Jesus Christ we should not have the holy and immaculate victim that we now offer to God. Justly, then, has St. Ambrose said: "Although Christ has suffered for all, he has especially suffered for us. But he that receives more, owes more. Let us render love to him for the blood that he has shed for us."[1]

Let us endeavor to understand the love that Jesus Christ has shown us in his Passion, and we shall certainly renounce the love of creatures. "Oh, if you knew the mystery of the cross!"[2] said the Apostle St. Andrew to the tyrant who tempted him to deny Jesus Christ. As if he said, O tyrant! if you knew the love that your God has for you, and his desire for your salvation, you would certainly cease to tempt me, and through gratitude for so much love, you would devote yourself to his love.

Happy, then, the man who keeps constantly before his eyes the wounds of Jesus Christ! *You shall draw waters with joy out of the Saviour's fountains.*[3] Oh, what waters of devotion, what lights and affections, do the saints draw from these fountains of salvation! Father Alvarez used to say, that the ignorance of the riches that we have in Jesus Christ is the cause of the ruin of Christians. The learned boast of their science, but the Apostle gloried in nothing but in the knowledge of Jesus Christ crucified: *For I judged not myself to know anything*

[1] "Etsi Christus pro omnibus mortuus est, pro nobis tamen specialiter passus est. Plus debet, qui plus accepit; reddamus ergo amorem pro sanguinis pretio."—*In Luc.* c. 7.

[2] "Oh! si scires mysterium Crucis!"

[3] "Haurietis aquas in gaudio de fontibus Salvatoris."—*Isa.* xii. 3.

[4] "Non enim judicavi me scire aliquid inter vos, nisi Jesum Christum, et hunc crucifixum."—I *Cor.* ii. 2.

among you, but Jesus Christ, and Him crucified.[1] Of what advantage are all sciences to him who knows not how to love Jesus Christ? *And if . . . I should know . . . all science*, said the same Apostle, *and have not charity, I am nothing.*[1] In another place he said that to gain Jesus Christ he esteemed all things as dung: *I count all things to be but loss, and count them but as dung, that I may gain Christ.*[2] Hence he gloried in calling himself the prisoner of Jesus Christ: *I, Paul, the prisoner of Jesus Christ.*[3]

Oh, happy the priest who, bound by these holy chains, gives himself entirely to Jesus Christ! God loves a soul that gives herself entirely to him, more than he does a hundred imperfect souls. If a prince had a hundred servants, ninety-nine of whom served him with little affection, always giving him some displeasure, and had one that served him through pure love, always seeking to please him to the utmost of his power, surely the prince would love that faithful servant more than all the others: *There are young maidens without number. One is my dove, my perfect one.*[4] The Lord loves the soul that serves him perfectly, as if he had no other to love but her. St. Bernard says: "Learn from Christ how to love Christ."[5] From his birth Jesus Christ has given himself entirely to us: *For a Child is born to us, and a Son is given to us.*[6] And he has given himself through love: *Christ also hath loved us, and hath delivered Himself*

---

[1] "Et si noverim omnem scientiam, charitatem autem non habuero nihil sum."—1 *Cor.* xiii. 2.

[2] "Omnia detrimentum feci, et arbitror ut stercora, ut Christum lucrifaciam."—*Phil.* iii. 8.

[3] "Ego Paulus, vinctus Christi Jesu."—*Eph.* iii. 1.

[4] "Adolescentularum non est numerus; una est columba mea, perfecta mea."—*Cant.* vi. 7.

[5] "Disce a Christo quemadmodum diligas Christum."—*In Cant.* s. 20.

[6] "Parvulus enim natus est nobis, et filius datus est nobis."—*Isa.* ix. 6.

*for us.*¹ It is just, then, that we also through love give ourselves entirely to Jesus Christ. He, says St. John Chrysostom, has given himself without reserve to you, bestowing upon you his blood, his life, his merits.² It is but just that you, too, give yourself without reserve to Jesus Christ, says St. Bernard.³

But if this holds for all, it applies in a special manner to priests. Hence, addressing particularly the priests of his Order, St. Francis of Assisi, knowing the special obligation of a priest to belong entirely to Jesus Christ, said: "Keep nothing back of yourselves, so that he who offers himself entirely may also receive you."⁴ The Redeemer has died for all, that each may live no longer to himself, but only to that God who has given his life for him: *Christ died for all; that they also, who live, may not now live to themselves, but unto Him who died for them.*⁵ Oh that each of us would continually say to God with St. Augustine: "May I die to myself that I may live only for Thee!"⁶ But to belong entirely to God, we must give him our whole, undivided love, says St. Augustine.⁷ He cannot belong entirely to God who loves anything which is not God, or loves it not for God, continues St. Augustine. "Let your soul," cries out St. Bernard, "be one, that you may serve God alone."⁸ Ah! redeemed soul, divide not your love

---

¹ "Dilexit nos, et tradidit semetipsum pro nobis."—*Eph.* v. 2.
² "Totum tibi dedit, nihil sibi reliquit."
³ "Integrum te da illi, quia ille, ut te salvaret, integrum se tradidit." —*De Modo bene viv.* c. 8.
⁴ "Nihil de vobis retineatis vobis, ut totos vos recipiat; qui se vobis exhibet totum."
⁵ "Pro omnibus mortuus est Christus, ut et qui vivunt, jam non sibi vivant, sed ei qui pro ipsis mortuus est."—2 *Cor.* v. 15.
⁶ "Moriar mihi, ut tu solus in me vivas."
⁷ "Minus te amat, qui tecum aliquid amat, quod non propter te amat."—*Conf.* l. 10, c. 29.
⁸ "Anima, sola esto, ut soli te serves."—*In Cant.* s. 40.

among creatures; keep yourself alone for that God who alone merits all your love. It was this that Blessed Egidius meant by the words *una, uni,* that is, the one soul which we have, we ought not to divide, but give entirely to that one God whose love for us exceeds the love of all others, and whose claims to our love surpass the claims of all.

II.

Means to be Employed for belonging Entirely to God.

1. Desire for Perfection.

Let us now see what a priest must do in order to belong entirely to God. First of all, he must have a great desire of sanctity: *For the beginning of her is the most true desire of discipline.*[1] Holy desires are the wings with which souls fly to God: *But the path of the just, as a shining light, goeth forward, and increaseth even to perfect day.*[2] The way of the just is like the light of the sun, which from his rising increases as he advances in his course; but, on the other hand, the light of sinners, like that of the evening, constantly grows more dim, until it is entirely lost, so that the miserable beings no longer see where they are going: *The way of the wicked is darksome; they know not where they fall.*[3]

Miserable, then, the man who is content with his conduct, and seeks not to advance. " Not to advance is to go backward,"[4] says St. Augustine. And St. Gregory has said,[5] he who remains in a river without making an effort to make way against the current, shall be carried

---

[1] " Initium enim illius, verissima est disciplinæ concupiscentia."— *Wisd.* vi. 18.

[2] " Iustorum autem semita, quasi lux splendens, procedit et crescit usque ad perfectam diem."—*Prov.* iv. 18.

[3] " Via impiorum tenebrosa; nesciunt ubi corruant."—*Ib.* 19.

[4] " Non progredi, reverti est."—*Ep.* 17, *E. B. app.*

[5] *Past.* p. 3, c. 1.

back by it. Hence St. Bernard said to a tepid soul, "You do not wish to advance. You will then go backward."[1] Are you unwilling to advance? Then you wish to go backward. You perhaps will answer: I wish to remain as I am, neither better nor worse. But this is impossible. "This," adds the saint, "is what cannot be done."[2] This cannot be, since Job has said, that man *never continueth in the same state*.[3] To win the prize that is, the eternal crown, we must run till we obtain it: *So run that you may obtain*.[4] He who ceases to run, shall lose all his labor and the crown of glory.

Blessed are they that hunger and thirst after justice.[5] For, as the divine mother said, God fills with his graces the souls that desire to become saints. *He hath filled the hungry with good things*. Mark the words, *the hungry, those that hunger*.[6] But to become a saint, a simple desire is not enough: a strong desire, and a certain hunger after sanctity, are necessary. As flame runs through a dry reed, so they who have this blessed hunger do not walk, but run in the way of virtue. *The just shall shine, and shall run to and fro like sparks among the reeds*.[7] Who, then, shall become a saint? He who wishes to become one: *If thou wilt be perfect, go*, etc.[8] But he must wish for sanctity with true humility. The tepid Christian, as the Wise Man says, also wills, but not with a sincere will. He desires, and always desires, but his desires bring him to destruction; for he feeds on them, and in

---

[1] "Non vis proficere; vis ergo deficere."
[2] "Hoc ergo vis, quod esse non potest."—*Ep*. 254.
[3] "Nunquam in eodem statu permanet."—*Job*, xiv. 2.
[4] "Sic currite, ut comprehendatis."—1 *Cor*. ix. 24.
[5] "Beati, qui esuriunt et sitiunt justitiam."—*Matth*. v. 6.
[6] "Esurientes implevit bonis."—*Magnif*.
[7] "Fulgebunt justi, et tanquam scintillæ in arundineto discurrent."—*Wisd*. iii. 7.
[8] "Si vis perfectus esse, vade . . . ."—*Matth*. xix. 21.

the mean time goes from bad to worse: *The sluggard willeth and willeth not.*[1]—*Desires kill the slothful.*[2]

Wisdom, that is sanctity, is easily found by them who seek it: *It is found by them that seek her.*[3] But to find sanctity it is not enough to desire it; we must desire it with a determined will to attain it: *If you seek, seek,*[4] says Isaias. He who desires sanctity with a resolute will of acquiring it, easily attains it. "Not with the feet of the body," says St. Bernard, " but with the desires of the soul; is God sought."[5] And St. Teresa has written: "Let our thoughts be great; from great thoughts our advancement shall come. Our desires must not be low and grovelling, but we must trust in God; that, gradually doing violence to ourselves, we shall, with the divine grace, arrive at the sanctity which the saints have attained."[6]

Open thy mouth wide, says the Lord, *and I will fill it.*[7] A mother cannot give suck to an infant if it open not its mouth to take the milk. *Open thy mouth wide;* that is, says St. Athanasius, "Increase thy desires."[8] By holy desires the saints have arrived at perfection in a short time: *Being made perfect in a short time, he fulfilled a long time.*[9] This was verified particularly in St. Aloysius Gonzaga, who in a few years attained such sublime sanctity, that to St. Mary Magdalene de Pazzi, who saw him in bliss, it appeared that his glory was scarcely surpassed by that of any of the saints. And

---
[1] " Vult et non vult piger."—*Prov.* xiii. 4.
[2] " Desideria occidunt pigrum."—*Prov.* xxi. 25.
[3] " Invenitur ab his qui quærunt illam."—*Wisd.* vi. 13.
[4] " Si quæritis, quærite."—*Isa.* xxi. 12.
[5] " Non pedum passibus, sed desideriis quæritur Deus."—*In Cant.* s. 84.
[6] *Life*, ch. 13.
[7] " Dilata os tuum, et implebo illud."—*Ps.* lxxx. 11.
[8] " Dilata desiderium tuum."
[9] " Consummatus in brevi, explevit tempora multa."—*Wisd.* iv. 13.

she was told that he attained to such glory by the ardor with which he desired, during life, to love God as much as he deserved to be loved.

Desires, says St. Laurence Justinian, give strength to the soul, and render labor light.[1] Hence the saint adds, that he who has an ardent desire of victory has already conquered.[2] St. Augustine has said: "For him that labors, the road is narrow; for him that loves, it is wide."[3] To him who has but little love for sanctity, the way is narrow and difficult to be trodden; but he who ardently loves perfection, finds the way broad, and walks in it without labor. The broadness, then, of the way is found not in the way, but in the heart; that is, in a determined will to please God: *I have run the way of Thy commandments, when Thou didst enlarge my heart.*[4] Blosius says that the Lord is not less pleased by holy desires than by ardent love.[5]

He that has not the desire of becoming a saint, let him at least ask it of God, and God will give it to him. And let us be persuaded that to become a saint is not difficult to him who desires it. In the world it is difficult for a vassal to obtain the friendship of his sovereign, however ardently he may desire it, but, said the courtier of the emperor mentioned by St. Augustine, to obtain the friendship of God it is enough to wish for it: "Behold, if I wish I am instantly his friend!"[6] And St. Bernard has written that a man cannot have a greater

---

[1] "Vires subministrat, pœnam exhibet leviorem."—*De Disc. mon.* c. 6.

[2] "Magna victoriæ pars est vincendi desiderium."—*De Casto Conn.* c. 3.

[3] "Laboranti angusta via est, amanti lata."—*In Ps.* 30, *en.* 2.

[4] "Viam mandatorum tuorum cucurri, cum dilatasti cor meum."—*Ps.* cxviii. 32.

[5] "Deus non minus sancto desiderio lætatur, quam si anima amore liquefiat."

[6] "Amicus Dei, si voluero, ecce nunc fio."—*Conf.* l. 8, c. 6.

proof of being the friend of God, and of enjoying his grace, than when he desires greater grace in order to please God.[1] And, adds the saint, it matters not that he should have been a sinner, for "God attends not to what a man has done, but to what he wishes to be."[2]

2. THE INTENTION OF PLEASING GOD IN ALL THINGS.

Secondly, the priest who wishes to be a saint, must do all his actions for the sole purpose of pleasing God. All his words, thoughts, desires, and actions must be an exercise of divine love. The spouse in the Canticles assumed at one time the character of a fowler; at another, of a warrior; now a gardener; again, a cultivator of the vine; but in all these occupations she presented the appearance of a lover, because she did all for the love of her spouse. So, in like manner, all the words, thoughts, sufferings, actions, of a priest, whether he says Mass or hears confessions, or preaches, or meditates, or assists the dying, or mortifies the flesh, or whatever else he does, should all proceed from the same love; for he ought to do all in order to please God.

Jesus Christ has said: *If thy eye be single, thy whole body shall be lightsome.*[3] By the eye the holy Fathers have understood the intention. Then, says St. Augustine, "The intention makes the work good."[4] The Lord said to Samuel: *Man seeth those things that appear, but the Lord beholdeth the heart.*[5] Men are satisfied with the works that they see, but God, who beholds the heart, is not content with any work unless he sees it performed with a view

[1] "Nullum omnino præsentiæ ejus certius testimonium est, quam desiderium gratiæ amplioris."—*De S. Andr.* s. 2.
[2] "Non attendit Deus quid fecerit homo, sed quid velit esse."
[3] "Si oculus tuus fuerit simplex, totum corpus tuum lucidum erit."—*Matth.* vi. 22.
[4] "Bonum opus intentio facit."—*In Ps.* 21, *en.* 2.
[5] "Homo enim videt ea quæ parent; Dominus autem intuetur cor."—1 *Kings*, xvi. 7.

to please himself. *I will offer up to Thee holocausts full of marrow*,[1] says David. Works performed without the proper intention, are victims without marrow, which God rejects. In the oblations made to him he regards not the value of the offering, but the affection with which it is presented. " God," says Salvian, " looks not so much at the value of the offering as at the disposition with which it is offered."[2] Of our Saviour it was justly said: *He hath done all things well.*[3] For in all his actions he sought only the pleasure of his eternal Father: *I seek not my own will, but the will of Him that sent me.*[4]

But, alas! only few of our works are perfectly pleasing to God; because few are done without some desire of our own glory. " It is rare," says St. Jerome, " to find a faithful soul that never acts out of vain-glory."[5] How many priests on the day of judgment shall say to Jesus Christ: *Lord, Lord, have we not prophesied, and cast out devils in Thy name, and done many miracles in Thy name?*[6] Lord, we have preached, we have celebrated Masses, we have heard confessions, we have converted souls, we have assisted the dying. The Lord shall answer: *I never knew you: depart from Me, you that work iniquity.*[7] He shall say: Begone, I have never known you as my ministers, for you have not labored for me, but for your own glory or interest.

Hence Jesus Christ exhorts us to conceal the works

[1] " Holocausta medullata offeram tibi."—*Ps.* lxv. 15.
[2] "Oblata Deo, non pretio, sed affectu placent."—*Adv. Avarit.* l. 1.
[3] " Bene omnia fecit."—*Mark*, vii. 37.
[4] " Non quæro voluntatem meam, sed voluntatem ejus qui misit me."—*John*, v. 30.
[5] " Rarum est, fidelem animam inveniri, ut nihil ob gloriæ cupiditatem faciat."—*Dial. adv. Luciferianos.*
[6] " Domine, nonne in nomine tuo prophetavimus, et in nomine tuo dæmonia ejecimus, et in nomine tuo virtutes multas fecimus ?"—*Matth.* vii. 22.
[7] "Nunquam novi vos; discedite a me, qui operamini iniquitatem."

which we perform: *Let not thy left hand know what thy right hand doth.*[1] The Son of God tells us to conceal our works, that, as St. Augustine remarks, what we do for God may not be afterwards lost through vanity.[2] God abominates rapine in the holocaust: *I the Lord . . . hate robbery in a holocaust.*[3] By rapine is meant precisely the seeking of our own glory, or of self-interest in the works of God. He who truly loves, says St. Bernard, merits a reward, but does not seek it: the only recompense that he demands is to please the God whom he loves.[4] In a word, as the same saint says in another place, "True love is content with itself;"[5] that is, with being love, and demands nothing more.

The marks by which a priest may know whether he acts with a pure intention are the following: 1. If he loves works that are attended with greater inconvenience and less glory. 2. If he preserves peace when he has not attained the object that he proposed. He who works for God has already attained his end, which is to please God; and, on the other hand, he who is disturbed when he fails in the attainment of his object shows that he has not labored solely for God. 3. If he rejoices in the good done by others as if it had been done by himself, and entertains no jealousy when others engage in the works that he performs, but desires to see all laboring to give glory to God, and says with Moses: *Oh that all the people might prophesy!*[6]

The days of the priest who performs all his actions

[1] "Nesciat sinistra tua quid faciat dextera tua."—*Matth.* vi. 3.
[2] "Quod facit amor Dei, non corrumpat vanitas."—*Serm.* 63, *E. B. app.*
[3] "Ego Dominus, . . . odio habens rapinam in holocausto."—*Isa.* lxi. 8.
[4] "Verus amor præmium non requirit, sed meretur; habet præmium, sed id quod amatur."—*De dil. Deo,* c. 7.
[5] "Verus amor seipso contentus est."
[6] "Quis tribuat ut omnis populus prophetet!"—*Num.* xi. 29.

for God are full days: *And full days shall be found in them.*¹ But of them who act for a selfish end, it is said that they do not reach even the half of their days: *Deceitful men shall not live out half their days.*² Hence St. Eucherius of Lyons has written, that we ought to consider ourselves to have lived only on the day on which we have denied our own will.³

Seneca says that he who makes us a small present through love, imposes on us a greater obligation than another who bestows great favors upon us through a motive of self-interest.⁴ Certainly the Lord is more pleased by a trifling act performed in order to do his will, than by the most splendid works done for our own satisfaction. Of the poor widow who gave two mites in the temple, Jesus Christ said that she gave more than all the others: *This poor widow hath cast in more than all.*⁵ On this passage St. Cyprian says: "The Lord does not regard how much is given, but with what sentiments it is given."⁶ The Lord regarded not the sum, but the affection with which it was given.

The Abbot Pambo, seeing a woman decked out in costly ornaments, began to weep. Being asked the cause of his tears, he said: "O God! how much more does this woman do to please men than I do to please God!" In the Life of St. Louis, king of France, it is related that a Father of the Order of St. Dominic, who was going to court, asked a woman whom he saw with

¹ "Et dies pleni invenientur in eis."—*Ps.* lxxii. 10.

² "Dolosi non dimidiabunt dies suos."—*Ps.* liv. 24.

³ "Illum tantum diem vixisse te computa; in quo voluntates proprias abnegasti."—*Ad Monach. hom.* 9.

⁴ "Magis nos obligat, qui exiguum dedit libenter, quam qui, non voluntatem tantum juvandi habuit, sed cupiditatem."—*De Benefic.* l. 1, c. 7.

⁵ "Vidua hæc pauper plus omnibus misit."—*Mark*, xii. 43.

⁶ "Considerans, non quantum, sed ex quanto dedisset."—*De Ope et Eleem.*

a lighted torch in one hand and a vessel of water in the other, why she carried these things; she answered: With this torch I wish to burn heaven, and with this water I desire to extinguish hell, that God may be loved solely because he deserves all love. Oh, happy the priest who labors only to please God! He who seeks only to please God imitates the souls in heaven, who, as the angelic Doctor says, "wish that He ,rather than themselves should be happy."[1] They rejoice more in the felicity of God than in their own happiness, because they love him more than themselves.

3. PATIENCE IN PAINS AND HUMILIATIONS.

Thirdly, the priest who wishes to be holy must be ready to suffer in peace for God all things—poverty, dishonor, infirmity, and death. The Apostle says: *You bear God in your body.*[2] In his comment on this text, Gilbert says: "Jesus Christ wishes to be carried by us in peace and joy. He who carries him with tediousness or complaint, carries not, but drags him by force."[3] The love that a soul bears to God is shown in embracing not delights, but insults and sufferings. This we learn from the words of our Redeemer when he went to meet the soldiers who came to capture him, in order to put him to death: *But that the world may know that I love the Father. . . . Arise, let us go hence.*[4] Hence the saints in imitation of Jesus Christ, have gone with joy to embrace torments and death. St. Joseph of Leonessa, a Capuchin, was once obliged to undergo a

[1] " Anima potius vult ipsum esse beatum, quam seipsam esse beatam."—*De Beatit.* c. 7.

[2] " Glorificate et portate Deum in corpore vestro."—1 *Cor.* vi. 20.

[3] " Portari vult a nobis Christum, sed gloriose, non cum tædio, non cum murmure; portari, non trahi: trahenti enim onerosus est Christus." —*In Cant.* s. 17.

[4] " Ut cognoscat mundus quia diligo Patrem, . . . surgite, eamus hinc."—*John*, xiv. 31.

painful operation. When some persons present spoke of binding him with cords, he took the crucifix into his hands and said: "What cords! what cords!" My Lord, who was nailed to the cross for my sake, binds me sufficiently to endure all pain for the love of him. Thus he bore the incision without complaint. St. Teresa said: "Who is there that can behold his Lord covered with wounds, and persecuted by enemies, without being willing to embrace and desirous of suffering every tribulation?"[1] St. Bernard writes: "To him who loves his crucified God, insults and pains are very acceptable."[2]

The Apostle says that in patience particularly we priests should make ourselves known as the ministers of Jesus Christ: *Let us exhibit ourselves as the ministers of God, in much patience, in tribulation, in necessities, in distresses, . . . in labors.*[3] Thomas à Kempis has written: "When the day of judgment cometh, it will not be asked of us what we have read, but what we have done."[4] Many men of learning are acquainted with many things, but know not how to bear anything for God; and what is worse, they are incapable of understanding the great fault which they commit by their impatience. *Who have eyes, and see not,*[5] says the Prophet Jeremias. What does learning profit the man who has not charity? says St. Paul. *And if . . . I should know all mysteries and all knowledge, . . . and have not charity, I am*

---

[1] *Life*, ch. 26.
[2] " Grata ignominia crucis ei qui Crucifixo ingratus non est."—*In Cant.* s. 25.
[3] " Exhibeamus nosmetipsos sicut Dei ministros in multa patientia, in tribulationibus, in necessitatibus, in angustiis, . . . in laboribus . . ." —2 *Cor.* vi. 4.
[4] " Adveniente die judicii, non quæretur quid legimus, sed quid fecimus."—*De Imit. Chr.* l. 1, c. 3.
[5] " Habentes oculos non videtis."—*Jer.* v. 21.

nothing.[1] But, as the same Apostle has observed, *Charity beareth all things*.[2] He who wishes to become a saint must suffer persecution. *All that live godly in Christ Jesus shall suffer persecution*.[3] And before him our Saviour said: *If they have persecuted Me, they will also persecute you*.[4] The life of a saint cannot, says St. Hilary, be a life of quiet and tranquillity: it must be often disturbed by contradictions and tried by patience.[5] The Lord chastises those whom he accepts for his children: *For whom the Lord loveth, He chastiseth: and He scourgeth every son whom He receiveth*.[6] *Such as I love I rebuke and chastise*.[7] And why? Because patience tries the love and perfect fidelity of a soul: *Patience hath a perfect work*.[8] It was this that the Archangel Raphael meant to say to holy Tobias: *Because thou wast acceptable to God, it was necessary that temptation should prove thee*.[9]

Sometimes we shall be reproved for a fault which we have not committed; but "what matter?" says St. Augustine; "we ought to accept the reproof in atonement for other sins to which we have consented."[10] Let us attend to the words of holy Judith, who says that in this life chastisements come from God, not for our de-

[1] " Et si . . . noverim mysteria omnia et omnem scientiam, charitatem autem non habuero, nihil sum."—1 *Cor*. xiii. 2.
[2] " Charitas omnia suffert."
[3] " Et omnes qui pie volunt vivere in Christo Jesu, persecutionem patientur."—2 *Tim*. iii. 12.
[4] " Si me persecuti sunt, et vos persequentur."—*John*, xv. 20.
[5] " Non otiosa ætas religiosi viri est, neque quietam exigit vitam; impugnatur sæpe, et hæc sunt quæ fidem probant."—*In Ps*. cxxviii.
[6] " Quem enim diligit Dominus, castigat; flagellat autem omnem filium quem recipit."—*Heb*. xii. 6.
[7] " Ego, quos amo, arguo et castigo."—*Apoc*. iii. 19.
[8] " Patientia autem opus perfectum habet."—*James*, i. 4.
[9] " Quia acceptus eras Deo, necesse fuit ut tentatio probaret te."—*Tob*. xii. 13.
[10] " Etsi non habemus peccatum quod nobis objicit inimicus, habemus tamen alterum, quod digne in nobis flagellatur."—*In Ps*. 68, s. 1.

struction, but that we may amend, and thus escape eternal vengeance: *They have happened for our amendment, and not for our destruction.*[1] If, then, on account of past sins, we find ourselves debtors to the divine justice, we should not only accept with patience the tribulations that befall us, but should also pray with St. Augustine: "Here burn, here cut, here do not spare, that Thou mayest spare us in eternity."[2]

Job said: *If we have received good things at the hand of God, why should we not receive evil?*[3] He said this because he well knew that we gain far more by patiently accepting the evils, that is, the tribulations of this life, than we do by temporal blessings. But whether we will or not, we must suffer the miseries of this life: he who bears them with patience merits heaven, but he who is impatient under them also suffers from them, but lays up merits for hell, says St. Augustine.[4] Speaking of the good and the wicked thief, the same saint says: "The cross united them; the manner of carrying the cross separated them."[5] Both suffered death, but one of them, because he accepted it with patience, was saved; the other, because he blasphemed in his suffering, was lost. St. John the Apostle saw that the saints who were in the enjoyment of the beatific vision came not from the delights of the earth, but from tribulations: *These are they who are come out of great tribulation; . . . therefore they are before the throne of God.*[6]

[1] "Ad emendationem, et non ad perditionem nostram, evenisse credamus."—*Judith*, viii. 27.
[2] "Hic ure, hic seca; hic non parcas, ut in æternum parcas."
[3] "Si bona suscepimus de manu Dei, mala quare non suscipiamus?"—*Job*, ii. 10.
[4] "Una eademque tunsio bonos perducit ad gloriam, malos redigit in favillam."—*Serm.* 52, *E. B. app.*
[5] "Quos passio jungebat causa separabat."—*Ep.* 185, *E. B.*
[6] "Hi sunt qui venerunt de tribulatione magna; . . . ideo sunt ante thronum Dei."—*Apoc.* vii. 14.

4. CONFORMITY TO THE WILL OF GOD.

Fourthly and lastly, he who wishes to be a saint must wish only what God wishes. All our good consists in uniting ourselves to the will of God: *And life in His good-will.*[1] St. Teresa says: "All that he who practises mental prayer should seek, is to conform his will to the divine will; let him be assured that in this consists the highest perfection."[2] All that the Lord demands of us is, that we give him our heart; that is, our will: *My son, give Me thy heart.*[3] St. Anselm says that God asks and, as it were, begs our heart; and when cast off, he does not depart, but repeats his petitions.[4] The most acceptable offering, then, that we can present to God is the oblation of our will, saying with the Apostle: *Lord, what wilt Thou have me to do?*[5] Hence St. Augustine has written: "We can do nothing more pleasing than to say to him, Do Thou possess us."[6] The Lord said that he had found in David a man according to his own heart. And why? Because David fulfilled all his divine wills: *I have found David, the son of Jesse, a man according to my own heart.*[7] Let us endeavor to say always with David: *Teach me to do Thy will.*[8] Lord, teach me to do nothing but what Thou willest. Hence we must frequently offer ourselves to God, saying with

[1] "Et vita in voluntate ejus."—*Ps.* xxix. 6.
[2] *Int. Castle*, d. 2, ch. 1.
[3] "Præbe, fili mi, cor tuum mihi."—*Prov.* xxiii. 26.
[4] "Nonne tu es Deus meus, qui tam crebro pulsas et mendicas ad ostium nostrum, dicens: Præbe, fili mi, cor tuum mihi?—imo, et sæpe repulsus, te iterum ingeris!"—*De Mens. cruc.* c. 5.
[5] "Domine, quid me vis facere?"—*Acts*, ix. 6.
[6] "Nihil gratius Deo possumus offere, quam ut dicamus ei: Posside nos."—*In Ps.* 131.
[7] "Inveni David, filium Jesse, virum secundum cor meum, qui faciet omnes voluntates meas."—*Acts*, xiii. 22.
[8] "Doce me facere voluntatem tuam."—*Ps.* cxlii. 9.

the same holy prophet: *My heart is ready, O God! my heart is ready.*[1]

But we must remember that our merit consists in embracing the divine will, not so much in things that are pleasing to us, as in those that are opposed to self-love. In these we show the strength of the love we bear to God. The Venerable John d'Avila used to say, that a single *Blessed be God*, in things that are opposed to our inclination, is of greater value than six thousand acts of thanksgiving in what is agreeable to us. And here it is necessary to understand that all that befalls us happens through the will of God, says St. Augustine.[2] This is the meaning of the words of Ecclesiasticus: *Good things and evil, life and death, poverty and riches, are from God.*[3] Thus when a person offends us, God wills not his sin, but he wills that we bear with the insult. When our reputation or property is taken away, we must say with holy Job: *The Lord gave, and the Lord hath taken away: as it hath pleased the Lord so is it done!*[4]

He who loves the will of God enjoys continual peace even in this life. *Delight in the Lord, and He will give thee the requests of thy heart*, said David.[5] Our heart, which has been created for an infinite good, cannot be satisfied by all creatures which are finite; and therefore, though it should possess all goods but God, the heart is not content; it always seeks after new enjoyments: but when it finds God, it possesses all things—he satisfies all its demands. Hence our Lord said to the Samaritan

[1] " Paratum cor meum, Deus, paratum cor meum."—*Ps.* lvi. 8.

[2] " Quidquid hic accidit contra voluntatem nostram, noveritis non accidere nisi de voluntate Dei."—*In Ps.* 148.

[3] " Bona et mala, vita et mors, paupertas et honestas, a Deo sunt." —*Ecclus.* xi. 14.

[4] " Dominus dedit, Dominus abstulit; sicut Domino placuit, ita factum est; sit nomen Domini benedictum!"—*Job*, i. 21.

[5] " Delectare in Domino, et dabit tibi petitiones cordis tui."—*Ps.* xxxvi. 4.

woman: *He that shall drink of the water that I will give him, shall not thirst forever.*[1] And in another place he said: *Blessed are they that hunger and thirst after justice, for they shall have their fill.*[2] Hence he who loves God is not afflicted at anything that happens: *Whatsoever shall befall the just man, it shall not make him sad.*[3] For the just man knows that whatever occurs, happens to him by the will of God. If, says Salvian, the saints are humbled, they wish for the humiliation; if they are poor, they rejoice in their poverty; in a word, they wish only what their God wishes, and therefore they enjoy continual peace.[4] In afflictions it is lawful to pray to be delivered from them, as Jesus Christ did in the garden: *My Father, if it be possible, let this chalice pass from Me.*[5] But we must also add with the Redeemer: *Nevertheless, not as I will, but as Thou wilt.*

It is certain that what God wills is best for us. Father John d'Avila once wrote to a sick priest: " Friend, think not of what you would do if you were in health, but be content to remain sick as long as it shall please God. If you seek the will of God, is it not as profitable to you to be sick as to be in health?"[6] We must be resigned in all things, even in the temptations by which we are impelled to offend God. The Apostle besought the Lord to deliver him from the many temptations which he suffered against chastity: *There was given me a sting of my flesh. . . . For which thing thrice I*

---

[1] " Qui autem biberit ex aqua quam ego dabo ei, non sitiet in æternum."—*John*, iv. 13.

[2] " Beati, qui esuriunt et sitiunt justitiam, quoniam ipsi saturabuntur."—*Matth.* v. 6.

[3] " Non contristabit justum, quidquid ei acciderit."—*Prov.* xii. 21.

[4] " Humiles sunt, hoc volunt; pauperes sunt, pauperie delectantur; itaque beati dicendi sunt."—*De Gub. Dei*, l. 1.

[5] " Pater mi, si possibile est, transeat a me calix iste; verumtamen, non sicut ego volo, sed sicut tu."—*Matth.* xxvi. 39.

[6] *Part* 2, *ep.* 54.

besought the Lord, that it might depart from me.[1] But in answer God said to him: *My grace is sufficient for thee.*[2] Let us be persuaded that God not only desires, but is also solicitous for our welfare. *The Lord is careful for me.*[3] Let us, then, abandon ourselves into the hands of God, for he has care of us: *Casting all your care upon Him, for He hath care of you.*[4]

Finally, how happy shall be the death of a soul perfectly conformed to the will of God! But he who wishes to die in sentiments of perfect conformity to the divine will must first conform to it in all things during life. Let us, then, in all contradictions and crosses that befall us accustom ourselves to acts of resignation, always repeating with the saints that great prayer which Jesus Christ has taught us: "Thy will be done; Thy will be done."[5] Or let us repeat the words of the same Saviour: *Yea, Father; for so hath it seemed good in Thy sight.*[6] And let us continually offer ourselves to God, saying with the divine Mother: "Behold the handmaid of the Lord."[7] Lord, behold your servant, dispose of me, and of all that belongs to me, as you please; I accept all from your hands. St. Teresa used to offer herself fifty times in the day to God. Let us also say to him, with the Apostle: *O Lord, what wilt Thou have me do.*[8] My God, make known to me what Thou wishest from me, and I will do it. The saints have done great things in order to accomplish the will of God. Some

---

[1] "Datus est mihi stimulus carnis meæ; . . . propter quod ter Dominum rogavi, ut discederet a me."—2 *Cor.* xii. 7.

[2] "Sufficit tibi gratia mea."

[3] "Dominus sollicitus est mei."—*Ps.* xxxix. 18.

[4] "Omnem sollicitudinem vestram projicientes in eum, quoniam ipsi cura est de vobis."—1 *Pet.* v. 7.

[5] "Fiat voluntas tua!"

[6] "Ita, Pater! quoniam sic fuit placitum ante te."—*Matth.* xi. 26.

[7] "Ecce ancilla Domini!" [8] "Domine, quid me vis facere?"

have fled into the desert, others have shut themselves up in the cloister, and others have suffered torments and death. Let us also who are priests, and are bound by stricter obligations to sanctity, unite ourselves to the divine will; let us become saints; let us not be diffident on account of past sins. "God does not attend," says St. Bernard, "to what man does, but to what he wishes to be."[1] A resolute will, with the divine aid, conquers all things.

Let us pray always: he who asks, receives: *For everyone that asketh, receiveth.*[2] Whatsoever we ask in prayer, we shall obtain: *You shall ask whatever you will, and it shall be done unto you.*[3] And among all prayers, let the beautiful prayer of St. Ignatius of Loyola be always dear to us; let us repeat it continually: "Grant me only Thy love with Thy grace, O Lord! and I shall be rich enough."[4] Lord, give me your love and your grace, and I desire nothing more. But, like St. Augustine, we must ask this gift of divine love continually and earnestly. The holy Doctor says: "Hear me, hear me, O my God, my King, my Father, my honor, my salvation, my light, my life,—hear, hear me! Thee only do I love, Thee only do I seek. Heal me, and open my eyes. Look upon him who has fled from Thee; long enough have I served Thy enemy. Command that I may be a pure, a perfect lover of Thy wisdom."[5] And in asking

---

[1] "Non attendit Deus quid fecerit homo, sed quid velit esse."
[2] "Omnis enim qui petit, accipit."—*Matth.* vii. 8.
[3] "Quodcunque volueritis, petetis, et fiet vobis."—*John*, xv. 7.
[4] "Amorem tui solum cum gratia tua mihi dones, et dives sum satis."
[5] "Exaudi, exaudi, exaudi me, Deus meus, Rex meus, Pater meus, Honor meus, Salus mea, Lux mea, Vita mea! exaudi, exaudi, exaudi me. Jam te solum amo, te solum quæro. Sana et aperi oculos meos. Recipe fugitivum tuum; satis inimicis tuis servierim. Jubeas me purum perfectumque amatorem esse sapientiæ tuæ."—*Solil.* l. 1, c. 1.

the divine graces, I add, with St. Bernard, let us always have recourse to the intercession of Mary, who obtains for her servants whatever she asks from God.[1]

[1] "Quæramus gratiam, et per Mariam quæramus; quia, quod quærit, invenit, et frustrari non potest."—*De Aquæd.*

INSTRUCTION XI.

DEVOTION TO MOST HOLY MARY.

(THIS instruction may serve either for an instruction or for a sermon; but whether it be given in the form of an instruction or of a sermon, the person who gives the spiritual exercises to the priests is entreated not to omit this discourse, which is, perhaps, the most fruitful of all; for without devotion to the divine Mother it is morally impossible for any one to be a good priest.)

Let us, first, consider the moral necessity of the intercession of Mary for priests; and secondly, the confidence which they ought to have in the prayers of this divine Mother.

I.

Moral Necessity of the Intercession of the Blessed Virgin.

With regard to the necessity of invoking her intercession, it is necessary to know that although the Council of Trent[1] has only declared that the invocation of the saints is useful, still St. Thomas has asked the question: "Whether we should ask the saints to pray for us,"[2] and has answered in the affirmative, saying, that the order of the divine law requires that we mortals be saved through the saints by obtaining, through their prayers, the graces necessary for salvation. The holy Doctor says: "Such is, after St. Denis the Areopagite, the order divinely established for the government of kings, that those far off should return to God through

---

[1] *Sess.* 25, *De inv. Sanct.*
[2] " Utrum debeamus Sanctos orare ad interpellandum pro nobis."

the mediation of those that are nearer."¹ "And as the saints in heaven are near God, we who are prisoners in the body and who travel far from God, we cannot, according to the order established, return to our supreme end except through the mediation of the saints."² Other authors, particularly the continuator of Tourney and Sylvius, hold the same opinion. He afterwards adds: "The natural law prescribes for us the order established by God. Now God wishes that inferior creatures in order to reach salvation should implore the help of superior creatures."³

But if it is a duty to ask the prayers of the saints, how much more strictly are we bound to invoke the intercession of Mary, whose prayers are more efficacious with God than the prayers of all the other saints! St. Thomas says that through the abundant grace which God has given them the saints can save many, but that the Blessed Virgin has merited grace sufficient to save all.⁴ St. Bernard has written that as we have access to the Father through his Son Jesus Christ, so we have access to the Son through the Mother.⁵ Hence he afterwards

¹ "Ordo est divinitus institutus in rebus, secundum Dionysium, ut per media ultima reducantur in Deum. Unde, cum Sancti, qui sunt in patria, sint Deo propinquissimi, hoc divinæ legis ordo requirit, ut nos, qui manentes in corpore peregrinamur a Domino, in eum per Sanctos medios reducamur."

² "Sicut, mediantibus Sanctorum suffragiis, Dei beneficia in nos deveniunt, ita oportet nos in Deum reduci, ut iterato beneficia ejus sumamus mediantibus Sanctis."—*In* 4 *Sent.* d. 45, q. 3, a. 2.

³ "Lege naturali tenemur eum ordinem observare, quem Deus instituit; at constituit Deus ut inferiores ad salutem perveniant, implorato superiorum subsidio."—*De Relig.* p. 2, c. 2, a. 5.

⁴ "Magnum est enim in quolibet Sancto, quando habet tantum de gratia quod sufficit ad salutem multorum; sed, quando haberet tantum quod sufficeret ad salutem omnium, hoc esset maximum, et hoc est in Christo et in Beata Virgine."—*Expos. in Sal. Ang.*

⁵ "Per te accessum habeamus ad Filium, o Inventrix gratiæ, Mater salutis, ut per te nos suscipiat, qui per te datus est nobis!"—*In Adv. Dom.* s. 2.

said that all the graces that we receive from God come to us through Mary: "God has placed in Mary the plenitude of all gifts. Acknowledge, then, that all that there is in us of hope, of grace, of salvation, we receive from her who is filled with delights. She is truly a garden of delights, so that from her are sent forth perfumes the most exquisite, that is, gifts and graces of God."[1] The saint assigns the following reason for asserting that all the divine graces come to us through the hands of Mary: "It is the will of God to grant us all the graces of which we stand in need."[2] This may be also inferred from all the texts of Scripture which the holy Church applies to Mary: *He that shall find me shall find life.*[3] *In me is all grace of the way and of the truth. . . . They that work by me shall not sin. They that explain me shall have life everlasting.*[4] The words of the holy Church, in the *Salve Regina*, in which she calls Mary *our life and our hope*,[5] are sufficient to confirm us all in this doctrine.

Hence St. Bernard exhorts us to have recourse to this divine Mother, with a secure confidence of obtaining the graces that we ask her to procure for us; because the Son knows not how to refuse anything to the Mother.[6] Hence the saint afterwards calls Mary the entire ground of his hope: "My children, she is the ladder for sinners;

[1] "Totius boni plenitudinem posuit (Deus) in Maria, ut proinde, si quid spei in nobis est, si quid gratiæ, si quid salutis, ab ea noverimus redundare, quæ ascendit deliciis affluens: hortus deliciarum, ut undique fluant et effluant aromata ejus, charismata scilicet gratiarum."—*De Aquæd.*

[2] "Sic est voluntas ejus qui totum nos habere voluit per Mariam."

[3] "Qui me invenerit, inveniet vitam, et hauriet salutem a Domino." *Prov.* viii. 35.

[4] "In me gratia omnis viæ et veritatis; in me omnis spes vitæ et virtutis. . . . Qui operantur in me, non peccabunt. Qui elucidant me, vitam æternam habebunt."—*Ecclus.* xxiv. 25.

[5] "Vita, Dulcedo, et Spes nostra."

[6] "Ad Mariam recurre; non dubius dixerim, exaudiet utique Matrem Filius."

she is the greatest motive of my confidence; she is the only cause of my hope."[1] He concludes by saying that we should ask all the graces of which we stand in need, through Mary, because she obtains whatever she asks, and her prayers cannot be rejected.[2] Before him St. Ephrem said the same: "O most sincere Virgin! only in thee do we repose confidence."[3] St. Ildephonsus teaches the same doctrine: "All the good decreed by the sublime majesty for the benefit of men, this she has decreed to be conveyed to them through the hands of Mary; for to thee, O Mary! has been intrusted treasures and ornaments of grace."[4] The same is held by St. Peter Damian: "In thy hands are all the treasures of divine mercies."[5] St. Bernardine of Sienna says: "Thou art the dispenser of all graces; our salvation rests in thy hands."[6] This, too, was the doctrine of St. John Damascene, of St. Germanus, of St. Anselm, of St. Antonine, of Idiota, and of so many other learned authors, such as Segneri, Pacciuchelli, Crasset, Vega, Mendoza, and Natalis Alexander, who says: "He [God] wishes that we should receive all the good that we wish from him through the mediation of his powerful Mother, by invoking her as we should."[7] Father Contenson has

[1] " Filioli, hæc peccatorum scala, hæc mea maxima fiducia est, hæc tota ratio spei meæ."

[2] "Quæramus gratiam, et per Mariam quæramus; quia, quod quærit, invenit, et frustrari non potest."—*De Aquæd.*

[3] "Nobis non est alia quam a te fiducia, o Virgo sincerissima!"—*De Laud. B. M. V.*

[4] "Omnia bona quæ illic summa Majestas decrevit facere, tuis manibus voluit commendare; commissi quippe sunt tibi thesauri . . . et ornamenta gratiarum."—*De Cor. Virg.* c. 15.

[5] "In manibus tuis sunt thesauri miserationum Domini."—*De Nativ.* s. 1.

[6] "Tu Dispensatrix omnium gratiarum; salus nostra in manu tua est."

[7] "Deus vult ut omnia bona ab ipso exspectemus, potentissima Virginis Matris intercessione, cum eam, ut par est, invocamus, impetranda."—*Ep.* 50 *in calce Theol.*

also held this opinion. Explaining the words of Jesus Christ on the cross to St. John, he says: "Behold thy Mother. As if he said: No one will participate in my blood except through the mediation of my Mother. My wounds are the fountains of all graces, but these fountains flow only through Mary upon you. O my disciple John, as much as you love her, so much shalt thou be loved by me."[1]

And if, on account of the moral necessity of Mary's intercession for all, every Christian ought to be devoted to the Mother of God, how much more should priests, who are bound by greater obligations, and stand in need of greater graces for salvation, practise devotion in her honor! We priests should remain always at the feet of Mary, asking the aid of her prayers. St. Francis Borgia had great doubts about the salvation of those that have not a special devotion to Mary; because, according to St. Antonine, he who expects graces from God without the intercession of Mary attempts to fly without wings.[2] St. Anselm has gone so far as to say: "It is impossible to be saved if we turn away from thee, O Mary."[3] St. Bonaventure has said the same: "He that neglects her will die in his sins."[4] Blessed Albertus Magnus says: 'The people that do not serve thee will perish."[5] And speaking of Mary, Richard of St. Laurence says: "All those whom this ship does not receive are lost in the sea

---

[1] " Ecce Mater tua ! (*John*, xix. 20); quasi diceret: Nullus sanguinis illius particeps erit, nisi intercessione Matris meæ. Vulnera gratiarum fontes sunt; sed ad nullos derivabantur rivi, nisi per Marianum canalem. Joannes discipule, tantum a me amaberis, quantum eam amaveris."— *Theol. ment. et cord.* t. 2, l. 10, d. 4, c. 1.

[2] " Sine alis tentat volare."—P. 4, tit. 15, c. 22.

[3] "Omnis a te aversus necesse est ut intereat."—*Orat.* 51.

[4] "Qui neglexerit illam, morietur in peccatis suis."—*Psalt. B. V. ps.* 116.

[5] " Gens quæ non servierit tibi, peribit."—*Bibl. Mar. Is.* n. 20.

of this world."[1] But, on the other hand, he who is faithful in the service of Mary will be certainly saved. "O Mother of God," says St. John Damascene, "if I put my confidence in you I shall be saved. If I am under your protection I have nothing to fear; for to be devoted to you is to have certain arms of salvation which God gives only to those whose salvation he wills in a special manner."[2]

II.

Confidence that we should have in the Intercession of the Mother of God.

Let us now pass to the confidence which we ought to have in the intercession of Mary, on account of her power and mercy.

I. As to her power. Cosmas of Jerusalem has called the intercession of our Queen not only powerful, but omnipotent.[3] And Richard of St. Laurence has written: "From the omnipotent Son the Mother was made omnipotent."[4] The Son is omnipotent by nature, the Mother by grace, inasmuch as she obtains from God whatsoever she asks. That this grace has been given to Mary we may infer from two reasons: first, because of all creatures Mary has been the most faithful, and the greatest lover of God. Hence, as Suarez says, the Lord loves Mary more than all the other saints and all the angels together. St. Bridget heard our Lord one day saying to his Mother: "Mother, ask what thou desirest

---

[1] "In mare mundi submerguntur omnes illi, quos non suscipit Navis ista."—*De Laud. B. M.* l. 11.
[2] *Crasset, Vér. Dév.* p. 1, tr. 1, q. 6.
[3] "Omnipotens auxilium tuum, o Maria!"—*Hymn.* 6.
[4] "Ab omnipotente Filio omnipotens Mater est effecta."—*De Laud. B. M.* l. 4.

of Me; for thy petition cannot be in vain. . . ." Then he added: "For since on earth thou didst deny Me nothing, I will not deny thee anything in heaven."[1] The second reason is, that Mary is a mother: hence St. Antonine has said, that her prayers partake of the nature of a command, because they are the prayers of a mother.[2] St. John Damascene says: "O Lady, thou hast all power to save sinners; thou needest no other recommendation to God, since thou art his mother."[3] And St. George of Nicomedia has written, that Jesus Christ, in order to discharge the obligations that he owed in a certain manner to Mary for having given him his human nature, grants whatever she asks from him.[4] Hence St. Peter Damian has gone so far as to say, that when Mary goes to Jesus to ask a favor for any of her clients "she approaches the altar of human reconciliation; not asking, but commanding, not as a servant, but as a mistress; for the Son honors her by not refusing her anything."[5]

From the time that Mary was on this earth she had the privilege of having all her prayers heard by her Son. Speaking of Mary's request[6] to Jesus to provide wine when it failed at the marriage of Cana in Galilee, St. John Chrysostom says, that though the Redeemer appeared to refuse the favor, saying: *Woman, what is to*

---

[1] "Mater, pete quod vis a me; non enim inanis potest esse petitio tua. Quia tu mihi nihil negasti in terra, ego tibi nihil negabo in cœlo." —*Rev.* l. 6, c. 23; l. 1, c. 24.

[2] "Oratio Deiparæ habet rationem imperii; unde impossibile est eam non exaudiri."—P. 4, t. 15, c. 17, §. 4.

[3] *In Dorm. B. V.* s. 2.

[4] "Filius, quasi exsolvens debitum, petitiones tuas implet."—*Orat. de Ingr. B. V.*

[5] "Accedis ante illud humanæ reconciliationis Altare, non solum rogans, sed imperans, Domina, non ancilla; nam Filius, nihil negans, honorat te."—*In Nat. B. V.* s. 1.

[6] "Vinum non habent."—*John,* ii. 3.

Me and to thee ? My hour has not yet come,[1] still he granted the petition of his mother.[2]

The prayers of Mary, says St. Germanus, obtain great graces for the most abandoned sinners, because they are prayers accompanied with the authority of a mother.[3] In a word, there is no one, however wicked, whom Mary does not save by her intercession when she wishes. Hence St. George, Archbishop of Nicomedia, says, O great Mother of God: "Thou hast insuperable strength, since the multitude of our sins does not outweigh thy clemency. Nothing resists thy power, for the Creator regards thy honor as his own."[4] To thee, then, O my Queen, says St. Peter Damian, nothing is impossible, since thou canst succor and save even those that are in despair.[5]

II. But if Mary is powerful, and able to save us by her intercession, she is equally merciful, and willing to obtain our salvation: "Neither the power nor the will is wanting to her,"[6] says St. Bernard. She is called the Mother of Mercy, because her compassion for us makes her love and assist us as a mother assists a sick child. The love of all mothers together, according to Father Nieremberg,[7] is not equal to the love which Mary bears

---

[1] "Quid mihi et tibi est, mulier? nondum venit hora mea."

[2] "Et licet ita responderit, maternis tamen precibus obtemperavit." —*In Jo. hom.* 21.

[3] "Tu autem, materna in Deum auctoritate pollens, etiam iis, qui enormiter peccant, gratiam concilias; non enim potes non exaudiri, cum Deus tibi, ut veræ et intemeratæ Matri, in omnibus morem gerat."—*In Dorm. Deip.* s. 2.

[4] "Habes vires insuperabiles, ne clementiam tuam superet multitudo peccatorum. Nihil tuæ resistit potentiæ; tuam enim gloriam Creator existimat esse propriam."—*Or. de Ingr. B. V.*

[5] "Nihil tibi impossibile, cui possibile est desperatos in spem beatitudinis relevare."—*De Nat. B. V.* s. 1.

[6] "Nec facultas ei deesse poterit, nec voluntas."—*In Assumpt.* s. 1.

[7] *De Aff. erga B. V.* c. 14.

a client that recommends himself to her. Hence she is compared to a fair olive tree: *As a fair olive tree in the plains.*[1] " In the plains," says Cardinal Hugo, " that all may look upon her, that all may have recourse to her."[2] As the olive gives oil, the symbol of mercy, to him who possesses it, so Mary pours her mercies on all who have recourse to her.

Blessed Amedeus has written, that our Queen is continually praying for us in heaven.[3] And before him Venerable Bede said: " Mary stands before her Son and does not cease to pray for sinners."[4] St. Bernard asks, What else but mercy can flow from the fountain of mercy?[5] St. Bridget once heard our Saviour saying to Mary: "Mother, ask what you wish of me."[6] Mary answered: "I ask mercy for the miserable."[7] As if she said: Son, since you have made me the Mother of Mercy, what will I ask of you? Nothing else than mercy for miserable sinners. The great charity, says St. Bernard, that reigns in the heart of Mary for all, obliges her to open to all the bosom of mercy.[8]

St. Bonaventure says that, looking at Mary, he appeared no longer to behold the divine justice that terrified him, but only the divine mercy that God has placed

---

[1] " Quasi oliva speciosa in campis."—*Ecclus.* xxiv. 19.

[2] " ' In campis,' ut omnes eam respiciant, omnes ad eam confugiant."

[3] "Adstat Beatissima Virgo vultui Conditoris, prece potentissima semper interpellans pro nobis."

[4] "Stat Maria in conspectu Filii sui, non cessans pro peccatoribus exorare."

[5] " Quid de fonte pietatis procederet, nisi pietas?"—*Dom.* 1 *p. Epiph.* s. 1

[6] " Mater, pete quod vis a me."—*Rev.* l. 6, c. 23.

[7] " Misericordiam peto miseris."—*Ib.* l. 1, c. 50.

[8] " Sapientibus et insipientibus copiosissima charitate debitricem se fecit; omnibus misericordiæ sinum aperit, ut de plenitudine ejus accipiant universi."—*In Sign. magn.*

in the hands of Mary, that she may assist the miserable.[1] And St. Leo has said that Mary is so full of mercy that she is called mercy itself.[2] And who after Jesus, exclaims St. Germanus, is so solicitous for our welfare as thou, O Mother of Mercy?[3] Speaking of Mary, St. Augustine says: "We acknowledge that one, namely, that thou alone, takest care of us in heaven."[4] As if he said: O Mother of God, it is true that all the saints love our salvation, but thy charity, in assisting us from heaven, with so much love, and heaping on us so many graces, which thou continually obtainest for us, compels us to confess, that it is thou alone who truly loves us, and anxiously seeks our welfare. St. Germanus adds: "Her defence of us is never satisfied."[5] Mary prays incessantly for us; she repeats her prayers, and is never tired praying in our defence.

Bernardine De Bustis says that Mary is more desirous of dispensing graces to us than we are of receiving them.[6] The same author says that as the devil, according to St. Peter, goes about seeking whom he may devour,[7] so Mary goes about seeking whom she may save.[8]

[1] "Certe, Domina ! cum te aspicio, nihil nisi misericordiam cerno; nam pro miseris Mater Dei facta es, et tibi miserendi est officium commissum."—*Stim. div. am.* p. 3, c. 19.

[2] "Maria adeo prædita est misericordiæ visceribus, ut, non tantum misericors, sed ipsa Misericordia dici promereatur."

[3] "Quis, post Filium tuum, curam gerit generis humani, sicut tu? Quis ita nos defendit in nostris afflictionibus? Quis pugnat pro peccatoribus? Propterea, patrocinium tuum majus est, quam comprehendi possit."—*De Zona Deip.*

[4] "Te solam, o Maria ! pro Sancta Ecclesia sollicitam præ omnibus Sanctis scimus."—*S. Bonav. Spec. B. V. lect.* 6.

[5] "Non est satietas defensionis ejus."—*De Zona Deip.*

[6] "Plus desiderat ipsa facere tibi bonum et largiri gratiam, quam tu accipere concupiscas."

[7] "Circuit quærens quem devoret."—1 *Pet.* v. 8.

[8] "Ipsa semper circuit quærens quem salvet."—*Marial* p. 2, s 5; p. 3, s. 1.

Who, I ask, receives grace from Mary?—he who wishes for them. A holy soul used to say, to obtain graces through Mary it is enough to ask them. And St. Ildephonsus has written, that we ought to ask nothing of Mary but to pray for us; for by her prayers she will obtain for us greater graces than we could ask.[1] How, then, does it happen that there are many who do not receive graces through the prayers of Mary? Because they do not wish for them. He who is attached to any passion, to self-interest, to ambition, to an inordinate affection, does not wish for grace to be delivered from it, and therefore he does not ask it: had he asked it of Mary, she would certainly have obtained it for him. But miserable and unhappy the man, said the Holy Virgin to St. Bridget, who, having it in his power to have recourse to me in this life, shall, through his own fault remain miserably in his sins and in the state of perdition.[2] A time shall come when he would wish, but will not be able, to have recourse to her.

Ah! let us not expose ourselves to this great danger. Let us always have recourse to this divine Mother, who knows not how to let any one who invokes her aid depart without consolation, says Blosius.[3] Mary is always ready, as Richard of St. Laurence says, to assist those who ask her prayers.[4] According to Richard of St. Victor, Mary's tenderness prevents our supplications, and procures aid for us before we pray to her. Because, adds the same author, Mary is so full of mercy that she

---

[1] "Majori devotione orabis pro me, quam ego auderem petere: et majora etiam impetrabis mihi, quam petere præsumam."—*De Rhet. div.* c. 18.

[2] "Ideo miser erit, qui ad misericordiam, cum possit, non accedit!"—*Rev.* l. 2, c. 23.

[3] "Adeo feci eam mitem, ut neminem a se redire tristem sinat."—*Alloq.* l. 1, p. 4, can. 12.

[4] "Semper paratam auxiliari."—*De Laud. B. M.* l. 2, p. 1.

cannot see our miseries without coming to our relief.[1]

And who, exclaims Innocent III., has ever had recourse to Mary without being heard?[2] Who, says Blessed Eutichianus, has ever sought her aid and has been abandoned by her?[3] St. Bernard has written: "O holy Virgin, if a man has been ever found who, after invoking your aid, remembers not to have obtained relief, I am satisfied that he should cease to praise your mercy."[4] No: such a case has never occurred, and never shall occur; for, says St. Bonaventure, Mary cannot but pity and relieve the miserable.[5] Hence the saint has said, that this Mother of mercy, who so ardently desires to assist us and to see us saved, is offended not only by those who do her a positive injury, but also by those who neglect to ask favors from her.[6]

Let us then have recourse to Mary; and in seeing that our sins render us unworthy to be heard, let us not distrust her clemency. Our Lord revealed to St. Bridget that Mary would have saved Lucifer by her intercession had that haughty demon humbled himself and had recourse to her.[7] And the Virgin herself said to the same

---

[1] "A Deo pietate replentur ubera tua, ut, alicujus miseriæ notitia tacta, lac fundant misericordiæ, nec possis miserias scire et non subvenire."—*In Cant.* c. 23.

[2] "Quis invocavit eam, et non est exauditus ab ipsa?"—*De Assumpt.* s. 2.

[3] "Quis, o Domina! fideliter omnipotentem tuam rogavit opem, et fuit derelictus? revera nullus unquam."—*Surius*, 4 *Febr. Vit. S. Theoph.*

[4] "Sileat misericordiam tuam, Virgo Beata, qui invocatam te in necessitatibus suis sibi meminerit defuisse."—*De Assumpt.* s. 4.

[5] "Ipsa enim non misereri ignorat, et miseris non satisfacere nunquam scivit."—*Stim. am.* p. 3, c. 13.

[6] "In te, Domina, peccant, non solum qui tibi injuriam irrogant, sed etiam qui te non rogant."

[7] "Etiam diabolo exhiberes misericordiam, si humiliter peteret."—*Rev. extr.* c. 50.

St. Bridget, that when a sinner casts himself at her feet she regards not his sins, but the intention with which he comes. If he comes with a determination to change his life, she heals and saves him.[1] Hence St. Bonaventure called Mary the salvation of them who invoke her.[2] He that has recourse to Mary shall be saved.

III.
Practice of Devotion to the Blessed Virgin.

I repeat, then, let us always have recourse to this great Mother of God, imploring her to protect us. But the better to gain her protection, let us endeavor to perform in her honor as many pious exercises as we can. That ardently devoted servant of Mary, Brother John Berchmans, of the Society of Jesus, being asked at death by his companions what they should do in order to obtain the favor of Mary, said: "However little it may be, provided it be done with perseverance."[3] Every little act of devotion is sufficient to secure the patronage of this divine Mother. She is content with any little exercise, provided it be constant; for, as St. Andrew of Crete says, she is so liberal that she is accustomed to reward the smallest homage by obtaining abundant graces.[4] But we should not be content with small things: let us at least offer her all the acts of devotion which her clients ordinarily perform in her honor; such as, to recite the Rosary every day, to perform the Novenas of

[1] "Quantumcumque homo peccet, si ex vera emendatione ad me reversus fuerit, statim parata sum recipere revertentem; nec attendo quantum peccaverit, sed cum quali voluntate venit; nam non dedignor ejus plagas ungere et sanare, quia vocor (et vere sum) Mater misericordiæ."—*Rev.* 1. 2, c. 23; 1. 6, c. 17.

[2] "O Salus te invocantium!"—*Cant. p. Psalt.*

[3] "Quidquid minimum, dummodo sit constans."

[4] "Cum sit magnificentissima, solet maxima pro minimis reddere."— *In Dorm. B. V.* s. 3.

her festivals, to fast on Saturday, to wear the Scapular, to visit some image every day in her honor, asking her to obtain some special grace, to read each day a book that treats of her praises, to salute her in leaving and returning home; rising in the morning and going to bed at night, to put ourselves under her protection, by saying three "Hail Marys" in honor of her purity.

Even seculars practise these devotions; but we priests can honor her much more by preaching her glories, and by inculcating to others the advantages of being devoted to her: *They that explain Me shall have life everlasting.*[1] She promises eternal life to him who endeavors in this life to make others know and love her. Blessed Edminco, Bishop, began every sermon by the praises of Mary. This was so pleasing to the divine Mother, that she one day said to St. Bridget: "Tell that prelate that I will be a mother to him, and that at death I will present his soul to my Son."[2] Oh, what pleasure would a priest give to Mary, if every Saturday he made a short discourse to the people on devotion to her, and especially on her tender compassion for us, and her desire to assist all who pray to her! For, as St. Bernard says, it is the mercy of Mary that inspires in the people the greatest affection for her devotion. Let preachers at least endeavor in every sermon, before the conclusion, to exhort the hearers to have recourse to most holy Mary, and to ask some favor from her.

In a word, Richard of St. Laurence says that he who honors Mary acquires treasures of eternal life.[3] For this purpose I published some years since a book entitled the *Glories of Mary*, and I endeavored to enrich it

---

[1] "Qui elucidant me, vitam æternam habebunt."—*Ecclus*. xxiv. 31.
[2] *Rev. extr.* c. 104.
[3] "Honorare Mariam, thesaurizare est sibi vitam æternam."—*De Laud. B. M.* l. 2, p. 1.

with authorities from Scriptures and the holy Fathers, with examples and devout practices, not only that it might be useful to all as a book for spiritual reading, but particularly that it might supply priests with abundant matter for preaching the praises of Mary, and inspiring the people with devotion to her.

APPENDIX.

St. Alphonsus himself has added, as an appendix to his Collection of Materials for Ecclesiastical Retreats, the three following little works: RULE OF LIFE, SPIRITUAL RULES, and SPIRITUAL MAXIMS. To them we have added an EXHORTATION TO YOUNG MEN WHO ARE DEVOTING THEMSELVES TO THE STUDY OF THE ECCLESIASTICAL SCIENCES.—EDITOR.

Rule of Life for a Secular Priest.

I.

Morning Exercises.

1. THE FIRST ACTS ON RISING.

IN the morning on rising the priest shall make acts of thanksgiving, of love, and of oblation of all that he is to do and to suffer during the day. He shall finish by a prayer to God and to the Blessed Virgin, in order to obtain the grace of not falling into sin.

These acts may be thus formulated:[1]

O my God! prostrate in Thy presence, I adore Thy infinite Majesty, and I submit myself entirely to Thee.

I believe in Thee, I hope in Thee, and I love Thee with my whole heart.

I thank Thee for all Thy benefits, and especially for having preserved me during this night.

I offer Thee all my thoughts, words, actions, and sufferings of this day in union with those of Jesus and of Mary.

I intend to gain all the indulgences that I can gain, and to apply them to the souls in purgatory.

O my God! for the love of Jesus Christ, deliver me from every sin. O my Jesus! by Thy merits make me live united to Thee. Mary, my Mother, bless me, and protect me under thy mantle. My holy guardian angel, and all my holy patrons, intercede for me. Amen.

Here recite the "Hail Mary" three times in honor of the purity of the Blessed Virgin Mary.

---

[1] We have thought it useful to add here the formula which the saint gives elsewhere in several places.—ED.

2. MENTAL PRAYER.

The priest shall begin the day by a half-hour's meditation on the eternal truths, or on the Passion of Jesus Christ. Meditation on the Passion of our Lord is more especially suitable to a priest before celebrating Mass, since he is about to renew at the altar the memory of it by offering to God the same victim and the same sacrifice. During meditation, after having read the subject, he should endeavor to make acts of sorrow and of love, and frequently offer to God prayers in order to obtain perseverance in his grace and his divine love. Let him guard against abandoning meditation, however great the disgust and the pain he may experience during it; if he abandons the practice of meditation, he will be exposed to the greatest danger of losing God. Even when he is able to say only these words: O my God, help me! O my Jesus, mercy!—his meditation will be excellent, and will profit him much.

In order to be more recollected in meditation, let him shut himself up in some place where he may find himself alone with the crucifix. For this purpose he shall endeavor to have a separate room; and if he cannot have it, let him go to the church to make his meditation there rather than make it at home amid the noise made by persons who pass in and out, and who talk.[1]

3. THE HOLY MASS.

After meditation, he shall recite the Little Hours as far as None; then he shall celebrate Mass. In order to say Mass with greater recollection, it would be expedi-

---

[1] To understand this passage and others of a like nature, we must know that many secular priests in Italy remained with their families, having no special employment; this was the case with St. Alphonsus himself at the beginning of his priestly life.—ED.

ent, if there be no obstacle, to say Mass before all other occupations of the day.

Besides the meditation one should not fail to make a short preparation for Mass by reanimating one's faith in the great mystery that one is about to celebrate; one should make at least three acts: of love, of contrition, and of desire to be united to Jesus Christ.

After Mass one should not omit to make thanksgiving, of an hour or at least of half an hour, by applying one's self during that time to the making of acts of love, of the offering of one's self, and of petition. The time that follows Mass is a time for amassing treasures of grace. When one is in a state of interior dryness, not knowing what to do with one's self, one may at least read out of some book pious affections to Jesus Christ.

4. CONFESSIONS AND STUDY.

After having made his thanksgiving,[1] the priest shall go to the confessional if he is a confessor. It must here be observed that on days on which there is a great concourse of people, as on festivals, he may shorten his thanksgiving in order to hear confessions; but this only holds good for similar cases that are rare. Usually the confessor should not omit his thanksgiving after Mass in order that penitents may not be obliged to wait for him. However, when there come to confession men that are not accustomed to frequent the sacraments, it will be better if he hears them before Mass; because such persons have not the patience to wait; and if they do not confess on that day, God knows when they will confess.

As for the priest who is not a confessor, he shall retire in order to attend to his studies. He should occupy

[1] We may remark that nothing is said about breakfast, because in Italy, generally, no meal is taken as in the countries of the north, but dinner is taken earlier.—ED.

himself in the study of Moral Theology, so as to become capable of administering the sacrament of penance, in the composition of sermons, or in similar things that may serve for his own instruction or for the good of souls.

5. REMARK IN REGARD TO THE ORDER OF THE EXERCISES.

It must here be observed that we do not ask that al the exercises of which this Rule speaks should be performed in the order in which they are here mentioned. Provided that they are performed in the course of the day, it is sufficient; it matters little whether one takes place before the other according to one's convenience. Thus, for example, in winter, when the days are longer, one may, after meditation and the Office, study for an hour or two. For the rest, a priest that wishes to lead a life worthy of his state should fix the time and the hour of all his exercises so that everything may be done in a regular order. Let him not act as some who follow no order in all that they do. The life that is without a rule is an image of hell, which is described by Job: *A land of misery and darkness, where the shadow of death, and no order, but everlasting horror dwelleth.*[1]

6. DINNER.

The hour of dinner having come, he shall eat moderately, as is becoming a priest: he should not imitate certain gluttonous priests who wish that the whole house should busy itself about preparing different kinds of food which they ordered in the morning, and when at dinner they do not find the food to be according to their taste, they grow angry, and excite a commotion among their servants and relatives. St. Philip Neri says: "He that seeks to gratify his palate will never become a saint."

[1] "Terram miseriæ et tenebrarum, ubi umbra mortis, et nullus ordo, sed sempiternus horror inhabitat."—*Job*, x. 22.

Rule of Life. 431

And if the priest should be temperate in eating, he should be particularly so in the use of wine, the excess of which is most pernicious to virtue, especially to the virtue of chastity.

On Saturdays, let him endeavor, in honor of the Blessed Virgin, to keep at least the common fast, if he thinks that he cannot fast on bread and water; let him, however, be content on that day with one course. Moreover, on some other days of the week, as on Wednesday and Friday, as also in all the Novenas of our Lady, let him at least deprive himself of something at table.

II.
Exercises after Dinner.
1. SPIRITUAL READING.

After the needed rest, the priest shall recite Vespers and Compline, and shall afterwards make a half-hour's spiritual reading. For the spiritual reading he may use the *Knowledge and Love of Jesus Christ* by Father St. Jure, or *Christian Perfection* by Father Rodriguez,— books that are filled with piety and unction. He may also read other works;[1] but let him, above all, read the lives of the saints, as the life of St. Philip Neri, of St. Francis Borgia, of St. Peter of Alcantara, and the like. In the books that treat of spirituality we see virtues in theory, while in the lives of the saints we see them in practice; and this will stimulate us more efficaciously to imitate the saints. St. Philip Neri never ceased to exhort his penitents to read the lives of the saints. How many saints, such as St. John Colombini, St. Ignatius Loyola, St. Teresa, have been induced by the

[1] It may perhaps be needless to recall here to mind the ascetical works written by St. Alphonsus himself. Many well-instructed priests avow that they seek no other books of piety, because they find all that they desire in those of the holy bishop, who seems to have provided for all the wants of the soul.—ED.

reading of such books to consecrate themselves entirely to God!

2. THE VISIT TO THE BLESSED SACRAMENT AND TO THE BLESSED VIRGIN.

After the spiritual reading he shall pay a visit to the Blessed Sacrament. Many of the faithful are very exact in performing this exercise every day, and never omit doing so, no matter how they may be inconvenienced thereby; but it is rare, and even very rare, to find secular priests who do so. It must be confessed that Jesus Christ is unfortunate in his priests! All this comes from the little love that priests have for him. He that tenderly loves a friend, seeks to see him as often as he can, especially when his visits are most agreeable to this friend.

By this visit I do not mean only a few " Our Fathers" said in passing and with distraction before the altar. It consists in occupying one's self during some time in making pious affections to Jesus Christ in the Blessed Sacrament, and in asking of him graces, especially the grace of final perseverance and of his holy love. Alas! who should entertain himself oftener and longer than a priest who every day makes Jesus come down from heaven to the earth, takes him in his hands, partakes of his adorable flesh, and moreover for his own benefit shuts him up in the tabernacle where he may find him present every time that he wishes?

After the visit to the Blessed Sacrament he should not omit to make, in the same church, his visit to the Mother of God, before some image that inspires him with the greatest devotion.[1]

[1] We all know the *Visits to the Blessed Sacrament and to the Blessed Virgin* which are found in Volume VI. This precious little work is also published separately.—ED.

3. RECREATION.

He may then recreate himself for some time by walking either in the country or on some solitary road, in company with a Father or some other spiritual person who speaks of God and not of the world. In the absence of such a person he should walk alone; for if he is accompanied by some secular he will soon lose all the recollection that he has found in his exercises of piety. If in his moments of leisure he visits the place where the moral conference is held, he will do better; he will find there recreation, and what will be profitable to him.

III.
Exercises of the Evening.
1. BEFORE SUPPER.

Towards evening it is befitting that the priest should make another half-hour's meditation; it will be better if he makes it when possible with all the persons of the house, reading the points of meditation himself, and finishing by reciting the Christian acts.

Then he should recite Matins and Lauds, and afterwards devote himself to another hour's study.

Afterwards he shall recite five decades of the Rosary, also with the people of the house, taking care to announce the mysteries on which the meditation should be made; he shall finish by saying the Litany of the Blessed Virgin

2. SUPPER.

The Rosary shall be followed by supper. He should observe greater sobriety at supper than at dinner; for if in the evening one takes too much food, it will happen that in the morning, when so many important duties are to be fulfilled,—meditation, the saying of Mass, the hearing of confessions,—one will suffer not only in the stomach, but also in the head, so that everything will be done with distraction and tepidity, and the half of it will be lost.

3. THE LAST ACTS BEFORE GOING TO BED.

After supper the priest shall make the examination of conscience, to be followed by the act of contrition and by other pious acts; then after having recited, with the face on the floor, the "Hail Mary" three times, and after the usual practices in honor of the holy patrons, he should go to bed.

The following is the act that we may recite before going to bed:[1]

O my God! I thank Thee for having preserved me this day, and I beseech Thee to vouchsafe to preserve me also this night, and to protect me from all evil. I take this repose in order to please Thee, and I intend each moment that I breathe to love and praise Thee, as is done by the saints and the elect in heaven.

Mary, my Mother, bless me, and protect me under thy mantle. My angel guardian, and all my holy Patrons, intercede for me.

IV.
Exercises that are not Performed Every Day.

1. CONFESSION.

The priest should confess twice or at least once a week. He should not fail to have a particular Director, on whom it will be his duty to depend in all his spiritual exercises, and even in all the temporal affairs that may be of profit to his soul.

2. THE MONTHLY RETREAT.

Every month he shall make a day of retreat; on this day he should keep aloof from all temporal affairs, and

[1] We add this simple formula as we have done above for the morning exercise.—ED.

Rule of Life. 435

even from spiritual occupations that regard his neighbor. Having retired to his own home or to some religious house, he shall occupy himself in silence only with himself, consecrating the whole day to prayer, to spiritual reading, to visiting the Blessed Sacrament, and to other similar exercises. Oh what strength does not the soul draw from these retreats, to be able to unite itself intimately with God, and to walk more fervently in the ways of the Lord on the following days![1]

3. SPECIAL COUNSELS.

In temptations, especially in those against purity, he shall renew the resolution to suffer rather a thousand deaths than to offend God; then he shall have recourse at once to Jesus and to Mary by invoking their holy names until the violence of the temptation has subsided.

He should be careful to dress modestly, always wearing long clothes, and never those that are of silk.

Let him keep from all banquets, the amusements of the world, the reunions with seculars, especially where there are women.

[1] There is no question here of the annual retreat.—ED.

Spiritual Rules for a Priest who Aspires to Perfection.

· I. TO AVOID SIN, AND TROUBLE AFTER SIN.

A PRIEST who aspires to perfection and desires to sanctify himself should, above all, endeavor to avoid more than death the least deliberate venial sin. In the present state of human frailty, since Adam's sin, no one can, and no one ever could, with the exception only of Jesus Christ and his most Blessed Mother, be exempt from all indeliberate venial faults. With the help of God, however, every one can avoid every deliberate fault; that is to say, committed with full advertence and consent; thus the saints have acted. He, therefore, who tends to perfection should make up his mind rather to allow himself to be cut to pieces than to tell, with full knowledge, a lie, or to commit any other venial sin, however small it may be.

Such should be his resolution; but if unfortunately he happens to fall into a fault, either deliberate or indeliberate, let him beware of troubling and disquieting himself. Disquietude does not come from God; it is a smoke that comes only from the abode of disquietude itself, namely, from hell; and it comes to us from that place because, as St. Aloysius has justly said, the devil always finds something to fish in troubled waters. When one has, for example, committed a fault one is troubled, and one is troubled because one has been troubled. In this state of disquietude we shall not only be unable to do any good, but we shall also easily commit many other faults, either of impatience or of some other kind. Hence, as soon as the fault has been com-

Spiritual Rules. 437

mitted, we must humble ourselves and immediately have recourse to God by making an act of love or of contrition with the firm purpose of amendment; then we ask with confidence for the grace of which we stand in need by saying: O Lord! see what I am able to do; and if Thou withdrawest Thy hand from me I shall do still worse. I love Thee; I repent of the displeasure that I have caused Thee, and I will do so no more; grant me the help that I hope to receive from Thy goodness.

After having done this we should be calm, as if we had not committed any fault; and if we fall back, even on the same day, let us do the same thing. Should we even fall a hundred times, we should always act in the same way, namely, we should humble ourselves, we should rise again, we must never remain down.

It must be observed that to trouble one's self after a fault has been committed is an effect not of humility, but of pride; since we are sorry for the fault not because we have offended God, but rather because we are ashamed to appear before him so defiled. The priest should, therefore, never trouble himself on account of the faults into which he falls; but let him humble himself, acknowledging himself capable of committing these and other faults. Let him then make an act of love of God; thus this sin, instead of removing him from God, will serve only the more to unite him more closely to him, according to what the Apostle says: *All things—* "even sins,"[1] the Gloss adds—*work together unto good.*[2]

2. EFFICACIOUS DESIRE TO ADVANCE IN THE LOVE OF GOD.

. Let him desire to advance without ceasing in the love of God. Not to wish to advance in perfection, which consists in the love of God, is to wish to go backward, says St. Augustine.[3] He that moves against the

[1] "Etiam peccata."
[2] "Omnia cooperantur in bonum."—*Rom.* viii. 23.
[3] "Non progredi, jam reverti est."—*Epist.* 17, *E. B. app.*

current of a river, and does not make continual efforts against the movement of the waters, will be driven back. The same thing happens to us when we cease to struggle with the concupiscence of the flesh.

Holy desires render our efforts easier, and help us to move forward; but it is necessary that these desires be firm and efficacious—that is to say, that they be put in practice as much as possible. They should not resemble the desires of those that are content with saying, for example: Oh! if I had no brothers, no nephews, I would enter religion; if I had health, I would do this or that penance; and in the mean time these persons do not take a step forward in the way of God: on the contrary, they always commit the same faults, always keeping up the same attachments and the same animosities, and go from bad to worse.

It is therefore necessary that we advance in divine love, but with the resolution to do on our part all that we can to attain this end. We must, however, entirely mistrust our own strength, and trust only in God; for as soon as we trust in ourselves we remain deprived of the help of grace.

3. DEVOTION TO THE PASSION OF OUR LORD AND TO THE BLESSED SACRAMENT.

To advance in perfection the priest must, moreover, entertain a great devotion to the Passion of Jesus Christ and to the Blessed Sacrament. When we consider these two great mysteries of love, in which a God, to make himself loved, gives his life and makes himself the food of a worm of the earth, his creature, we cannot live without being inflamed with love for Jesus Christ. *For the charity of Christ presseth us.*[1] He that thinks of the love of Jesus Christ will feel himself, as it were, forced to love him. St. Bonaventure call the wounds

---

[1] " Charitas enim Christi urget nos."—2 *Cor*. v. 14.

Spiritual Rules. 439

of Jesus the wounds that wound the most hardened hearts, and that inflame with love for God the coldest souls.[1]

Let the priest, then, always make as a usual thing, every day, a half-hour's meditation on the Passion of Jesus Christ. Let him, besides, make during the day frequent acts of love to this good Master, beginning them on awakening in the morning, and endeavoring at night to fall asleep while making them. St. Teresa said that acts of love are the wood that keeps up in the heart the sweet fire of divine love. The act of love of God that is more especially agreeable to God is the offering that we make to him of ourselves by offering to do and to suffer all that will please him. St. Teresa repeated this act at least fifty times a day.

4. THE INTENTION OF DOING ALL FOR GOD.

The priest should in all his actions take care to make his intention to do for God alone all that he does. The right intention is called by the masters of spiritual life a heavenly alchemy, which converts into gold all our actions, even corporal alleviations, such as sleep, eating, and recreation. But it is particularly necessary that the exercises of piety should be performed only to please God, and not for any interested motive, either of vainglory or self-satisfaction; otherwise all will be lost, and instead of a reward we shall receive only punishment. This is the reason why, in order to do surely for God all that we do, it is important that we always act in dependence on our director.

5. LOVE OF SOLITUDE AND OF SILENCE.

It is necessary that the priest should be a friend of solitude and of silence. He that treats too much with

[1] "Vulnera corda saxea vulnerantia, et mentes congelatas inflammantia."—*Stim. div. am.* p. 1, c. 1.

men, and speaks too much with them. will do well to be cautious; he will with difficulty escape sin: *In the multitude of words there shall not want sin.*[1] For this reason the Lord says: *In silence and in hope shall your strength be.*[2] Our strength against temptations is in confidence in God and in detachment from the society of creatures. Moreover, he that speaks much with men will rarely speak and treat with God. In solitude the Lord speaks and converses familiarly with souls, in accordance with the saying of St Jerome: "O solitude, in which God familiarly converses with his creatures!"[3] And he himself has informed us that it is in solitude that he speaks to our hearts: *I will lead her into the wilderness; and I will speak to her heart.*[4] Thus we see souls that burn with the love of God always seeking solitude. The saints went to bury themselves in the forests and in the most frightful caverns, in order not to be troubled by the noise of the world and in order to converse only with God. "Silence and rest from noise," said St. Bernard, "as it were, forces the soul to converse with God."[5]

Nevertheless the virtue of silence does not consist in always keeping silence, but in being silent when it is expedient. A good priest is silent when he should be silent, and speaks when he should speak; but he speaks only of God or of what concerns the glory of God and the good of souls. Often a word about God spoken familiarly in conversation will produce more fruit than many sermons. We should therefore be careful in all our conversations, however indifferent they may be, to allow some edifying word to glide into it on the eternal truths

[1] "In multiloquio non deerit peccatum."—*Prov.* x. 19.
[2] "In silentio et in spe erit fortitudo vestra."—*Is.* xxx. 15.
[3] "O solitudo, in qua Deus cum suis familiariter loquitur ac conversatur!"
[4] "Ducam eam in solitudinem, et loquar ad cor ejus."—*Os.* ii. 14.
[5] "Silentium, et a strepitu quies cogit cœlestia meditari."—*Epist.* 78.

or on the love of God. When we love a person, we always wish to speak of him and to hear others speak of him; when we love God, we do not wish to speak of any one but of God, and we do not wish to hear any one spoken of except God.

6. CONFORMITY TO THE WILL OF GOD.

The love of God consists above all in conformity to his holy will, especially in regard to things that are mostly contrary to self-love, such as sickness, poverty, contempt, persecutions, spiritual aridities. We should be persuaded that all that comes from God is useful to us, since all that he does, he does for our own good; for there is no one that loves us more than God. If we wish to sanctify ourselves, let us say in all that happens to us: May Thy will be done! May the name of the Lord be blessed. O Lord! what wilt Thou have me do? As it pleases the Lord, so let it be done. Let it be thus, O Father! because it was thus pleasing to Thee.

In all the occurrences of life, whether agreeable or disagreeable, let us endeavor to preserve this continual peace and this unalterable tranquillity, of which the saints have given us the example, always saying: *In peace in the self-same I will sleep and I will rest.*[1] A soul that loves God, always united with its Lord, leads a uniform life. This is what is said by that great servant of God, Cardinal Petrucci, when speaking of the words of the Holy Ghost: *Whatsoever shall befall the just, it shall not make him sad.*[2]

Thus a priest that loves God will never be afflicted. Sin only should cause him sorrow; but even this sorrow, as we have said above, should be a tranquil sorrow, that does not trouble the peace of the soul.

[1] " In pace in idipsum dormiam et requiescam."—*Ps.* iv. 9.
[2] " Non contristabit justum quidquid ei acciderit."—*Prov.* xii. 21.

7. DESIRE FOR DEATH.

The priest should often desire paradise, and consequently death itself, in order promptly to go to heaven, where he may love Jesus Christ with all his strength and during all eternity, without fear of ever losing him. In the mean time he should conduct himself towards God without reserve, not refusing him anything that he knows will be more agreeable to him; and he should be continually attentive to banish from his heart all that is not God or for God.

8. DEVOTION TO THE BLESSED VIRGIN.

He should endeavor to conceive a great confidence and a tender devotion to the Blessed Virgin. All the saints are always fond of nourishing in their hearts a filial piety towards this divine Mother. He should take care to make every day a spiritual reading out of a book that treats of the great confidence that we should have in her powerful protection. He should never fail as well as he is able to fast on Saturdays in her honor; and in all her novenas he should at least practise some abstinence and some other mortification. He should never omit to pay her a visit once or several times a day before some devout image. He should speak to others as much as he can of the confidence that we should have in the protection of Mary, and should endeavor on Saturdays to address in the church a little instruction to the faithful, so as to excite their devotion towards this charitable Queen; at least he should speak of her in a special manner in every one of his sermons, and recommend the same devotion to all his penitents and to all persons. The more one loves Mary, the more one loves God; for Mary draws to God all that love her. St. Bonaventure says: "Because she was inflamed with love, she also inflames all those that love her, and makes them like herself."[1]

9. TO BE HUMBLE OF HEART.

Let the priest endeavor to be humble of heart. Many are humble in their speech, but not in their hearts; they say that they are the greatest sinners in the world, that they merit a thousand hells: nevertheless they wish to be preferred, esteemed, and praised; they strive after honorable employments; they cannot suffer a contemptuous word. The humble of heart do not act in this manner: they never speak of their talents, of their nobility, of their riches, or of anything that may be turned to their advantage.

He should, therefore, love those employments and those works that are most humble and are less conspicuous. He should receive affronts without being troubled; he should even feel interior pleasure in seeing that he has become similar to Jesus Christ, who was filled with reproaches. Therefore, when he meets with some contradiction that wounds and irritates his pride he should do violence to himself not to speak nor act at that moment, even if he held the office of Superior, and as such is obliged to reprimand the insolence of him that offers the outrage. As long as he feels himself agitated he should keep silence and wait till he becomes calm, otherwise the smoke produced by his trouble will obscure his vision; he will believe that what he says or what he does is right, while all is faulty and disorderly. Moreover, when the correction is made amid agitation, the inferior will not receive it as a deserved reprimand, but as a passionate outbreak of temper on the part of the Superior; and this will make the correction useless, or nearly so. For the same

[1] "Quia tota ardens fuit, omnes se amantes, eamque tangentes, incendit."—*De B. V. M.* s. 1.

reason, when the Superior perceives that the inferior is troubled, he should put off the reprimand and wait till he has become calm; otherwise the inferior, blinded by his passion, will not only not receive the correction, but will even be moved to greater passion.

10. TO RENDER GOOD FOR EVIL.

The priest should try to be ready to assist every one, and especially to do good to him that has done him wrong, at least by recommending him to God. This is the way in which the saints take revenge.

11. INTERIOR AND EXTERIOR MORTIFICATION.

Let the priest be attentive to the practice of interior and exterior mortification. It was recommended by Jesus Christ when he said: *Let him deny himself*.[1] This is absolutely necessary in order to attain sanctity.

Interior mortification exacts of us that we know how to conquer ourselves by refusing all that satisfies only our self-love. We should therefore abstain from every action that has no other object than to satisfy curiosity, ambition, or self-love.

We should also love exterior mortification, namely, fasting, abstinence, disciplines, and the like. The saints macerated their flesh as much as possible, that is to say, as much as obedience permitted, and obedience is the rule of the saints. As to him who, on account of ill-health, cannot impose upon himself exterior mortifications, he should embrace the pains and the inconveniences that he has to suffer by endeavoring to support them patiently and peacefully, and by refraining from making them known without necessity, and from complaining about the want of care on the part of the physicians or persons of the house.

[1] "Abneget semetipsum."—*Matt.* xvi. 24.

12. To Pray without Ceasing.

We must always pray and recommend ourselves to God. All our good resolutions and all our promises end in smoke when we neglect to pray; for by not praying we are deprived of the necessary graces to carry them out. *I will cry like a young swallow.*[1] We should always have the mouth open for prayer by saying: O Lord, help me! O Lord, mercy! O Lord, have pity on me! Thus the saints have acted, and it is thus that they sanctified themselves.

We should above all ask Jesus Christ for the gift of his holy love. St. Francis de Sales said that this gift includes all other gifts; for when we love God we try to avoid all that which is disagreeable to him, and to do all that we can do to please him. Let us also ask always for the grace of having great confidence in the Passion of Jesus Christ and in the intercession of Mary. Let us, moreover, not cease to recommend to God the poor souls in purgatory and poor sinners; for such prayers are most pleasing to God.

[1] "Sicut pullus hirundinis, sic clamabo."—*Is.* xxxviii. 14.

Spiritual Maxims for Priests.

1. To lose all rather than to lose God.
2. To displease every one rather than to displease God.
3. It is only sin that we have to fear, and that should grieve us.
4. To die rather than knowingly to commit a sin, even if it were only a venial sin.
5. All things come to an end; the world is a scene that passes very quickly.
6. Every moment is a treasure for eternity.
7. Everything that pleases God is good.
8. Do what you would wish to have done at the hour of death.
9. Live as if there were no other beings in the world except God and yourself.
10. God alone makes man contented.
11. There is no other good than God; there is no other evil than sin.
12. Never do anything for your own gratification.
13. The more one mortifies one's self in this life, the more joy one shall have in the next.
14. To the friends of God the bitter is sweet, and the sweet bitter.
15. He that wishes what God wishes has all that he wishes.
16. The will of God renders sweet all that which is bitter.
17. In sickness one may see who has real virtue.
18. Whoever desires nothing of this world has no need of anything.

19. Do not defer carrying out your good resolutions if you do not wish to retrograde.

20. To trouble one's self about faults committed is not humility, but pride.

21. We are only that which we are before God.

22. He that loves God desires to love rather than to know.

23. He that wishes to sanctify himself should banish from his heart all that which is not God.

24. One is not entirely for God when one seeks something that is not God.

25. Pain, poverty, and humiliation were the companions of Jesus Christ; may they also be ours.

26. Mental agitation, whatever may have been the cause, does not come from God.

27. The humble man believes himself unworthy of all honor, and worthy of contempt.

28. When one thinks of hell, which one has deserved, one suffers with resignation every pain.

29. Forget yourself, and God will think of you.

30. Love contempt, and you will find God.

31. He that contents himself with that which is less good is not far from evil.

32. God esteems but little him who seeks to be esteemed.

33. The saints always speak of God; they always speak ill of themselves, and always well of others.

34. The curious are always distracted.

35. Woe to him that loves health more than sanctity.

36. The devil is always in pursuit of the idle.

37. A vain priest is but the sport in the hand of the devil.

38. He that wishes to live in peace ought to mortify all his passions without excepting any one of them.

39. St. Joseph Calasanctius used to say: "The servant of God speaks little, works much, bears all."

40. The saints try to be saints, and not merely to appear to be saints.

41. We shall never reach any high degree of perfection as long as we are not fond of prayer.

42. One must first be a reservoir to collect, and then only can we be a canal to pour out.

43. Every attachment hinders us from belonging entirely to God.

44. The priest should not perceive anything but Jesus Christ and the good pleasure of Jesus Christ.

45. In our actions that become conspicuous pride is often hidden.

46. To offer one's self entirely to God is an excellent preparation for Communion.

47. When you walk in places that are inhabited keep your eyes cast down; think that you are a priest, and not a painter.

Exhortation to Young Men who Devote Themselves to the Study of the Ecclesiastical Sciences.*

They should, above all, endeavor to make Progress in the Science of the Saints.

ST. PAUL says, in speaking of worldly science: *Knowledge puffeth up; but charity edifieth. And if any man think that he knoweth anything, he hath not yet known as he ought to know.*[1] Worldly science when united with divine love is of great use for us and for others; but when it is separated from charity, it causes us great injury by rendering us proud and inciting us to despise others; for as much as the Lord is lavish of his graces towards the humble, so much is he chary of them towards the proud.

Happy the man to whom God gives the *science of the saints*, as he gave it to Jacob: *She gave him the knowledge of holy things.*[2] Scripture speaks of this gift as greater than all other gifts. Oh how many men live full of themselves because of their knowledge of mathematics, belles-lettres, foreign languages, and antiquities, which are of no service to religion, and are of no help as to spiritual profit! Of what use is it to possess such a science, to know so many fine things, if one does not

[1] "Scientia inflat, charitas vero ædificat. Si quis autem se existimat scire aliquid, nondum cognovit quemadmodum oporteat eum scire."—1 *Cor.* viii. 1.

[2] "Dedit illi scientiam sanctorum."—*Wisd.* x. 10.

---

* In the Italian editions this Exhortation is joined as an appendix to the *Rules for Seminaries*, which may be found in a subsequent volume.—ED.

know how to love God and to practise virtue? The wise men of this world, who seek only to acquire a great name, are deprived of the celestial lights that the Lord gives to the simple: *Thou hast hid these things from the wise and prudent* (the wise and prudent of the world), *and hast revealed them to the little ones.*[1] The *little ones* are the simple minds that bestow all their care on pleasing God alone.

St. Augustine proclaims him happy who knows God, his grandeur, his goodness, even though he should be ignorant of all other things: "Happy he that knows Thee, although he knows nothing of those things."[2] He that knows God cannot but love him; now he that loves God is wiser than all the men of letters that know not how to love him. "The unlettered," exclaims the same holy Doctor, "will rise up and bear away heaven."[3] How many rustics, how many poor villagers, reach sanctity and obtain eternal life, the enjoyment of which for a moment is better than the acquisition of all the goods of this world! The Apostle wrote to the Corinthians: *For I judged not Myself to know anything among you but Jesus Christ, and Him crucified.*[4] How happy should we be if we succeed in knowing Jesus crucified, in knowing the love that he has borne us and the love that he has merited for us by sacrificing for us his life on the cross, and if by studying such a book we succeed in loving him with an ardent love!

A great servant of God, Father Vincent Caraffa, writing to some young ecclesiastics who were engaged in studying to qualify themselves for the work of sav-

---

[1] "Abscondisti hæc a sapientibus et prudentibus, et revelasti ea parvulis."—*Matt.* xi. 25.

[2] "Beatus, qui te scit, etiamsi illa nesciat."—*Conf.* l. 5, c. 4

[3] "Surgunt indocti, et cœlum rapiunt!"—*Conf.* l. 8, c. 8.

[4] "Non enim judicavi me scire aliquid inter vos, nisi Jesum Christum, et hunc crucifixum."—I *Cor.* ii. 2.

ing souls, said to them: "To bring about great conversions among souls it is better to be a man of much prayer than a man of great eloquence; for the eternal truths that convert souls are preached differently by the heart than they are by the lips." The true ministers of the Gospel should, therefore, lead a life that shows itself to be in agreement with what they teach; they should, in a word, appear like men who, detached from the world and the flesh, seek only to procure the glory of God and to make him loved by all. This is the reason why Father Caraffa added: "Bestow all your care on giving yourself up to the exercise of divine love; only the love of God, as soon as it possesses our heart, detaches it from all inordinate love, and renders it pure by stripping it of earthly affections." "A pure heart," says St. Augustine, "is a heart empty of all cupidity."[1] In fact, adds St. Bernard, he that loves God, thinks only of loving him, and desires nothing else: "He that loves, loves and knows nothing else."[2] When one burns with the love for God, one knows not how to devote one's self to the love of any earthly object.

Hence, just as students should give from year to year proofs of their advancement in the sciences, so those that wish to sanctify themselves should labor to acquire not only from year to year, but from day to day, a great love for God. They should endeavor to increase in themselves holy love by often repeating acts of love, by offering to God every action that they begin, with the intention of performing it only to please him, and by always begging him to grant them the light and the strength necessary to accomplish the good desires with which he inspires them.

— St. Thomas of Villanova used to say: "To convert

[1] "Cor purum est cor vacuum ab omni cupiditate."
[2] "Qui amat, amat, et aliud novit nihil."—*In Cant.* s. 83.

sinners and make them come forth from the mire of their iniquities, we need arrows of fire; but how can these arrows of fire come forth from an icy heart that is not animated by the love of God?" Experience permits us to see that a priest with moderate science, but burning with love for Jesus Christ, draws more souls to God than many learned and excellent orators who charm people by their eloquence. The latter, with their beautiful thoughts, their rare acquirements, and their ingenious reflections, send away their hearers greatly satisfied with the discourse that they have heard; but they go away deprived of the love for God, and perhaps colder than when they came. But is such a success of profit to the common good? and what profit does the preacher draw therefrom, if it is not to be more full of himself and more responsible before God, since instead of the fruit that his sermon could have produced, he obtains only vain praises that yield nothing? He who, on the contrary, preaches Jesus crucified in a simple manner, not to be praised, but only to make him loved, descends from the pulpit rich in the merit of all the good that he has done, or at least that he desired to do for his hearers.

All that has been said above concerns not only preachers, but also those that are charged with teaching and those that hear confessions. How much good cannot a professor do in teaching sciences, in instilling into his pupils the maxims of true piety! The same thing holds good of confessors.

To this must be added the happy fruits that one may produce in conversing with others. We cannot always preach; but what good may not be done in conversation by a priest, who is well instructed and who is holy, when he speaks adroitly, when an occasion presents itself, of the vanity of worldly grandeur, of conformity to the will of God, of the necessity of recommending one's self without ceasing to the protection of Heaven in the midst of so many temptations with which we have to struggle!

May the Lord deign to give us the light and the strength of which we stand in need in order to employ the days that still remain to us in loving him and in doing his will, since only this is profitable, and all the rest is lost!

Discourse on the Necessity of Mental Prayer for Priests.*

If we do not try to become saints, it will be difficult to sanctify others. If therefore we wish to produce much fruit in souls, we must necessarily practise meditation, and practise it much. Without this practise what good can we ever hope for ourselves and for others? *With desolation is all the land made desolate*, says the Holy Ghost, why?—*because there is none that considereth in the heart*.[1] The Holy Ghost speaks thus of the neglect of mental prayer; and if it is this that causes the ruin of every one, with how much greater reason should not this defect cause the ruin of the priest!

If you desire to see what is the necessity of mental prayer for the priest, you should this evening consider with me these two points: I say, in speaking of a priest without mental prayer:

First, it is difficult for him to save his soul;
Secondly, it is impossible for him to attain perfection.
Let us pray to the Holy Ghost to enlighten us.

---

[1] "Desolatione desolata est omnis terra: quia nullus est qui recogitet corde."—*Jer*. xii. 11.

---

* This discourse, which remained unpublished till 1869, was found among the manuscripts of St. Alphonsus preserved at Rome. From its context we see that it was composed for retreats that are given to priests and to candidates for Holy Orders, and it seems that it was composed before 1737, since the author gives on page 446 only the title of *Blessed* to St. John Francis Regis, canonized at this time by Pope Clement XII.—Ed.

I will speak to my Lord, whereas I am dust and ashes.[1] Ah! how happy should I be, O my God! if I were but dust and ashes! I am worse than that: I am a rebel, having had the boldness to offend Thee, who art the supreme good! But Thou hast come into this world in order that poor sinners *may have life, and may have it more abundantly.*[2] Enlighten me, therefore, O Lord! speak to me, for I wish to listen to Thee: *Speak, Lord, for Thy servant heareth.*[3] Tell me what I have to do to please Thee and to sanctify myself.

Mary, my hope; thou dost fulfil the beautiful office, so conformable to thy heart all full of love and mercy, of being pacifier between sinners and God; for pity's sake, exert thyself also in my behalf, O my Sovereign Lady!

I.

Without Mental Prayer it is Difficult for a Priest to Save his Soul.

With desolation is all the land made desolate, because there is none that considereth in the heart. These last words, *considereth in the heart*, I understand to mean mental prayer: it is to meditate on the law of God, on eternity, on one's own duties, on the things of God. Let us see how difficult it is for a priest to save his soul without prayer; here is the way in which I reason:

It is certain that a priest, in order to save his soul, must fulfil all the duties of a priest,—duties of which we have already shown the greatness; and to fulfil all these duties he needs to be continually aided by the hand of the all-powerful God. It is true that God is ready to aid us; but what does the Lord desire? He

---

[1] "Loquar ad Dominum meum, cum sim pulvis et cinis."—*Gen.* xviii. 27.
[2] "Ut vitam habeant, et abundantius habeant."—*John*, x. 10.
[3] "Loquere, Domine, quia audit servus tuus."—1 *Kings*, iii. 9.

desires that we should continually ask all the help that is necessary for us; and if we do not ask him for it he will not give it to us. You know the common opinion of theologians, that prayer,—that is to say, the asking for graces,—on the part of every one that has attained the age of reason, is necessary as a means of salvation; otherwise we cannot be saved. *Ask, and you shall receive*, He that does not ask will not receive.

Now a priest that does not make mental prayer, when will he reflect on his duties as a priest? under what circumstances will he ask God for the necessary help? It will happen, that walking blindly without looking where or how he walks, he will hardly think of asking God's help; he will hardly think of the necessity in which he is of asking for it; or rather, without prayer he will not even think of his duties as a priest; and so how will he save his soul? Cardinal Bellarmine thinks it to be morally impossible for any Christian to fulfil the duties of a simple Christian without mental prayer; for how much greater reason should we not believe that this is impossible for a priest who has greater duties than a simple Christian! My dear patroness St. Teresa also says that to obtain God's grace the only door is mental prayer, and she speaks expressly of mental prayer: " This door being closed," she says, " I know not how grace will reach the soul."[1] If the saint does not know, I declare that I know much less how a priest without mental prayer will receive all the graces necessary to save his soul.

Let us consider, in the first place, how much light a priest needs for himself and for others so as to save his soul. He must keep himself pure in the midst of the seductions of the flesh; he must avoid the occasions in which he is exposed to lose God; he must give wise counsel to others, since he is the master of the people,

[1] *Life*, ch. 8.

especially if he is a confessor; he has to place souls on the road that leads to God, so often to resolve doubts unexpectedly, to give advice in every confession, and then to render an account of all to Jesus Christ.

Now how will he receive this light unless he makes mental prayer?

Mental prayer, says St. Bonaventure,[1] is a torch which on this earth of darkness shows us the road on which we should walk. St. Bernard, treating of the same subject, says that mental prayer is like a mirror: this comparison pleases me much. If one has a stain on one's countenance and one looks in the mirror, one sees it and takes it away; without this mirror, the stain remains, and will always remain; as one does not see it, one does not take it away. So it is with mental prayer: if we have a defect, if we find ourselves in a dangerous occasion, when we go to mental prayer, as if going before the mirror, we see in our conscience this defect that we have, we see this danger of losing God; we see it and we take it away.

Even though one should have had the misfortune of falling over the precipice, if one practises mental prayer with perseverance, one will surely come forth from it. Hence we quote the remark made by a master of the spiritual life: With sin there can often be united some act virtuous in itself, as, for instance, to be in the state of sin and to give alms, to be worldly and to be patient; but mental prayer and sin cannot remain united together. Why? Because if we begin voluntarily to make mental prayer,—there are some that go to mental prayer by force, and then it will do them no good,—if, I say, we go to it voluntarily, either we shall give up mental prayer, or we shall give up sin. And according to St. Teresa,[2] however great may be the ruin of a soul, if it perseveres in mental prayer, it is sure that the Lord will

[1] *Diæt. sal.* tit. 2, c. 5.   [2] *Life*, ch. 8.

bring it back to the haven of salvation. But if this soul does not go to mental prayer, because it does not think of it, or thinks of it but little, it will continue to live in its faults, in the dangerous occasions in which it finds itself, and it will end by falling into the abyss. Why? Because it walks in darkness, without light; it will find itself at the bottom of the precipice without knowing in what manner it fell over it.

Come ye to Him and be enlightened.[1] What light would we wish to have if we do not approach God by means of mental prayer? Where have so many saints, I ask, where, without studying theology, have so many simple men and women, so well learned divine things if it was not in mental prayer, this school of the saints? Such was a St. Hildegarde, who composed several books about holy Scripture; a St. Magdalene de Pazzi, who spoke so admirably of the perfection of God; a St. Teresa, who wrote so well on mental prayer that she has become the admiration of the whole world, and the Church wishes us to ask God for the grace of profiting by her heavenly doctrine: "So we feed to our ghostly health upon her heavenly teaching."[2] Let us add a St. Thomas Aquinas, who confessed that all that he knew he had learnt in mental prayer; likewise a St. Bonaventure, who said that he never had any other Master than Jesus crucified. *Come ye to Him and be enlightened.*

Let us, moreover, consider how much strength a priest needs to overcome so many enemies, both exterior and interior, that are continually laying snares for his soul. These enemies are the world, persecutions, human respect, passions, evil inclinations, temptations of the devil. Oh, how much more trouble does not the devil take to make a priest fall than to make a secular fall!

---

[1] " Accedite ad eum, et illuminamini."—*Ps.* xxxiii. 6.
[2] " Cœlestis ejus doctrinæ pabulo nutriamur."

Necessity of Mental Prayer. 459

And why? Because if he succeeds in bringing to his fall a priest, he obtains a greater prey, and causes greater displeasure to God Again, the fall of a priest is accompanied by the fall of many others; for a bad priest by falling into the precipice does not fall into it alone; he drags down with him many others. and this is the reason why the devil makes so many efforts to ruin a priest. How, then, can he undertake without mental prayer to overcome all these temptiatons, especially if he is a secular priest, who has to live in the midst of the world, exposed to the danger of meeting with so many dangerous objects—at times in the same house in which he lives? and if he is a confessor, when hearing the confessions of young persons, of children, of women; when hearing the history of their miseries, of their frailties? But then you will say, The priest takes the place of God. Ah! dear Fathers, while receiving the sacerdotal character, we neverthless remain earthly beings, weak, frail, liable to fall. How often must we not, as it were, sweat blood in order to overcome a suggestion of the devil! And without mental prayer how shall we do this? how shall we acquire the strength to resist so many enemies? Let us hear what St. Teresa says: " He that neglects mental prayer has no need of being taken to hell by demons: he will cast himself into it." [1]

When, on the contrary, we apply to mental prayer, what strength do we not continually derive from this holy exercise in order to resist all the attacks of hell! *What shalt thou see in the Sulamitess but the companies of camps?* The Sulamitess represents the soul given to mental prayer, which by this powerful means becomes for all its enemies *terrible as an army set in array.*[3] The soul is then able to conquer all its passions, all bad inclinations.

[1] *Life*, ch. 19.
[2] " Quid videbis in Sulamite nisi choros castrorum ?"—*Cant*. vii. 1.
[3] " Terribilis ut castrorum acies ordinata."—*Cant*. vi. 3.

These vicious tendencies are produced only by our corrupt nature, and it is very difficult to conquer them without much mental prayer; but by means of this prayer we overcome them easily. The soul in mental prayer is like iron in the fire: when the iron is cold it is difficult to work; but when it is put into the fire it becomes soft, and allows itself to be easily worked: so it is with the soul. A master of the spiritual life calls it a furnace, because as the fire softens the iron and renders it easy to work, so mental prayer makes it easy for the soul to overcome its passions. For example, some one receives an affront, an injury that wounds his self-love: before mental prayer, it is very difficult to him to overcome the passion that incites him to grow angry, to defend himself, and even to furnish him at times with pretexts to make him believe that this is necessary. The iron is yet cold, it must be put into the fire. Let this troubled soul enter mental prayer, and at once the sweet flame of the Holy Ghost touches it, and an interior voice tells him: Is it not better to bear that without resenting it? Leave rather your defence to God, as your divine Master did when he was calumniated,—he who was more innocent than you! At once the iron loses its hardness; the soul is softened, is appeased: without mental prayer, it would have been otherwise.

St. John Chrysostom [1] says that in a soul mental prayer is as a fountain in a garden. Oh, how beautiful is a garden when a fountain continually waters it with its vivifying waters! how fresh the verdure, how resplendent the flowers, how abundant the fruit! Take away the fountain, and everything will languish and dry up —grass, flowers, fruits, and plants. Hence how quickly does one recognize a priest who makes mental prayer! See his manner of saying Mass, of preaching, of conversing! See his humility and modesty in his actions, in

[1] *Ad pop. Ant.* hom. 79.

his whole conduct! He is the garden of the Lord, a garden enclosed.[1] It is closed to vices, to passions; it is filled with flowers and fruits of virtues; it is a paradise: *Thy plants are a paradise of pomegranates with the fruits of the orchard.*[2] And why? Because it is *the fountain of gardens*, the *well of living waters.*[3] Mental prayer is the source of living waters that continually waters the garden. Take away mental prayer, take away the fountain, and then we say Mass and the Office with precipitation; we preach in a different manner. Show me your beautiful detachment, your beautiful humility, your beautiful modesty, . . . after the fountain has been taken away. A priest without mental prayer is a garden without water, just as David said of himself in reference to the time when he was far from God: *My soul is as earth without water unto Thee.*[4] He is not even a priest; he is the corpse of a priest, according to the saying of St. John Chrysostom: "As the body cannot live without the soul, so the soul without prayer is dead and malodorous."[5] Oh, how one perceives even from afar the bad odor of a priest who does not make mental prayer! Happy, on the contrary, he who meditates on the law of God, who applies himself to the holy exercise of mental prayer. The Holy Ghost compares him to a tree planted by the rivers of water.[6]

[1] "Hortus conclusus."—*Cant.* iv. 12.
[2] "Emissiones tuæ, paradisus malorum punicorum, cum pomorum fructibus."—*Ibid.* 13.
[3] "Fons hortorum, puteus aquarum viventium."—*Ibid.* 15.
[4] "Anima mea sicut terra sine aqua tibi."—*Ps.* cxlii. 6.
[5] "Sicut corpus, sine anima, non potest vivere, sic anima, sine oratione, mortua est, et graviter olens."—*De or. Deo*, l. 1.
[6] *Ps.* i. 3.

II.
Without Mental Prayer it is Impossible for the Priest to Attain Perfection.

We now enter upon the second point, in which we must consider that, as it is difficult for a priest to save his soul without mental prayer, so it is impossible for him to attain perfection.

I suppose that, without dwelling specially on this point, every priest well knows the obligation under which he is of striving to attain perfection. Let us therefore come to the point.

Observe, says the Holy Spirit to us, that the trees planted far from the water, dry up, grow but little, or do not grow straight, while those that are found on the banks of a stream are vigorous, straight, and high. Thus men of mental prayer show themselves full of life and strength: they are straight, having only God before their eyes; they attain a great height, growing always in virtue: *Like a tree which is planted near the running waters, which shall bring forth its fruit in due season; and his leaf shall not fall off.*[1] They will not lose a leaf, that is, they will not lose a moment of their life, because either actually or virtually they always advance in perfection or in divine love,—holy charity,—which is the cause of perfection in our soul, as St. Paul says: *Have charity, which is the bond of perfection.*[2] The sweet furnace in which souls are inflamed by this celestial fire, with which the saints on earth and the blessed in heaven are burning, is mental prayer: *In my meditation a fire shall flame out*, says David.[3]

[1] "Tamquam lignum quod plantatum est secus decursus aquarum, quod fructum suum dabit in tempore suo; et folium ejus non defluet."—*Ps.* i. 3.

[2] "Charitatem habete, quod est vinculum perfectionis."—*Col.* iii. 14.

[3] "In meditatione mea exardescet ignis."—*Ps.* xxxviii. 4.

We complain that we are lukewarm and feeble; but need we be astonished at this if we remain from mental prayer? Why do we not try to enter often this happy cellar of love, where, having been scarcely introduced, the Spouse of the Canticles feels herself all set on fire with charity? *He brought me into the cellar of wine, He set in order charity in me.*[1]

We feel ourselves cold in divine love: why, then, do we not often go to converse with God? Why do we not approach Him who is called a devouring fire: *Thy God is a consuming fire.*[2] We approach God by means of mental prayer, says St. John Climacus.[3] Let us suppose the heart to be very cold, entirely deprived of love towards God: if it perseveres in mental prayer, it is certain that this God, who is so faithful and never allows himself to be outdone in generosity, will end by inflaming it with his holy love; the fire should produce its effect. If at times, while conversing with a person who truly loves God, we feel ourselves excited by the ardor that he communicates to us to love God also, how much more shall we not be inflamed with this celestial fire by often conversing with God himself!

God speaks, yes, God speaks to souls that seek him sincerely; but when does he speak to them? Is it in society, in visits, where we lose whole hours in useless conversation? No; there God does not speak. If a soul wishes to hear me, says the Lord, let it leave the society of men, let it retire into solitude, and make mental prayer; it is there that I wish to speak to it: *I will lead her into the wilderness, and I will speak to her heart.*[4] There I will make the soul hear my word, this

---

[1] " Introduxit me in cellam vinariam, ordinavit in me charitatem."
—*Cant.* ii. 4.
[2] " Deus tuus ignis consumens est."—*Deut.* iv. 24.
[3] " Oratio est hominis conjunctio cum Deo."—*Scala par.* gr. 28.
[4] " Ducam eam in solitudinem, et loquar ad cor ejus."—*Os.* ii. 14.

word full and substantial, which in making itself heard, produces the effect that it signifies, and is not only an exhortation, but a power that makes others act rightly.

Where, in fact, have the saints learned to love God if it was not in mental prayer? Where did a St. Philip Neri receive a love so ardent, that his poor heart, not being able to support it, two ribs expanded so as to give more space to its palpitations? Where was a St. Peter of Alcantara inflamed with such a love for God that, in order not to die of this love, he was obliged to go into the field, and sometimes throw himself upon the ice? Where was a St. Mary Magdalene de Pazzi inflamed with the same fire, she going nearly out of herself on account of this love? Where was a St. Teresa wounded,—she who has written of herself, that when she began to practise mental prayer, only then she began to feel what it is to love God?

Ah! dear Fathers, let us not think that mental prayer is an exercise only peculiar to solitaries, and not to those that are occupied in an active life. Tertullian calls all priests "persons devoted to prayer and contemplation."[1] The Apostles were not solitaries; they were very great workers of the Gospel throughout the world. Now what did they do in order to have time to devote themselves to mental prayer? They appointed deacons who were charged with the care of inferior things, and they said: *But we will give ourselves continually to prayer, and to the ministry of the word.*[2] Note the words, *prayer and the ministry of the word;* at first prayer, and then preaching, because without prayer we can do no good. What matters it that we are not solitaries, called to a contemplative life? If we wish to sanctify ourselves by becoming good evangelical laborers, it will be neces-

---

[1] "Genus deditum orationi et contemplationi."

[2] "Nos vero orationi et ministerio verbi instantes erimus."—*Acts*, vi. 4.

Necessity of Mental Prayer. 465

sary that we apply ourselves to mental prayer, and much mental prayer; not a quarter, or half an hour in passing, but *much more, much more;* otherwise it will, morally speaking, be impossible for us to become saints.

In the midst of our greatest labors we must always find time to give a little rest to our soul, as Jesus Christ has enjoined upon the Apostles: *Rest a little.*[1] In retreat and in mental prayer the soul sits down, as it were, and takes rest, and gathers new strength to work better. *He shall sit solitary, and hold his peace, because he hath taken it upon himself.*[2] When a soul comes forth from mental prayer it is quite changed. Hence I think highly of the good practice of those that reserve for themselves every week a day of retreat, a day entirely consecrated to the repose of the soul. On this day we do not hear confessions, we do not study: we apply only to mental prayer, to spiritual reading, to holy solitude. There are religious institutes that allow every week a day of recreation for the body, in order that the body may have more strength to work, and be better able to resist fatigue. Why should we not also give to the soul a day of spiritual recreation, so that it may be better able to bear the fatigue, considering that in exterior works it becomes always a little dissipated?

Yes, I repeat, we stand much in need of mental prayer, of not a quarter of an hour, nor half an hour, but much more. Show me an apostolic laborer who has sanctified himself without much mental prayer; as for myself, I can find none. I see that St. Francis Xavier, the wonder of apostolic workers, spent most of the night in the churches to make mental prayer, and that after a short rest which he took in the sacristy he went to pour out the affections of his heart before the Blessed Sacrament, where the Lord so filled him with his con-

[1] "Requiescite pusillum."—*Mark*, vi. 31.
[2] "Sedebit solitarius, et tacebit, quia levavit super se."—*Lam.* iii. 28.

solations that he cried out: "It is enough, O Lord, it is enough!"[1] I read of the Blessed John Francis Regis, the great missionary of France, that after having spent the whole day in preaching and hearing confessions, instead of resting, he went before the door of the church, which was closed, and conversed there with his God during the whole night. You know what were the labors of a St. Philip Neri, and what was his love for prayer. St. Vincent Ferrer, the apostle of Spain, used to make before preaching an hour's meditation. All evangelical laborers have only imitated in this their model and chief, Jesus Christ, who spent sometimes the whole night in prayer: *He passed the whole night in the prayer of God.*[2]

Undoubtedly, when God commands us to leave mental prayer in order to labor for the salvation of souls we must obey by leaving God for God. Let us then apply ourselves to the good of our neighbor as much as it is necessary; but let us not lose time: let us avoid useless conversations, and not listen to vain discourses. The time lost is a thing that God does not command. As soon as we are free let us return to prayer. And even in the midst of our occupations, while hearing confessions, preaching, or doing anything else, we must always preserve in our hearts the little cell of St. Catharine of Sienna, where we may be anxious to enter from time to time in order to speak to God by an act of love or some ejaculatory prayer. We must also take care not to lose sight of holy solitude, and not cease to love it. We should imitate the Spouse of the Canticles, who said to his Well-beloved: *Flee away, O My beloved, . . upon the mountains of aromatical spices.*[3] She did not wish that the divine Spouse should depart from her and

---

[1] " Sat est, Domine, sat est!"
[2] " Erat pernoctans in oratione Dei."—*Luke*, vi. 12.
[3] " Fuge, Dilecte mi . . . super montes aromatum."—*Cant.* viii. 14.

abandon her; but knowing that he was accustomed to speak in solitude, she begged him to retire to the solitary mountains, so that she might be able to converse with him alone. It is thus that in our labors, and then more than ever, we should sigh after happy solitude, desiring ardently, as a thirsty hart desires the fountain of waters, to see the moment of prayer arrive in order to go to converse alone with God.

And how long should we converse with God? Would it be a very great thing to give ourselves up to prayer for two hours a day, one hour in the morning, the other in the evening? Let us devote ourselves to it at least for an hour every day. Ah! I would regard it as a success if, with God's help, I should obtain as the fruit of this retreat that some among you, even if it were only one of you, would desire to increase a little the time given to prayer. You at least who are candidates for ordination do so; increase the time of mental prayer; all depends on the good habit that you acquire in the beginning. For those who for a number of years have the habit of making, for example, a half-hour's meditation, and not more, it would be difficult to add more to it; they would believe that it would be an injury to them to add more mental prayer.

No, I repeat, it is not a great sacrifice to spend every day two hours in conversing with Jesus Crucified or with the Blessed Sacrament. *I sat down under His shadow, whom I desired.*[1] Oh! what a paradise to be able to speak with Jesus Christ exposed during the Forty Hours' devotion, or under other circumstances, or to visit some solitary church where the Blessed Sacrament is kept! Seculars, to our shame be it said, spend there sometimes whole hours. It is precisely to converse often with us that our dear Saviour remains on earth in

---

[1] "Sub umbra illius quem desideraveram, sedi."—*Cant.* ii. 3.

the Blessed Sacrament; when he is shut up there, he asks, he prays, so to speak, that we go to speak to him.

But you will perhaps say, Two hours!—that is too much. How! it would be too much, two hours of mental prayer! Do you not then know what mental prayer is? It consists in speaking familiarly with God, as a friend speaks with a friend, says St. Teresa. In mental prayer we find those wings so greatly desired by the Royal Prophet, by the aid of which he raised himself up to perfection: *Who will give me wings like a dove, and I will fly and be at rest?*[1] What perfection could we ever acquire without mental prayer? It is an excellent school in which one learns the heavenly science of the saints. Permit me still to say before finishing, So many studies to which we devote ourselves, so many languages that we wish to know, so much knowledge, so many various sciences that we try to master, are without doubt good: no one denies that; they may be useful. It would, however, be better first to study Holy Scripture, the Canons, Dogmatic Theology, to be ready to satisfy also this modern erudition that is diffused throughout the world. But what is above all necessary to us is the beautiful science of the saints, which consists in loving God; a science that we learn, not in books, but before the Crucifix, before the Blessed Sacrament.

Mental prayer, then, dear Fathers, mental prayer! The more we desire to labor for the salvation of souls, the more we need light and strength, since we are to give light and strength to others. What warmth and what light can be communicated to other lamps by a lamp that scarcely burns, that is in danger of being extinguished? Ah! would to God that it would not occur daily that a priest who devotes himself to the salvation

[1] " Quis dabit mihi pennas sicut columbæ, et volabo, et requiescam." —*Ps.* liv. 7.

Necessity of Mental Prayer. 469

of souls, having himself but little fervor, little love for God, becomes more and more lukewarm, even falls sometimes over the precipice, and ends by losing God! How many examples of a similar misfortune do exist! Do you not yourselves know of some priest, who, wishing to hear confessions, to convert others, has afterwards succumbed to the occasions, and in them has lost God?

After this we say that it is too much to spend two hours in mental prayer! Such was not the thought of a St. Francis Borgia, who after eight hours of prayer asked the favor of a quarter of an hour more; a St. Rose of Lima, who spent twelve hours a day in prayer; a St. Anthony the Abbot, who, after having devoted the whole night to prayer, complained in the morning that the sun arose so soon and obliged him to finish. And how many young virgins, how many seculars, even mechanics, make four, five, and six hours of mental prayer! Is this not a subject of confusion for us who are priests? Will they not have to judge us on the last day? Ah, priests of the Lord! let us not allow ourselves to be surpassed by others in the love for God, while as priests we are under greater obligations than others to love him. Let us not lose any more time; who knows how many days are still left us to live? Let us love God, at least on account of the great desire and the firm will that he has of being loved by us who are his priests.

O my God! it is then true that Thou wishest to be loved by me. And of what use will life be if I do not employ it entirely to love Thee, who art my Lord and my God, my supreme and only good? I am not worthy to love Thee; but Thou art infinitely worthy of being loved; Thou hast all the qualities that render Thee amiable: Thou art beautiful, loving, beneficent, faithful; what dost Thou need more to be loved? There remains only one thing to be done: it is, that I love Thee. But why should I not love Thee, O my God! Why? what should I love if I do not love Thee? Outside of Thee, to whatever side I turn, I find nothing amiable; I see only creatures, earthly objects; I see only smoke and misery. "O fire that dost always burn," I will say with St. Augustine, "inflame me!"[1] O God, who art all afire with love, thoroughly inflame me, consume me with love for Thee!

Have we a better means to love God than continually to ask him for his holy love? I desire, says Jesus Christ to us, I desire to inflame thy heart as thou desirest, thou who art my priest; but come to mental prayer: *Arise, My love, my beautiful one, and come.*[2] I expect thee in solitude; it is there that I have prepared for thee the abundance of my favors.

Ah, dear Fathers, of what advantage is it not to love God! The only thing that we find at the moment of death will be to have loved God—nothing more. If we have obtained honors, possessed a convenient house, succeeded in our undertakings, at the end what shall we find? Nothing but that we have loved God. Alas! what are we doing in this world, if we are not occupied therein in loving God? Should we seek to amass riches, to gain the esteem of others, to enjoy pleasures, to acquire honors? What interest have we in the world? *I have chosen you out of the world.*[3] God has withdrawn us from the world, and we should wish to throw ourselves again into it? Ah! the world, honors, pleasures! let us live, and let us live only in order to love God; and to do this, let us devote ourselves to prayer, to prayer. By this means we shall have the

---

[1] "O ignis qui semper ardes! accende me."—*Solil. an. ad D.* c. 19.

[2] "Veni, columba mea in foraminibus petræ, in caverna maceriæ."—*Cant.* ii. 13.

[3] "Elegi vos de mundo."—*John*, xv. 19.

Necessity of Mental Prayer. 471

happiness of leaving this world while thanking God, like the glorious martyr St. Agatha, who said at the moment of her death: " O Lord, who hast taken from me the love of the world! receive now my soul."[1] Ah! a thousand times happy shall we be if we can then also say: " The kingdom of this world and all the beauty of life I have esteemed as nothing, for the excellency of the love of Jesus Christ my Lord."[2]

O Mary, my tender Mother! thou whose whole life was a continual prayer, since even sleep did not hinder thee from keeping thyself united with God, deign to remember us. Thou didst do to St. Rose the charity to awaken her when it was time for prayer: in the same way, when thou seest us fallen asleep in negligence, in lukewarmness, have the kindness to come to awaken us, and to recall us to the duty of attending to prayer, which should inflame us with love for God and for thee, so that afterwards we may be able to go to love thee for all eternity in paradise.

Live Jesus and Mary: with Joseph and Teresa!

[1] "Domine, qui abstulisti a me amorem sæculi, accipe animam meam."—*Off.* 5 *febr.*

[2] " Regnum mundi et omnem ornatum sæculi contempsi, propter amorem Domini mei Jesu Christi!"—*Comm. non Virg.*

INDEX.

A

ABNEGATION, see *Interior Mortification.*
AMBITION, it causes the ruin of souls, 351.
ANGER, it must be repressed, 323.
APPETITE, see *Taste.*
AVARICE, horror that a priest should have of it, 345.

B

BISHOPS, their responsibility with regard to Masses celebrated without due respect, 223. As to what concerns the candidates for ordination, see *Vocation.*
BLESSED SACRAMENT, daily visit to it, in what it consists, 432.
BLINDNESS of the soul caused by impurity, 113.

C

CHARITY, we should render good for evil, 444. Charity that a confessor should have, 274.
CHASTITY, the merit of this virtue, 243; its necessity in the priest, 108, 243, and in the candidate for the priesthood, 197; means of preserving chastity, 247, 309, 375, 435; dangers to be avoided, 252, 276, 435.
CLERIC, what this name signifies, 54.
COMMUNION, it effaces venial sins, 103; after Communion the Lord dispenses his grace most abundantly, 227.
COMPANY, DANGEROUS, we must avoid it, 254, 257, 435.
CONFESSORS: power that they exercise, 26; charity and firmness which they must have, 274; many err by too great rigor or too great indulgence, 20, 277; how to act in regard to those living in the occasion of sin, 281, and those who are relapsing sinners, 283, 285, and habitual sinners, 285. Obligation for every priest to hear confessions, and to render himself capable of doing so, 158, 182, 265, 271. The knowledge required to hear confessions

well, 273. When one may shorten the thanksgiving to go to hear confessions, 429.

CONFIDENCE with which sinners should be animated, 21 Our faults should not make us lose confidence, 318, 436. Confidence that one should have in the Blessed Virgin, 414.

CONFORMITY to the will of God, a principal means of sanctifying one's self, 403, 441.

CONTEMPT must be borne, 320, 330; those that love God are delighted when receiving contempt, 334.

D

DEATH, we should wish for it in order to go promptly to heaven and to be delivered from the danger of losing it, 442. We should assist the dying, 181, 193.

DESIRE for perfection, first means of sanctifying one's self, 391. Desire for death, 442.

DESOLATIONS, spiritual, they cannot prevent us from making meditation, 293.

DIGNITY of the priest, 23, 154; see *Priest*.

DIRECTOR, spiritual, one should obey him as one obeys God, 357, 358, 434.

DISTRUST of one's self, necessary to evangelical laborers, 315.

DRESS of priests, should be modest, 373, 435.

E

ELOQUENCE simple and popular, the most profitable manner of preaching, even when the people are well instructed, 269; see *Preaching*.

END of the priesthood, 39, and of the works of the priest, 19, 177, 217, 267.

END, final, the people as well as priests, should often be put in mind of it, 20.

EXAMPLE, or good example which the priest must give, 62, 140, 230, 239, 266, 451, 454.

EXAMPLES quoted: the respect that princes should show to the priest, 30; even the angels honor him, 31; the saints dreaded the sacerdotal office, 39, 186; zeal for the salvation of souls, 170; reward of this zeal, 174; zeal in regard to the saying of Mass, 228; scandal given by saying Mass without devotion, 221, and without making thanksgiving, 226; tepidity in the service of God, 100; blindness of the soul produced by an impure passion, 116; punishment of this vice, 117, 119; means to conquer it, or the recitation of the "Hail Mary," 263; indiscreet severity, 327; flight from dangerous occasions, 253, 256; temptations caused by looks, 365; modesty of the eyes, 370; consequences of vanity and of pride, 310, 312; false humility, 319; sobriety, 374; penances self imposed, 377; patience amid inconveniences and humiliations, 330, 332, 335, 366, 379, 399.

EXERCISES, spiritual, admonitions necessary for him who gives the spiritual exercises to priests, 19. Monthly retreat, recommended, 434.

EYES, we should mortify them, 367.

F

FIRMNESS, necessary to the confessor, 274.
FORTITUDE, necessary in the confessor, 276.

G

GAMES: there are some that are simple, and the others are not suitable for priests, 251.
GLUTTONY, a pernicious vice, which should be overcome before all things, 374, 430.

H

HABITUAL sinners, how the priest should treat them, 285.
HAIR, modesty in wearing it, 373.
HONORS, the priest should be detached from them, 351.
HUMILITY, a necessary virtue in the priest, 305, especially to obtain and to preserve chastity, 260, 309. Practice of humility: to have a horror of pride, 309; not to glory in the good that we do, 312; we must distrust ourselves, 315, accept humiliation, 319, 444. False humility, 319, 443.

I

IDLENESS, dangerous to chastity, 258.
INCONTINENCE, the evil that it creates, 107; its malice in a priest, 109; its sad consequences. blindness of the soul, 113; obstinacy of the will, 117; eternal damnation, 119. Decrees against incontinent ecclesiastics, 108. Remedies against this vice, 120; see *Chastity*.
INTENTION required to enter holy Orders, 192. Intention or end that the evangelical laborer should have, 19, 177, 396. The intention of pleasing God in all things is a great means of sanctifying one's self, 395, 439.

J

JESUS CHRIST died to institute the priesthood, and he gives himself up into the priest's hands. 26. Price that is attached to the souls of men, 167. We must love him in order to preach well, and it is the science of the saints, 296, 450. How much he deserved to be loved, 386; and how much he loves a soul that is devoted to him, 389. He wishes us to think of his Passion, and we cannot often think of it without loving him, 215, 387, 438. When we love him, we suffer all with joy, 334. We find in him a model of devotion to prayer, 289, of meekness, 322, of mortification, 339.

L

LAW-SUITS, the priest should not take charge of those of others, nor of his own, 349.

LOVE, divine, science of the saints, true wisdom which we should prefer to everything else, 295, 449, 470; it procures joy in sufferings and humiliations, 394; how one acquires it, 391, 395, 436, 438. The priest should belong entirely to God, 384. See *Jesus Christ* and *Sanctity*.

M

MANIPLE, its origin, 217.

MARY, Mother of God, necessity of her intercession, 409, and confidence that we should have in it, 414, how good is devotion to Mary in order to obtain and preserve purity, 263. Practice of devotion to Mary, 421, 442; fasts in her honor, 431, 442; visits, 432, 442. A priest should strive to make her loved and honored, 421, 442.

MASS, whence its name, 217. Mass renders to God an infinite honor, 25, 122, 209. Benefit that confers upon the world, 210, 224, and what it should above all confer upon the celebrant, 213, 225. In Mass, Jesus Christ obeys the priest, 26. Sanctity that it requires of the priest, 48, 110, 122, 212, 214. The respect and devotion with which he should celebrate Mass, 217. How great a crime of the priest who celebrates in the state of mortal sin, 125; he commits four mortal sins, 129. Faults that many priests commit in celebrating, 218, Mass said in less than a quarter of an hour cannot be excused from a grievous sin, 220. The preparation, 213, 428; one should propose to one's self three ends, 217. Thanksgiving, 226, 428; when one may shorten it, 429. Priests who abstain from saying Mass through humility, 228. Responsibility of bishops in regard to Mass, 223.

MAXIMS, spiritual, for a priest, 446.

MEEKNESS, merit of this virtue, 322. It gains hearts for God, 332. Its practice: to repress anger, 323; to bear with contempt 330. It does not prevent one from being just and severe, 325. We should practise it also towards ourselves, 328.

Index. 477

MENTAL prayer, how necessary it is to the priest, 214, 267, 289, 428, 454; without mental prayer it will be difficult for a priest to be saved, 455, and impossible for him to attain perfection, 462. Mental prayer and mortification are the principal means to sanctify one's self, 340. The time that we should give to mental prayer, 214, 467. Answer to excuses: spiritual desolation, 294; study, 295; labors, 299. We should often meditate on the Passion of Jesus Christ, 215, 387, 438.

MODESTY, a virtue necessary to the priest, 240, 372; modesty in words, 372, in dress, in his hair, 373, and above all in his looks, 252, 367.

MORTIFICATION in general, how necessary it is, 337; it is the first means to acquire sanctity, 258, 339; practice: detachment from property, 345, from honors, 351, from relatives, 354, from self-will, 357; means of conquering self-will, 360. Necessity of exterior mortification, 362; its fruits, 365; practice: in the pains that happen to us, and in lawful pleasures, 365; the eyes, 367; in the whole exterior, 371; in the taste or appetite, 374; in the touch, 377, in the pains that happen of themselves, 379, 399. Summary, 444. The good that is derived from a mortified life, 383.

O

OCCASION, necessity of avoiding it to preserve chastity, 248, 369. Remote, proximate, voluntary, necessary occasion, 281. How the confessor should act in regard to those in the occasion of sin, 282.

OFFICE, divine, how to recite it, 302.

ORDERS, sacred, see *Priest, Vocation.*

P

PARENTS, one need not obey them when there is question of vocation, 190. The priest should be detached from his relatives, 354.

PARISH PRIESTS, their responsibility in regard to candidates for ordination, 197.

PASSIONS should be subjected to reason, 341, and one should apply one's self to the subjugation of the dominant passion, 343.

PATIENCE in pains and humiliations, a great means of sanctifying one's self, 379, 399.

PENANCE administration of the sacrament of penance, see *Confessor.* The priest should often confess, and obey his spiritual director, 357, 358, 434. Penitential works that should be practised, 377.

PERFECTION, see *Sanctity.*

PRAYER, should often be recommended, 21; it is particularly necessary for the priest, 289. It is a great means to obtain and to preserve chastity, 261. We should pray without ceasing, 445. To pray well we should practise mental prayer, 292.

PREACHING, it is a duty of the priest, 181, 265. We should begin by preaching by example, 238, 266, 451, 454. Intention that one should have, 20, 177, 267. Success should be expected from the divine mercy, 21, 317. It is necessary that the preacher makes the discourse his own, 19. He should adopt a simple and popular manner, 269, and renounce vain ornaments, 20, 268, 452. Respect and sweetness are necessary in order to convince any one, 21. He must inspire sinners with confidence, and often recommend prayer, 21; frequently remind them of the last things, and speak of practical things, 20, 271.

PREPARATION for Mass, its importance, 213, 429. Preparation is twofold: remote and proximate, 214. The priest should propose to himself three ends, 217.

PRIDE, a vice incompatible with chastity, 260, 309. God detests the proud, 307.

PRIEST, SACERDOS and PRESBYTER, explanation of these names, 46, 157, 234. Dignity of the priest, 23, 154. His power over the real body and the mystical body of Jesus Christ, 26, 32, 34. Chief titles which, besides that of priest, express his dignity and his offices: ambassador of the Church with God, 24; leader of the flock of Jesus Christ, 187, 231; creator of his Creator, 35; the husbandman of the vineyard of the Lord, 160; a God on earth, 67, 156; dispenser of the sacraments, 60, and of the royal house of God, 187; a celestial man, 78, a man of God, 54; interpreter of the divine law, 187; judge, having the power of the keys, 27, 34; light of the world, 140, 232; spiritual physician, 160; mediator between God and men, 34, 59, 179, 216; minister, ambassador, and co-operator of God, 43, 54, 65, 155; minister of the altar, 55; mirror of the world, 239; model of virtues, 62, 139, 230; father of Christians, 144, 160, 234; the salt of the earth, 140, 159, 232; the temple, the house of God, 109, 160; the vicar of Jesus Christ, 34, 42, 59, 123. He belongs not to himself, but to God, 185. His charge is formidable, 39, 43, 48, 157, 178; his duties, see *Mass, Preaching, Confessors, Sanctity*, etc. Reward of his zeal, 172. If he is a sinner or tepid, he will not easily be converted, 21, 77, 93. When God wishes to chastise a people, he begins with the priests, 83.

PROPERTY, earthly, one must be detached from it, 345.

PURITY, see *Chastity*.

R

READING, spiritual, to be made every day, 431.
RELAPSING SINNERS, how the priest should treat them, 283, 285.
RETREAT, monthly, recommended to priests, 434.
RUBRICS of the Mass, they bind under pain of sin, 218, 220.
RULE of life for a secular priest, 427.
RULES spiritual for a priest who aspires to perfection, 436.

S

SANCTITY which a priest should have, 48, 97, 110, 122, 178, 230, 286. Perfection required for admission to holy Orders, 192; it should be greater than that of the simply religious, 192. See *Chastity, Mortification, Mental Prayer, Vocation*. Rule of life, 427. Spiritual Rules, 436. Spiritual Maxims, 446. The priest should labor for the sanctification of souls, see *Souls*.
SCANDAL given by the priest, its gravity, its consequences, 138, 231.
SCIENCE requisite in order to take holy Orders, 193; in order to hear confessions, 273. The science of the saints necessary before all, 296, 449, 468.
SERMON, see *Preaching*.
SEVERITY, sometimes just and necessary, 326.
SILENCE, one should love it, and should speak only to edify others, 371, 439.
SIN. gravity of the sins of the priest, 70, 109, 128, 142; chastisement, 75, 113; the sin of scandal, 138. See *Incontinence*. The little faults about which one cares not disposes one to grievous faults, 89, 93, 103. A priest cannot be satisfied with avoiding grievous sins, 97. How venial sins are cancelled, 102. Sin is incompatible with mental prayer, 292. We should avoid every sin, and being troubled after sin, 329, 436. The sin of him who enters holy Orders without a vocation, 198. The confessor should avoid judging lightly that a sin is a mortal sin, 278.
SOBRIETY, always necessary, 374. 430, especially at supper, 433.
SOLITUDE, how much one should love it, 439.
SOULS, the priest should labor for their salvation, 154, 161, 266; means to be employed, 178, 265, 422; pleasures that it gives to God when we labor for the salvation of souls, 166; reward of his zeal, 172. He should, above all, sanctify himself, 298; he should fear offices to which the care of souls is attached, 253.
SPEECH, the priest should speak little and in a proper manner, 371.
STUDY: it is necessary for the priest to study Moral Theology, 273; study does not prevent one from practising mental prayer, 295;

we should, above all, apply ourselves to making progress in the science of the saints, 450, 468.

T

TASTE, mortification in eating and drinking, 374, 430, 433.

TEMPTATIONS: the devil tempts one priest more than a hundred seculars, 85, 101. We must before all pray in temptations, 261. What he must do amid carnal temptations, 262, 435.

TEPIDITY, a priest is not easily converted from tepidity, 21, 93; his state, his conduct, 92. Tepidity disposes one to grave faults, 88, 97. How does God begin to vomit forth the tepid priest, 96.

THANKSGIVING after Mass, its importance, the time and the care to be given to it, 226, 428; when we may abridge it, 429.

THEOLOGY, moral, a difficult science and necessary for the priest, 273.

TOUCH, the sense that must be mortified, 377.

TRAFFIC, forbidden to ecclesiastics, 348.

V

VANITY, its dangers and its consequences, 312, 316, 396.

VISITS to be made to the Blessed Sacrament and to the Blessed Virgin, 432.

VOCATION, divine, its necessity for taking holy Orders, 185, 198. Vocation is also necessary for every state of life, 201. Marks of vocation to the priesthood, 189. What a priest should do who has entered Orders without a vocation, 206.

W

WILL of God, we should conform to it in all things, 403, 441; it is manifested to us by Superiors and spiritual directors, 359. Self-will, one should be detached from it, 357.

WINE, dangerous to chastity, 259, 431.

WOMEN: one must avoid looking at them and conversing with them, 250, 367, 435.

Z

ZEAL which the priest should have, 43, 154; end, means, and labors, 177; how much this zeal pleases God, 166; his reward, 172.

www.ingramcontent.com/pod-product-compliance
Lightning Source LLC
Chambersburg PA
CBHW051852300426
44117CB00006B/368